# THE CRIMINAL JUSTICE SYSTEM
# AND HEALTH CARE

# The Criminal Justice System and Health Care

Edited by
CHARLES A. ERIN
and
SUZANNE OST

OXFORD
UNIVERSITY PRESS

# OXFORD
## UNIVERSITY PRESS

Great Clarendon Street, Oxford, OX2 6DP,
United Kingdom

Oxford University Press is a department of the University of Oxford.
It furthers the University's objective of excellence in research, scholarship,
and education by publishing worldwide. Oxford is a registered trade mark of
Oxford University Press in the UK and in certain other countries

Published in the United States of America by Oxford University Press
198 Madison Avenue, New York, NY 10016, United States of America

British Library Cataloguing in Publication Data
Data available

Library of Congress Control Number: 2007034283

ISBN 978-0-19-922829-4

For Emma Victoria, and Mélisande
'Millie' Ottoline, and Lily Jorja

# *Foreword*

Times change. Prior to the middle of the nineteenth century, doctors were not held in particularly high regard. The discovery of anaesthesia, the development of surgery, and greater understanding of the causes of diseases and their effective treatment led to a demand for more and better health care. The creation of the National Health Service in the UK in 1948, and similar systems in other countries marked the high point. As the literature of the period, and contemporary films and television programmes show, doctors were the modern heroes, able to perform modern miracles, and incapable of poor practice. Society in general, and the criminal justice system in particular, adopted a tolerant attitude to the profession, and to clinical practice.

Over the last twenty-five years, however, the criminal law has increasingly become invoked to resolve ethical dilemmas, and to protect patients from poor professional practice. The number of doctors prosecuted has risen steadily in recent years in this country, and in many others. There are many explanations for this increase. It has, however, not been the result of a considered strategy, and its effects have not until now been considered. Is recourse to the criminal court the best way of addressing such ethical issues as abortion and euthanasia? Will prosecuting more doctors for manslaughter result in better medical practice, or inhibit practitioners from discussing and learning from their errors, and the mistakes of others? What is the appropriate balance between admission, audit, learning, and prevention on the one hand, and criminal prosecution on the other? How best does society deal with these complex issues in a way that is acceptable both to the individual patient and the general public while being fair to the practitioner? And, of course, similar considerations influence the way society deals with members of the public who have broken the law. Some are characterized as criminals, and dealt with through the courts; others are treated as patients outwith the criminal justice system. The effects on prisons and mental hospitals are clear.

This book is an enjoyable and fascinating read. The issues are presented in a lucid and accessible way by experts in the field. Perhaps, inevitably, there are few right and wrong answers. It is, however, essential that we understand more clearly just what we might expect if we as a society continue to make more use of the criminal law in our attempts to resolve health care and medical practice dilemmas. Personally, I believe that we should ask the criminal justice system to answer specific questions. Society itself, not the judiciary and lawyers, however eminent, must address the broader ethical and professional issues. But read the book, consider the arguments, and come to your own conclusions. The scope is impressively wide. The remarkable interest in medical ethics, medico-legal issues, and the criminalization of health care is most certainly a healthy development.

Graeme Catto

# General Editor's Preface

This volume presents a much-needed critical examination of the interface between the criminal law and practices in the health care system. It focuses on the use of the criminal law against those alleged to have perpetrated medical malpractice, and on the use of the criminal law to resolve—or to intrude into—some of the ethical conflicts that beset modern health care. It includes searching examination of medical manslaughter, corporate liability for medical errors, the necessity defence, euthanasia, abortion, HIV transmission and more. The volume also presents comparative perspectives, but certainly does not take for granted the criminal law's involvement in these ethically troublesome issues. Indeed, the editors have ensured that from beginning to end this is a self-reflective volume, always asking whether the criminal law should be used in that way or to this extent. It is therefore not only the subject-matter but also the questioning approach that makes this volume an important addition to the monographs series.

Andrew Ashworth

# *Acknowledgements*

The genesis of this edited volume involved various informal conversations with our friend and colleague Margaret Brazier, often in breaks from teaching duties, usually over coffee and tea. We had each, it is fair to say, intuited, rather than consciously noticed, an increase of criminal law activity in regard of health care in recent times, but it was only through these chats with Margot that we acquired the confidence to voice our perceptions as a discernable trend. And, as in all areas of our academic lives, Margot has been our rock during the development of this book. 'Thank you' seems a rather feeble way of expressing our gratitude for her advice, encouragement, and constant support, but it is heartfelt.

Our discussions with Margot grew into a project, and that project gained added impetus when, with Margot, we arranged an international conference, *Criminalising Medicine—Doctors in the Dock*, which was convened at the University of Manchester on 26 and 27 May 2005, and for whose support we are grateful to the School of Law at the University of Manchester, and to the British Academy. The idea for this volume preceded that conference, and a great deal of thought was put into identification of specific themes, and appropriate speakers, with this book never far from our minds. As it turned out, many of the authors who have contributed their work to this collection were speakers at that conference, and several of the chapters have been developed from views originally expressed there. We would like to thank the speakers at that conference, but also everyone who contributed to the discussion sessions, for confirming that we were not barking up the wrong tree, and that this is, indeed, an interesting, worthwhile, and important line of research.

Anyone who has ever edited a collection, or contributed to an edited volume, will be aware of the burdens involved, and how much easier it is to produce a single author book! The contributors to this collection are a distinguished group, who have all shown great dedication and energy, and have given of their time and wisdom with grace and good heart. We thank you all.

And, finally, but not least, we would like to express our gratitude to Rebecca Smith and Benjamin Roberts at the Press for their understanding natures, kindly manner, and for their patience in dealing with us during the production of this book.

Charles A. Erin and Suzanne Ost
Manchester and Lancaster, 2007

# Contents

# Contributors

**Mr Neil Allen**, Clinical Teaching Fellow, School of Law, University of Manchester, UK.

**Dr Rebecca Bennett**, Senior Lecturer in Bioethics, Centre for Social Ethics & Policy, School of Law, University of Manchester, UK.

**Professor Margaret Brazier**, OBE, Professor of Law, and Director, Centre for Social Ethics & Policy, School of Law, University of Manchester, UK.

**Professor Sir Graeme Catto**, President, General Medical Council, Chair in Medicine & Therapeutics, School of Medicine, University of Aberdeen, UK.

**Professor Robert A. Destro**, Professor of Law, and Director of the Interdisciplinary Program in Law & Religion, Columbus School of Law, Catholic University of America, Washington DC, USA.

**Dr Charles A. Erin**, Senior Lecturer in Applied Philosophy, Centre for Social Ethics & Policy, School of Law, University of Manchester, UK.

**Professor John Griffiths**, Professor in Theory of Law, Faculty of Law, University of Groningen, the Netherlands.

**Professor Alan Forbes Merry**, Professor of Anaesthesiology, and Head of Department, Department of Anaesthesiology, Faculty of Medical & Health Sciences, University of Auckland, and President of the Auckland Medico-Legal Society, New Zealand.

**Professor Jonathan Montgomery**, Professor of Health Care Law, School of Law, University of Southampton, UK.

**Dr Suzanne Ost**, Senior Lecturer in Law, Law School, Lancaster University, UK.

**Dr Oliver Quick**, Lecturer in Law, School of Law, University of Bristol, UK.

**Dr Sergio Romeo-Malanda**, Postdoctoral Research Fellow, Centre for Law and Genetics, University of Tasmania, Australia.

**Dr Stephen Smith**, Lecturer in Law, and Deputy Director of the Institute of Medical Law, School of Law, University of Birmingham, UK.

**Dr Elizabeth Wicks**, Senior Lecturer in Law, School of Law, University of Birmingham, UK.

**Dr Michael Wilks**, Chairman, Representative Body, British Medical Association, President-elect, Standing Committee of European Doctors (CPME), and Principal Forensic Medical Examiner, Metropolitan Police, London, UK.

# Table of Cases

# Table of Legislation

# 1

# An Ill-Suited and Inappropriate Union? Exploring the Relationship Between the Criminal Justice System and Health Care

*Suzanne Ost and Charles A. Erin*

## 1. Introduction

This volume seeks to provide an exploration and analysis of the increasing intervention of the criminal law and the criminal justice system in health care and the impact of the criminalization of medical malpractice. More so in today's society than ever, it seems that the uneasy relationship between criminal law and health care and practice is becoming ever more prominent, and the tensions to be found at the intersection of the domains of each offer great potential for both ethical and legal academic analysis.

What we first seek to do in this introductory chapter is to address the wider picture of law's increased intervention in health care, before proceeding to focus upon the greater involvement of the criminal law in the medical arena. We then endeavour to tease out the themes that are explored in the essays contained in this work, and to offer readers an account of the main arguments the authors raise.

## 2. The increasing intervention of criminal law in health care and medical practice

The civil law has a long-standing relationship with health care and medical practice. Yet, whilst it is true that for some time the courts have played a role in resolving ethical conflicts relating to medical practice and medical accountability through the civil law, more recently there have been some significant changes in the judiciary's approach when adjudicating upon such issues. In the past, when faced with cases involving often tragic, ethical dilemmas, the judiciary was inclined to leave the question of what should constitute patients' best interests largely in the hands of the medical profession itself.[1] In a number of recent cases, however, judges have reminded the medical profession that the ultimate decision as to the patient's best interests rests with the courts.[2] Previous years saw the judiciary consistently express a definite lack of enthusiasm for casting judgement upon the medical profession, and be quick to state their desire to leave matters of serious ethical concern to Parliament and the medical profession's own regulator, the General Medical Council (GMC).[3] But it can no longer be said that the regulation of the medical profession is the sole province of the GMC. Our modern day society demands that its medical practice is accountable to the public, and, consequently, in a number of cases over recent years, our judges have been cautiously dipping their toes into the seemingly uninviting waters of medical practice. The last ten years have seen judicial analysis and critique of the basis of medical opinion in medical malpractice cases, albeit to a somewhat limited degree,[4] and a more patient-orientated approach to causation.[5] Unsurprisingly, such developments have led to fears that an increase in legal actions will cause the UK to see a rise in the practice of defensive medicine.[6]

Whilst in the past, legal control over medical practice tended to be exercised through the civil law, over the past twenty-five years the *criminal* law has increasingly come to play a larger role in regulating the medical profession and determining moral and ethical conflicts. Thus, we have witnessed doctors being prosecuted for gross negligence manslaughter,[7] and for murder, and attempted murder.[8] We have seen, for example, legal proceedings brought in an attempt to challenge the decision not to prosecute doctors who performed an abortion under the 'serious handicap' ground of the Abortion Act 1967 in a case where the fetus

---

[1] See, for example, *Airedale Trust v Bland* [1993] 1 All ER 821. See also M. Brazier, 'Patient autonomy and consent to medical treatment: The role of the law', *Legal Studies*, 7 (1997), 169–93.
[2] *Re S (Adult Patient: Sterilisation)* [2000] 3 WLR 1288 and *Re A (Medical Treatment: Male Sterilization)* [2000] 1 FLR 549. See also H. Woolf, 'Are the courts excessively deferential to the medical profession?', *Medical Law Review*, 9 (2001), 1–17.
[3] See, for example, Lords Browne-Wilkinson and Mustill in *Airedale Trust v Bland*, at 878 and 889.
[4] *Bolitho v City and Hackney Health Authority* [1997] 4 All ER 771, *Marriott v West Midlands Health Authority* [1999] Lloyd's Rep. Med. 23, *Penney v East Kent Health Authority* [2000] Lloyd's Rep Med 41 and *Pearce v United Bristol Healthcare Trust* (1999) 48 BMLR 118. See M. Brazier & J. Miola, 'Bye-bye Bolam: A Medical Litigation Revolution?', *Medical Law Review*, 8 (2000), 85. Note, however, the view held by some commentators that the judiciary still relies to a heavy extent upon the views of medical experts when formulating the appropriate standard of care. See, for example, A. MacLean, 'The doctrine of informed consent: Does it exist and has it crossed the Atlantic?', 24/3 (2004) *Legal Studies* 386–413, at 409.
[5] *Chester v Afshar* [2004] 3 WLR 927. See Sarah Devaney's commentary upon the case: 'Autonomy rules ok', *Medical Law Review*, 13/1 (2005), 102–7.
[6] See, for example, D. Kessler, 'Effects of the Medical Liability System in Australia, the UK and the USA', *The Lancet*, July 368/9531 (2006), 240–6.
[7] *R v Prentice, R v Adomako, R v Holloway* [1993] 4 All ER 935, CA.
[8] A. Arlidge, 'The Trial of David Moor', (2000) Crim LR, 31–40, *R v Cox* [1992] BMLR 38.

had a bilateral cleft lip and palate.[9] Moreover, Parliament also seems increasingly prepared to criminalize the medical profession's activities where there has been a failure to meet the relevant regulations in the wake of scandals such as those relating to the practice of removing and storing organs at Bristol Royal Infirmary and Alder Hey Hospital.[10] And it is not only medical professionals who have found their conduct scrutinized under the microscope of the criminal law. Disruptive patients have become the subjects of Anti-Social Banning Orders, and the criminalization of the transmission of HIV has arguably added to the stigmatization of patients with this condition.[11] The trend to prosecute in the medical arena is pervasive, and has undoubtedly had a major impact upon medical professionals and patients, and there is little evidence to suggest that it has been a reflective, carefully measured development.

Placing the criminalization of medical practice within a wider social and cultural context may perhaps shed some light upon the reasons for the growing intervention of the criminal justice system. Ashworth notes that 'the frontiers of criminal liability are not given but are historically contingent'.[12] In the past, medical professionals' actions did not often come under the scrutiny of the criminal law, and in cases where they did, it was rare that criminal liability was found.[13] However, in the current social climate, medical professionals' mistakes are increasingly visible because of the media coverage and political publicity they now attract,[14] aggrieved patients are more empowered to challenge doctors, and

---

[9] *Jepson v The Chief Constable of West Mercia Police Constabulary* [2003] EWHC 3318. It was announced on 16 March 2005 that the doctors in question would not face prosecution by West Mercia CPS as they had acted in good faith, believing that a substantial risk existed that the child would be seriously handicapped. See the Crown Prosecution's website, 'CPS decides not to prosecute doctors following complaint by Rev Joanna Jepson', available at <http://www.cps.gov.uk/news/pressreleases/archive/2005/117_05.html> (accessed 7 May 2007).

[10] The Human Tissue Act 2004. See *Learning from Bristol: the report of the public inquiry into children's heart surgery at the Bristol Royal Infirmary 1984–1995* (CM 5207, 2001), and *Royal Liverpool Children's Inquiry Report* (Stationery Office, 2001). As Ashworth notes, 'The idea of a crime is that it is something that rightly concerns the State, and not just the person(s) affected by the wrongdoing' (A. Ashworth, *Principles of Criminal Law*, 5th edn. (Oxford: Oxford University Press, 2006), 1).

[11] *R v Dica* [2005] EWCA Crim 2304, [2004] 3 All ER 593. Following Dica's conviction for 'biological' grievous bodily harm, the National Aids Trust chief executive, Derek Bodell, stated: 'Treating cases like this as a criminal offence will not prevent such incidents in the future, and on the contrary may be counterproductive. People with HIV should feel able to disclose their HIV status without fear of rejection or discrimination.' See Anon, 'HIV man guilty of infecting lovers', BBC News Online at <http://news.bbc.co.uk/1/hi/england/london/3190626.stm> (accessed 11 April 2007). There is, as may be expected, a large literature on stigmatization and associated issues concerning HIV and AIDS, but see, for example, Catherine Manuel, 'HIV screening: Benefits and harms for the individual and the community', in Rebecca Bennett, & Charles A. Erin (eds.), *HIV and AIDS: Testing, Screening, and Confidentiality—Ethics, Law, and Social Policy* (Oxford: Oxford University Press, 1999) 61–74.

[12] Ashworth, *Principles of Criminal Law*, 22.

[13] See A. Ashworth, 'Criminal liability in a medical context: the treatment of good intentions', in A. P. Simester, & A. T. H. Smith, (eds.), *Harm and Culpability* (Oxford: Clarendon Press, 1996).

[14] M. Brazier 'Editorial: Times of change?', *Medical Law Review*, 13 (2005), 1–16, at 3. In Ashworth's view, 'the growth of the criminal law may reflect particular phases in contemporary social history, as written by the mass media and politicians.' (Ashworth, *Principles of Criminal*

the privileged and haloed status that medical practitioners previously enjoyed no longer protects them from civil and criminal liability. Undoubtedly, a consequence of this is that the public does not consider medical professionals to be infallible, and in the milieu of our modern day 'blame-culture', and in the wake of media coverage of medical scandals such as those mentioned above, much more is expected and demanded of health care providers.[15] Today's public wants justice to be seen to be done, perhaps more so in the health care context than in any other, because of the greater likelihood of serious harm to health if medical professionals do fail to meet their expectations.

The intersection between the criminal justice system and health care is then, clearly ripe for both ethical and legal academic analysis. Yet, to date, little attention has been paid to the questions of whether the criminal justice system is the most apposite forum for determining health care matters and of the impact that the intervention of criminal law has had upon professionals and the delivery of health care in the UK. What do the demands of justice require in the health context? Through greater criminalization of health care, is society aiming to deter other medical professionals from committing medical malpractice, or simply to punish the negligent health care professional, or to rehabilitate him, or all three?

### 3. Themes, cases, and concerns

In its focus upon the role of the criminal justice system in regulating medical practice and the development of health care, this collection of essays aims to fill an important gap in the literature, addressing these issues through a combination of theoretical analyses and key case studies, drawing upon the insights offered by the experiences of other carefully selected jurisdictions. We believe that this volume should be of particular interest to health care and criminal lawyers, criminologists, clinicians, bioethicists, and jurists, but also to patient groups and the general public. There is a particular emphasis upon the *appropriateness* of the involvement of the criminal justice system in health care, the limitations of this developing trend, and suggesting solutions to the problems it is creating. For example, is it appropriate that our society should respond to instances of medical malpractice by attempting to 'stamp them out with the jackboots of the criminal law'?[16] Does this ensure the effective regulation of health care? To adopt a

---

*Law*, 23). For a critique of the media's portrayal of doctors, see V. Harpwood, *Medicine, Malpractice and Misapprehensions*, (Oxford: Routledge-Cavendish, 2007).

[15] M. Brazier 'Do no harm—Do patients have responsibilities too?' (2006) 65 *Cambridge Law Journal* 397–422, at 400, and see M. Brazier & N. Glover, 'Does medical law have a future?' in D. Hayton (ed), *Law's Future(s)* (Oxford: Hart, 2000) 371–88. See also Oliver Quick's chapter in this volume, 'Medical Manslaughter: The Rise (and Replacement) of a Contested Crime', at section 3.

[16] We are borrowing a phrase from Ronald Dworkin here. See his *Life's Dominion: an Argument about Abortion and Euthanasia* (Harper-Collins, 1993) 15.

Benthamite utilitarian approach, is the pain caused to the medical professional by being brought before the criminal law,[17] and punished, justifiable because in treating him in this way, society is deterring other medical professionals from negligently traversing the same terrain? As part of this collection's analysis of whether the increased intervention of the criminal law is appropriate, in several of the chapters, a critical approach to legal reasoning in cases involving health care and medical practice is adopted. For, as Alan Norrie argues, '[i]f we want to understand the nature and logic of developments in the criminal law...we should...seek to understand the *limits* of legal reasoning.'[18]

The themes of the book are explored through a focus upon four areas which serve as primary exemplars of the issues with which we are concerned: the criminalization of medical malpractice, euthanasia and end–of–life cases, neonaticide, and disease transmission. Readers may perhaps have been expecting some consideration of the relationship between criminal law and mental health. However, our omission to deal with this matter in this collection is deliberate; tensions between criminal justice and mental health have been extensively examined[19] and we wished to examine the intervention of the criminal law in areas that have been neglected until now.

The first four chapters in this collection offer a critical and illuminating assessment of the criminal law's increased intervention in cases of medical malpractice. In the first chapter, Margaret Brazier and Neil Allen provide a perceptive analysis of the circumstances in which a doctor's civil liability for negligently caused death transforms into criminal liability. For Brazier and Allen, the utilization of the gross negligence manslaughter offence to deal with doctors whose gross carelessness causes their patients' deaths, in particular, raises significant questions concerning the circumstances in which it is appropriate to consider medical errors to be criminal and highlights the significance of an element of chance in terms of the criminalization of the doctor's conduct. Brazier and Allen draw readers' attention

[17] In his chapter in this volume, Alan Merry provides an affecting account of the markedly more severe impact of a criminal prosecution, irrespective of whether the accused is ultimately convicted, as compared to a civil case, or to professional disciplinary proceedings.

[18] A. Norrie, *Crime, Reason and History: A Critical Introduction to Criminal Law* (2nd edn., London: Butterworths, 2001), 31.

[19] See, for example, N. Gray, J. Laing, & L. Noaks, (eds), *Criminal Justice, Mental Health and the Politics of Risk* (London: Cavendish, 2001); J. Harding, B. Littlechild, & D. Fearns (eds.), *Mental Disorder and Criminal Justice: Policy Provision and Practice* (Dorset: Russell House Publishing, 2005); E. W. Mitchell, *Self-Made Madness: Rethinking Illness and Criminal Responsibility* (Aldershot, Hampshire: Ashgate, 2004); J. Winstone, & F. Pakes, 'Marginalised and disenfranchised: Community justice and mentally disordered offenders', in J. Winstone, & F. Pakes, (eds.), *Community Justice: Issues for Probation and Criminal Justice* (Cullompton: Willan, 2005); J. Winstone, 'Insanity, mental health and the criminal justice system: Criminalised by diagnosis?', in J. Winstone, & F. Pakes, *Psychology and Crime: Understanding and Tackling Offending Behaviour* (Cullompton: Willan, 2007); J. Peay (ed.), *Seminal Issues in Mental Health Law* (Aldershot: Ashgate, 2005); R. A. Lart, *Crossing Boundaries: Accessing Community Mental Health Services for Prisoners on Release* (Bristol: The Policy Press, 1997); I. Cummins, 'A path not taken?: Mentally disordered offenders and the criminal justice system', *Journal of Social Welfare and Family Law*, 28 (2006), 267–81.

to the question of whether, in criminalizing the actions of a medical professional
who negligently causes death, the law is tackling behaviour that warrants punishment. The themes Brazier and Allen identify weave throughout the following
three chapters. Oliver Quick offers a searching critique of the legal response to
medical manslaughter. His analysis suggests that the issue of declining trust may
provide an explanation for the increased trend in prosecutions and an increased
cultural recognition of the phenomenon of negligently caused patient deaths.
Quick has argued for the abolition of the current gross negligence manslaughter offence elsewhere[20] and thus, his critical analysis of the Law Commission's
recently proposed 'killing by gross carelessness' offence, and his consideration of
whether relying upon subjective recklessness liability would be a better alternative in his contribution to this volume is of particular interest.[21] His conclusion is
that the current offence of gross negligence manslaughter should be replaced with
an involuntary manslaughter offence that focuses culpability upon recklessness.
Quick argues that such reform would be likely to reduce the number of prosecutions, but would also be more likely to lead to the criminalization of behaviour in
the most appropriate cases.

In the following chapter, Neil Allen turns his attention to the question of
whether, in cases where patients' deaths are caused by managerial errors, the
criminal law can and should be utilized to hold National Health Service Hospital
Trusts to greater corporate accountability. Allen proposes that difficulties involved
in prosecuting hospital Trusts on the basis of the controversial 'principle of identification' element of corporate liability could be avoided if culpability is established upon the basis that Trusts owe a direct duty of care to patients. He raises a
persuasive argument that the criminal justice system would offer more effective
regulation of medical practice if the judiciary can be convinced to adopt such a
direct liability approach to corporate killing and consequently, we were to witness
an increase of hospital Trusts standing as corporate defendants in the dock.

The increased tendency to resort to criminal prosecutions of health care professionals following the death of a patient is not uniquely a British concern. Such
a trend was particularly noticeable in New Zealand during the late 1980s and
the 1990s. In 'When are errors a crime?', Alan Forbes Merry provides an account
of developments in New Zealand, both before, and after the introduction of the
Crimes Amendment Act 1997 which reformed that country's Crimes Act 1961.
Interestingly, while, prior to this, simple negligence had sufficed for a conviction
for manslaughter, the Crimes Amendment Act raised the threshold in line with
the requirement of gross negligence in England, and this reform had a noticeable
impact in reducing the likelihood of such prosecutions. From the New Zealand
perspective, then, the increase in the frequency of health care professionals facing

---

[20]  O. Quick. 'Prosecuting "gross" medical negligence: Manslaughter, discretion and the Crown
Prosecution Service', *Journal of Law and Society*, 33 (2006), 421–50.
[21]  Law Commission, *A New Homicide Act for England and Wales*, (Law Com CP No 177, 2006).

manslaughter prosecutions that we are currently witnessing in England comes as something of a surprise.

One of Merry's foci is the empirical and theoretical evidence on the mechanisms leading to, and the nature of human error. This helps to ground his analysis of the appropriate legal response to the accidental harming of a patient. Ultimately, the conclusions to which Merry's arguments lead him are critical of prosecution policy in England. Earlier in this chapter, we asked: 'Through greater criminalization of health care, is society aiming to deter other medical professionals from committing medical malpractice, or simply to punish the negligent health care professional, or to rehabilitate him, or all three?' As Merry's analysis shows, some human error is inevitable, and deterrence is ineffectual here. While Merry accepts that punishment does have a place in health care regulation, it must be seen to be just punishment, and, ideally, where appropriate, those responsible for the system, and able to remedy its deficiencies, should also be brought to account. Moreover, if the reduction of harm due to medical error is our priority, the aim should be to improve the system, and criminal prosecution will not provide a reliable way to achieve this. Using the criminal law to regulate normal medical practice, argues Merry, is not desirable for patients, or for society.

The focus of the volume then turns from the criminalization of medical malpractice to the criminal law's involvement in resolving ethical conflicts in health care. As the decriminalization of euthanasia in this jurisdiction seems unlikely, at least for the imminent future, in Chapter 6, Suzanne Ost looks to see whether the existing criminal law could better deal with a medical professional's hastening and/or inducement of death. The inherent difficulties that she identifies with the current legal application of the doctrine of double effect cause her to look to the potential that the doctrine of necessity could hold for doctors who administer lethal treatment to their patients, at their explicit request, in order to relieve severe suffering. The possibility of the defence of necessity being applicable in cases of euthanasia in the medical setting has been increased, Ost argues, by the Court of Appeal's decision in *Re A*.[22] She proposes that a reframed defence of necessity could be available to a medical professional who carries out an instance of euthanasia when 'he acts both reasonably and proportionately and ends the patient's life because he believes that it is immediately necessary to prevent the continuation of severe pain and suffering of the patient, this belief being reasonable and held in good faith'.[23] However, notwithstanding the potential that a revamped doctrine of necessity holds, it remains the case that the criminal law may not be the most effective method of dealing with euthanasia in the medical context.

Ashworth has drawn our attention to the fact that '[t]he criminal law is a preventative mechanism, but there are others'.[24] The particular problems that

---

[22] *Re A (Children) (Conjoined Twins: Medical Treatment) (No 1)* [2001] Fam 147.
[23] S. Ost, 'Euthanasia and the Defence of Necessity: advocating a more appropriate legal response', in this volume.
[24] Ashworth, *Principles of Criminal Law*, 33.

the criminal law creates in its attempted regulation of the practice of euthanasia are explored by John Griffiths in the subsequent chapter. The focus of Griffiths' analysis of the problems posed by the criminal law's intervention is the current system of legal regulation and the criminal control of 'medical behaviour that potentially shortens life' (MBPSL) in the Netherlands. The Netherlands is, of course, almost iconic in its long history of regulated permission of euthanasia, and its more recent legislation governing the practice of euthanasia,[25] as evidenced by a House of Lords Select Committee's visit to the country when considering Lord Joffe's Assisted Dying for the Terminally Ill Bill.[26] Notwithstanding the distinctive approach to the regulation of euthanasia in the Netherlands, Griffiths contends that his essential argument regarding the criminal law is a general one that can be made in relation to other legal systems. His consideration of the significantly different understandings of MBPSL held by the prosecuting authorities and members of the medical profession, and his analysis of why this variance in understanding means that the reporting and regulation of euthanasia under the criminal law will always be problematic, lends credence to the argument that it is now time for the Netherlands and indeed, other jurisdictions, to seriously consider a different direction in their regulation and control of the practice of euthanasia.

In the third of the chapters focusing upon legal intervention in health care at the end of life, Robert Destro analyses the legal sanctioning of the termination of medical treatment in the much-publicized US case of *Schiavo*.[27] Destro who (inter alia) acted as co-counsel for Mrs Schiavo's parents, writes with passion, acting as an advocate for a woman whom he perceives was 'sentenced to death' without due process. His role allows him to offer a revealing insider's insight into the theatre of the judicial process, an insight not often available in academic literature. He is highly critical of the 'conventional wisdom' argument that the judiciary reached a decision in the *Schiavo* case which was within the established Florida legal framework. His view is that the judiciary went beyond the limits of their moral and legal authority, as the trial court served as her substituted decision-maker. According to Destro, legal intervention did not ensure that Terri Schiavo was treated justly. Significantly, he presents an argument that can be perceived to be the converse

[25] The Termination of Life on Request and Assisted Suicide (Review Procedure) Act, effective 1 April 2002. Available online at <http://www.minbuza.nl/binaries/en-pdf/pdf/euth-amendedbill-en.pdf> (accessed 9 May 2007).

[26] The Select Committee was appointed on 30 November 2004. The Committee's Report, *Assisted Dying for the Terminally Ill Bill—First Report*, H.L Paper 86—I, (London: The Stationary Office, 2005), is available online at <http://www.publications.parliament.uk/pa/ld/ldasdy.htm> (accessed 9 May 2007). The text of Lord Joffe's Assisted Dying for the Terminally Ill Bill (HL Bill 36) (as revised following the Select Committee's Report and ordered to be printed on 9 November 2005) can be found at <http://www.publications.parliament.uk/pa/ld200506/ldbills/036/2006036.htm> (accessed 9 May 2007). The Bill was defeated in the House of Lords by 148 votes to 100 in May 2006.

[27] *In re Guardianship of Theresa Marie Schiavo*: *Schindler v Schiavo* 780 So 2d 176, 177–8 (Fla 2d DCA 2001).

of the claim that the criminal law's intervention in health care is inapposite: the US courts in the *Schiavo* case failed to address what to him was the crucial ethical question of whether the decision not to appoint a guardian *ad litem* meant that Terri Schiavo did not receive a fair trial. Yet, he argues, if the court had been hearing a criminal case involving a person facing the death penalty, the due process argument would have been taken more seriously. Approaching the *Schiavo* case from the point of view of the patient, Destro is therefore claiming that her interests would have been better protected had the matter of whether it was appropriate to end her life been one for the criminal as opposed to civil law. This argument is thought-provoking in light of the conclusions reached by other authors in this volume that the criminal justice system is not the appropriate forum in which to decide ethical conflicts regarding health. Destro's chapter also fills an important gap in the existing UK literature, since little has been written about the *Schiavo* case, despite the huge international media coverage it attracted.

That the rising number of prosecutions for medical manslaughter generates concern within the medical profession is well known, and understandable. The complex ethical issues with which a medical professional must contend when confronted by a patient's request for assisted dying can only be exacerbated by the knowledge that his consequent actions may educe criminal liability. At the British Medical Association (BMA) conference in June 2005, doctors dropped their former opposition to changes in the law which would permit assistance with dying, and opted for an essentially neutral stance.[28] It is worth noting, however, that '[t]hey agreed that the question of the criminal law in relation to assisted dying was "primarily a matter for society and for Parliament"'.[29] The fact that, at the 2006 BMA conference, 65 per cent of the 500 doctors present voted to overturn the 2005 decision[30] gives some indication, we think, of the difficulties this issue raises in doctors' minds. It is against this kind of background that Michael Wilks gives a British doctor's perspective on medical treatment at the end of life. As demonstrated by Griffiths, there are various conceptions of MBPSL, and it can take more than one form. While Ost's and Griffiths' primary focus is on 'active' euthanasia,[31] and Destro's on withdrawal of life-sustaining treatment, Wilks' assessment encompasses both.

In terms of recent developments regarding the way ethical principles impact upon clinical practice at the end of life, Wilks identifies three influences as key: the increased demand for 'patients' rights'; medical advances that can prolong

---

[28] Anon, 'BMA drops euthanasia opposition', BBC News Online, 30 June 2005 at <http://news.bbc.co.uk/1/hi/health/4637835.stm> (accessed 9 May 2007).

[29] Ibid.

[30] Anon, 'Doctors change euthanasia stance', BBC News Online, 29 June 2006 at <http://news.bbc.co.uk/1/hi/health/5123974.stm> (accessed 9 May 2007).

[31] A term we use for brevity here, although it is not our preferred term for referring to the situation where a doctor administers lethal treatment to her patient at the patient's request. See S. Ost, *An Analytical Study of the Legal, Moral and Ethical Aspects of the Living Phenomenon of Euthanasia*, (Lewiston, New York: Edwin Mellen Press, 2003) 50.

life; and the Human Rights Act 1998. In concert, these elements can lead to tensions for a doctor trying, at one and the same time, to respect his patient's vulnerability, assist the patient in articulating his or her authentic wishes, and to follow these wishes while remaining within the law. While the starting point for all therapeutic encounters is the clinical perspective, over the last thirty years or so, what would normally follow has changed in that what now constitutes the best interests of a competent patient may incorporate the patient's expressed autonomous wishes which are not in line with what would be perceived as a 'good' outcome in clinical terms alone. Such developments, and the level of confusion that seems to abound over distinctions between, for example, assisted dying and palliation, and between euthanasia and withdrawal of treatment, cannot but frustrate the doctor's attempts at good clinical practice and make his situation parlous in the eyes of the law. Moreover, Wilks challenges the established, and, again, often confusing application of the doctrine of double effect, and demonstrates that many of the beliefs about the consequences of withdrawing artificial nutrition and hydration are based on a misunderstanding of the clinical scenarios involved.

With Stephen W. Smith's chapter, we move to the third of our exemplars, that of neonaticide. The Abortion Act 1967 imposes no time limit for the termination of a severely disabled fetus. However, if a doctor were to comply with a mother's wish to terminate the life of a severely disabled neonate, he would face a charge of murder. This raises an interesting philosophical question: why is it apparently acceptable to terminate a fetus for severe disability, while it is not acceptable to terminate a neonate for the same disability? Smith begins by exploring this apparent inconsistency from the perspectives of two popular arguments, the argument that life begins at conception, and the argument from personhood, and demonstrates why each is to be found wanting in this regard. He then adopts a somewhat less popular theoretical template, and applies the so-called dignitarian approach, as laid down by Beyleveld and Brownsword.[32] Their work is, in no small part, predicated upon Alan Gewirth's theory of ethical rationalism, and the principle of generic consistency (PGC). His *Reason and Morality*[33] was first published in 1978, and the theoretical approach laid out there has attracted many critics,[34] and some notable proponents, including Deryck Beyleveld.[35] Both sides will likely be fascinated by Smith's application of this approach to the issue at hand.

Smith's aim is to discover whether it is possible to 'create *a logical ethical distinction* between allowing the termination of a fetus for severe disability prior to birth

---

[32] D. Beyleveld and R. Brownsword *Human Dignity in Bioethics and Biolaw* (Oxford: Oxford University Press, 2001).

[33] A. Gewirth, *Reason and Morality* (Chicago, IL: Chicago University Press, 1978).

[34] See, for example, E. R. Jr (ed.), *Gewirth's Ethical Rationalism: Critical Essays with a Reply by Alan Gewirth* (Chicago, IL: Chicago University Press, 1984).

[35] See, for example, Deryck Beyleveld, *The Dialectical Necessity of Morality: an Analysis and Defence of Gewirth's Argument to the Principle of Generic Consistency* (Chicago, IL: Chicago University Press, 1991).

while maintaining that the intentional killing of a newborn after birth for the same severe disability is not acceptable'.[36] Finding that the PGC, in its standard, Gewirthian form, which can assign 'partial agency' to fetuses and neonates, takes us no further than the argument from personhood, Smith follows Beyleveld and Brownsword's line on agency (as a threshold concept), and adopts their refined 'precautionary principle' to make room for our imperfect knowledge of the world. Effectively, a probability exercise allows us to distinguish between entities that are more likely agents and those things that are less likely agents. From this basis, Smith shows how, with some manipulation, the dignitarian approach will provide a logically consistent ethical justification for the distinction we endorse, intuitively, and in law, between our positions on the fetus with severe disability and the neonate with severe disability.

In today's rights-orientated society, almost all areas of law have been pervaded by human rights concerns, so much so that readers would no doubt have been surprised had this aspect of law not been explored in a volume that addresses crucial matters of life and death and criminal justice. It is to the matter of human rights that Elizabeth Wicks turns in her chapter upon the termination of fetal and neonatal life. Following her analysis of whether the significance of birth can justify the fact that the criminal law treats the termination of fetal life and the killing of a neonate differently, Wicks then proceeds to critically evaluate whether the law's differential treatment of the fetus and the neonate rests easily with human rights concerns. It is her conclusion that the criminal law's intervention in these two contexts does in fact reflect the status ascribed to fetal and neonatal life and the way in which the right to life is applied to the fetus and to the neonate in human rights law.

It is the significance of viability, rather than the point of birth that features prominently in Sergio Romeo-Malanda's chapter, and its examination of whether medical professionals in Spain can be held criminally responsible if they withdraw life-sustaining treatment from severely disabled newborn babies. The focus on the Spanish jurisdiction here is significant, since, in contrast to the legal position in the UK, America, Australia, and elsewhere, Romeo-Malanda explains that the position under Spanish law is currently much more ambiguous. Thus, medical professionals faced with making the decision of whether to discontinue medical treatment or to omit to treat severely disabled newborns must reach this decision in a climate of uncertainty as to whether their actions will attract criminal liability, and in the absence of any clear guidelines. His analysis and application of the Spanish criminal law leads Romeo-Malanda to conclude that it is the distinction between viability and non-viability that marks the point at which the law will intervene to criminalize the medical professional's actions, since a non-viable

---

[36] S. Smith, 'Dignity: The Difference Between Abortion and Neonaticide for Severe Disability', in this volume [our emphasis].

human being is not recognized as a newborn infant under Spanish law, and thus does not enjoy the protection of the criminal law.

The last of our four exemplars is the criminalization of disease transmission. Rebecca Bennett considers whether the convictions we have witnessed, since 2003, for reckless transmission of HIV during consensual sexual intercourse constitute an appropriate legal response. These convictions have been obtained under section 20 of the Offences Against the Person Act 1861, which previously had been interpreted as allowing a charge of grievous bodily harm only for acts involving violence. However, this changed, in 1998, with a House of Lords ruling[37] that established that grievous bodily harm can involve non-violent behaviour.

Bennett shows that the judgments in these cases 'effectively establish a legal duty upon HIV-positive persons to disclose their HIV-status before engaging in activities which are considered to pose a high risk of transmission of the virus'.[38] Bennett's analysis proceeds from the question of what the imposition of such a duty under the criminal law sets out to achieve. She shows that, while reduction of the incidence of HIV transmission is a clear public health goal, the threat of prosecution will not necessarily lead to a reduction in risky behaviour, and criminalization actually runs the risk of being counter-productive in this area. Bennett then scrutinizes the retributive aim of criminalization, and demonstrates that the correspondence of the moral situation with the legal stance is not as straightforward a matter as some perceive. The moral wrong involved in such cases can vary, argues Bennett, according to, for example, the level of risk involved, and the nature of the parties' relationship. At the moral level, not all cases, certainly, will deserve punishment by the criminal law. Bennett concludes that attempts to quantify the level of moral wrong in each case are fraught with difficulty, and often inappropriate, and that the criminalization of reckless sexual transmission of HIV should be resisted.

Like Bennett, Erin is an applied philosopher, and he makes no claim to possession of a 'legal mind', an embarrassment which he tries to harness to good effect in offering a lay perspective on the law. The cases analysed by Bennett take the issue of forewarning as central, and establish that, under the current interpretation of the Offences Against the Person Act 1861, consent to the risk of HIV transmission through sexual intercourse will stand as a valid defence in the criminal law. Erin's starting point is *R v Brown*, in which the mutual consent of the actors was *not* allowed as a valid defence. In essence, Erin's chapter constitutes a plea for consistency in the law, or, at the very least, a plea for reasonable explanation and resolution of why the inconsistencies the lay eye perceives are not just that, *inconsistencies*. Why is it, he asks, that the likes of the defendants in *Brown* suffered grave penalties from the criminal law for mutually consensual acts of harm,[39]

---

[37] *R v Ireland; R v Burstow* [1998] AC 147.
[38] R. Bennett, 'Should We Criminalize HIV Transmission?', in this volume.
[39] *R v Brown* [1993] 2 All ER 75.

while doctors who perform 'operations' such as labia trimming do not? Consent seems clearly to be the core issue. And the lay person is left wondering why the consent of the defendants in *Brown* was seen to be irrelevant, and why there exists a medical exemption to this attitude.

Allowing the likes of John Stuart Mill and Joel Feinberg to make the running for him, Erin concludes that it is the *harm principle* that sketches the rightful domain of the criminal law, and applying these jurisprudential considerations to *Brown*, shows that the defendants there did not fall foul of the harm principle. The comparison with various medical procedures, including several involved in aesthetic surgery, does seem to throw up inconsistencies between the way the criminal law deals with similar acts according to whether they are done by private citizens or by qualified medical professionals. Erin argues that the presumption in favour of liberty and autonomy should prevail, and, thus, not that we should see more doctors in the dock, but, rather, that the likes of the defendants in *Brown* should be freed of the risk of criminal law penalties.

In the concluding chapter, Jonathan Montgomery draws together the broad themes of the book, utilizing two of the areas of focus (the criminalization of medical malpractice and disease transmission) as case studies. He undertakes a socio-legal analysis of whether the intervention of the criminal law in health care is defensible, and whether it can, in fact, achieve the realization of social goals. Montgomery argues that the role of the criminal law in health matters should necessarily be limited by the interests of justice. An issue of great interest that Montgomery raises is whether media constructions of those who transmit diseases such as AIDS have given rise to a moral panic about which individuals pose the greatest danger of deliberate infection. We would like to take Montgomery's analysis further here by raising the possibility that such a moral panic may have been formed as a result of an availability cascade. As the public does not have all the precise information or the personal experience to reach a careful, informed judgement about the dangers of individuals deliberately transmitting diseases such as AIDS, we rely instead upon the representations most readily available from the media. The media's coverage and focus upon those individuals who transmit disease and share particular racial and sexual characteristics,[40] the ease with which we can access this coverage, and our consequent acceptance of this as shorthand to enable us to decide upon the extent of the problem of disease transmission, means that it is easy for us to bring to mind the prevalence of the deliberate transmission of AIDS by individuals sharing certain racial and sexual characteristics as a real and prominent danger.[41]

---

[40] As highlighted by Jonathan Montgomery in his chapter, 'Medicalizing Crime—Criminalizing Health?: The Role of Law', in this volume.

[41] 'Availability cascades' are defined as 'social cascades, or simply cascades, through which expressed perceptions trigger chains of individual responses that make these perceptions appear increasingly plausible through their rising availability in public discourse.' T. Kuran & C. Sunstein, 'Availability Cascades and Risk Regulation', *Stanford Law Review*, 51 (1999), 683–768, at 685.

Whilst it should be apparent from the above discussion of the direction and focus of each of the chapters that they are connected by the broad theme of the criminalization of health care and the impact of this criminalization upon medical professionals and society, needless to say, there is a wide divergence of views between authors. Yet, there is one argument that is reflected in several of the chapters; that it is appropriate for the criminal law to intervene when the medical professional acts in a way that is *subjectively* culpable. For instance, Quick contends that the fault element of gross negligence manslaughter should be replaced with subjective recklessness to better ensure the criminalization of the actions of medical professionals who cause their patients' deaths in the most appropriate cases, a view that is echoed by Brazier and Allen. The recommendation in Allen's chapter is that the offence of corporate manslaughter be modified so that it becomes easier to prosecute hospital Trusts rather than individual medical professionals in circumstances where it is system failures that lead to tragic deaths, rather than subjective culpability on the part of medical professionals. Destro finishes his chapter with an admonition to medical professionals that they should take personal responsibility for their actions in order to avoid the intervention of the criminal and the civil law. According to Romeo-Malanda, it is the lack of general legal guidelines laying down the boundary between criminal and non-criminal behaviour that poses a real problem for Spanish doctors who seek guidance as to their personal responsibility when deciding whether to withdraw life-sustaining treatment from severely disabled neonates. For Montgomery, in health matters, it is the deliberate causing of harm rather than the inadvertent infliction of injury that should be subject to the criminal law, and he goes so far as to argue that the intervention of the criminal justice system in the context of the latter poses a real and significant risk to society's health.

One dissenter appears to be Griffiths. For the practical and pragmatic reasons he identifies in his chapter, he argues that the regulation and control of MBPSL should be placed outside the reach of the criminal law, and a system of professional self-control, backed up by monitoring by the Netherlands Health Inspectorate instead be put in place. Thus, under Griffiths' suggested scheme, the medical profession itself would bear responsibility for ensuring its members face up to their subjective responsibilities and conform to their ethical duties towards their patients, and indeed, society. Thus, whatever else this volume achieves, it should cause readers to pause and reflect upon the case for and against dealing with errant medical professionals and resolving ethical dilemmas through the criminal justice system.

# 2

# Criminalizing Medical Malpractice

*Margaret Brazier and Neil Allen*

## 1. Introduction

I imagine that you will think long and hard before deciding that doctors, of the eminence we have heard, representing to you what medical ethics are ... have evolved standards which amount to committing crime.[1]

In this key part of his direction to the jury in the trial of Dr Leonard Arthur for the attempted[2] murder of a disabled newborn infant, Farquharson J seemingly encapsulates a tradition of deference towards the medical profession. In 1981, it may sometimes have appeared that doctors enjoyed a special status close to immunity from the usual rigours of the law. Relatively few doctors faced even civil claims.[3] When such claims were brought by patients, judges tended to defend the doctors.[4] Farquharson J's words echoed much earlier judicial pronouncements. In 1859, Pollock CB directing the jury on a charge of manslaughter, in a case in

---

[1] *R v Arthur* (1981) 12 BMLR 1, 22.

[2] Dr Arthur was initially charged with the murder of an infant boy born suffering from Down's syndrome. After consultation with the parents, Dr Arthur ordered that the baby be given nursing care only and prescribed a drug that would suppress the baby's appetite. The prosecution contended that Dr Arthur in effect starved the baby to death. In the course of the trial, expert evidence established that Dr Arthur's actions had not caused the baby's death. He died of natural causes. Thus, mid-trial, the charge against Dr Arthur was reduced to attempted murder. See H. Benyon, 'Doctors as Murderers', *Criminal Law Review*, [1982], 17–28; M. Gunn, and J. C. Smith, 'Arthur's Case and the Right to Life of a Down's Syndrome Child', *Criminal Law Review* [1985], 705–15.

[3] Although a rise in the number of what were described then as medical negligence claims was noted in 1957 (see P. C. Nathan, and A. R. Barrowclough, *Medical Negligence* (London: Butterworths, 1957) 5), it was not until the 1980s that the number of claims began to rise rapidly prompting alarm among the medical profession. The number of claims initiated doubled between 1983 and 1987; see C. Ham, R. Dingwall, P. Fenn, and D. Harris, *Medical Negligence, Compensation and Accountability* (London and Oxford: King's Fund Institute and Centre for Socio-Legal Studies, 1988). And, see generally, M. A. Jones, *Medical Negligence* (3rd edn, London: Sweet & Maxwell, 2003).

[4] See, for example, Lord Denning in *Hatcher v Black* The Times (2 July 1954); and *Whitehouse v Jordan* [1980] 1 All ER 650, 658, CA. And see *Maynard v West Midlands RHA* [1984] 1 WLR 634, 639 per Lord Scarman. And see generally M. Brazier and E. Cave, *Medicine, Patients and the Law*, (4th edn, London: Lexis-Nexis/Penguin, 2007) paras 7. to 7.7.

which an unqualified health practitioner had administered a dangerous medicine with fatal results, said this:

If the prisoner had been a medical man I should have recommended you to take the most favourable view of his conduct for *it would be most fatal to the efficiency of the medical profession if no-one could administer medicine without a halter round his neck.*[5]

In 2007, the picture looks very different. Although there is some evidence that the crude number of civil claims for clinical negligence may be levelling out,[6] medical practitioners have witnessed a revolution in terms of vulnerability to malpractice claims.[7] The judges too have moved some way from earlier attitudes of protectionism towards medical 'brethren' voicing more strongly a culture of accountability[8] and patient rights.[9] Of especial concern however to the medical profession, will be the rise in the number of prosecutions for 'medical manslaughter'. Reliable statistics are not readily available. Ferner,[10] however, has found evidence of just forty-one prosecutions for gross negligence manslaughter brought against doctors between 1795 and 1974. Yet forty-four were prosecuted between 1975 and 2005.

In this introductory essay, we begin to examine the role that the criminal justice system does, and should play in ensuring accountability for medical malpractice. When are medical errors rightly crimes? If England and Wales prove to be moving towards a greater role for the criminal law—if in truth we are criminalizing medical malpractice, *cui bono*—will patients sleep easier in their beds in the knowledge that more doctors face ending up in the dock? In the following essay, Oliver Quick[11] expands upon our analysis of 'medical manslaughter', and considers the Law Commission's[12] proposals to replace gross negligence manslaughter by an offence of 'killing by gross negligence'. Quick develops a critical analysis of why resort to prosecution has become more common. He argues for the abolition

---

[5]  *R v Crick* (1859) 1 F&F 519 (our emphasis).

[6]  The number of claims received by the National Health Service Litigation Authority (NHSLA) fell to 5,609 in 2004–05 from 6,251 in 2003–04. The figures for 2005–06 indicate a small increase in numbers again to 5,697. See *NHSLA Factsheet 3: information on claims* (July 2006) at <http://www.nhsla.com>.

[7]  It was reported that in 1996, 36 per cent of consultants and senior registrars had been sued at least once; see *Hansard*, cols 165–6 (24 March 1998).

[8]  See, for example, *Bolitho v City & Hackney Health Authority* [1997] 4 All ER 771, HL. See M. Brazier, and J. Miola, 'Bye-Bye Bolam: A Medical Litigation Revolution?', *Medical Law Review* 8 (2000), 85–114.

[9]  Notably in *Chester v Afshar* [2005] 1 AC 134, HL.

[10]  R. Ferner and S. McDowell 'Doctors charged with manslaughter in the course of medical practice, 1795–2005: a literature review', *Journal of the Royal Society of Medicine*, 99 (2006), 309–14. And see R. Ferner, 'Medication errors that have led to manslaughter charges', *British Medical Journal*, 321 (2000), 1212–16.

[11]  See Oliver Quick's chapter in the current volume, 'Medical Manslaughter: The Rise (and Replacement) of a Contested Crime'.

[12]  Law Commission, *A New Homicide Act for England and Wales?* (Law Com CP No 177, 2006); discussed by Quick in 'Medical Manslaughter', in this volume.

of gross negligence manslaughter and considers the merits of appropriate alternatives to address the most serious incidence of medical malpractice. In this essay, we address only the criminal liability of individual practitioners, not the corporate liability of NHS Trusts or other NHS authorities. Neil Allen tackles the thorny question of corporate manslaughter in the NHS in the third essay of this collection.[13] We limit our discussion to crimes of negligence and eschew questions of intentional harm or killing.[14] Harold Shipman is not our central concern, albeit his undoubtedly evil and criminal conduct may be a factor influencing public attitudes to criminalizing medicine.

## 2. Medical error: medical crime[15]

English law (unlike Scottish law) has never treated negligence, even gross negligence or recklessness, as a crime per se. A doctor may make the most egregious error[16] yet escape criminal liability unless he or she (and the patient) are unlucky and his or her patient dies. Statute has criminalized certain kinds of negligence, notably in relation to careless driving and matters of health and safety.[17] 'Among common law crimes, only manslaughter rests on liability for (gross) negligence.'[18] What constitutes the requisite degree of negligence to render negligent 'killing' a crime has long troubled the courts. In *R v Bateman*,[19] a doctor faced trial after his patient died in childbirth. Directing the jury, the judge simply advised that they must be satisfied that 'the negligence of the accused went beyond a mere matter of compensation between subjects and showed such disregard for the life and safety of others as to amount to a crime against the state and conduct deserving punishment'.[20]

*Bateman* begs the question of what sort of conduct merits punishment. The language of disregard might seem to connote what lay persons would consider to be recklessness. The doctor indifferent to his patient's welfare, or one who goes ahead with a course of treatment regardless of risk, might well be seen to merit punishment.[21] In the 1970s, it appeared for a short while that gross negligence

---

[13] See Neil Allen's chapter in the current volume, 'Medical or Managerial Manslaughter?'.

[14] See W. Hesketh, 'Medico-Crime: Time For a Police-Health Professions Protocol', *Police Journal*, 76 (2003), 121–34.

[15] For an early discussion of this tendentious question see A. McCall Smith, 'Criminal Negligence and the Incompetent Doctor', *Medical Law Review*, 1 (1993), 336–49.

[16] See, for example, *Kay v Ayrshire and Arran Health Board* [1987] 2 All ER 417, HL discussed below.

[17] See Quick, 'Medical Manslaughter', in this volume.

[18] A. Ashworth, *Principles of Criminal Law*, (5th edn, Oxford: Oxford University Press, 2006) 190.

[19] [1925] All ER Rep 45; approved in *Andrews v DPP* [1937] AC 576, HL.

[20] Ibid, at 48.

[21] *R v Saha and Salim* (1992) (unreported) discussed in J. K. Mason, and G. T. Laurie, *Mason & McCall Smith's Law & Medical Ethics*, (7th edn, Oxford: Oxford University Press, 2005) 345.

manslaughter in general was mutating into a crime requiring proof of recklessness.[22] Mere inadvertence was not sufficient; recklessness as defined by Lord
Diplock in *R v Caldwell*[23] must be proven.[24] As Ashworth notes,[25] it came to be
'widely assumed that gross negligence manslaughter had been absorbed into and
replaced by reckless manslaughter'.

Any such assumption soon proved mistaken. And the crucial judgment
derived from the most (in)famous of all medical manslaughter prosecutions. In
*R v Adomako,*[26] the House of Lords firmly reinstated gross negligence as the
requisite pre-condition to transform death caused by negligence into homicide.
*Adomako* represented the culmination of two separate prosecutions against doctors whose negligence resulted in the death of their patient. The first case involved
the prosecution of two junior doctors, Dr Sullman and Dr Prentice. The second
concerned a Dr Adomako, a locum anaesthetist. The facts of both cases need to
be briefly recapped.[27]

Dr Sullman and Dr Prentice were caring for a 16-year-old boy, admitted to
Peterborough General Hospital for his monthly chemotherapy. The patient
had suffered from leukaemia since the age of four. His regime required him to
receive two drugs—vincristine (to be administered intravenously) and metho-
textrate (administered intrathecally). Dr Prentice was a pre-registration house
officer; Dr Sullman a house officer. The former had never administered such
drugs before, nor had he received relevant training, whilst the latter had very
limited relevant experience. The drugs were brought down to the ward on a trolley. Dr Prentice asked Dr Sullman to supervise him in administering the lumbar
puncture. Dr Sullman believed he was just supervising the procedure itself.
Dr Prentice injected the vincristine into the boy's spine. The boy died some days
later in agony. Careful reading of the labels on the vials of both drugs would have
indicated the proper route of administration, though not necessarily the disastrous
effect of administering vincristine intrathecally. Both doctors were convicted of
manslaughter, albeit the judge told them 'you could have been helped more than
you were helped—You are far from being bad men'. They were guilty, the trial
judge said, of momentary recklessness, but that sufficed to make them criminals.

Dr Adomako was an anaesthetist. He had worked as a locum for 15 years,
rarely staying more than a few months in any job. His command of English was
poor. In the course of minor eye surgery he failed to notice for over four minutes
that the tube carrying oxygen to his patient had become dislodged. His standard
of care was said to be abysmal. Dr Adomako was also convicted of manslaughter.

[22] See Ashworth, *Principles of Criminal Law*, 291.
[23] [1982] AC 341.
[24] See *R v Seymour* [1983] 1 AC 624, HL; *R v Kong Cheuk Kwan* (1985) 82 Cr App R 18, PC.
[25] See Ashworth, *Principles of Criminal Law*, 292.
[26] [1995] 1 AC 171, HL.
[27] See M. Brazier, 'Wilfred Fish Lecture: The Tooth Fairy in the Dock', *British Dental Journal*,
193 (2002), 193–7.

His appeal was consolidated into one hearing together with the appeals of Dr Prentice and Dr Sullman.[28] Their appeal succeeded. Dr Adomako's failed.

The Court of Appeal[29] outlined the following test for gross negligence manslaughter:

(i)   Did the doctor show indifference to an obvious risk of injury to his patient?
(ii)  Was he (or she) aware of the risk but decided (for no good reason) to run the risk?
(iii) Were efforts to avoid a recognised risk so grossly negligent as to deserve punishment?
(iv)  Was there a degree of inattention or failure to have due regard to risks going beyond mere inadvertence?[30]

At least one of these questions must be answered affirmatively before a doctor can be convicted of manslaughter.

The appeal court ruled that in the cases of Dr Sullman and Dr Prentice there was insufficient evidence of gross negligence. Dr Adomako's conviction was upheld. The appeal judges said he failed in 'his essential and ... sole duty to see that his patient was breathing satisfactorily and to cope with the breathing emergency ... his failure was more then mere inadvertence and constituted gross negligence of the degree necessary for manslaughter'.[31]

Dr Adomako appealed to the House of Lords without success.[32] The Law Lords neither reviewed the appeal court's four-part test of gross negligence, nor offered a helpful definition, Lord Mackay LC merely saying that '[t]he jury will have to consider whether the extent to which the defendant's conduct departed from the proper standard of care incumbent upon him ... was such that it should be judged criminal'.[33] What the Law Lords did do was to remove (at least in theory) any requirement for subjective fault from liability for gross negligence manslaughter. Dr Adomako was in effect convicted of being an extremely incompetent doctor.

In *Adomako*, Lord Mackay declined to offer any greater precision about just how incompetent a doctor must be to face criminal conviction, saying that this was 'likely to achieve only a spurious precision'. He acknowledged that the test he advanced involves an 'element of circularity'.[34] Dr Becker faced the same fate as Dr Adomako. Dr Becker attended a patient suffering the excruciating pain of

---

[28] A third case, consolidated into the one appeal hearing related to an electrician, Stephen Holloway. Mr Holloway was convicted of manslaughter following a retrial, after his alleged negligence in fitting the electrical components of a central heating system resulted in a member of the household suffering a fatal electric shock. The wiring had been wrongly connected, and even after members of the family had suffered electric shocks and Mr Holloway had revisited the house, the error was not discovered by him. Mr Holloway's appeal succeeded.

[29] *R v Prentice, R v Adomako, R v Holloway* [1993] 4 All ER 935, CA.

[30] Ibid, at 943–4.

[31] Ibid, at 954.

[32] [1995] 1 AC 171.

[33] Ibid, at 187.

[34] Ibid. Attempts to review *Adomako* by asking the Law Lords to reconsider their decision have so far failed; see *R v Mark (Alan James)* [2004] EWCA Crim 2490 and see Mason and Laurie, *Mason & McCall Smith's Law & Medical Ethics*, 346.

renal colic. He decided to combine two painkilling drugs, volterol and diamorphine, to ensure rapid relief. But he wrongly selected a 30mg dose of diamorphine rather than the correct dose of 10mg. He injected the diamorphine intramuscularly together with the correct dose of volterol. The overdose of diamorphine resulted in respiratory failure and the patient died. The doctor was convicted of manslaughter and his appeal failed.[35] The judge had followed exactly the directions in *Adomako*. The jury were instructed that they must be satisfied that Dr Becker's negligence was criminal. No further definition of 'gross' was required of the judge.

Dr Misra and Dr Srivastava[36] were convicted of manslaughter after their patient died when they failed to treat a post-operative infection after surgery to repair the patella tendon. Over a period of 48 hours the doctors omitted to act on evidence that the patient was critically ill. They failed to chase up the results of blood cultures and ignored warnings from nurses and a third medical colleague. The patient died of toxic shock. The two senior house officers appealed (inter alia) on the grounds that manslaughter by gross negligence was an offence offending against Article 7[37] of the European Convention of Human Rights because the offence lacked certainty. Their appeal failed. Gross negligence manslaughter requires that the accused must be shown to have failed to act to avert a risk of death, or have acted in such a way as to exacerbate that risk. Risk of bodily harm or risk to health alone will not suffice. That said, once breach of duty in relation to that risk to life was shown, the jury must be directed to consider whether the accused's negligence was gross and *consequently* criminal. The hypothetical citizen seeking to know his potential liability for criminal conviction could simply be advised that if he owed a duty of care to the deceased which he negligently breached he would be liable for manslaughter if, on all the evidence, a jury was satisfied his negligence was gross. There was thus no uncertainty violating Article 7.

The Court of Appeal addressed three key issues:

(i) They made it clear that proof of gross negligence alone transforms 'simple' negligence engaging only civil liability into crime. It was not the case that juries should decide (a) was the negligence gross and (b) was that gross negligence *additionally* criminal? Criminal liability did not depend on the jury's purely subjective perception of the defendant's conduct.

(ii) In determining whether the relevant negligence was gross the jury must consider 'all the relevant circumstances in which the breach of duty occurred. In each case, of course, the circumstances are fact specific'.

[35] *R v Becker* (2000) WL 877688.
[36] *R v Misra and Srivastava* [2005] 1 Cr App R 21; discussed in O. Quick, 'Prosecuting Medical Mishaps' *New Law Journal*, 156 (2006), 394–5.
[37] Article 7 requires that any criminal offence must be framed in sufficiently clear terms so that people may be aware of what does, and does not, constitute criminal conduct.

(iii) Gross negligence manslaughter is not a crime without *mens rea*. *Mens rea* may properly be used to describe an element of fault or culpability which the exceptionally bad nature of the relevant negligence supplies as opposed to the defendant's state of mind.

*Misra and Srivastava* sought to limit the circularity of the crime of gross negligence manslaughter while openly acknowledging the presence of an element of circularity.[38] But do the arguments convince? Can an adequate boundary be identified explaining why Dr Prentice and Dr Sullman were merely 'simply' negligent while Dr Adomako, Becker, Misra and Srivastava were grossly careless? Readers of the reported judgments lack access to the evidence available to the jury. But could it be argued that Adomako and Becker fell the wrong side of the line? The Court of Appeal in *R v Prentice* judged Dr Prentice and Dr Sullman merely momentarily inadvertent. Dr Adomako was dreadfully incompetent. Dr Becker made an awful error in the heat of the moment. Dr Misra and Dr Srivastava failed in their duty to their patient over a sustained period. The appeal judges approved the trial judge's direction that the jury should be satisfied that the doctors' conduct fell so far below the standard to be expected that 'it was something . . . truly exceptionally bad, which showed . . . indifference to' an obviously serious risk to the life of the patient.[39] Is that where a line can be drawn? Or is to do so to seek (yet again) to reinstate reckless manslaughter?

## 3 Crime and carelessness

In attempting to evaluate when medical error should rightly become medical crime, the relationship between crime and careless conduct more generally must be addressed, together with the proper role of criminal law in society. The increasing exposure of doctors to prosecution for manslaughter may simply be reflective of a more general trend in the development of English law. As Jean Hampton has commented we live in a society where '[a]ccusing, condemning and avenging are part of our daily life'.[40]

To the doctor in the dock, accused of gross negligence manslaughter, the element of chance may loom large.[41] Others may have been more grossly negligent than he, yet not faced prosecution. In *Kay v Ayrshire and Arran Health Board*[42] doctors

---

[38] In *R v Misra* [2004] All ER (D) 150, the Court of Appeal refused leave to appeal to the House of Lords but certified that a point of law of general importance was involved in the case—'Does the offence of gross negligence manslaughter comply with the European Convention on Human Rights?'.
[39] See n 36 above, para 66.
[40] J. Hampton, 'Mens rea' in E. F. Paul, F. D. Miller, and J. Paul (eds.), *Crime, Culpability and Remedy*, (Oxford: Basil Blackwell, 1990), 1–28, at 1.
[41] On which see the seminal article, J. C. Smith, 'The Element of Chance in Criminal Liability', Criminal Law Review, [1971], 63–75.
[42] See above, n 16.

negligently administered an overdose of 30 times the proper dosage of penicillin to a little boy suffering from meningitis. The skill and dedication of other doctors saved the boy's life and saved their colleagues from the dock. When death results from medical malpractice then, and then alone, does the careless doctor risk criminal redress. The consequences of the careless conduct, not the degree of carelessness alone, transform error into crime. As Smith notes in his example of the careless father who keeps colourless weedkiller in a lemonade bottle within his child's reach and the child drinks the poison mistaking it for lemonade: 'My moral culpability and my dangerousness as a father and a member of society is no less the case where no harm is done than in the case where death occurred.'[43]

Dr Becker was no more blameworthy or a danger to his patients than his luckier brethren in *Kay*. Dr Becker's conviction must be justifiable because the greater harm justifies the punishment. In *Misra*, the Court of Appeal invoked the law's duty to protect the right to life.[44] Smith[45] cites Stephen J who overtly acknowledged the emotional and symbolic components of the criminal law. Giving the example of two people guilty of exactly the same carelessness but only one of whom causes a fatal accident Stephen J opined:

In one sense, each has committed an offence, but one has had the bad luck to cause a horrible misfortune, and to attract public attention to it, and the other the good fortune to do no harm. Both certainly deserve punishment but *it gratifies a natural public feeling to choose out for punishment the one who has actually caused great harm and the effect in the way of preventing a repetition of the offence is much the same as if both were punished.*[46]

In these words uttered well over a century ago Stephen J encapsulated today's emphasis on retribution. In 1971, JC Smith forthrightly disagreed. He commented that if criminal law is to be based on emotional reactions, '[i]s this not naked retribution—and a very crude form of retribution, the degree of punishment being based not on the moral culpability but on the harm done?'[47] Smith proposed that either gross negligence manslaughter should be abolished or a new crime of inflicting non-fatal injury by gross negligence be created. His own preference leaned towards the former course of action in line with his philosophy that '[w]e should only have as much criminal law as we have to have. The enforcement of the criminal law, as such, benefits no one—except possibly the lawyers engaged in the case.'[48]

Cogent arguments could be, and are, advanced for granting the criminal law a broader role in deterring negligent behaviour endangering others.[49] The model of

---

[43] Smith, 'The Element of Chance in Criminal Liability', 66.
[44] See n 36 above at para 52, per Judge LJ.
[45] Smith, 'The Element of Chance in Criminal Liability', 71–2.
[46] *History of the Criminal Law,* vol III ( Macmillan, 1883), 311 ff (our emphasis).
[47] Smith, 'The Element of Chance in Criminal Liability', 73.
[48] Ibid.
[49] See Ashworth, *Principles of Criminal Law*, 191–5.

specific negligence-based offences, well established in the contexts of road safety and safety at work, could be extended to health care.[50] In the absence of such changes we would argue that criminal liability for medical malpractice resulting in death must thus either be rooted in a framework endorsing retribution or be based on evidence of effective deterrence. For Smith, only the latter would suffice. For Stephen, retribution is valid but somehow also operates as deterrence. Merry and McCall Smith,[51] writing expressly about medical error, fall into Smith's camp. They contend that society should distinguish between two kinds of mistakes; *errors* which are not morally culpable and *violations* which involve deliberate wrongdoing, including deliberately unjustifiable risk-taking. Good people make terrible errors. Those who suffer as a result may have a proper claim for redress in terms of compensation. Society is not endangered by those errors, so it is not just to criminalize those individuals in error. They add a caveat. Society might judge that certain sorts of errors are so lamentably common that criminal law should be invoked to aid in deterring such errors. Merry and McCall Smith noted that since the prosecution of Dr Sullman and Dr Prentice, identical errors involving injecting vincristine into the spine occurred on a further ten occasions prior to 2001.[52] At least two further such incidents have occurred, the most recent leading to the conviction and imprisonment of Dr Mulhem.[53] Would the conviction of Dr Prentice and Dr Sullman have sent out signals deterring their successors? Evidence based answers are not forthcoming.[54]

## 4. Deterrence and the 'blame culture'

In the context of medical error, a trend to put more doctors, and other health care professionals, 'in the dock' runs counter to the series of initiatives within the NHS to redress the allegedly adverse effects of the 'blame culture'. The Bristol

---

[50] See Quick, 'Medical Manslaughter', in this volume.

[51] A. Merry, and A. McCall Smith, *Errors, Medicine and the Law* (Cambridge: Cambridge University Press, 2001).

[52] Ibid, 2. The number is now at least fourteen; see Ferner and McDowell, 'Doctors charged with manslaughter'.

[53] See a series of papers regarding the conviction of Dr Mulhem; S. Dyer, 'The facts of R v Mulhem', *AVMA Medical and Legal Journal*, 10 (2004), 28–9; A. narrow C. Elias-Jones, 'Medical Manslaughter or systems failure?' *AVMA Medical and Legal Journal*, 10 (2004), 29–31; S. Levy, 'Drawing the line: medical practitioners and manslaughter', *AVMA Medical and Legal Journal*, 10 (2004), 31–2; P. Balen, 'Wayne Jowett (deceased)', *AVMA Medical and Legal Journal*, 10 (2004), 25–7. And see *R (on the application of the Council for the Regulation of Healthcare Professionals) v General Medical Council* [2004] EWHC 3115 (Admin) concerning his resulting professional standing.

[54] Useful hypotheses are advanced in R. Wheeler, 'Medical Manslaughter: Why This Shift from Tort to Crime?', *New Law Journal*, 152 (2002), 593–4. An excellent analysis of the use of discretion by the Crown Prosecution Service is offered by O. Quick, 'Prosecuting "Gross" Medical Negligence: Manslaughter, Discretion and the Crown Prosecution Service', *Journal of Law and Society*, 33 (2006), 421–50; and see Quick, 'Medical Manslaughter', in this volume.

Inquiry Report[55] was forthright, proposing the abolition of civil claims for clinical negligence, declaring:

The system of clinical negligence is now ripe for review … [W]e take the view that it will not be possible to achieve an environment of full, open reporting within the NHS when, outside it, there exists a litigation system the incentives of which press in the opposite direction. We believe that the way forward lies in the abolition of clinical negligence litigation, *taking the clinical error out of the courts and the tort system.*[56]

In somewhat less radical proposals for reform of clinical negligence claims, the Chief Medical Officer[57] echoed Kennedy's call to move away from a 'blame culture'.[58] The fruit of his labours, the NHS Redress Act 2006, diluted his proposals yet further. A raft of initiatives[59] within the NHS, notably the creation of the National Patient Safety Agency,[60] depends on a similar philosophy. A 'blame culture' is perceived as counter-productive to the laudable objective of creating a culture where health care professionals feel able to acknowledge error openly. Doctors and nurses should be empowered to learn from their own mistakes and be encouraged to report others' mistakes without fear that they are sending their colleague to 'gaol'.[61] Merry and McCall Smith lent further support to the case against 'blame':

An important barrier to progress in reducing the incidence of medical injuries and in finding better ways of handling these injuries when they occur is an undue emphasis on blame. Blame promotes an adversarial response which in turn feeds upon blame. A sophisticated and constructive approach to the attribution of blame is required.[62]

A common feature of proposals to abolish or attenuate the 'blame culture' is an emphasis on a duty of candour. Professionals must not only report mistakes (or even near misses) to their employers and their regulators, they should acknowledge their mistake to their 'victim', the patient. Fear of litigation on the part of the patient will inhibit such candour.

As we have noted earlier, this key debate on blame, safety, and candour takes place largely in the context of civil claims. Fear of criminal redress might well be

---

[55] I. Kennedy (chair), *Learning from Bristol: The Report of the Public Inquiry into Children's Heart Surgery at the Bristol Royal Infirmary 1984–95* (CM 5207(1), (London: HMSO, 2001).
[56] Ibid, 367 (our emphasis).
[57] Chief Medical Officer (CMO), *Making Amends: A Consultation Paper Setting Out Proposals for Reforming the Approach to Clinical Negligence in the NHS* (London: Department of Health, 2003).
[58] Kennedy, *Learning from Bristol*, 363–4.
[59] See (inter alia) Department of Health Expert Group, *An Organisation with a Memory* (London: Department of Health, 2000); *Building a Safer NHS for Patients: Improving Medication Safety* (London: Department of Health, 2004).
[60] National Patient Safety Agency (Establishment and Constitution) Order 2001, SI 2001/1743.
[61] Though note that condemnation of the 'blame culture' in *Learning from Bristol* and elsewhere appears to focus exclusively on the adverse effects of the civil justice system. We discuss the analogies to be drawn between civil and criminal justice below.
[62] Merry and McCall Smith, *Errors, Medicine and the Law*, 248.

seen as yet more damaging. A doctor employed within the NHS facing a civil claim need fear no direct impact on his own pocket. His employers pick up the tab covering both the cost of litigation and any award of compensation.[63] The self-employed general practitioner and doctors in private practice will be indemnified by their chosen medical defence organization.[64] The doctor prosecuted for manslaughter after a fatal error confronts the prospect of criminal conviction, possible imprisonment and (often) the end of his of her professional career.[65] So might it be argued that if patient safety is undermined by the prospect of 'blame' within civil redress, the spectre of the criminal process doubles or triples that risk?

Such an argument must be treated with caution. Proposals to abolish or limit civil redress are invariably coupled to proposals for alternative means to compensate patients injured by medical error. The infant left seriously disabled after the obstetrician erroneously delays Caesarean surgery is not simply to be 'sacrificed' to the greater good of abolishing the blame culture. Proposals for reform, in theory, offer the infant's parents swifter and cheaper access to a secure income to provide for the child. Alternative compensation schemes would meet the right to compensation (currently provided by the law of tort). Effective means of investigating medical accidents reinformed by the duty of candour would meet tort's old role in ensuring accountability. The elimination of the fear engendered by the 'blame culture' would be more effective in preventing repetition of error than any deterrent effect currently offered by civil redress. We make no judgement here about whether a brave new 'no blame' world would live up to expectations. Our concern is whether the arguments touching on blame culture cross over from the civil to the criminal process.

Civil redress endorses the rights of, and protects the interests of, the individual citizen. Loss occasioned by us to us by the fault of others responsible for our welfare should not simply lie where it falls. The criminal process protects society's interests. If gross negligence resulting in death is properly such a cause of danger to society, and so heinous a fault as to deserve society's condemnation, can any special case for exemption be made for doctors? Can we properly conclude that, albeit such errors ought individually to be the subject of the criminal process, in the context of medicine the good of all depends on excusing the malpractice of the few?

---

[63] The introduction of NHS Indemnity in 1990 provided that NHS Trusts would indemnify doctors against liability and take over funding and managing all such claims; see HC (89) 34 'Claims of Medical Negligence against NHS Hospitals and Community Doctors and Dentists'; as amended by HCG (96) 48. See generally, Brazier and Cave, *Medicine, Patients and the Law*, para 8.3.'

[64] Membership of a medical defence organization is not mandatory but it would be a foolish doctor who failed to ensure he had such cover. See Brazier, ibid.

[65] *Kewal Krishnan Abrol v The General Dental Council* (1983) Privy Council No 46 of 1983; *R (on the application of the Council for the Regulation of Healthcare Professionals) v General Medical Council* [2004] EWHC 3115 (Admin); *R (on the application of General Medical Council) v Syed* [2005] EWHC 1209 (Admin); *General Medical Council v Walker* [2005] All ER (D) 23.

Even if the answer to that question is 'yes', other problems must be addressed. Were we to conclude that in the interests of candour and the elimination of an adverse blame culture, doctors should be especially exempt from prosecution for gross negligence manslaughter, why should doctors alone be so privileged? Health care professionals are not the only people who risk prosecution for a misjudgement in their job. The third defendant in the Court of Appeal in *Adomako* was an electrician. An architect whose poor maintenance of an air-conditioning system in Barrow allegedly led to seven deaths from Legionnaire's Disease was ultimately acquitted at a second trial for manslaughter after the first jury failed to agree.[66] In a number of cases, workers leading youth adventure schemes have been convicted of manslaughter.[67] In 2003, a teacher, Paul Ellis, whose poor planning of a school trip to the Lake District resulted in the death of a 10 year-old boy, was jailed for a year.[68] The judge described his decision to allow pupils to jump into a mountain stream at full spate as 'unbelievably negligent and foolhardy behaviour'.[69]

Doctors are by no means alone in facing criminal liability for fatal error. So, what (if anything) is so special about doctors? One argument that might be advanced is this. The unfortunate teacher, Mr Ellis, and the adventure scheme leaders also convicted of manslaughter enjoyed some element of choice in relation to risk-taking as much as risk assessment. Seeing the stream at full spate, Mr Ellis could have called off the expedition. A surgeon cannot usually refuse to operate; risk (even risk of death) is an inherent part of medicine. Judgements have to be made instantly. The risk averse doctor may do more harm than good. Yet the risk of all such arguments to safeguard doctors from the dock becomes that we in effect simply re-enforce Pollock CB's[70] deference to medical paternalism dressed up in modern jargon so that:

... it would be most detrimental to the efficiency of health care if no-one could practise medicine without fear of the dock looming in her mind.

## 5. Recklessness encore

Whether compelling social reasons should require separate, and different treatment when determining whether a doctor who makes a fatal error should be

[66] *R v Beckingham and Barrow Borough Council* The Times (1 August 2006). See G. Forlin, 'Directing Minds: Caught in a Trap', *New Law Journal*, 154 (2004), 326–7.
[67] See Y. Jacobs, 'Safety at adventure activities centres following the Lyme Bay tragedy: What are the legal consequences', *Education and the Law*, 8 (1996), 295–306; G. Parry, and L. Clarke, 'Risk assessment and geography teachers: a survey' *Education and the Law*, 16 (2004), 115–31; *R (on the application of Brown) v HM Coroner for County Borough of Neath and Talbot* [2006] EWHC 2019 (Admin).
[68] *The Times* (24 September 2003).
[69] See Parry and Clarke, 'Risk assessment and geography teachers', 120.
[70] *R v Crick.*

convicted of medical manslaughter, requires further research. Perhaps the res-
urrection of gross negligence manslaughter per se was in error? Carelessness,
incompetence, and error should not, save in exceptional cases, be the business
of the criminal law. Only such conduct pursued with disregard for the life of
others should merit punishment. Recklessness, not negligence of any degree,
should transform mishap into crime. Or is such a claim simply another attempt
to revive old heresy? Speaking of heresy though, modern doctors are not as badly
treated by the cruel legal system as they sometimes believe. In the seventeenth
century, suits for medical negligence were rare. Dissatisfied patients simply
sought to have their physicians or apothecaries arraigned for witchcraft.[71]

[71] B. Woolley, *The Herbalist* (Hammersmith: Harper Perennial, 2005) 213–15.

# 3

# Medical Manslaughter: The Rise (and Replacement) of a Contested Crime?

*Oliver Quick*

## 1. Introduction

This essay considers the increase of, explanations for, and alternatives to prosecutions of health care professionals for manslaughter following fatal error. The imposition of negligent criminal liability is controversial, particularly as it applies to the serious offence of manslaughter, and this essay begins by analysing the arguments for and against such criminalization. The process by which this crime has received cultural acceptance is considered and particular attention given to the context of the changing landscape of regulating quality in health care. Shifting perceptions and understandings of the notion of trust are considered central to this. It is argued here that the difficulties of interpretation and the potential vagaries of discretion renders this offence incapable of clear and objective measurement and that consequently, it ought to be abolished. However, whilst the argument for abolition is perhaps an easy one to make, agreeing on an appropriate alternative is an altogether tougher task. The final part of this essay considers available (yet under used) alternatives in the form of health and safety law, and from within the existing and proposed structure of homicide. It is concluded that there are persuasive philosophical and practical arguments for pitching liability at the level of recklessness.

## 2. 'Medical Manslaughter': History of a contested crime

It seems scarcely necessary to rehearse the well-known rationales for the imposition of criminal law. That said, in an era where criminal justice policy dominates the domestic legislative agenda,[1] it is pertinent to re-examine the appropriateness

---

[1]  See A. Sanders, and R. Young, *Criminal Justice* (3rd edn, Oxford: Oxford University Press, 2006) 18.

of imposing negligent liability upon health professionals (and others) who fatally err in the course of their work. Manslaughter is by no means unique as an example of objective criminal liability; in fact, crimes of negligence are on the increase.[2] However, its position near the apex of serious offences and the absence of a lesser charge or an inchoate crime for manslaughter renders this an unsatisfactory 'all or nothing' scenario, often hinging on issues of moral luck[3] and prosecutorial performance in terms of the outcome.[4] The question about the appropriateness of criminal negligence has mainly exercised legal philosophers, who have, as Jerome Hall noted, found it an 'inordinately troublesome' area.[5] Hall was responding (and rejecting) Hart's celebrated general theory of guilt in which he defended negligent criminal liability, reasoning that providing an individual was of normal capacity, such liability was warranted in principle and as a practical deterrent.[6] For Hall, the imposition of such liability loses sight of the notion of blame, which is the proper foundation for criminal law. In terms of more contemporary scholarship, Hart's view finds an echo in the work of Andrew Ashworth who advocates the extension of negligence to other areas of criminal law.[7] Jeremy Horder explains that the preoccupation with subjective fault is a relatively modern development, something that judges were relatively unconcerned about during the emergence of the concept of gross negligence in the nineteenth-century.[8] And despite its general commitment to a subjectivist vision of criminal law, the Law Commission endorses criminal sanction for culpable inadvertence, albeit abandoning the label 'manslaughter' for its favoured formulation of 'killing by gross carelessness'.[9] However, others have argued along the lines of Hall's objection

---

[2] For example, supplying intoxicating substances to the underaged (Intoxicating Substance (Supply) Act 1985, s 1(1)); causing death by dangerous driving (Road Traffic Act 1988, s1); insider trading (Criminal Justice Act 1993), (s 529(2)(a)); harassment (Protection of Harassment Act 1997, ss 1(1) and 2(1)); providing money or property for the purposes of terrorism (Terrorism Act 2000, ss 15–18); money laundering (Proceeds of Crime Act 2002, s 330(2)(b)); and causing or allowing the death of a child or vulnerable adult (Domestic Violence, Crime and Victims Act 2004, s 5).

[3] See J. C. Smith, 'The Element of Chance in Criminal Liability' [1971] *Criminal Law Review*, [1971], 63–75 and T. Nagel, *Mortal Questions* (London: Canto, 1991).

[4] This section draws on material from O. Quick, 'Prosecuting "Gross" Medical Negligence: Manslaughter, Discretion and the Crown Prosecution Service', *Journal of Law and Society*, 33 (2006), 421–50.

[5] J. Hall, 'Negligence and the General Problem of Criminal Responsibility', *Yale Law Journal*, 81 (1972), 949–79, at 952, and see also J. Hall, 'Negligent Behaviour Should be Excluded from Penal Liability', *Columbia Law Review*, 63/4 (1963), 632–44.

[6] H. L. A. Hart, 'Negligence, Mens Rea and Criminal Responsibility' in *Punishment and Responsibility: Essays in the Philosophy of Law* (Oxford, Oxford University Press, 1968), 136–57, at 147.

[7] See A. Ashworth, *Principles of Criminal Law* (5th edn, Oxford: Oxford University Press, 2006) 194.

[8] J. Horder, 'Gross Negligence and Criminal Culpability', *University of Toronto Law Journal*, 47 (1997), 495–521.

[9] Involuntary Homicide Bill Clause 2(1) in Law Commission, *Legislating the Criminal Code: Involuntary Manslaughter* (Law Com No 237, 1996); and see Law Commission, *A New Homicide Act for England and Wales*, (Law Com CP No 177, 2006), discussed further later in this chapter.

to penalizing negligence.[10] Yet amidst the arguments on the issue of principle, surely all would agree that the range of conduct and culpability encompassed by involuntary manslaughter is such that, as Clarkson has argued, 'the crime label has become morally uninformative',[11] and that reform is required.

Medical manslaughter prosecutions are not a new phenomenon. The first known case occurred in 1329 where a practitioner 'was commended to God' at a court in Newcastle.[12] The emergence of 'gross' negligence as a basis for prosecuting unlawful killing emerged in the nineteenth-century, and it is here that we find the first cluster of cases. Although such cases have traditionally been very rare, their tendency to challenge the very basis of liability has often led them to the appeal courts and into law reports as the leading authorities on the law of manslaughter. The first of these concerned the conviction of a Dr Bateman who mistakenly and fatally removed part of his patient's uterus whilst delivering her baby.[13] This was endorsed by the House of Lords in *R v Adomako*,[14] where in dismissing an appeal of an anaesthetist who fatally mismanaged a routine eye operation it set out a much criticized circular test of liability.[15] In fact, this offence category appeared particularly vulnerable following the House of Lords' rejection of objective recklessness in the context of criminal damage.[16] However, in 2005, it survived a challenge to its compatibility with Articles 6 and 7 of the European Convention on Human Rights (ECHR) in *R v Misra*,[17] where two junior doctors failed to adequately respond to a patient's obvious signs of infection, which proved fatal.[18]

---

[10] A. McCall Smith, 'Criminal Negligence and the Incompetent Doctor', Medical Law Review, 1 (1993), 336–49.

[11] C. M. V. Clarkson, 'Context and Culpability in Involuntary Manslaughter: Principle or Instinct?' in A. Ashworth, and B. Mitchell, (eds.), *Rethinking English Homicide Law* (Oxford: Oxford University Press, 2000) 133–65, at 142. Clarkson persuasively argues for the creation of a more nuanced approach to involuntary manslaughter with the creation of separate offences, and in this context, favours the Law Commission's formulation of 'killing by gross carelessness'.

[12] I am grateful to Mr Ian Barker, former Honorary Legal Secretary of the Medico-Legal Society, for providing me with the information about this case (personal communication, 21 August 2000).

[13] *R v Bateman* (1925) 19 Cr App R 8. His conviction was quashed on appeal.

[14] [1995] 1 AC 171.

[15] See S. Gardner, 'Manslaughter by Gross Negligence', *Law Quarterly Review*, 111 (1995), 22–27; G. Virgo, 'Reconstructing Manslaughter on Defective Foundations', *Cambridge Law Journal*, 54/1 [1995], 14–16; Clarkson, 'Context and Culpability'. See also the chapter in the current volume by M. Brazier and N. Allen, 'Criminalizing Medical Malpractice'.

[16] *R v G* [2004] 1 AC 1034, 1055, where Lord Bingham stated that 'it is a salutary principle that conviction of serious crime should depend on proof not simply that the defendant caused (by act or omission) an injurious result to another but that his state of mind when so acting was culpable. This, after all, is the meaning of the familiar rule *actus non facit reum nisi mens sit rea* ... It is clearly blameworthy to take an obvious and significant risk of causing injury to another. But it is not clearly blameworthy to do something involving a risk of injury to another if ... one genuinely does not perceive the risk. Such a person may fairly be accused of stupidity or lack of imagination, but neither of those failings should expose him to conviction of serious crime or the risk of punishment.'

[17] *R v Misra* [2005] 1 Cr App R 21.

[18] See O. Quick, 'Prosecuting Medical Mishaps' *New Law Journal*, 156 (2006), 394–5 and Brazier and Allen, 'Criminalizing Medical Malpractice'.

A decade on from *Adomako*, prosecutors, judges, and juries are left to grapple with this difficult and loosely defined concept. Given the obvious concern and controversy about this offence, and the issue of its compatibility with Articles 6 and 7 of the ECHR, it is disappointing that an application for leave to appeal to the House of Lords was rejected. This represents a missed opportunity for a possible declaration of incompatibility which would prompt a rethink about the appropriateness of this much criticized offence or, at the very least, the setting out of more detailed guidance for prosecutors, trial judges, and juries.

Although no real advance in terms of clarifying the law, the failed appeals in *Adomako* and *Misra* affirmed the status of this offence and presumably paved the way for further prosecutions. But just how many prosecutions for medical manslaughter have there been? Whilst it is commonly reported that prosecutions have risen, this has not been examined in detail.[19] In order to establish the increased incidence of medical manslaughter prosecutions, a search was conducted of the indexes of *The Times* (1970–2005), *The Guardian* and *Observer* (1990–2005), and the *Daily* and *Sunday Telegraph* (1994–2005). The BBC news website was also searched from January 2000 to January 2007, as well as *The Lancet* and the *British Medical Journal* (1966–2007).[20] A trawl through these sources uncovered 65 cases of 'medical manslaughter'.[21] This included cases where individuals were investigated but not charged. Clearly, the number of cases investigated is likely to be significantly higher (yet probably unknowable). The bulk of the incidents identified from the above sources (40) occurred between 1996–2005. There were nineteen convictions, although six of these were quashed on appeal. Two practitioners received custodial sentences. In the period between 1986–2005, the conviction rate (in terms of the cases that were prosecuted) was thirty nine per cent, considerably lower than that for manslaughter prosecutions generally.

## 3. Explanations: Risk, trust, and safety in health care

The statistics in Table 1 demonstrate that manslaughter prosecutions (and the consideration of such prosecutions) are no longer such rare events. This has occurred within the context of a heightened awareness of risk in society,[22] and the new realization within health care about the scale of medical harm and the variety of factors affecting this, such as individual clinical performance, the effectiveness of teamwork, mechanisms for monitoring quality, and prevailing cultures of safety. There has been an explosion of interest in health care quality

---

[19] With the exception of R. Ferner, 'Medication errors that have led to manslaughter charges', *British Medical Journal*, 321 (2000), 1212–16 and R. Ferner, and S. McDowell, 'Doctors charged with manslaughter in the course of medical practice, 1795–2005: a literature review', *Journal of the Royal Society of Medicine*, 99 (2006), 309–14.

[20] Key words chosen included manslaughter, coroner, medical, doctor, hospital, and error.

[21] The vast majority involved doctors, with a sizeable minority of nurses and a few dentists.

[22] U. Beck, *World Risk Society* (Cambridge: Polity Press, 1999).

**Table 1.** Number investigations/convictions in ten-year periods

| Cases | 1976–1985 | 1986–1995 | 1996–2005 |
| --- | --- | --- | --- |
| Total number of incidents investigated | 7 | 13 | 40 |
| Total number of individual health care professionals (HCPs) investigated | 9 | 13 | 50 |
| Total number of individual HCPs convicted | 1 | 6 | 7 |

and safety, with terms such as 'medical error' and 'medical negligence' gaining common currency and possessing powerful connotations; language usage may be an important factor in shaping responses here, as Wells argues in the context of corporate manslaughter:

If they are called accidents then they are less likely to be seen as potentially unlawful homicides; if they were seen as potentially unlawful homicides they would be less likely to be called accidents. Enforcement processes are influenced and partly determined by stereotypes of crime and criminals: corporations are not stereotypical deviant offenders.[23]

Likewise, health care professionals are non-stereotypical defendants and represent a challenge for the criminal justice system in terms of law enforcement processes. However, whilst Ashworth has noted that 'courts have striven to exculpate doctors for decisions taken in medical contexts which would probably, in almost all other situations, lead to the imposition of criminal liability',[24] the statistics in relation to prosecutions suggest that the crime of medical manslaughter, like that of corporate manslaughter, is beginning to achieve cultural recognition and acceptance. Although this trend has not gone unnoticed by the profession,[25] and indeed the Government,[26] there has been little reflection on the reasons for this.[27] As Table 1 suggests, this increased incidence of prosecution appears to coincide with the establishment of the Crown Prosecution Service (CPS) in 1986. This is particularly interesting given that the introduction of the CPS saw a higher threshold for deciding on whether to continue with prosecutions as compared with the previous police-run system—a shift from there being a prima facie case

[23] C. Wells, *Corporations and Criminal Responsibility* (Oxford: Oxford University Press, 2001) 12.

[24] A. Ashworth, 'Criminal Liability in a Medical Context: the Treatment of Good Intentions' in A. P. Simester, and A. T. H. Smith, (eds.), *Harm and Culpability* (Oxford: Clarendon Press, 1996) 192.

[25] Ferner, 'Medication errors'.

[26] It was reported in July 2005 that the Home Office were considering investigating this as part of its review of the law of murder (BBC News online at <http://news.bbc.co.uk/1/hi/health/4642743. stm> (accessed 12 January 2006), although it has not formed part of the Law Commission's work: Law Commission, *Legislating the Criminal Code* and *A New Homicide Act*.

[27] For a recent analysis see O. Quick, 'Outing Medical Error: Questions of Trust and Responsibility', *Medical Law Review*, 14/1 (2006), 22–43. This section draws on some material from this article.

to a 'realistic prospect of conviction'.[28] Under this different evidential test, one would perhaps have expected a decrease rather than increase in the number of prosecutions. How then to account for this increase?

Certain explanations can be discounted with a reasonable degree of confidence. For example, increased prosecution is unlikely to reflect a marked increase in the frequency of medical mishaps or negligent episodes; manslaughter prosecutions bear no necessary relation to the number of 'accidental' or even 'negligent' deaths in the medical setting. However, research has revealed that the true toll of medical error is substantial. A small-scale pilot study of adverse events in hospitalized patients in the UK found that 10.8 per cent of patients experienced an adverse event, with half of these judged to be preventable given ordinary standards of care. Extrapolated to the NHS in England, based on the 8.5 million inpatient episodes per annum, it was calculated that there are potentially 850,000 adverse events each year in NHS hospitals in England. From this, it was estimated that there were 70,000 deaths per annum in hospital that were partly due to error. The financial cost in terms of additional bed-days was calculated at up to two billion pounds.[29] The fact that not all mistakes lead to adverse outcomes, and that many patients remain unaware of errors, suggests that the true toll of medical error is even higher.

It has long been recognized that patients are sometimes victims of harm at the hands of their health care professionals.[30] However, attention to the many costs of error in health care has intensified following a series of high-profile disasters. The very high mortality rates of a paediatric heart unit,[31] a gynaecologist who caused substantial morbidity to the women on whom he operated,[32] and a series of murders committed by a general practitioner[33] were graphic illustrations of both medical harm and the failure of self-regulation. Unsurprisingly, such troubling episodes attracted extensive publicity,[34] led to two major public inquiries,[35] and caused consternation for a beleaguered profession.[36]

[28]  See A. Ashworth, and M. Redmayne, *The Criminal Process* (Oxford University Press: Oxford, 2005) 179–80.

[29]  See C. Vincent, G. Neale, and M. Woloshynowych, 'Adverse events in British hospitals: preliminary retrospective record review', *British Medical Journal*, 322 (2001), 517–19. See also National Audit Office, *A Safer Place for Patients: Learning to improve patient safety* (London: Department of Health, 2005).

[30]  I. Illich, *Limits to Medicine: Medical Nemesis—The Expropriation of Health* (London: Penguin, 1977).

[31]  I. Kennedy (chair), *Learning from Bristol*: The Report of the Public Inquiry into Children's Heart Surgery at the Bristol Royal Infirmary 1984–95 (CM 5207(1), (London: HMSO, 2001).

[32]  J. Ritchie *The Report of the Inquiry into Quality and Practice Within the National Health Service Arising from the Actions of Rodney Ledward* (London: Stationery Office, 2000).

[33]  J. Smith, *Fifth Report—Safeguarding Patients: Lessons from the Past—Proposals for the Future* (Cm 6394, 2004).

[34]  H. T. O. Davies and A. V. Shields, 'Public Trust and Accountability for Clinical Performance: Lessons from the National Press Reportage of the Bristol Hearing', *Journal of Evaluation in Clinical Practice*, 5 (1999), 335–42; M. Brazier, 'Times of Change?', *Medical Law Review*, 13 (2005), 1–16.

[35]  Kennedy, *Learning from Bristol*, and Smith, *Fifth Report*.

[36]  R. Tallis, *Hippocratic Oaths: Medicine and Its Discontents* (London: Atlantic Books, 2004).

Until recently, however, it was assumed that harms in the context of health care were rare and either unavoidable or attributable to the incompetence, malice, or negligence of a few individual health professionals—so-called 'bad apples'.[37] There was little concerted effort to investigate and address the problem of harms occurring in the course of health care. Traditionally, health care professionals have preferred to closet errors, fearing loss of trust and status should they 'come out'. The traditional culture of medicine has been resistant to confronting error, with doctors being schooled in the unrealistic ideal of error-free practice.[38] This, combined with the threat of damaging malpractice litigation, led them to cover up their mistakes, so that even if it allowed individual learning, this was not shared. Recent attention to medical error has seen the eschewal of the model of individual blame which has characterized the approach to health care errors in favour of encouraging a culture of open disclosure and reporting.[39]

Systematic attempts to investigate error-related harms did not emerge until the second half of the twentieth-century, although studies of the relationships between health care interventions and outcomes had preceded these.[40] From the 1960s onwards, data started to accrue suggesting that a high proportion of hospital patients experienced potentially preventable iatrogenic harm. This attracted little attention until the 1990s, when the data was converted into estimates of the number of people in the USA who died each year from iatrogenic injury (180,000), and of what this equated to in terms of jumbo jet crashes (three every two days).[41] Media coverage of these estimates greatly raised public awareness of the scale of the problem.[42] These ideas were taken up in several initiatives to improve health care safety, and were moved into mainstream thinking about health care quality with the publication of the Institute of Medicine's report, *To Err is Human*, and the Department of Health's report, *Organisation with a Memory*.[43] These influential reports emphasized the scale of the problem of errors

[37] D. M. Berwick, 'Continuous Improvement as an Ideal in Health Care', *New England Journal of Medicine*, 320 (1989), 53–6.

[38] D. Hilfiker, 'Facing our Mistakes', *New England Journal of Medicine*, 310 (1984), 118–22.

[39] Department of Health, *An Organisation with a Memory: Report of an Expert Group on Learning from Adverse Events in the NHS chaired by the Chief Medical Officer* (London: HMSO, 2000). The Kennedy inquiry into paediatric heart surgery at Bristol also called for a duty of candour on professionals to admit and explain mistakes to their patients. See Kennedy, *Learning from Bristol*. For a fuller discussion of the process whereby medical error has been outed, see Quick, 'Outing Medical Error'.

[40] V. A. Sharpe, and A. I. Faden, *Medical Harm: Historical, Conceptual and Ethical Dimensions of Iatrogenic Illness* (Cambridge: Cambridge University Press, 1998). This section draws on material from V. A. Entwistle, and O. Quick, 'Trust in the Context of Patient Safety', *Journal of Health Organization and Management*, 20/5 (2006), 397–416.

[41] L. L. Leape, 'Error in Medicine', *Journal of the American Medical Association*, 272/23 (1994), 1851–7.

[42] M. L. Millenson, 'Pushing the Profession: How the News Media Turned Patient Safety into a Priority', *Quality and Safety in Health Care*, 11 (2002), 57–63.

[43] L. Kohn, J. Corrigan and M. Donaldson, (eds.), *To Err is Human: Building a Safer Health System* (Washington: National Academy Press, 1999); Department of Health, *An Organisation with a Memory: Report of an Expert Group on Learning from Adverse Events in the NHS* chaired by the Chief Medical Officer (London: HMSO 2000).

and harms in health care and the fact that these problems were for the most part attributable to features of health care delivery systems rather than individual health professionals. Beyond this, these reports drew on research into the sociology and psychology of error to highlight the accepted classification of errors into slips, mistakes, and violations.[44]

Governments and international agencies have responded by developing wide-ranging policies and laws to ensure improvements in patient safety.[45] In the UK, the National Patient Safety Agency (NPSA), created in 2001, coordinates a National Learning and Reporting System for adverse events. Since April 2005, it has incorporated the National Clinical Assessment Service, an advisory body which undertakes assessments of individual practitioners whose performance is in question. This has taken place amidst a wealth of reform of the system of regulating health care quality, with the creation of a number of initiatives and agencies with various and often overlapping responsibilities for monitoring quality in health care. The scale of reform and rebranding has been enough to confuse even the committed student of health care regulation and makes the task of summary somewhat difficult.[46] However, at bottom, it reflects a shift from light touch self-regulation to a government-driven interventionist approach towards managing quality in health care.[47] It is also underpinned by changes to relationships of trust, and it is to understandings of this important concept that I will now turn.

In her 2002 Reith lectures, Onora O'Neill remarked that discussion of a 'climate of suspicion' is something of a cliché of our times.[48] Widespread lay knowledge of risks and errors leads to an awareness of the limits of expertise, and represents a public relations problem for those seeking to maintain trust in expert systems.[49] This has been problematic for a medical profession troubled by a series of high-profile disasters, and has attracted attention to trust, a relatively under-researched issue compared with its conceptual cousin of risk, although now the subject of a substantial literature.[50] Significantly, recent conceptualization of trust has

---

[44] For an attempt to conceptualize a scale of culpability in relation to medical error see A. Merry and A. McCall Smith, *Errors, Medicine and the Law* (Cambridge: Cambridge University Press, 2001).

[45] R. Watson, 'EU to tackle issues of patient safety', *British Medical Journal*, 330 (2005), 866; D. Pittet, and L. Donaldson, 'Challenging the World: Patient safety and health care-associated infection', *International Journal for Quality in Health Care*, 18 (2006), 4–8.

[46] The confusing collection of overlapping organizations has been acknowledged by the Department of Health in its review of arm's length bodies: Department of Health, *Reconfiguring the Department of Health's Arm's Length Bodies* (Department of Health, 2004).

[47] A. C. L. Davies, 'Don't Trust Me I'm a Doctor: Medical Regulation and the 1999 NHS Reforms', *Oxford Journal of Legal Studies*, 20/3 (2000), 437–56.

[48] O. O'Neill, *A Question of Trust 2002 BBC Reith Lectures* (Cambridge, Cambridge University Press, 2002).

[49] A. Giddens, *The Consequences of Modernity* (Cambridge, Polity Press, 1990) 130.

[50] For a review of the literature see M. Calnan and R. Rowe, *Trust in Health Care: An Agenda for Future Research* (London: The Nuffield Trust, 2004) and see (2006) 20/5 *Journal of Healthcare Organisation and Management* (Special Edition).

revealed the true complexity of understanding the different types of trust and how they relate to the complex relationships and contexts within health care.[51] Most obviously, it may be classified into interpersonal trust and social or organizational trust, although even this distinction is a slightly crude one requiring careful unpacking in terms of the different contexts and cultures within health care.

There is something of a paradox that whilst opinion polls demonstrate that health care professionals remain highly trusted,[52] the literature suggests that important questions and doubts linger over the issue of trust. Whilst the notion of a 'crisis of trust' may be an exaggerated claim lacking hard evidence, there is certainly a perception of this, and arguably it is the perception that is important. At bottom, it is difficult to divorce discussion of declining trust from the many recent debates about the work of the medical profession and its regulation. And in terms of potential medical manslaughter cases, prosecutors work within this climate of increased suspicion of professionals which is likely to impact on the 'frames' they adopt in exercising their discretion. Arguably, this is more probable given the public pressure associated with cases involving fatalities,[53] coupled with the fact that the very definition of this offence depends on the use of discretion by prosecutors.

## 4. The argument for abolishing gross negligence manslaughter

There is nothing new in arguing against the imposition of negligent criminal liability in the medical setting.[54] However, such arguments have been based on a principled objection to the unfairness of this offence, and particularly as this applies to well-intentioned professionals working in high-risk (and often unsafe) systems. There has been little empirical investigation into the actual enforcement of this offence. A study by this author examining quantitative and qualitative data on medical manslaughter prosecutions observed that the offence is vague and vulnerable to the vagaries of discretion and discrimination, and concluded that it is incapable of clear and objective measurement and ought to be abolished.[55] Although retaining the support of the appeal courts and the Law Commission—albeit in its revised formulation of 'killing by gross carelessness' discussed below, several reasons of principle and practice point to its abolition. If one accepts the principled objection to negligent criminal liability, then it is

---

[51] See Entwistle and Quick 'Trust in the Context of Patient Safety'.

[52] See Ipsos MORI, 'Public Trust In Doctors Is Still High' (1 November 2006) at <http://www.ipsos-mori.com/polls/2006/rcp.shtml>, although this is framed in terms of truth telling as opposed to trust in competency.

[53] See A. Hoyano, L. Hoyano, G. Davis, and S. Goldie, 'A Study of the Impact of the Revised Code for Crown Prosecutors', *Criminal Law Review*, [1997], 556–64.

[54] For example, see McCall Smith, 'Criminal Negligence and the Incompetent Doctor'.

[55] This section summarizes the findings from Quick, 'Prosecuting "Gross" Medical Negligence'.

arguable that this points to a general abolition of this offence category. Although obtaining a detailed breakdown of the statistics is difficult, this offence would seem to apply almost exclusively to individuals whose performance of a workplace duty causes death.[56] However, the argument advanced here rests in part on empirical findings pointing to the unfairness and lack of objectivity in terms of the enforcement of the offence in the health care setting. Yet, without enough empirical evidence of its application in other settings, the argument will be confined to destabilizing the offence in this context.[57]

In terms of medical manslaughter, whilst it may be said that malleability for mounting a prosecution is an advantage, in reality the offence is too broad for prosecutorial judgment to be consistently applied, and this translates into particular harshness for those operating in error-ridden activities who are exposed to risk of prosecution by virtue of their socially vital work, and are often at the mercy of moral luck.[58] An analysis of interviews with crown prosecutors at an office of the casework directorate of the CPS suggested that no real meaningful hierarchy of seriousness was adopted in relation to classifying errors as gross. Respondents struggled to pin down their understanding of the term gross, often initially relying on gut instinct. Whilst there was some recognition of a distinction between tragic slips (excusable) and reckless mistakes (condemned), there was no reference to the developing literature on understanding the causes of medical error, and the accepted classification of slips, mistakes, and violations and no obvious or objective system for classifying episodes as gross or not gross.[59]

A closer analysis of the data, both statistical and qualitative, presents further reasons for abolishing this offence. The statistics reveal that a disproportionate number of non-white practitioners feature in medical manslaughter prosecutions; this is a troubling finding and one that may be understood with reference to a number of sociological explanations, such as the training and language skills of overseas trained overseas, as well as their ability to gain employment and superior supervision in better performing hospitals. The high number may also be related to racist attitudes that creep in to the decisions to complain about and consider investigating individuals in the first place. The notion of a principled, rational and just system of discretion is difficult when much depends on the possibly discriminatory decisions that inform the process of complaining and filtering such cases for investigation. Of course, there is no shortage of evidence of the effect

---

[56] Thus we find a motley crew of electricians (*R v Holloway* (Stephen John) [1993] 3 WLR 922), teachers (Anon, 'Teacher jailed over drowned boy', BBC News Online (23 September 2003) at <http://news.bbc.co.uk/1/hi/england/lancashire/3132102.stm>), truck drivers (*R v Wacker* [2003] 1 Cr App R 329, and architects (*R v Beckingham and Barrow Borough Council*—see G. Forlin, 'Directing Minds: caught in a trap', *New Law Journal*, 154/7118 (2004), 326–7).

[57] The Corporate Manslaughter and Corporate Homicide Bill 2006 also proposes to abolish the offence of gross negligence manslaughter in its application to organizations that the Bill applies to (see cl 20).

[58] See Smith, 'The Element of Chance in Criminal Liability' and Nagel, *Mortal Questions*.

[59] See Quick, 'Prosecuting "Gross" Medical Negligence'.

of prejudicial attitudes within the criminal justice system[60] yet, coupled with the vagueness and seriousness of this offence category, the consequences may be particularly unfair. The statistics also suggest a possible geography of prosecution, with unexplained regional variation of the number of prosecutions. Whilst the numbers are small, and *may* be explained by normal random distributions, it may also be a sign of increased prosecutorial confidence in certain regions which have 'got home' on *Adomako* and achieved a successful conviction, arguably significant given the overall low conviction rate. Ultimately, the legal frame (in other words the measurement of 'gross negligence'), is effectively handed over to medical experts. The fact that expert evidence appears to effectively determine, as opposed to merely inform, what is supposedly a legal term of art, is inappropriate. Furthermore, reflecting the difficult task of interpretation, expert discretion is itself an uncertain and fluctuating process of framing and reframing, and something which we know little about. Finally, this study showed prosecutorial unease with the fairness of gross negligence, and the reality of prosecutors navigating around the *Adomako* test in search of subjective fault. The cases which are prosecuted, and certainly those which result in conviction, would be more appropriately accommodated within subjective recklessness. In mopping up a range of unintentional killings it also washes over issues of fair labelling. Despite *Misra*, the issue of compatibility with Articles 6 and 7 of the ECHR cannot be considered settled. And the relatively low conviction rate suggests that juries are reluctant to convict.[61] Why continue to struggle with the vagueness and vagaries of interpreting gross negligence when nobody is really convinced about what it means, and whether it actually should be a crime? The argument for abolition is clear and compelling.[62]

## 5. Appropriate alternatives?

Agreeing an appropriate alternative is an altogether tougher task. However, before considering possible 'new' offences to replace gross negligence manslaughter, existing—albeit under-used—mechanisms for responding to fatal negligent error should be considered. The landmark reports into medical error noted above emphasized the true toll of error and harm in health care and the fact that these problems are mainly attributable to features of health care delivery systems rather than individual health professionals. However, formal legal mechanisms for responding to medical errors are largely based on a model of individual fault with

---

[60] For example, see M. Fitzgerald, and R. Sibbitt, *Ethnic Monitoring in Police Forces: A Beginning* (Home Office Research Study 173 (London: Home Office, 1997) and W. Macpherson, *The Stephen Lawrence Inquiry* (Cm 4262I, 1999).

[61] See Ferner and McDowell, 'Doctors charged with manslaughter' and Quick, 'Prosecuting "Gross" Medical Negligence'.

[62] See Quick, 'Prosecuting "Gross" Medical Negligence'.

knowledge about the psychology of understanding errors yet to translate into legal responses.[63] In terms of civil law, whilst trusts are vicariously liable for the negligence of their employees, cases alleging breaches of their primary or direct duty for ensuring safety are unusual.[64] Clearly this raises the issue of what forms of collective accountability are appropriate? In terms of health care errors, in what ways are we able to hold organizations accountable for medical error, in this case fatal and potentially 'criminal' error? Of course, prosecuting NHS Trusts for corporate manslaughter remains a theoretical if not entirely practical possibility,[65] although this would seem more realistic under the draft corporate killing proposals,[66] and given the position set out by Neil Allen's contribution to the current volume.[67] However, here I consider the forgotten role of health and safety law, before evaluating the other options within the existing and proposed structure of homicide.

## 5.1 Health and safety law

Recent attention to the subject of safety in health care can make it seem something of a new concern. However, relevant legislation has existed for over thirty years in the form of the Health and Safety at Work Act 1974, albeit under-used in the context of patient safety. Section 3(1) of 1974 Act states that:

It shall be the duty of every employer to conduct his undertaking in such a way as to ensure, so far as is reasonably practicable, that persons not in his employment who may be affected thereby are not thereby exposed to risks to their health or safety.

Prosecutions against health care providers for breaches under this section are very unusual, and certainly less prevalent than manslaughter prosecutions against individual practitioners. Given the consensus that most errors reflect problems at organizational rather than individual level, and that excessive workloads, inadequate supervision, misunderstandings, and poor systems of communication are common features of medical manslaughter cases, it is perhaps surprising that the Health and Safety Executive (HSE) has not exercised its discretion to investigate hospital Trusts more than it appears to have done. This is likely to be tied up with issues of territory in terms of the HSE's perception of whether such cases represent its turf, and to issues of capacity and resources. However, three convictions of NHS Trusts in 2006 for breaches under the 1974 Act in relation to the

[63] See Merry and McCall Smith, *Errors, Medicine and the Law*.
[64] *Wilsher v Essex AHA* [1986] 3 All ER 801; *Bull v Devon AHA* [1993] 4 Med LR 117. See Brazier and Allen, 'Criminalizing Medical Malpractice' for discussion of civil redress.
[65] M. Childs, 'Medical Manslaughter and Corporate Liability', *Legal Studies*, 19/3 (1999), 316–38.
[66] See Home Office, *Corporate Manslaughter and Corporate Homicide Bill*, HC Bill 236 (London: The Stationery Office, 2006). The Bill was at the report stage of the House of Lords at the time of writing.
[67] 'Medical or Managerial Manslaughter?'.

deaths of two patients illustrate the potential application of health and safety law here, and possibly pave the way for further such prosecutions.

The first of these, *R v Southampton University Hospitals NHS Trust*,[68] arose out of the same events that led to the conviction of Dr Misra, with the result that the Trust was fined £100,000. In the second case, the Welsh Ambulance Service and Cardiff and Vale NHS Trust both pleaded guilty following the death of a patient who sustained injuries after being left at an incorrect address by an ambulance crew.[69] The Trusts were fined £20,000 and £7,500 respectively. These three convictions, believed to be amongst the first of their kind, are symbolically important as an official recognition of organizational fault, and remind us of the wide scope of health and safety offences as applied to the context of medical manslaughter cases. The initial indictment in the *Southampton* case included allegations that the trust employed one of the doctors without taking up references or conducting a face-to-face interview, failed to organize ward rounds properly, and to encourage nurses to report concerns about colleagues. Although these were dropped from the indictment, it indicates a prosecutorial preparedness to probe wider aspects of the system and its responsibility for safety lapses. It is possible to envisage a wide variety of problems stemming from failing systems as opposed to flawed individuals, and the potential greater use of health and safety law here. For example, the case transcript in *Misra* refers to misunderstandings about the correct procedures for obtaining blood results—one of the doctors relied on the laboratory to flag up abnormalities, whilst the prosecution maintained that the onus was on the doctors to chase up the results. It is not hard to imagine the investigatory lens being broadened to encompass a variety of important organizational issues involving the recruitment and training of staff, as well as planning and communication problems which are currently relegated to the background context of prosecutions against individual practitioners. In terms of likely deterrent effect, the fact that trusts are unable to insure against the payment of criminal fines may be an important factor in terms of helping to improve prevailing systems of safety.

These prosecutions are particularly significant given the underlying philosophy and practical implementation of the Act, with its preference for compliance over penalty, what Hawkins termed 'law as last resort.'[70] Furthermore, the Act was originally designed to protect the health and safety of *workers*—as opposed to being used as a response to patient safety incidents; thus prosecutions for breaches of duties owed to non-employees under the Health and Safety at Work Act 1974 are rare. A recent high profile (and bizarre) use of this law is found in the fallout from the mistaken killing on the London underground of Jean Charles de Menezes on 22 July 2005 in relation to suspected acts of terrorism. Although deciding not to

---

[68] *R v Southampton University Hospital NHS Trust* [2006] EWCA Crim 2971.
[69] *South Wales Echo*, 8 April 2006.
[70] K. Hawkins, *Law as Last Resort: Prosecution Decision Making in a Regulatory Agency* (Oxford: Oxford University Press, 2002).

prosecute individuals for gross negligence manslaughter,[71] the CPS declared they would be prosecuting the Office of the Commissioner of Police for an offence under sections 3 and 33 of the Health and Safety at Work Act 1974 of failing to provide for the health, safety, and welfare of the victim. Arguably, this recent recourse to health and safety prosecutions partly reflects a sense of unease with the unfairness of gross negligence manslaughter and is perhaps emblematic of the future use of health and safety law in relation to patient safety episodes. However, such prosecutions are likely to sit alongside, rather than replace, individual criminal liability and we are still left with the task of agreeing an appropriate alternative to gross negligence manslaughter, which is workable in practice, decreases discretion, and dampens down professional disquiet.

## 5.2  Killing by gross carelessness

The Law Commission favour replacing gross negligence manslaughter with the offence of 'killing by gross carelessness',[72] which would be committed where:

(1) a person by his conduct causes the death of another;
(2) a risk that his conduct will cause death or serious injury would be obvious to a reasonable person in his position;
(3) he is capable of appreciating that risk at the material time; and
(4) either
    (a) his conduct falls far below what can reasonably be expected of him in the circumstances, or
    (b) he intends by his conduct to cause some injury, or is aware of, and unreasonably takes, the risk that it may do so [and the conduct causing (or intended to cause) the injury constitutes an offence]

This was endorsed in 2005 as part of the Commission's proposed overhaul of the law of homicide, subject to limiting paragraph (2) to the risk of causing death and not serious injury.[73] Apart from confirming the Law Commission's preoccupation with the term 'gross',[74] it is unclear whether this revised formulation represents an improvement. The eschewal of the emotive term manslaughter is to be welcomed, as is the reference to capacity. Less convincing is the belief that

[71] Although the family are reportedly seeking to judicially review the CPS decision not to prosecute: see V. Dodd, 'De Menezes family push for charges against police' *The Guardian*, 16 October 2006.
[72] Law Commission, *Legislating the Criminal Code: Involuntary Manslaughter*.
[73] Law Commission, *A New Homicide Act*, 251, 10.12, para 3.2(4) (killing by gross carelessness) and 10.13, para 3.2(4) (unlawful act manslaughter). This will form part of a law of homicide restructured as follows: 'A top tier of "First degree murder" requiring an intention to kill; an intermediate tier of "Second degree murder" requiring intention to cause serious harm or reckless indifference to causing death; and a lower tier of "Manslaughter" requiring gross negligence as to causing death, or causing death through a criminal act intended to cause injury, or where there was recklessness as to causing injury' (at 93).
[74] It also appears used in its proposals for the partial defence of 'gross provocation', and for assessing the culpability of corporations for manslaughter.

this tackles one of the central criticisms of *Adomako*: the problem of circularity. The current struggle to make sense of 'gross negligence' would be replaced by the similarly tricky task of assessing whether 'conduct falls far below what can reasonably be expected in the circumstances'.[75] It is difficult to imagine that, in practice, this offence would not be beset by the same problems as gross negligence manslaughter. Prosecutors (and their experts) would surely still struggle with what amounts to 'conduct falling far below reasonable expectations. The aim of providing a clearer jury-friendly formulation appears to have failed. Furthermore, this reformulation is arguably broader than the current test for liability, and whilst surely not an intended effect, would likely lead to an increase of prosecutions. On the whole, it is difficult to see that this tackles the fundamental objection to this type of liability, or that it would make much of a difference in practice. The option of fleshing out this statutory formulation with reference to a notion such as 'extreme indifference', whilst purporting to promise greater clarity, would probably only further complicate an already difficult task.[76]

## 5.3 Reckless manslaughter/killing

The most appropriate (and easiest) alternative would be to consider such cases within the category of subjective reckless manslaughter. The legal line drawn between subjective recklessness and gross negligence has always been at best blurry; as Horder points out, in the nineteenth-century, judges were less concerned about committing to a subjective vision of criminal law and observing a neat separation between recklessness and negligence.[77] The quest for a strict separation of these related terms is a product of more modern criminal law scholarship and its pursuit of conceptual clarity.[78] And it is not entirely clear why the term 'gross' emerged as the dominant epithet, given that 'criminal' or 'wicked' are arguably more closely connected with the notion of individual fault. Nevertheless, given that historically these terms have been used interchangeably, the current confusion is somewhat easier to understand. Arguably, it also makes it easier to justify the abolition of gross negligence, and to place our trust in the concept of recklessness to work here.

Despite a series of convictions for gross negligence manslaughter through the nineteenth and twentieth-century, the decision in the infamous case of *Stone and Dobinson*[79] appeared to place the bar above gross negligence manslaughter

---

[75] Involuntary Homicide Bill, cl 2(1).

[76] See Clarkson, 'Context and Culpability', 156. The attempt in cl 8 of the proposed Corporate Manslaughter and Corporate Homicide Bill 2006 to flesh out the factors for assessing grossness has similarly been criticized: see C. Wells, 'Corporate Manslaughter: Why Does Reform Matter?', *South African Law Journal*, 122 (2006), 646–62.

[77] Horder, 'Gross Negligence and Criminal Culpability'.

[78] For example, the Law Commission's Codification project: Law Commission, *Codification of the Criminal Law: A Report to the Law Commission* (Law Com No 143, 1985).

[79] [1977] QB 354.

and resurrect recklessness by requiring 'reckless disregard of danger to the health and welfare... [and that] mere inadvertence is not enough. The defendant must be proved to have been indifferent to an obvious risk of injury to health, or actually to have foreseen the risk but to have determined nevertheless to run it.' In line with the prevailing *Caldwell*[80] recklessness of the day, the case of *Seymour*[81] seemed to suggest that recklessness replaced (or subsumed) negligent manslaughter. Although the House of Lords actually ditched *Caldwell* reckless-ness in favour of gross negligence in the leading case of *Adomako*, Lord Mackay stated that 'it is perfectly open to the trial judge to use the word "reckless" in its ordinary meaning as part of his exposition of the law if he deems it appropriate in the circumstances of the particular case'.[82] The Law Commission has recently endorsed this by stating that:

[R]ecklessness falling short of reckless indifference can really be regarded as a kind of gross negligence... The fact that... the defendant saw a risk and wrongly discounted it or stupidly thought it insignificant is simply compelling evidence of the grossness of his or her negligence.[83]

On this basis, perhaps the term gross negligence is really just recklessness in dis-guise? Either way, it is probably no accident that recklessness lurks in the back-ground in judicial opinion about gross negligence. This reflects a sense of judicial reluctance with leaving liability at the lower level of gross negligence. A closer reading of recent reported medical cases confirms judicial support for incorpor-ating subjective recklessness into the task of assessing gross negligence. The case of *Rowley* concerned an unsuccessful judicial review of a CPS decision not to prosecute following a death in a care home. The CPS argued, and the High Court agreed, that evidence (or lack of evidence) of subjective recklessness was relevant in determining gross negligence.[84] This was actually endorsed in *Misra*, where whilst shielding gross negligence manslaughter from a human rights challenge, the Court of Appeal stated that evidence of the defendant's state of mind is 'not irrelevant' to the issue of gross negligence, in fact, adding that it will often be a 'critical factor in the decision'.[85] This support for subjectivism was also apparent in its approval of the trial judge's direction that the jury should be satisfied that the doctors' conduct fell so far below the expected standard that 'it was some-thing... truly exceptionally bad, which showed... indifference to an obviously serious risk to the life of the patient'.[86] Such comments suggest judicial unease with the potential unfairness of gross negligence, and demonstrate the alterna-tive and arguably more appropriate liability based on subjective recklessness. This may also be understood alongside the evidence that prosecutors are more

[80] [1982] AC 341.                    [81] [1983] 2 All ER 1058.
[82] *R v Adomako*, at 118.            [83] Law Commission, *A New Homicide Act*, 90, para 3.182.
[84] *R (Rowley) v DPP* [2003] EWHC 693.
[85] *R v Misra*, at para 56.
[86] Ibid, at para 25.

comfortable working to the notion of recklessness, which whilst representing a tougher task of 'getting home',[87] appears to correspond with some prosecutorial practice. Certainly, the few cases which result in conviction would seem to be cases where the CPS could have proceeded on the basis of establishing subjective recklessness—for example, where a doctor has continued with a dangerous operation in the face of colleague advice to the contrary,[88] or administered a large and lethal overdose which would have been obvious but for the refusal to look at the patient's medical history and current medication chart.[89] And given the outright rejection of objective recklessness in criminal law,[90] framing the crime in terms of subjective recklessness benefits from conceptual coherence with other offence categories.

In their 1996 proposals, the Law Commission proposed to replace subjective reckless manslaughter with the offence of 'reckless killing' which would be committed when:

(1) a person by his or her conduct causes the death of another;
(2) he is aware of a risk that his conduct will cause death or serious injury;
(3) it is unreasonable for him to take that risk, having regard to the circumstances as he believes them to be.

As Clarkson has noted, this is 'simply a clearer articulation of the one species of involuntary manslaughter that presently exists uncontroversially' and is thus difficult to criticize.[91] The situation would be somewhat different following the Law Commission's wider review of the law of homicide, where reckless killings could fall within 'second degree murder' ('[r]ecklessly indifferent killing, where the offender realised that his or her conduct involved an unjustified risk of killing, but pressed on with that conduct without caring whether or not death would result') or manslaughter by '[k]illing through an intentional act intended to cause injury or involving recklessness as to causing injury'. [92] Medical cases under consideration here could theoretically be captured by both of these, but in terms of the cases envisaged here we are primarily concerned with manslaughter liability.

The most important question for present purposes is whether we can place our trust in the concept of (subjective) recklessness to work here? For defenders of gross negligence liability, raising the bar to subjective recklessness risks placing cases which are currently prosecuted outside the reach of the criminal justice system. However, this is not necessarily the case in the context of medical treatment, where professionals would surely be conscious of the risks of death associated with their work. Obviously this will differ depending on the circumstances such as the type of treatment or non-treatment, but it is simply untrue that the

---

[87] Quick, 'Prosecuting "Gross" Medical Negligence'.
[88] 'Doctor who killed patient on operating table escapes jail', *The Independent*, 24 June 2004, 19.
[89] 'GP jailed for giving lethal morphine overdose', *The Guardian*, 6 April 2004.
[90] *R v G.*      [91] Clarkson, 'Context and Culpability', 148.
[92] Both quotes taken from: Law Commission, *A New Homicide Act*, 7.

prosecution would be unable to present evidence suggesting that defendants must have foreseen the risk of death associated with behaving in the way that they did. For example, as Tadros suggests, where a doctor has special knowledge that certain types of procedures carry with them certain risks and fails to investigate that risk, then criminal responsibility might be properly attributed, given that such conduct suggests the vice of being insufficiently motivated by the patient's interests.[93] Tadros offers the following test for recklessness which represents a 'middle way' between subjective and objective requirements, and thus addresses the concerns over the ability to prosecute cases where establishing evidence of foresight of consequences *at the time* of action/inaction is difficult:

(a)   the action was of a kind that might carry risks with it according to the beliefs of the individual;
      and either
(bi)  given those beliefs the agent failed to fulfil his duty of investigating the risks;
      or
(bii) the agent wilfully blinded himself to the existence of the risks.[94]

This places the moral bar at the correct level and would arguably work well in the context of prosecuting medical manslaughter. Whilst predicting the practical effect in terms of numbers of prosecutions is difficult, committing to a form of subjective reckless liability would likely lead to a decrease in individual prosecutions. If the net effect of this change is to deter prosecutions in the cases of momentary slips and lapses in concentration, then this should be welcomed rather than creating cause for concern.

## 6. Conclusion

This essay has charted the increased prosecution of health care professionals for fatally erring in the performance of their work duties. It has noted that whilst the crime of medical manslaughter has achieved cultural recognition, the basis of the liability of this crime has remained controversial and somewhat unclear. Whilst there has long been a principled objection to pitching criminal liability at the level of gross negligence—particularly for an offence of homicide—empirical evidence pointing to practical unfairness and the vagaries of prosecutorial discretion strengthen the case for abolition. However, arguing for abolition of this offence category also calls for consideration of appropriate alternative criminal law responses. First, there is the thus far under-used option of prosecuting trusts

---

[93] V. Tadros, 'Recklessness and the Duty to Take Care', in S. Shute and A. P. Simester (eds.), *Criminal Law Theory: Doctrines of the General Part* (Oxford: Oxford University Press, 2002) 227–58, at 255. See also V. Tadros, *Criminal Responsibility* (Oxford: Oxford University Press, 2005), for further elaboration of this argument to criminal liability generally.

[94] Tadros, 'Recklessness and the Duty to Take Care', 258.

for breaches of the Health and Safety at Work Act 1974. Three convictions in 2006 are significant from a symbolic and practical level in holding organizations criminally liable for failing to ensure patient safety—albeit through a less stigmatized and less visible prosecution compared with manslaughter. In terms of the proposed new law of homicide, the Law Commission's intended replacement of gross negligence manslaughter—killing by gross carelessness—is nothing more than a linguistic modernization of the status quo, and fails to address the fundamental objection to negligence-based criminal liability. Further, it would surely be hampered by all the same problems as the current 'test' of liability in the sense of causing confusion and anxiety for prosecutors, judges and juries. It is argued that the easiest and most appropriate basis for liability is that based on the existing (and proposed) form of reckless manslaughter. This would be welcome as a matter of principle and in practical terms would seem to reflect some prosecutorial preference, and also be consistent with a closer reading of judicial comments in key cases. In the context of involuntary manslaughter, concepts of gross negligence and recklessness have never been sharply separated. Clearly, they have always been closely related terms. However, it is cases on the cusp of the elusive notion of gross negligence which present particular problems—and sometimes lead to inappropriate prosecutions. Considering cases of fatal medical error within the confines of subjective recklessness, and alongside forgotten forms of organizational liability, is a more measured and meaningful approach for criminal law.

# 4

# Medical or Managerial Manslaughter?

*Neil Allen*

## 1. Introduction

In Chapter 2, Brazier and I chart the rising number of prosecutions against doctors for gross negligence manslaughter, a development which has prompted mixed reactions.[1] The medical profession evinces alarm and cites as a warning the unhappy precedent of New Zealand's flirtation with far-reaching criminal liability for 'simple' negligence manslaughter.[2] The families of patients may see the prosecution of doctors as securing justice for their deceased relative, but are often unhappy to witness so many prosecutions fail and so few convictions result in imprisonment. On one point, however, a degree of consensus may exist. Many of the reported judgments on medical manslaughter demonstrate that a failure in the hospital system was as much (if not more) at fault as the doctor in the dock. Relatively little attention has been given to the potential criminal liability of National Health Service (NHS) Hospital Trusts,[3] when in other contexts deaths caused by corporate error have led to calls for prosecution, albeit few convictions.[4] Where corporate manslaughter within the health service is discussed, the prospects of a successful prosecution have seemed remote.[5] This chapter thus

---

[1] See Chapter 2 in the current volume by M. Brazier and N. Allen, 'Criminalizing Medical Malpractice'; see also R. Wheeler, 'Medical Manslaughter: Why this Shift from Tort to Crime?', *New Law Journal*, 152 (2002), 593–4.

[2] P. D. G. Skegg, 'Criminal Prosecutions of Negligent Health Professionals: The New Zealand Experience', *Medical Law Review*, 6 (1998) 220–46. See also *R v Yogasakaran* [1990] 1 NZLR 399, where a junior doctor who omitted to check the label of an ampoule was convicted of manslaughter for failing to show 'reasonable knowledge, skill and care'. For an in-depth analysis of the legal position in New Zealand, see Alan Merry's chapter in the current volume (Chapter 5), 'When Are Errors a Crime?—Lessons from New Zealand'.

[3] G. Slapper, 'Manslaughter, Mens Rea and Medicine', *New Law Journal*, 144 (1994), 941.

[4] See G. Forlin, 'Corporate Killing—Will Directors Ever Be Held to Account?', *Medico-Legal Journal*, 71/4 (2003), 159–64; G. Slapper, 'Corporate Manslaughter: An Examination of the Determinants of Prosecutorial Policy', *Social and Legal Studies*, (1993), 423–43.

[5] M. Childs, 'Medical Manslaughter and Corporate Liability', *Legal Studies*, 19(3) (1999), 316–38.

explores the possibility of prosecuting NHS Trust and Foundation Trust hospitals for gross negligence manslaughter. The complex issues surrounding sentencing are not my concern.

Why should the NHS have escaped the growing public demands for corporate accountability? First, NHS authorities enjoyed Crown immunity from prosecution until 1990. Secondly, until the House of Lords' decision in *R v Adomako*,[6] it was thought that an individual's guilty state of mind was an essential element of gross negligence manslaughter. It followed from this that, thirdly, the judicially invented 'doctrine of identification' was considered to require the Crown Prosecution Service (CPS) to identify, as a precondition to corporate liability, the necessary criminal culpability on the part of a particular employee who was sufficiently senior to fall within the entity's 'directing and controlling mind'.[7] Finally, in terms of prosecution policy, difficult questions arose concerning the utility of prosecuting hospitals when the cause of systemic failures may have stemmed, in part, from inadequate financial resources. Fining the Trust might simply exacerbate the problem.

In 1990, Parliament removed the immunity from prosecution of hospital Trusts[8] and declared them to be corporate bodies.[9] Furthermore, it is now arguable that the objective nature of gross negligence manslaughter no longer requires the Crown to adduce evidence of a guilty state of mind on the part of the defendant as a prerequisite to a conviction.[10] I shall therefore contend that the troublesome principle of identification is not applicable to the *sui generis* nature of hospital Trusts because, unlike many corporate bodies, they owe a *direct* duty of care to patients. Finally, society now seems to be more prepared to challenge the actions of public authorities than in times gone by; perhaps due to an ebbing of public trust.[11] NHS Trusts find themselves in the line of fire. This sentiment is reflected in the Government's belief,[12] contrary to that of the Law Commission,[13] that the new offence of corporate manslaughter should be extended to cover not just corporations but also 'undertakings' such as hospital Trusts. To date, the CPS

---

[6] [1995] 1 AC 171.

[7] *Attorney-General's Reference (No 2 of 1999)* [2000] 3 WLR 195.

[8] National Health Service and Community Care Act 1990, s 60 and Sch 2, para 18.

[9] Ibid s 5(5); see also Health and Social Care (Community Health and Standards) Act 2003, s 1(2) in relation to Foundation Trust hospitals.

[10] As accepted by Rose LJ in *Attorney-General's Reference (No 2 of 1999)*. See also *R v Misra and Srivastava* [2005] 1 Cr App R 21, at para 57.

[11] Wheeler, 'Medical Manslaughter'; see also O. Quick's chapter in the current volume (Chapter 3), 'Medical Manslaughter: The Rise (and Replacement) of a Contested Crime?'.

[12] See Home Office, *Corporate Manslaughter and Corporate Homicide Bill* (HC Bill 236, London: The Stationery Office, 2006) explanatory note 26; see also Home Office, *Corporate Manslaughter: the Government's Draft Bill for Reform* (Cm 6497, London: HMSO, March 2005) explanatory note 22 and Home Office, *Reforming the Law on Involuntary Manslaughter: The Government's Proposals*, (London: HMSO, May 2000) para 3.2.5.

[13] *Legislating the Criminal Code: Involuntary Manslaughter* (Law Com No 237, 1996) paras 8.54 and 8.55.

has shied away from initiating a number of such manslaughter prosecutions,[14] but there is Dutch precedent for them.[15]

## 2. Should health care be subject to crime control?

There can be no doubt that certain types of wrongful activity on the part of health care professionals are so serious as to justify the rigours of the criminal law. If a drunken surgeon avoidably causes the death of his patient,[16] or a doctor dangerously waves a scalpel cutting his patient's throat,[17] society's indignation clearly justifies them being brought before the criminal courts. Yet, less flagrant negligence has placed doctors in the dock, even though there are usually organizational or systemic factors contributing to their behaviour. In Chapter 2, it was suggested that perhaps only recklessness can ever justify a doctor's arraignment.[18] What about a grossly negligent hospital system, which may pose more serious, widespread, and continuous risks to patients?

Estimates of deaths resulting from 'patient safety incidents'[19] range from 840[20] to 34,000[21] per year 'but in reality the NHS simply does not know'.[22] It will come as little comfort to grieving families to learn that around half of these incidents are entirely avoidable.[23] Proactive hindsight in health care, coupled with a retreat from its blame culture, seems an attractive way of minimizing the risks to patients without recourse to the criminal law. However, despite the Government's current

[14] For example, see *The Times*, 1 June 2002, where there was considered to be insufficient evidence to charge the NHS Trust governing Leeds General Infirmary and St James' Hospital. See also *The Daily Mail*, 16 February 2002, in relation to Whiston Hospital, Merseyside.

[15] A Dutch hospital was convicted of negligent homicide following a patient's death resulting from out-of-date anaesthetic equipment, inadequate supervision, and control: Hospital case, Rechtbank Leeuwarden, 23 December 1987, partially reported at (1988) *Nederlandse Jurisprudentie* 981 and discussed in N. Jorg and S. Field, 'Corporate Liability and Manslaughter: Should we be going Dutch?' *Criminal Law Review*, [1991], 156–71.

[16] See *Doherty* (1887) 16 Cox CC 306, 309 per Stephen J. See also D. Brahams, 'Death of a Remand Prisoner' (1992) 340 *The Lancet* 1462, where doctors Saha and Salim over-prescribed a heavy regime of drugs which led to the death of a man in police custody.

[17] *R v Larkin* [1943] KB 174.

[18] See Brazier and Allen, 'Criminalizing Medical Malpractice'.

[19] Defined as 'any unintended or unexpected incident that could have or did lead to harm for one or more patients receiving NHS-funded healthcare' (National Patient Safety Agency, *Seven steps to patient safety* (London: National Patient Safety Agency, 2004)).

[20] *Building a memory: preventing harm, reducing risks and improving patient safety. The first report of the National Reporting and Learning System and the Patient Safety Observatory* (London: National Patient Safety Agency, 2005).

[21] Department of Health, *Doing Less Harm*, draft guidance (London: Department of Health, 2001).

[22] National Audit Office, *A Safer Place for Patients: Learning to improve patient safety* (London: Department of Health, 2005), 1.

[23] Ibid.

emphasis on clinical governance, financial incentives behind the NHS Litigation Authority's clinical negligence scheme, and the culture of greater openness promoted by the National Patient Safety Agency, the NHS 'has not yet fully embraced the culture of patient safety'.[24] Many lessons are not being learnt. For example, since 1985, fourteen patients have died during chemotherapy treatment as a result of doctors erroneously injecting a toxic drug into their spines rather than their veins.[25] The Department of Health issued national guidance and safety alerts in 2001 requiring the nineteen Trusts administering such treatment to comply within a month. Yet, an independent inspection revealed that forty seven per cent of those visited were still non-compliant in 2005, with three having previously reported compliance.[26] Might the opprobrium of a criminal conviction better quench the deceased's families' understandable thirst for justice[27] and serve to overcome such institutional reluctance to learn from the benefits of hindsight?

Some might find it unpalatable to brand hospital Trust boards as 'criminals'. Are they not responsible bodies, better able to compensate a bereaved family rather than face criminal proceedings? From a taxpayer's point of view, privately funded civil litigation would certainly be a cheaper alternative to expensive State-sponsored prosecution. But this ignores the differing functions of civil and criminal liability. If a hospital's gross negligence results in death, this societal wrong requires a form of public censure for which civil liability is ill-suited. Bearing in mind society's collective interest in maintaining safe standards of health care, it seems inappropriate to require individual claimants to bear the risks and costs of uncertain civil or private criminal proceedings.[28] Furthermore, the prosecuting authorities' ability to gather evidence of corporate wrongdoing is more likely to uncover gross negligence if it exists.

Smith has demonstrated the way in which the intervention of the criminal law depends upon the element of chance.[29] Dangerous hospital systems may enable two surgeons to make the same mistake, in separate incidents, which create a risk of death. Yet the wrath of the criminal law will only be encountered by the individual (or hospital) that was unfortunate enough to witness the realization of that risk. Rather than resorting to the law of manslaughter to punish unlucky results, might it not be better therefore to pursue preventative measures through the use of regulatory legislation?

[24] *Learning How to Learn: Compliance with patient safety alerts in the NHS*, Chief Medical Officer's Annual Report 2004 (London: Department of Health, 2004), 49.
[25] J. Holbrook, 'Criminalisation of fatal medical mistakes', *British Medical Journal*, 327 (2003), 1118–19.
[26] *Learning How to Learn*, 54.
[27] B. Fisse, 'The Use of Publicity as a Criminal Sanction Against Business Corporations', *Melbourne University Law Review*, 8 (1971), 107–50.
[28] See, for example, *R (on the application of Rowley) v DPP* [2003] EWHC 693. Section 11 of the Civil Evidence Act 1968 enables a criminal conviction to be adduced in subsequent civil proceedings.
[29] J. C. Smith, 'The Element of Chance in Criminal Liability', *Criminal Law Review*, [1971], 63–75.

In the last two decades, at least twenty NHS Trusts in the UK have been fined for health and safety offences.[30] Three such incidents were fatal in 2006 alone.[31] Health care management is inherently a risky business that is often hampered by inadequate financial resources and poor levels of staffing which may justify a more regulatory approach. However, Celia Wells notes that safety laws are often dismissed as dealing only with 'quasi-crime' rather than 'real crime' and fail to reflect the seriousness of the harm caused.[32] The compliance approach of the under-resourced enforcement agency, the Health and Safety Executive, also encourages a propensity not to prosecute.[33] It is therefore likely that the criminality of an NHS Trust would be 'diverted into the calmer waters of health and safety investigation, with low prosecution rates, little stigma and derisory penalties'.[34] Such 'moral-neutrality' seems an inadequate way of properly assessing and assigning societal disapprobation. These concerns may, to some extent, be assuaged by the enactment of new offences where death or serious injury results from the breaching of safety regulations, as proposed by Glazebrook.[35] Nevertheless, a health and safety conviction seems to be an unfair label to ascribe to those rare cases where a patient's death results from gross systemic negligence.

The public service provided by hospital Trusts should not absolve them from prosecution any more than airline or railway industries might similarly be absolved. To prosecute for manslaughter is thus to pursue both the moral objective of denouncing socially unacceptable conduct and the utilitarian aims of crime prevention and deterrence. Whilst regulatory legislation may identify the *fact* of corporate wrongdoing, the main function of the criminal law is to express the *degree* of that wrongdoing,[36] thereby acting as a powerful form of public condemnation. Regulatory offences should therefore be viewed as complementing the criminal law rather than displacing it.

A sensible way forward might be to prosecute Trusts for health and safety offences where the standard of health care falls *below* what can reasonably be expected, and to prosecute for manslaughter (if the common law so permits) where that standard falls *far below* reasonable expectations. This complementary approach would ensure that, where societal norms are breached to varying degrees

---

[30] Section 3 of the Health and Safety at Work etc Act 1974 imposes a duty on hospital Trusts to ensure, so far as is reasonably practicable, that patients are not exposed to risks to their health or safety.

[31] See Quick's discussion of these in his chapter in the current volume (Chapter 3), 'Medical Manslaughter'.

[32] C. Wells, 'Corporate Manslaughter: A cultural and legal form', *Criminal Law Forum*, 6/1 (1995), 45–72, 51.

[33] See A. Sanders, 'Class Bias in Prosecutions', *Howard Journal of Criminal Justice*, 24/3 (1985), 176–99.

[34] C. Wells, 'Corporate Manslaughter: A cultural and legal form', 54.

[35] P. R. Glazebrook, 'A Better Way of Convicting Businesses of Avoidable Deaths and Injuries?', *Cambridge Law Journal*, 61/2 [2002], 405–22. See also Chapter 3, Quick, 'Medical Manslaughter'.

[36] A. Ashworth, *Principles of Criminal Law* (5th edn, Oxford: Oxford University Press, 2006) 35.

resulting in death, the level of misconduct receives an appropriately graded reproach. Whilst it may be difficult to transform hospital managerial behaviour by the threat of criminal punishment, an organizational focus might at least lead to the modifying of practitioners' working conditions, thereby reducing the likelihood of human error.[37] In this way, the prospect of corporate liability might make for better patient care.


## 3. Gross negligence manslaughter

In order to determine whether the law presently permits such an approach, I shall first summarize the general law of gross negligence manslaughter and corporate liability before turning my attention to NHS Trusts in particular.


### 3.1 Human culpability

Involuntary manslaughter has experienced a somewhat unstable judicial upbringing. In *R v Williamson*[38] Lord Ellenborough held that 'the prisoner must have been guilty of criminal misconduct arising either from the grossest ignorance or the most criminal inattention'. Hewart CJ held in *R v Bateman*[39] that the negligence must have gone 'beyond a mere matter of compensation between subjects and showed such disregard for the life and safety of others, as to amount to a crime against the State and deserving of punishment.' The unanswered question remained whether such conduct required recklessness, be it subjective or objective, or whether something less would suffice. Lord Atkin attempted to resolve the issue in *Andrews v DPP*[40] by stating that 'a very high degree of negligence is required' and '[p]robably of all the epithets that can be applied "reckless" most nearly covers the case'.[41] But his Lordship then ambiguously remarked that recklessness suggests an indifference to risk, 'whereas the accused may have appreciated the risk and intended to avoid it and yet shown such a high degree of negligence in the means adopted to avoid the risk as would justify a conviction'.

The recklessness requirement reached its high watermark in *R v Seymour*[42] where the House of Lords held that, for motor manslaughter, a *Lawrence*[43]

---

[37] In the USA, there are examples where criminal prosecution has prompted dramatic improvements in corporate behaviour; see B. Fisse, 'Reconstructing Corporate Criminal Law: Deterrence, Retribution, Fault and Sanctions', *Southern California Law Review*, 56 (1983), 1141–246, 1161.

[38] (1807) 3 C & P 635. Similarly in *R v Long* (1831) 4 C & P 423, it was stated that a doctor is not criminally responsible 'unless his conduct is characterised either by gross ignorance of his art, or gross inattention to his patient's safety'; see also *R v Finney* (1874) 12 Cox CC 625, 626, where Lush LJ directed the jury that there had to be 'such a degree of culpability as to amount to gross negligence'.

[39] (1925) 19 Cr App R 8, 11.       [40] [1937] AC 576.

[41] Ibid, 583.       [42] [1983] 2 All ER 1058.

[43] [1981] 1 All ER 974.

recklessness direction should be given along the lines of *Caldwell*.[44] Recklessness would thus be inferred where the accused had created an obvious risk of some bodily injury and given no thought to it. Therefore, 1983 to 1995 proved to be a demanding era for the prosecuting authorities, especially in their attempts to prosecute companies, as *mens rea* in the form of recklessness had to be established for manslaughter.

That was until the House of Lords resuscitated the concept of gross negligence in *R v Adomako*,[45] discussed elsewhere.[46] Lord Mackay LC expressly disapproved of *Seymour*, considered a *Lawrence* direction to be unnecessary, and abandoned the need for recklessness by stating that the offence did not require proof of *any* blameworthy state of mind. Confirming *Andrews v DPP*,[47] his Lordship defined the elements of the offence, making it plain that one should apply 'the ordinary principles of the law of negligence' to confer criminal liability.[48] So, first, a duty of care must be owed by the defendant to the deceased; secondly, there must be a breach of that duty; thirdly, the breach must be a substantial cause of death; and finally, the circumstances must be so reprehensible as to amount to gross negligence. Thus, *any* tortious duty of care could be relied upon, subject to two conditions; the duty must have been owed to the deceased and the actions or omissions[49] must have involved a risk of death.[50] It follows that, where death results from medical negligence, the boundary line between civil and criminal liability is supremely a jury question.[51] Negligent behaviour will constitute a crime where the jury considers the defendant's conduct to have so departed from the proper standard of care as to amount to a crime.

## 3.2 Corporate culpability

Before examining the NHS, we need to consider the development of corporate liability more generally. The legal consensus in the sixteenth and seventeenth centuries was that corporate bodies simply could not commit criminal offences.

---

[44] [1981] 1 All ER 961. The House of Lords departed from this decision in *R v G* [2004] 1 AC 1034.

[45] [1995] 1 AC 171. For commentary see J. C. Smith, 'Involuntary Manslaughter — involuntary manslaughter by breach of duty—ingredients of offence', *Criminal Law Review*, [1994], 757–60 and S. Gardner, 'Manslaughter by Gross Negligence' *Law Quarterly Review*, 111 (1995), 22–7. See also J. Stannard, 'From *Andrews* to *Seymour* and Back Again', *Northern Ireland Legal Quarterly*, 47 [1996], 1–11.

[46] Brazier and Allen, 'Criminalizing Medical Malpractice'.

[47] [1937] AC 576.

[48] See n 45 above, 187.

[49] See *R v Stone and Dobinson* (1977) 64 Cr App R 186; *R v Harrhy and Harrhy* (unreported) 16 October 1998; *R v Hood* [2004] 2 Cr App R (S) 73.

[50] The nature of this risk has been confirmed in *R (on the application of Gurphal) v Singh* [1999] *Criminal Law Review* 582 and the matter was finally settled in *R v Misra and Srivastava*, para 52. See also Law Commission, *A New Homicide Act for England and Wales?* (Law Com CP No 177, 2006) para 3.189.

[51] Brazier and Allen, 'Criminalizing Medical Malpractice'.

Lord Holt commented that a 'corporation is not indictable, but the particular members of it are'.[52] Similarly, Baron Thurlow remarked, '[d]id you ever expect a corporation to have conscience, when it has no soul to be damned and no body to be kicked?'[53] Our perceptions have shifted significantly since then; so much so that they can now be seen as one of the most influential of social groupings.[54]

In the nineteenth and early twentieth century, vicarious liability was readily used for non-violent crimes, even though company directors were entirely innocent of any wrongdoing.[55] However, it was considered impossible for a corporation to commit homicide as this required the killing of one human by another.[56] Running parallel to these developments was the birth of the identification principle in civil law. In *Lennard's Carrying Co Ltd v Asiatic Petroleum Co Ltd* Viscount Haldane stated:

A corporation is an abstraction. It has no mind of its own any more than it has a body of its own; its active and directing will must consequently be sought in the person of somebody who . . . is really the directing mind and will of the corporation, the very ego and centre of the personality of the corporation.[57]

The Second World War marked a legal watershed for corporate liability as this theory of attribution dipped its toes into the tempestuous waters of the criminal law.[58] In *R v ICR Haulage Ltd*[59] Stable J held that whether a managing director's conspiracy to defraud could amount to that of the company 'must depend on the nature of the charge, the relative position of the officer or agent, and the other relevant facts and circumstances of the case'.[60] Denning LJ purported to harmonize this theory as a general principle of civil and criminal liability when he commented that 'the guilty mind of the directors or the managers will render the

[52] *Anonymous Case* (No 935) (1701) 88 Eng Rep 1518.
[53] Quoted in: J. C. Coffee Jr, 'No Soul to Damn: No Body to Kick. An Unscandalized Inquiry into the Problem of Corporate Punishment', *Michigan Law Review*, 79/3 ( 1980–1981), 386–459. See also, C. M. V. Clarkson, 'Kicking Corporate Bodies and Damning Their Souls', *Modern Law Review*, 59 (1996), 557–72.
[54] See Clarkson, ibid.
[55] For example, in *Mousell Brothers v London & North Western Railway Company* [1916–17] All ER 1101, the criminal acts and intent of the company's branch manager were imputed to the company which was held to be criminally liable for the statutory offence of giving a false account with intent to avoid the payment of tolls. See also *Mullins v Collins* (1874) LR 9 QB 292; *Bond v Evans* (1888) 21 QBD 249; *Coppen v Moore (no 2)* [1898] 2 QB 306; *Pearks, Gunston and Tee Ltd v Ward* [1902] 2 KB 1; *Allen v Whitehead* [1930] 1 KB 211.
[56] In *R v Birmingham and Gloucester Railway Company* (1842) 3 QB 223, Patteson J held that 'as a general proposition . . . a corporation may be indicted for breach of a duty imposed upon it by law, though not for a felony, or for crimes involving personal violence, as for riots or assaults'. This reasoning was also the basis for Finlay J's decision, in *R v Cory Brothers and Company Limited* [1927] 1 KB 810, to quash an indictment containing, inter alia, a count of manslaughter.
[57] [1915] AC 705, 713.
[58] In *DPP v Kent and Sussex Contractors* [1944] KB 146, DC, the identification doctrine seems to have been applied without clear guidance to a statutory offence under a motor fuel rationing order, as a result of which, the company was held liable for the fault of its transport manager.
[59] [1944] KB 551, CA where the act of the managing director was attributed to the company.
[60] Ibid, 559.

company itself guilty'.[61] Then, in 1965, the Bar and judiciary finally accepted that a company could be prosecuted for the common law offence of manslaughter.[62]

The supposed leading authority on corporate liability centred upon an issue of statutory construction. In *Tesco Supermarkets Ltd v Nattrass*[63] a shop manager failed to notice that his store had run out of specially marked low-price packets of washing powder. The company was prosecuted for advertising their sale at a price less than that at which they were in fact being offered. The issue did *not* concern the circumstances in which a company could be criminally liable at common law for the actions of its employees; the company accepted that it was strictly liable under the Trade Descriptions Act 1968. Rather, the question was whether it could rely upon the statutory defence of due diligence. The Law Lords were therefore called upon to determine whether the manager's lack of diligence should be attributed to the company.

Referring to section 20 of the 1968 Act,[64] Lord Morris stated that 'an indication is given (*which need not necessarily be an all-embracing indication*) of those who may personify "the directing mind and will" of the company'.[65] Similarly, Lord Pearson considered it to afford 'a useful indication of the grades of officers who may for some purposes be identifiable with the company, *although in any particular case the constitution of the company concerned should be taken into account*'.[66] The most commonly cited dicta of Lord Reid states:

> Normally the board of directors, the managing director and perhaps other superior officers of a company carry out the functions of management and speak and act as the company. Their subordinates do not. They carry out orders from above and it can make no difference that they are given some measure of discretion.[67]

The House of Lords unanimously held that the shop manager was not part of the directing and controlling mind of Tesco, nor had the company delegated to him its duty to take precautions and exercise due diligence.[68] Therefore, his failures could not be attributed to it and the company was entitled to rely upon the

---

[61] *HL Bolton (Engineering) Co Ltd v TJ Graham & Sons Ltd* [1957] 1 QB 159, 172; see also *Vane v Yiannopoullos* [1964] 2 All ER 829; *John Henshall (Quarries) Ltd v Harvey* [1965] 1 All ER 725; *R v McDonnell* [1966] 1 QB 233.

[62] *R v Northern Strip Mining Construction Co Ltd* The Times 2, 4, 5 February 1965 at Glamorgan Assizes, although it was acquitted on the facts.

[63] [1972] AC 153.

[64] This stated that a company could be prosecuted where this particular offence was committed 'with the consent and connivance of, or [was] attributable to any neglect on the part of, any director, manager, secretary or other similar officer of the body corporate '.

[65] [1972] AC 153, 180 (emphasis added).

[66] Ibid at 191 (emphasis added); see also Lord Diplock at 199.

[67] Ibid at 171.

[68] cf P. Cartwright, 'Corporate Fault and Consumer Protection: A new approach for the UK', *Journal of Consumer Policy*, 21/1 (1998), 71–89. Cartwright argues that the *mens rea* of the store manager should have been imputed to the company. For a competing view see A. Hainsworth, 'The case for Establishing Independent Schemes of Corporate and Individual Fault in the Criminal Law', *Journal of Criminal Law*, 65 (2001), 420–34.

statutory defence. If this reasoning is embraced more generally as circumscribing the conditions in which a corporate prosecution becomes feasible, it will admittedly make it extremely difficult to prosecute NHS Trusts for gross negligence manslaughter.

The archetypal approach of the CPS has been to sculpt a prosecution with the duty of care of a sufficiently senior employee, embodying the company, as its centrepiece.[69] Any deviation from such a policy seemed bound to fail. Thus it was not surprising that, following the capsizing of the *Herald of Free Enterprise* in which 193 people lost their lives, Turner J directed the acquittal of *P&O European Ferries (Dover) Ltd*,[70] as the prerequisites of manslaughter had not been proven against its controlling mind. Despite being thoroughly 'infected with the disease of sloppiness',[71] the company avoided liability because no individual was found to be criminally culpable. Being 'one of the bluntest legal tools ever to emerge from the courts' shed',[72] the identification principle 'works best in cases where it is needed least and works least in cases where it is needed most'.[73] Whilst small companies have been successfully targeted,[74] larger organizations are enjoying de facto immunity from prosecution.

The mid-1990s witnessed a judicial retreat from this position in relation to statutory offences as the theory of direct liability emerged to circumvent any need to identify blameworthy individuals; the company would be directly liable for failing to do what the law required of it.[75] At the same time, the identification theory was being redefined.[76] This looked like the beginning of the end for *Nattrass*. Confirmation of the objective nature of gross negligence manslaughter in *Adomako* and further corporate convictions[77] served only to raise such hopes.

[69] In accordance with the obiter comments of Bingham LJ in *R v HM Coroner for East Kent, ex parte Spooner* (1989) 88 Cr App R 10.

[70] (1991) 93 Cr App R 72.

[71] Sir B. Sheen, *MV Herald of Free Enterprise: Report of Court no. 8074 Formal Investigation* (London: HMSO for Department of Transport, 1987) 14.

[72] Hainsworth, 'The Case for Establishing Independent Schemes', 422.

[73] J. Gobert, 'Corporate Criminality: Four Models of Fault', *Legal Studies*, 14 (1994), 393–410, at 401.

[74] For example *R v Kite and OLL Ltd* [1996] 2 Cr App R (S) 295. The Managing Director and his outdoor leisure company were found to be grossly negligent in failing to establish a proper system of safety which led to the drowning of four school students in a canoeing accident at sea.

[75] *Nattrass* was distinguished in *Tesco Stores Ltd v Brent LBC* [1993] 2 All ER 718 where the beliefs of sales staff as to the age of persons buying videos was imputed to the company. See also *R v British Steel plc* [1995] 1 WLR 1356 (for commentary see J. C. Smith, 'Health and Safety at Work Act 1974 s 3(1)—corporate liability', *Criminal Law Review*, [1995], 654–6) and *R v Associated Octel Co Ltd* [1996] 1 WLR 1543, 1547.

[76] In *El Ajou v Dollar Land Holdings plc* [1994] 2 All ER 685 Rose LJ held that 'a company's directing mind and will may be found in different persons for different activities' which may even include non-directors. The House of Lords critically undermined the *Nattrass* reasoning in *Re Supply of Ready Mixed Concrete (No 2)* [1995] 1 All ER 135 (see C. A. Ong and R. J. Wickins, 'Confusion Worse Confounded: The End of the Directing Mind Theory', *Journal of Business Law*, (1997), 524–56, at 546–7).

[77] In *R v Jackson Transport (Ossett) Ltd* (1996) unreported, a company employing 40 people was convicted of manslaughter for failing to provide proper equipment, training and supervision which

Following the Southall rail crash in which seven commuters were killed, a novel attempt was made in *Attorney-General's Reference (No 2 of 1999)*[78] to attribute direct liability to Great Western Trains at common law. However, in a myopic, unreasoned riposte, Rose LJ simply stated that the civil negligence rules were 'not apt to confer criminal liability on a company'[79] and re-established the identification principle as the sole basis for proving gross negligence manslaughter. Bruised by this setback, the CPS reverted to its conventional approach but sought to expand the scope of the principle in pioneering the first prosecution for manslaughter of a local authority in *R v Beckingham and Barrow Borough Council*.[80] The alleged cancellation of a maintenance contract led to an outbreak of Legionnaire's Disease, killing seven and infecting 172. However, the trial judge directed an acquittal, doubting whether even the Chief Executive Officer could properly be described as the part of the Council's 'controlling mind'.

## 4. NHS Trusts in the dock

The NHS is the largest employer in Europe, employing over one million people, and forms an integral part of English society. Hospital care and community health services are usually provided by NHS Trust hospitals and Foundation Trust hospitals. The former, despite being subject to direction by the Secretary of State, were given corporate status in 1990[81] whilst the latter have been classified as 'public benefit corporations'.[82] The CPS has contemplated their prosecution for gross negligence manslaughter;[83] but would such prosecutions succeed as the law presently stands?

It will be exceptionally rare for any member of a hospital's 'directing and controlling mind' to commit a gross breach of a duty of care owed to the deceased. Thus, if the *Nattrass* reasoning were to apply, the complex internal structure of hospital Trusts would undoubtedly preclude any finding of managerial culpability. Conversely, to attribute criminal liability using vicarious principles is almost

---

resulted in the death of an employee who was cleaning behind a tanker containing toxic chemicals. In *R v Roy Bowles Transport Ltd* (1999) unreported, two directors were similarly convicted for failing to regulate the working hours of one of the haulage company's drivers who fell asleep at the wheel killing two people.

[78] [2000] QB 796. G. Slapper, 'Corporate Homicide and Legal Chaos', *New Law Journal*, 149 (1999), 1031. For a critique of the decision see S. Parsons, 'The Doctrine of Identification, Causation and Corporate Liability for Manslaughter', *Journal of Criminal Law*, 67/1 (2003), 69–81.

[79] Ibid at 815. Mackay J similarly dismissed manslaughter charges against Railtrack (September 2004) and Balfour Beatty (July 2005) following the Hatfield rail disaster in October 2000, which claimed the lives of four passengers. See also *R (on the application of W) v HM Deputy Coroner for Northamptonshire* [2007] EWHC 1649 (Admin) at para 28.'

[80] See G. Forlin, 'Directing Minds: Caught in a Trap', *New Law Journal*, 154 (2004), 326–27.

[81] National Health Service and Community Care Act 1990, ss 5(5), 60, and Sch 2, para 18.

[82] Health and Social Care (Community Health and Standards) Act 2003, s 1(2).

[83] See above, n 14.

unprecedented at common law.[84] Penalizing Trusts, in the absence of fault, for the crimes of their employees would be entirely unjust. However, a carefully chartered middle course, based on direct liability, may avoid these two brinks.

Trust Boards enter into contracts and can be sued and ordered to pay compensation for civil wrongdoing. They own property and hire and fire staff. Their legal persona in civil law is therefore distinct from that of the individuals they employ. Legal responsibility and resulting liability flow from the senior employees to the Trust and can be found in the hospital's managerial structures themselves.[85] Should this persona be disguised when faced with the prospect of criminal liability? This depends on whether the judiciary persists with its old-fashioned 'atomic approach' to corporate structures or whether it is prepared to develop the 'organic approach' currently in vogue.[86] Should hospital Trusts be treated as nothing more than a collection of individuals? Or are they independent entities, different to the sum of their parts?[87] To persevere with too atomistic a view would be to linger in the restrictive shadows left by the *Nattrass* decision. To embrace the following theory of direct liability would be to infuse corporate accountability with a degree of legal realism.[88]

The many fatalities resulting from errors in the administration of intrathecal chemotherapy treatment may provide fertile territory for the CPS. For example, the unsafe system at Peterborough General Hospital required a consultant to 'borrow' junior doctors Prentice and Sullman from a fellow consultant, both of whom were inexperienced with this procedure.[89] Furthermore, none of the nurses present was competent to deal with cytotoxic drugs. There was a fundamental misunderstanding between the doctors as to what Sullman was supposed to supervise. Neither of them checked the labelled syringes containing the toxic drugs, both of which were injected into the patient's spine with fatal results. Without access to the evidence made available to the jury, it is difficult to assess whether a corporate conviction would have been feasible.[90]

Prosecuting those doctors for manslaughter failed to deter other Trusts from using dangerous hospital systems. A corporate-focused investigation by multifarious agencies is more likely to uncover institutional negligence of the kind demonstrated by the Queen's Medical Centre where Doctor Mulhem mistakenly

---

[84] One of the few exceptions is the rarely used offence of public nuisance; see *R v Rimmington* [2006] 1 AC 459.

[85] C. Wells, *Corporations and Criminal Responsibility* (2nd edn, Oxford: Oxford University Press, 2001) 157.

[86] Ibid, 75.

[87] As Wells puts it, eventually '2+2=5'; see ibid, 79.

[88] For a contrasting view, see V. Todarello, 'Corporations Don't Kill People—People Do: Exploring the Goals of the United Kingdom's Corporate Homicide Bill', *New York Law School Journal of International and Comparative Law*, 19/1 (2003), 481–96, 486.

[89] *R v Prentice and Sullman* [1994] QB 302 (CA).

[90] Although, Childs considers that these facts might show a degree of overall fault sufficient to justify a conviction if the law permitted them to be aggregated. See Childs, 'Medical Manslaughter', 326.

instructed a junior doctor to perform the same tragic procedure. Professor Toft's report into Wayne Jowett's death revealed a plethora of contributory factors including inadequate and incompetent levels of staffing.[91] Cytotoxic drug protocols were either not issued or not followed. There was insufficient staff training relating to the risk of death associated with chemotherapy treatment. Similarity in the design of intravenous and intrathecal syringes also compounded the risk of human error. Mulhem was said to be responsible for only three of the forty-eight contributory failures.

The ordinary civil rules of negligence determine which organizations can be prosecuted. Whether hospitals owe an appropriate duty of care is generally 'a matter for the jury once the judge has decided that there is evidence capable of establishing a duty'.[92] A 'managerial manslaughter' prosecution against a hospital may be an exceptional case where the judge can direct the jury that a duty exists.[93] In *Gold v Essex County Council*[94] Lord Greene MR ruled that the local authority (responsible for the hospital) owed its patient a direct, non-delegable duty of care to nurse and treat her properly and was liable for the negligent treatment provided by its radiographer. Moreover, 'it is no answer to say that the obligation is one which on the face of it they could never perform themselves'.[95] The other judges seemed more inclined to base civil liability on traditional vicarious principles. Nonetheless, the Master of the Rolls' reasoning was followed in *Collins v Hertfordshire CC*[96] where a surgeon's order for 'procaine' was mistaken for 'cocaine' which he inadvertently injected as an anaesthetic. Hilbery J held that the hospital had breached its direct duty of care by permitting a system to be in operation which was 'utterly defective and dangerous' and caused the patient's death.

The direct, rather than vicarious, nature of this duty was reaffirmed in *Cassidy v Ministry of Health*.[97] The patient was undergoing post-operative treatment during the course of which his hand was rendered useless. The Court of Appeal ruled that hospital authorities owe their patients the same duty of care as a doctor. They were therefore liable for any failure to give proper treatment on the part of anyone they employ. Denning LJ commented, obiter, that 'whenever they accept a patient for treatment, they must use reasonable care and skill to cure him of his ailment'.[98] Similarly, Singleton LJ denounced the need to prove negligence

---

[91] Prof. B. Toft, *External Inquiry into the adverse incident that occurred at Queen's Medical Centre, Nottingham, 4th January, 2001*, (London: Department of Health, 2001).

[92] *R v Willoughby* [2005] 1 Cr App R 29, para 24 per Rose LJ. See also *R v Khan & Khan* [1998] *Criminal Law Review* 83.

[93] *R v Willoughby* [2005] 1 Cr App R 29, para 23.

[94] [1942] 2 KB 293.

[95] Ibid at 301. It is arguable that the majority decision did not rest on direct liability principles. MacKinnon LJ was clearly thinking in terms of vicarious liability (at 305–6) whilst Goddard LJ had both direct and vicarious approaches in mind (at 312–13).

[96] [1947] KB 598.

[97] [1951] 2 KB 343.

[98] Ibid at 360. See also *Jones v Manchester Corporation* [1952] 2 All ER 125, 132, per Denning LJ.

against any particular individual when all those concerned were employees of the corporation.[99]

In *Roe v Ministry of Health and others*[100] two patients were injected with a spinal anaesthetic which resulted in spastic paraplegia. Their claims failed, but Denning LJ remarked generally that a hospital was directly liable for the whole of its staff except those consultants or anaesthetists privately employed by the patient.[101] However, Somervell LJ appeared to favour vicarious liability whilst Morris LJ embraced the concept of direct liability but based his decision on vicarious liability.[102] After much debate,[103] the existence of this duty in the law of negligence is now beyond doubt. Lord Browne-Wilkinson in *X v Bedfordshire County Council* put it thus:

> It is established that those conducting a hospital are under a direct duty of care to those admitted as patients to the hospital (I express no view as to the extent of that duty). They are liable for the negligent acts of a member of the hospital staff which constitutes a breach of that duty, whether or not the member of staff is himself in breach of a separate duty of care owed by him to the [claimant].[104]

Whether a corporate prosecution could be mounted on the back of this special duty is likely to depend upon the judicial will to rein in the scope of the *Attorney-General's Reference* decision. For Rose LJ to question the applicability of the ordinary civil rules of negligence was to affront the House of Lords' reasoning in *Adomako*.[105] Why should these rules not be 'apt to confer criminal liability on a company' when, as Parsons notes, the identification doctrine and gross negligence manslaughter are both founded on the law of negligence?[106] Indeed Kay LJ has reaffirmed the *Adomako* principles in stating that Lord Mackay 'was doing no more than holding that . . . the question whether there was a duty of care was to be judged by the same legal criteria as governed whether there was a duty of care in the law of negligence'.[107] So for Rose LJ to deny the civil basis of the criminal offence was to jettison gross negligence manslaughter from its intellectual moorings, as no distinction can logically be drawn in this context between individual and corporate defendants.

---

[99] Ibid at 355.        [100] [1954] 2 All ER 131.
[101] Ibid at 137.        [102] Ibid at 135 and 140.
[103] See I. Kennedy and A. Grubb, *Principles of Medical Law* (2nd edn, Oxford: Oxford University Press, 1998) 460–2; C. Newdick, *Who Should We Treat?* (2nd edn, Oxford: Oxford University Press, 2005) 234–8.
[104] [1995] 2 AC 633, 640. See also *A (A Child) v Ministry of Defence* [2004] 3 WLR 469, at para 63 per Lord Phillips MR; *New Zealand Guardian Trust Co Ltd v Brooks* [1995] 1 WLR 96 (PC) per Lord Keith. In *Bull v Devon Area Health Authority* [1993] 4 *Medical Law Review,* 117, the hospital was liable for implementing an unreliable and essentially unsatisfactory system.
[105] It also runs counter to the Government's interpretation of the law, on the basis of which Parliament enacted the Corporate Manslaughter and Corporate Homicide Act 2007.
[106] Parsons, 'The Doctrine of Identification'.
[107] *R v Wacker* [2003] QB 1207, 1217. In *R v Willoughby* [2005] 1 Cr App R 29, at para 20, Rose LJ does not dissent from this approach.

As will be discussed below, the long-awaited statutory offence of corporate manslaughter will supersede this questionable ruling. In the meantime, it could be distinguished, for the CPS relied upon an employer's duty of care[108] to establish liability. But this duty was owed only to the train company's employees; not to the deceased rail passengers.[109] Contrarily, hospital Trusts owe a direct duty to those patients accepted for treatment over whom they exercise control.

All successful corporate prosecutions to date have also identified a culpable human defendant. However, an individual's state of mind 'is not a prerequisite to a conviction for manslaughter by gross negligence'.[110] A corporate conviction can be secured, if necessary, despite an empty Crown Court dock. Subjective recklessness on the part of the Trust's 'directing mind' may strongly indicate the necessary degree of fault. However, the hospital's negligence may still be criminal, in the absence of human recklessness, if on an objective basis it demonstrated, for example, a 'failure to advert to a serious risk going beyond mere inadvertence in respect of an obvious and important matter which the defendant's duty demanded [it] should address'.[111]

To determine the circumstances which may give rise to managerial negligence will depend upon what the hospital Trusts' direct duty of care requires. Trusts must use reasonable care to provide access to health care and to implement a system which provides a safe level of service.[112] Competent staff must be used and adequate facilities and equipment provided. An adequate system of communication between staff must be in place[113] which must enable appropriate staff to be summoned in response to particular emergencies.[114] Moreover, the Court of Appeal has recognized, obiter, that there are strong policy arguments for holding Trusts responsible 'for the care with which that treatment is administered, regardless of the status of the person employed or engaged to deliver the treatment'.[115] Even if the civil rules of negligence have not so far developed, the criminal law 'may very well step in at the precise moment when civil courts withdraw because of [its] very different function'[116] of protecting citizens by trying those who have deprived patients of their right to life. With such public

[108] As formulated in *Wilsons & Clyde Co Ltd v English* [1938] AC 57.
[109] Such a view is substantiated by *R v Director of Public Prosecutions, ex parte Jones (Timothy)* [2000] IRLR 373; [2000] *Criminal Law Review* 858. See also *R v Crow (Alistair)* [2002] 2 Cr App R (S) 49; *R v Dean* [2002] EWCA Crim 2410, at para 20; *R v Clothier and Dennis Clothier & Sons Ltd* [2004] EWCA Crim 2629.
[110] [2000] QB 796, 809 per Rose LJ.
[111] Lord Mackay quoting the Court of Appeal in *Adomako*, as described at page 183C. See also *R v Director of Public Prosecutions, ex parte Jones (Timothy)* [2000] IRLR 373, at para 24 per Buxton LJ.
[112] *A (A Child) v Ministry of Defence* [2005] QB 183.
[113] *Robertson v Nottingham Health Authority* [1997] 8 *Medical Law Review* 1.
[114] *Bull v Devon Area Health Authority* [1993] 4 *Medical Law Review* 117.
[115] *A (A Child) v Ministry of Defence*, at para 63 per Lord Phillips MR.
[116] *R v Wacker* [2003] QB 1207, at para 33 per Kay LJ.

policy considerations influencing recent judicial generosity in finding 'duty-situations',[117] this approach might be particularly welcome during an era which sees the NHS making increasing use of agency staff[118] and referring patients for treatment in private clinics.

Where systemic negligence is alleged to have resulted in a patient's death, the troublesome issue of causation may ultimately determine whether prosecuting authorities pursue a 'managerial manslaughter' or a health and safety prosecution. For example, in *R v Southampton University Hospital NHS Trust*[119] the CPS accepted that the serious failings in the Trust's management and supervision of Doctors Misra and Srivastava did not cause Sean Phillips' death. Could the Queen's Medical Centre's negligent system be said to have caused Wayne Jowett's death?[120] Was the specialist registrar to blame? Or the junior doctor he instructed? Allegations of manslaughter will inevitably result in management blaming staff in a bid to break the chain of causation which may undermine the profession's efforts to rid itself of a blame culture. It is therefore important to bear in mind that the system need only be *a* cause, not necessarily *the* cause, of death.

Pursuant to *Adomako*, only that conduct of an NHS Trust which involved a serious and obvious risk of death will be relevant. To be properly characterized as criminal, the Trust's negligence must have been 'gross' in the sense that, having regard to this risk, its conduct must have fallen *far below* what could reasonably be expected. Account should therefore be taken of all the relevant circumstances including, importantly, the Trust's culture of safety and any measures taken to minimize the risk.[121] Conversely, breaches of regulatory legislation and any failures to adhere to the guidance, safety alerts, or protocols issued by patient safety stakeholders[122] will assist the prosecution in establishing the requisite degree of 'grossness'. Because of the direct nature of the duty of care, there is no reason in principle why the prosecution should not be able to present evidence of the acts and omissions of any of the hospital staff, past and present, provided their conduct is relevant to the risk of death.

---

[117] It was accepted in *R v Khan (Rungzabe)* [1998] *Criminal Law Review* 830 that a drug supplier could owe a duty of care to his customer, despite both being participants to a criminal enterprise. In *R v Wacker*, it was held that a defendant lorry driver owed a duty of care to illegal Chinese immigrants whose suffocated bodies were discovered in the back of his container.

[118] For example, see *Clark v Oxfordshire Health Authority* [1998] IRLR 125. However, an assignment of at least twelve months may now give rise to an implied contract of employment between agency workers and end users; see *Dacas v Brook Street Bureau UK Ltd* [2004] IRLR 358: *James v Greenwich Council* [2007] 1 RLR 168.

[119] [2006] EWCA Crim 2971.

[120] See n 91 above.

[121] The organizational reality approach is readily used in civil negligence claims. See *W B Anderson and Sons Ltd v Rhodes (Liverpool) Ltd* [1967] 2 All ER 850; *Robertson v Nottingham Health Authority* [1997] 8 *Medical Law Review* 1.

[122] For example, the Department of Health, the National Patient Safety Agency, the Health Protection Agency, and the Medicines and Healthcare Products Regulatory Agency.

## 5. A glimpse at the legislative horizon

NHS Trusts will still be susceptible to prosecution when the Corporate Manslaughter and Corporate Homicide Act 2007 comes into force towards the end of 2008 (as expected).[123] Endorsing the direct liability approach, the new offence attributes systemic negligence to the hospital Trust itself without the need to identify culpable individuals. Although the present common law offence of gross negligence manslaughter will be abolished,[124] insofar as it applies to corporations, the scope of the statutory offence will continue to be governed by the law of negligence.[125]

A trust will be guilty 'if the way in which its activities are managed or organised (a) causes a person's death, and (b) amounts to a gross breach of a relevant duty of care owed by the organisation to the deceased'.[126] Using the civil rules of negligence, the judge will be able to direct the jury of the hospital's direct duty of care that was owed to the deceased as discussed above.[127] Reflecting the suggested threshold for the current offence, the Trust will commit a 'gross breach' if its conduct 'falls far below what can reasonably be expected' in the circumstances[128] which causes a person's death.

This new offence may, perversely, serve to limit a Trust's criminal liability. First, must there be some form of 'senior management' failure in the way the hospital's activities were managed or organized.[129] Fault will need to be established against those play who a significant role in strategic decision-making or operational management for the whole or a substantial part of the hospital's activities. What do the terms 'significant' and 'substantial' mean? Overworked junior doctors create a risk of death but in what circumstances will their dangerous working conditions be attributable to the failure of senior management? Contrast this

---

[123] The Law Commission initially proposed a new statutory offence of 'corporate killing' in *Legislating the Criminal Code*. This was endorsed, with some modifications, in the Government's Consultation Paper *Reforming the Law on Involuntary Manslaughter*. See also Home Office, *Corporate Manslaughter: The Government's Draft Bill for Reform* (Cm 6497, 2005). For a more detailed analysis of the 2005 Bill, see C. M. V. Clarkson, 'Corporate Manslaughter: Yet More Government Proposals', *Criminal Law Review*, [2005], 677–89.

[124] Corporate Manslaughter and Corporate Homicide Act 2007 s 20.

[125] A Trust's supply of medical services will fall within s 2(1)(c)(i) of the Act.

[126] Ibid, s 1(1).

[127] Ibid, s 2(5).

[128] Ibid, s 1(4)(6). Section 8 provides a non-exhaustive list of factors to be taken into account. The jury *must* consider any failure to comply with relevant health and safety legislation, the seriousness of that failure and how much of a risk of death it posed. They *may* also consider the extent to which the Trust's attitudes, policies, systems, or accepted practices were likely to have encouraged any such failure or to have produced tolerance of it. Regard may also be had to any health and safety guidance and any other relevant matters.

[129] Ibid, s 1(3). A literal interpretation of 'senior management' as a collective body would emasculate the legislation. It is therefore suggested that it should be interpreted as referring to one or more persons who play the requisite significant role.

with the present position, which enables the entire organizational reality of the Trust to be taken into account.

Secondly the failure must be a *substantial element* in the breach of the duty of care.[130] This statutory interference with the usual principles of causation in the criminal law threatens to undermine the effectiveness of the offence. Imagine a middle management failure which *prima facie* amounts to corporate manslaughter. Although the Trust Board is likely to be responsible for managing or organizing the fomer's activities, it could argue that its failure to do so was not a substantial element of the breach and thereby avoid criminal liability. Is this really what Parliament intended?

The final limitation is that the consent of the Director of Public Prosecutions will be required before the commencement of criminal proceedings,[131] although it is hoped that such discretion will not be exercized in an unduly restrictive manner.

## 6. Conclusion

In the absence of long-awaited legislative reform on corporate liability, the common law's offence of gross negligence manslaughter has striven to confine 'legal persons' (be they human or corporate bodies) into the same criminal strait-jacket. By criminalizing extreme inadvertence, thereby sidestepping the need to prove subjective wrongdoing, its unique objective nature makes it sufficiently loose-fitting. But do these conjoined heads of human and corporate culpability sit comfortably with one another? Convicting doctors without proof of recklessness seems morally unsettling; convicting Trusts without the adoption of direct liability has appeared impossible hitherto. But if subjectivity is to govern the former, and objectivity the latter, separating the two may offend the principle of legal consistency.

The 2007 Act seeks to bisect human from corporate culpability. Yet the duty of care for the latter will continue to be based upon the common law of negligence. Human errors are inevitable but a hospital's inadequate resilience to risk should not be. With over £3m per year being spent on patient safety incidents, surely the time has come to target systemic failures rather the individuals who do their best to shield patients from them. It has been suggested that the direct duty of care owed by Trusts proffers a direct liability approach. How ironic it would be if the Corporate Manslaughter and Corporate Homicide Act 2007, designed to overcome the doctrine of identification, was to limit corporate accountability.

[130] Ibid.
[131] Corporate Manslaughter and Corporate Homicide Act 20079 s 17.

# 5

# When Are Errors a Crime?—Lessons from New Zealand

*Alan Forbes Merry*

## 1. Introduction

It is a truism that all human beings make errors. Allnutt puts the matter thus:

... all human beings, without any exception whatsoever, make errors, and ... such errors are a completely normal and necessary part of human cognitive function.[1]

Doctors are no exception, and their errors contribute to harm (known as *iatrogenic* harm) caused by health care. In some two per cent of acute care admissions, this iatrogenic harm contributes to the death or permanent injury of patients (possibly as many as 96,000 per year in the USA).[2] Some of the patients who die are essentially healthy and undergoing treatment which ought to have been relatively straightforward. These are circumstances in which an avoidable death is particularly tragic. A proportion of the deaths involve very sick patients with complex medical conditions whose life expectancy would be limited even in the absence of any failure in their care.[3] This fact places the data in context, but does not exonerate those responsible. From a legal perspective, the point is that people die as a result of errors in health care, and the number of these people is very large.

Health professionals have faced criminal prosecution for alleged negligence from time to time. This is perhaps to be expected. However, in England, there has been a recent and substantial increase in the rate of prosecutions of doctors for manslaughter.[4] A similar marked increase occurred in New Zealand during the last decade of the Twentieth century.[5] In both countries, many of the cases

---

[1] M. F. Allnutt, 'Human factors in accidents', *British Journal of Anaesthesia*, 59 (1987), 856–64.

[2] L. T. Kohn, J. M. Corrigan, and M. S. Donaldson, (eds.), *To Err Is Human: Building a Safer Health System* (Washington DC: National Academy Press, 1999).

[3] R. A. Hayward, 'Counting deaths due to medical errors', *JAMA*, 288/19 (2002), 2404–5.

[4] R. E. Ferner and S. E. McDowell, 'Doctors charged with manslaughter in the course of medical practice, 1795–2005: a literature review', *J R Soc Med*, 99/6 (2006), 309–14.

[5] P. D. G. Skegg, 'Criminal prosecutions of negligent health professionals: the New Zealand experience', *Medical Law Review*, 6 (Summer, 1998), 220–46.

involved simple errors, sometimes in emergencies, sometimes under difficult circumstances. In New Zealand, this change in prosecution policy precipitated vigorous debate. After intense lobbying on the part of members of the medical profession, the Crimes Amendment Act 1997 was passed: simple, or civil negligence had been sufficient for a conviction of manslaughter; this threshold was raised to equate with the requirement for gross negligence in England (amongst other countries). This change has substantially reduced the likelihood of such prosecutions in New Zealand. The subsequent run of manslaughter charges against doctors in England is therefore surprising.

In this chapter, I will begin by considering the harsh nature of criminal prosecution. I will remind readers that the perceived need to fear the criminal law as a result of the accidents which can sometimes occur during normal clinical work is a recent development for doctors. I will briefly outline the relevant legal developments in New Zealand and England, with reference to selected cases. I will review the establishment and objectives of the New Zealand Medical Law Reform Group (NZMLRG). I will consider the appropriate response to the accidental harm of a patient, and show that the criminal law usually achieves only one element of this response (that is, it punishes the practitioner). I will outline arguments relevant to England today which led to a change in the law in New Zealand. These arguments are based on considerations of social policy, justice, and the law, informed by science. I will conclude that the situation which has developed over the last fifteen years in England is undesirable for patients and for society, and that action is needed to reverse the trend towards using the criminal law as an instrument for regulating normal medical practice.


## 2. The harsh implications of a criminal prosecution

In the end, does it really matter if an accident in health care is dealt with through a civil law suit, through disciplinary proceedings, or through prosecution in the criminal courts by the State? The extent of the difference between these processes may not always be appreciated. There is no doubt that a civil action can be very stressful to all concerned, but in the end it is one of the normal interactions between individuals within society and does not in itself necessarily imply serious moral blameworthiness. Disciplinary proceedings may also damage a doctor's reputation and cause great stress, but at least they lie explicitly in the realm of professional regulation. Being prosecuted by the State for a serious crime is quite different from either of these, and carries strong connotations of moral opprobrium. Whatever view one takes of error in health care, it is important to really understand the implications of a criminal prosecution.

This difference can perhaps be better appreciated by reflecting on certain consequences of criminal charges that do not apply to these other processes. Criminal charges imply being arrested, taken to the police station, and formally charged by police officers. Photographs and fingerprint impressions will be required. It has not been common for doctors to spend prolonged periods in jail, but going to jail is a possible outcome of conviction, and even while awaiting trial it is necessary to apply for bail. It is usual for travel to be restricted while a trial for manslaughter is pending, and this may involve surrendering one's passport as part of bail conditions. Many countries ask visitors about past criminal convictions, and may well restrict entry if the answer is in the affirmative. During a manslaughter trial, the defendant is in the position of a prisoner and will typically be taken into custody at the start of each day and during the time of jury deliberations and attend court under the supervision of a prison officer. The name of the defendant at a depositions hearing will often be included on a list of other people charged with crimes, and these crimes are likely to be of an obviously egregious nature, such as rape, theft, and assault.

The importance of these differences is reflected in the required standard of proof: in general, civil cases are determined on the balance of probabilities, whereas criminal charges must be proven beyond reasonable doubt (the requirements for disciplinary proceedings may vary between countries).

The 'Granny Test' is illustrative here. This test involves telling one's Grandmother that one is in trouble. It is likely that she will understand a civil law suit as an unfortunate, but relatively normal transaction between individuals, and disciplinary proceedings as primarily a professional matter, but it may be difficult to persuade her that being prosecuted by the State for a serious crime does not imply that one is (at least allegedly) a bad person.

## 3. The way things used to be

In medicine, in England, and in New Zealand, the idea has long held sway that the doctor who practises to a reasonable standard has little to fear from the criminal law. In the past, this attitude has no doubt been grounded in a very real understanding of the challenges faced by medical practitioners, and of the limitations of their abilities to combat disease. This situation is well illustrated by the story of the first recorded death under anaesthesia.

### 3.1 An ingrowing toenail

It is easy, today, to forget the horrors of surgery without anaesthesia. The demonstration of ether anaesthesia by William TG Morton in 1846 was an advance, the significance of which is encapsulated in his epitaph:

> *Inventor and Revealer of Anaesthetic Inhalation*
> *Before Whom, in All Time, Surgery Was Agony*
> *By Whom Pain in Surgery was Averted and Annulled*
> *Since Whom Science Has Control of Pain*[6]

---

[6] R. J. Wolfe, *Tarnished Idol: William Thomas Green Morton and the Introduction of Surgical Anesthesia : A Chronicle of the Ether Controversy* (San Anselmo: Norman, 2001) 493.

However, this advance was not achieved without cost. It was not long before the first report of a death under anaesthesia was published, in the pages of the *London Medical Gazette*, during 1848.[7] A 15-year-old girl, Hannah Greener, was having an ingrowing toenail removed. The surgeon, a Dr Meggison, administered chloroform. Unfortunately, Hannah collapsed, and attempts to resuscitate her (which included throwing water in her face, pouring brandy down her throat, and bleeding her) failed.

After evidence from a number of experts, some supportive of the surgeon (who had administered the anaesthetic), some less so, it took the jury only a short time to find that 'no blame could be attached to Dr Meggison or his assistant'.[8] The coroner then mentioned 'what he had not thought it right to name before, that Dr Meggison, immediately after the fatal event, informed the police of it, and suggested that it would be necessary to hold an inquest'.[9]

In the story of Hannah Greener, there is a strong sense that if a doctor provided conscientious care and was open and honest about things which went wrong, he[10] had little to fear from the courts. This was the medico-legal situation in New Zealand and Britain during the first seven decades of the twentieth-century. During the 1980s and 1990s, however, a very different approach has emerged. The change probably took place a little earlier in New Zealand than in Britain.


## 4. New Zealand from 1840 to 1997

New Zealand was first settled hundreds of years ago by Maori, who called it Aotearoa. The later integration of peoples from other countries, and of their laws and cultures has been unusual in having at least some basis on a founding document, the Treaty of Waitangi, signed in 1840 by a large number of Maori Chiefs and the Lieutenant Governor, William Hobson. Hobson had been charged with the task of establishing a government in the British tradition. To this end, he appointed (amongst others) an Attorney General and a Police Magistrate. Despite the importance of the Treaty, and ongoing influence from Maori and other cultures, New Zealand criminal law is strongly grounded in the common law of England.

In England, the law in relation to negligently caused harm has developed since the industrial revolution, when accidents became very common and accountability for the new risks associated with rapid and unrestrained advances in engineering was the priority, to a more balanced position in which notions of absolute

---

[7] P. R. Knight III and D. R. Bacon, 'An unexplained death: Hannah Greener and chloroform', *Anesthesiology*, 96/5 (2002), 1250–3.

[8] Anon, 'Medical trials and inquests: Death from cholorform during a surgical operation', *London Medical Gazette*, VI (1848), 254.

[9] Ibid.

[10] In those days, it would not often have been 'she'.

liability have given way to the concept of the reasonable person. In 1879, the English criminal code commissioners drew up a code of criminal law, called Stephen's Code.[11] This was never enacted in England, but was the basis of the Criminal Code Act of 1893 in New Zealand, and was adopted in several other jurisdictions. The relevant sections (under different numbers) passed unchanged into the Crimes Acts of 1908 and 1961. These sections are 151 to 157, which relate to doing dangerous acts, being in charge of dangerous things, providing the necessities of life, and so forth. Note that these sections are not restricted to doctors, or to medical or surgical treatment. The section generally cited in manslaughter charges against doctors is section 155:

155. Duty of persons doing dangerous acts—Every one who undertakes (except in the case of necessity) to administer surgical or medical treatment, or to do any other lawful act the doing of which is or may be dangerous to life, is under a legal duty to have and to use reasonable knowledge, skill, and care in doing any such act, and is criminally responsible for the consequences of omitting without lawful excuse to discharge that duty.

Lawyers will recognize this as a statement of the civil standard of negligence.

## 4.1 The first New Zealand prosecution of a doctor for manslaughter

In 1981, a Doctor McDonald was recruited from Australia to work in a small provincial hospital in the South Island of New Zealand. On his first day, he anaesthetized an 11-year-old boy for acute appendicitis. Unfortunately, he confused the knob on the unfamiliar anaesthetic machine, and gave carbon dioxide in place of oxygen, with fatal results. He had apparently familiarized himself with local equipment the night before, but in a different operating theatre. The result was that he failed to appreciate that the machine in question supported a carbon dioxide cylinder. He was also colour blind, which may have contributed to his error. He was charged with manslaughter. After a nine-day trial in the High Court, and almost ten hours of deliberation by the jury, he was found guilty. The jury recommended that leniency be shown: he was fined NZ$2,500, and ordered to pay costs of NZ$2,000.

Slightly more than a century had passed since the original drafting of the legislation, so the intention of the legislators in relation to the interpretation of what had become section 155 of the Crimes Act is a matter of speculation. However, it had been established in the early (motoring) cases of *R v Dawe*[12] and *R v Storey*[13] that the standard of negligence required under sections 155 and 156 of the Crimes

---

[11] F. B. Adams (ed.), *Criminal Law and Practice in New Zealand* (2nd edn, Wellington: Sweet & Maxwell, 1971).
[12] *R v Dawe* (1911) 30 NZLR 673.
[13] *R v Storey* [1931] NZLR 417, 432.

Act 1961 was no greater than that needed for civil actions. In *R v Storey,* Myers CJ stated explicitly:

[I]t seems to me clear that the decision in Bateman's case is not law in New Zealand so far as the criminal responsibility of a medical practitioner is concerned ... [I]n New Zealand the same standard applies in regard to both civil and criminal responsibility.[14]

Dr McDonald's conviction caused some concern amongst the medical profession. However, little more happened in this context for nearly a decade.

## 4.2  A tragic emergency

In 1987, another anaesthetist, Dr Yogasakaran, came to New Zealand. He obtained a position in a small, peripheral hospital where he was called upon to anaesthetize a 'high-risk' patient for the removal of her gall bladder. At the end of the procedure, while emerging from anaesthesia, this patient began to bite on her endotracheal tube, had difficulty breathing, and became hypoxic. Dr Yogasakaran decided to administer an analeptic drug, doxapram (or Dopram). This is a neurological stimulant which hastens arousal. A third person, never identified, had unfortunately stocked the drug drawer of the anaesthesia trolley incorrectly. In the compartment which should have contained doxapram, an ampoule of dopamine (of similar appearance) had been placed. This is a powerful cardiac stimulant, or inotrope, used to support the failing heart. It is provided in concentrated solution and must be diluted before administration (usually as a continuous infusion). Under pressure to act, Dr Yogasakaran injected the entire contents of this ampoule into the patient, whose heart arrested.

Dr Yogasakaran managed to resuscitate the patient, and to transfer her to the Intensive Care Unit (ICU) at a base hospital where she was placed on a ventilator. On returning to his own hospital, he went back to the operating room and discovered his error from the empty ampoules. He immediately informed the doctors in the ICU, and was honest and open about his error, then, and later. Unfortunately the patient went on to die, and Dr Yogasakaran was charged with manslaughter. He was found guilty. In summing up, the High Court Judge said this to the jury:

The Crown says Dr Yogasakaran is a highly trained, experienced, responsible man whom the Crown says made a mistake, through carelessness, on this one occasion.[15]

This seems an extraordinary basis for convicting a doctor of (arguably) one of the worst crimes on the books.

Once again, this case involved a tragic death—that of an adult in the prime of life, being operated on for an entirely recoverable condition. There were several systematic issues that contributed to these unfortunate events, and these

---

[14]  Ibid, 432; *R v Bateman* (1925) 19 Cr App R 8, discussed below.
[15]  *R v Yogasakaran* [1990] 1 NZLR 399.

have been outlined elsewhere.[16] In particular, Dr Yogasakaran's error was made in circumstances that many anaesthetists would consider to be an emergency. Dr Yogasakaran was not helped by one of the witnesses called by the defence. This anaesthetist was asked whether he would ever administer a drug without checking it. He said he would not, but then sought to qualify his evidence by reference to cognitive psychology in relation to the proposition that anyone can misread a label. This was disallowed on the grounds that the witness was not a psychologist.[17] It might be thought that the defence ought to have anticipated this objection, or at least responded to it by calling a psychologist. It might even be thought (at least to lay commentators) that some responsibility lay with the judge to ensure that the relevant issues were aired even if this required some delay. One take on these events is that a legal error contributed to convicting this doctor for a medical error, which, if true, would be ironic to say the least.

In a more general sense, immunity on the part of lawyers in relation to errors made in the heat of a court case was at that time sacrosanct for both barristers and the judiciary. This recognition of the realities of human error (see below) as it applies to lawyers was not extended to Dr Yogasakaran. The law does seem to make provision for those undertaking dangerous acts in an emergency: the duty prescribed by the Crimes Act is not breached in the case of 'necessity'. Collins has indicated that there is authority for the contention that necessity equates with emergency, citing *R v Rogers*,[18] a decision of the Court of Appeal of British Columbia.[19] In *Yogasakaran*, the jury was instructed as follows:

In the context of medical treatment necessity is a situation which is an emergency involving such urgency and immediate peril that the only available option is to respond. In any way whatever. So that it would be completely unjust that whatever action was taken should even be challenged. Particularly, of course, with the benefit of hindsight and the comfort of time for consideration.[20]

In the judgment of the Court of Appeal, this suggestion was rejected:

That exception [necessity] is plainly intended to cover the case of persons unqualified or insufficiently qualified who in emergencies undertake surgical or medical treatment or the like. It is not intended to emancipate a professional medical practitioner from the exercise of reasonable professional care and skill in an emergency... The statutory exception... was needlessly introduced into the present case.[21]

This ruling by the New Zealand Court of Appeal appears to take the position (in effect) that emergencies do not occur in hospitals, but only in situations such as

[16] A. F. Merry and A. McCall Smith, *Errors, Medicine and the Law* (Cambridge: Cambridge University Press, 2001).

[17] See Skegg, 'Criminal prosecutions of negligent health professionals', 227–8.

[18] *R v Rogers* (1968) 65 WWR 193.

[19] D. B. Collins, *Medical Law in New Zealand* (Wellington: Brooker & Friend, 1992).

[20] Summing up of Justice Anderson, Case no 56/88 (HC Hamilton Registry), 8–9.

[21] *R v Yogasakaran* [1990] 1 NZLR 399, at 405.

(for example) motor vehicle accidents at the side of the road. This notion certainly
engaged the minds of those doctors who regularly find themselves faced with
what they view as emergencies in hospitals. The Court of Appeal upheld the finding; the Privy Council (at that time, the final Court of Appeal in New Zealand)
refused leave to appeal on the grounds that the stance taken by the New Zealand
Court of Appeal was a matter of 'policy', and that the Privy Council should not
interfere with 'policy' decisions of the New Zealand courts. In 2003, the Supreme
Court of New Zealand was established. This Court might well have heard the
appeal, had it been in existence at the time. Had the appeal been successful, it is
possible that subsequent events in New Zealand may have followed a very different
course. It seems very probable that success in the prosecutions of Dr McDonald
and Dr Yogasakaran contributed to the decisions of Crown Prosecutors to pursue
the cases which followed in quick succession.

## 4.3 A change of pace

By 2004, ten health professionals had faced charges for manslaughter for alleged
negligence in the normal conduct of their work (see Table 1). New Zealand has
fewer than four million inhabitants, perhaps one fifteenth the population of the
UK. Of course, there is nothing remarkable per se in the fact that a few doctors,
a dentist, and a nurse have faced criminal charges, even in a small country. The
remarkable point is that these were not crimes in the common sense (for example,
fraud, rape, or assault), or even wilful violations of expected standards of professional behaviour: in no case was it suggested (for example) that the practitioner was
under the influence of alcohol or other drugs, or absent when on duty. One could
debate the finer points of each of these cases, but it is clear that the level of negligence in the majority was very low. In this context, the number is extraordinary.

## 4.4 The New Zealand Medical Law Reform Group (NZMLRG)

The NZMLRG was established in response to increased anxiety on the part of
many doctors about the perceived 'inappropriate criminal prosecutions of doctors'[22] in relation to 'the type of error inherent in medical work'[23] to coordinate
initiatives from organizations of the medical profession seeking 'a proper balance
between the criminal code and other means of accountability in medicine'.[24]
There was little support for this objective from outside the medical profession. In
part, this reflected a misunderstanding. It is often overlooked that a number of
people other than doctors, had been convicted for manslaughter under the same
legislation; the negligence involved in some of these cases was obviously gross, but

[22] See Skegg, 'Criminal prosecutions of negligent health professionals', 244.
[23] Ibid.
[24] The New Zealand Medical Law Reform Group, Crimes Amendment Bill (No 5) 1996,
'Medical Manslaughter', Submission (1997).

**Table 1:** Health professionals who have faced criminal prosecution for alleged negligence during their normal clinical practice in New Zealand

| Date of Event | Date of Trial | Health Professional | Alleged Incident | Charge | Outcome | Sentence if applicable | Reference |
|---|---|---|---|---|---|---|---|
| 1981 | 9–20 November 1982 | Anaesthetist | Patient administered $CO_2$ instead of oxygen. | Manslaughter | Guilty with recommendation for leniency | Fine $2,500 Costs $2,000 | *R v McDonald*, 19 November 1982, T 24/82, High Court, Christchurch; P. D. G. Skegg, 'Criminal prosecutions of negligent health professionals: the New Zealand experience', *Medical Law Review*, 6 (1998) 220–46. |
| 1987 | | Anaesthetist | Patient administered Dopamine instead of Dopram. | Manslaughter | Guilty | Discharged without sentence | Skegg, 'Criminal prosecutions of negligent health professionals'; *R v Yogasakaran* [1990] 1 NZLR 399. |
| 1990 | 1991 | Dentist/oral and maxillo-facial surgeon | Patient died following administration of cocktail drugs, patient left unattended. | Manslaughter | Dismissed | | Skegg, 'Criminal prosecutions of negligent health professionals'. |
| 1991 | April 1991 | Radiologist | Patient injected with incorrect contrast medium preparatory to myelogram. | Manslaughter | Pleaded guilty, discharged | | *R v Morrison*, 23 April 1991, S 7/91, High Court, Dunedin. |

**Table 1:** (*Continued*)

| Date of Event | Date of Trial | Health Professional | Alleged Incident | Charge | Outcome | Sentence if applicable | Reference |
|---|---|---|---|---|---|---|---|
| 1994 | | Nurse | Patient's epidural pump set to same rate as antibiotic drip. | Manslaughter | Guilty, discharged | | *R v Brown*, 6 May 1994, S 27/94, High Court, Wellington. |
| 1993 | 1995 | Anaesthetist | Patient died from air embolism injected during rapid intravenous infusion. | Manslaughter | High Court Judge granted application that no indictment be presented (same effect as acquittal) | | *R v Long* [1995] 2 NZLR 691; *R v Long* 13 CRNZ 124. |
| | | Cardiac surgeon | Clamp left for too long on arteries in the head of newborn child. | Manslaughter | Charges withdrawn | | Report of Sir Duncan McMullin to Hon Douglas Graham, Minister of Justice, on sections 155 and 156 of the Crimes Act 1961 (1995). |
| 1991 and 1992 | 24 September 1996 | Cardiothoracic surgeon | Incompetence resulting in the deaths of three patients either during or shortly after surgery for cancer or suspected | Manslaughter | Guilty in relation to one patient, not guilty in relation to two others (Appealed to | Six months imprisonment, suspended for six months | *R v Ramstead*, 22 October 1996, T 26/96, High Court, Wellington; *R v Ramstead*, CA 428/96, 12 May 1997. |

| | | | | | |
|---|---|---|---|---|---|
| 1996 | | cancer. The case for which the manslaughter conviction was entered involved the incorrect placement of a clamp. | | Court of Appeal and subsequently Privy Council) | |
| March 1998 | Anaesthetist | 13-year-old patient inhaled vomit, and then died as a result of a blocked filter. | Manslaughter | Not guilty | *R v Hugel* (1998). |
| February 1999 | General Practitioner practising appearance medicine | Patient died following the application of Exoderm (phenol-based preparation) to her face during cosmetic procedure. | Failing to provide the necessaries of life | Pleaded guilty   Fined $30,000 | *R v Little* (2001). |
| May 2001 | | | | | |
| 14 March 2003 | Midwife | Baby died shortly after birth of hypoxia from cord compression. Allegations of failure to adequately monitor fetal heart during labour. | Manslaughter | Not guilty | *R v Crawshaw* (2006). |
| 6–21 March 2006 | | | | | |

in others it was very low indeed, and entirely comparable with the medical examples. A key principle adopted early in the campaign of the NZMLRG was that there should be no special deal for doctors. Any change in the law should apply to everyone; it is the level of blameworthiness that should determine whether or not criminal prosecution follows an accidental death, not the profession of the person causing that death. Many other people become involved in dangerous and essential activities. This position would apply equally to England; the judge in *Bateman* said:

The law is that anybody who causes the death of anyone else—it does not only apply to a doctor, it applies to motor drivers, railway men, or signalmen, to a number of people—is criminally responsible.[25]

Those who understood this point were more easily persuaded of the need for change. Other arguments advanced by the NZMLRG are discussed below.

In 1997, the Crimes Act 1961 was amended by the insertion of the following provision:

**150A. Standard of care required of persons under legal duties**
    (1) This section applies in respect of the legal duties specified in any of sections 151, 152, 153, 155, 156, and 157.
    (2) For the purposes of this Part, a person is criminally responsible for—
        (a) Omitting to discharge or perform a legal duty to which this section applies; or
        (b) Neglecting a legal duty to which this section applies—only if, in the circumstances of the particular case, the omission or neglect is a major departure from the standard of care expected of a reasonable person to whom that legal duty applies in those circumstances.[26]

The duty-imposing provisions of the law remained, but the new 'major departure' requirement for a conviction for manslaughter aligned the New Zealand position with that of countries (notably England) in which the requirement is for gross negligence. The new provisions were not retrospective in their effect.

## 5. England—a conflict between precedent and policy

In England, the common law is that gross negligence is required to warrant conviction for manslaughter. This test was established in the case of Dr Percy Bateman, who was called to assist a midwife with an obstructed labour in 1924.

[25] *R v Bateman* [1925] All ER 45, at 49. The quotation is from Shearman J's direction to the jury in the Central Criminal Court. Shearman's direction was alleged to be a misdirection by counsel for Bateman. However, looking at Shearman's summing up as a whole, the appeal judges decided that there was no misdirection.
[26] Available at <http://www.legislation.govt.nz/browse_vw.asp?content-set=pal_statutes> (accessed 5 May 2007).

In the process of delivering the (by then dead) baby, it seems he removed a portion of the uterus along with the placenta. He continued to visit his patient at home in the following days, but did not initially transfer her to the local infirmary. She died, and he was charged with, and convicted of manslaughter. In the Court of Appeal, Lord Hewart CJ said:

> In explaining to juries the test which they should apply to determine whether the negligence, in the particular case, amounted or did not amount to a crime, judges have used many epithets, such as 'culpable,' 'criminal,' 'gross,' 'wicked,' 'clear,' 'complete.' But, whatever epithet be used and whether an epithet be used or not, in order to establish criminal liability the facts must be such that, in the opinion of the jury, the negligence of the accused went beyond a mere matter of compensation between subjects and showed such disregard for the life and safety of others as to amount to a crime against the State and conduct deserving punishment.[27]

There was subsequently a brief period in which the English position appeared to become uncertain, notably in relation to *Prentice and Sullman*,[28] but, in *Adomako*,[29] a case involving an anaesthetist, the House of Lords confirmed gross negligence as the correct test in cases of negligent manslaughter. It seemed as if there had been a brief flirtation with the criminal law in response to medical deaths, but that henceforth this law would be reserved for clearly egregious circumstances. Subsequent events have shown that perception to have been incorrect.

Between 1900 and 1989, only fifteen doctors were prosecuted for manslaughter in the UK. In the next fifteen years, thirty-eight were prosecuted. Thirty-four of these took place after 1994 (the date of *Adomako*). Ferner and McDowell have evaluated twenty-two in which a conviction for manslaughter was obtained (see Figure 1).[30] Fourteen of these involved an error rather than a violation (see below). This implies a low level of negligence. The situation in England today seems very reminiscent of that in New Zealand ten years ago. At least some doctors are facing prosecution for manslaughter (although not necessarily always conviction) for failures that amount to little, if anything more than the simple (or 'civil') negligence.

It is particularly instructive to consider the series of tragic accidents in the management of patients receiving the anti-cancer drug vincristine. Vincristine is properly administered intravenously. It is typically used in combination with drugs (notably methotrexate) administered into the cerebrospinal fluid (that is, intrathecally). If vincristine is inadvertently given intrathecally, the result is usually a slow and painful death.

---

[27]  *R v Bateman* (1925) 19 Cr App R 8, at 11.
[28]  *R v Prentice* [1993] 3 WLR 927.
[29]  *R v Prentice, R v Sulliman, R v Adomako, R v Holloway* [1994] QB 302.
[30]  Ferner and McDowell, 'Doctors charged with manslaughter in the course of medical practice'.

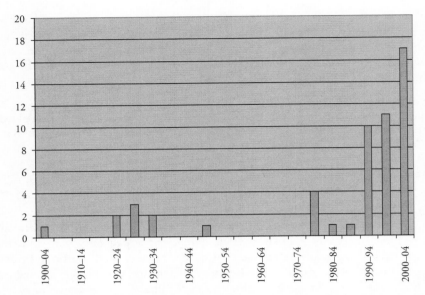

**Figure 1:** Number of doctors prosecuted for manslaughter in the UK in five-year periods from 1900 to 2004.

## 5.1 The vincristine cases

In 1990, a 16-year-old boy was admitted to Peterborough District Hospital for his monthly treatment for leukaemia, from which he had suffered since the age of four. At post-mortem, it was found that his disease was actually in remission. Dr Prentice, a pre-registration house officer, was asked to administer the drugs. He saw his registrar and explained that he was reluctant to do so because of his inexperience. The registrar told him to ask for supervision from Dr Sullman, a house officer with full medical registration. A misunderstanding developed: Dr Sullman believed himself to be supervizing the necessary procedure (a lumbar puncture, or insertion of a needle through the back into the spinal fluid), while Dr Prentice understood that he was being supervized in the overall undertaking of administering the patient's treatment for cancer. The ward sister left the two doctors to their task. Two labelled syringes were supplied in a single container, one with methotrexate and one with vincristine. Neither doctor read the labels. Dr Sullman handed the two syringes in turn to Dr Prentice who injected them both intrathecally. The consultant arrived a little later, and discovered the mistake. The young man died two weeks later.

It is worth reflecting on just how terrible this experience would have been for the patient and his family. It would also have been very bad for the doctors. If anything characterizes the cases for which manslaughter charges have been laid, in the UK and in New Zealand, it is the particularly poignant nature of the events in question. In many of these cases, the requirement for a substantive response is obvious; the only question is what kind of response. The fact that something terrible has happened is, without doubt, reason to take steps to ensure, so far as is possible, that it does not happen again. It may or may not be reason for a criminal prosecution.

These two junior doctors were convicted of manslaughter, and given nine-month suspended prison sentences. The similarity with the summing up in the case of Dr Yogasakaran is striking; the judge said:

You are far from being bad men; you are good men who contrary to your normal behaviour on this one occasion were guilty of momentary recklessness.[31]

Given the known serious risks associated with this therapy, this is an understatement. The practice of supplying the two syringes in a single container was clearly flawed, and was discontinued, at least in that hospital. The organizational approach to a hazardous and highly specialized treatment was not adequate. Accountability was called for, clearly, but why only from the most junior players, particularly when one of them had expressly stated that he was inexperienced and wanted to be supervized? Why were the senior doctors not taken to task? What about the hospital administrators? The juniors would have been in no position to address the deficiencies in the system and reduce the risk of recurrence, whereas those with more administrative authority could possibly have done so. Removing the last person in the chain of errors without fixing the predisposing factors simply sets the stage for the same thing to happen again to someone else.

The conviction was overturned on appeal. This was a reassuring development, but it was based on a technicality that most non-lawyers would find subtle. The trial judge instructed the jury that they should convict if they found the defendants had created a serious risk of harm to the patient, and had done so without giving thought to that risk. This seems to be a description of objective recklessness. On appeal, Lord Taylor CJ held that this was the wrong test of manslaughter. The proper test was one of gross negligence. Had this been applied, the jury could have taken into account the mitigating circumstances (and the judge acknowledged that there were several).[32] Of course, the disconcerting point is that the jury were not asked to judge matters against this standard, so it is only possible to speculate on the outcome if they had been. At the House of Lords, this Appeal Court finding was upheld; at the same hearing, the conviction of another anaesthetist (Dr Adomako) for manslaughter was upheld, because in that case the jury had been instructed to apply the test of gross negligence.[33]

---

[31] *R v Prentice* [1993] 3 WLR 927.
[32] *R v Prentice, R v Sulliman, R v Adomako, R v Holloway*, 328–9.
[33] Even in this case, there were circumstances suggesting liability on the part of those responsible for the system. Dr Adomako had worked as a locum tenens for 15 years, mostly on six-monthly

The very high profile prosecution and initial conviction of these two junior doctors appears to have had no impact at all on preventing further occurrences of the same accident. In 1997, this time at the famous Great Ormond Street Hospital for Children, two more junior doctors (registrars on this occasion) were involved in a very similar mistake, resulting in the death of a 12-year-old child.[34] System errors abounded. Charges of manslaughter were laid, and received a great deal of publicity, even though they were eventually dropped on the basis of expert evidence. Despite this publicity, any effect in improving the system appears to have been minimal. In 2001, at Nottingham, with one junior doctor supervizing another, vincrisitine was administered intrathecally yet again, and again to a patient (18 years' old) in remission from leukaemia.[35] This was the fifteenth occurrence of an intrathecal injection of vincristine in Britain, and the fifth criminal prosecution to arise from these events. This doctor pleaded guilty and was sentenced to eight months in prison.

## 5.2 The problem—the law or prosecution policy?

It is fairly obvious that a change occurred in prosecution policy in both New Zealand and England between 1980 and 2000. It is not altogether obvious why this occurred. It may be that the public has forgotten what it used to know: how bad the alternatives were before the advances of modern medicine.[36] As the ability of doctors to provide effective care has increased, so too has the expectation that this care will be provided safely. In addition, a number of public inquiries have occurred in both countries which have seriously eroded trust in the medical profession (the Cartwright Inquiry[37] in New Zealand, and, in England, the Bristol Inquiry,[38] and the case of Dr Shipman,[39] for example). In New Zealand,

---

contracts. He was also working at weekends at a different hospital, and had slept only a few hours before the day in question. The systemic issues of the overall suitability of locum appointments for unsupervized work in potentially dangerous activities (and anaesthesia is certainly such an activity), and of measures to ensure appropriate hours of work, were not addressed by prosecuting the doctors at the end of the chains of events.

[34] C. Dyer, 'Doctors cleared of manslaughter', *British Medical Journal*, 318 (1999), 148.

[35] C. Dyer, 'Doctor sentenced for manslaughter of leukaemia patient', *British Medical Journal*, 327/7417 (2003), 697.

[36] Recall the story of Hannah Greener, above, for example.

[37] S. Cartwright, *The Report of the Cervical Cancer Inquiry* (Auckland: Government Printing Office, 1988).

[38] The Report of the Public Inquiry into children's heart surgery at the Bristol Royal Infirmary 1984–1995: *Learning from Bristol* (Cm 5207, 2001). See also R. Smith, 'All changed, changed utterly: British medicine will be transformed by the Bristol case', *British Medical Journal*, 316 (1998) 1917–18.

[39] T. Richards, 'Chairwoman of Shipman inquiry protests at lack of action', *British Medical Journal*, 332 (2006), 1111. See also *The Shipman Inquiry*, available online at <http//:www.the-shipman-inquiry.org>.

the Accident Compensation and Rehabilitation Act of 1972 provided a statutory bar on actions for damages for personal injury covered by this Act, and this may also be relevant.

The most obvious difference between the situation in New Zealand in the 1990s and that in England today is that in the former, the level of negligence needed for a conviction of manslaughter was no higher than that generally required for a civil action, whereas in the latter, gross negligence is required (at least in theory). It was suggested to the NZMLRG that it would be easier to seek a change in prosecution policy than a change in the law.[40] This may have been true, but prosecution policy ought to reflect the law, and there was no easy argument against prosecuting doctors for civil negligence with the law as it stood. The prosecutors were applying the law: it was the law that was at fault, not the policy. Establishing local precedent to the effect that the interpretation of the law ought to be similar to that in Australia (see below) might perhaps have provided a way forward, but, instead, case after case consolidated the legal position in New Zealand. If the trend towards increased prosecutions of health professionals for manslaughter was to be reversed, a change in the law to bring it into line with the more usual requirement for gross negligence was essential. It was assumed that a change in prosecution policy would follow, partly in response to the signal from Parliament implicit in such law reform, and in part because it would be harder to obtain convictions.

In England today, the law itself is not the problem. It is clear that gross negligence is needed for a conviction of manslaughter. It seems, therefore, that the primary requirement in England is for a review of prosecution policy. Ferner and McDowell have pointed out that:

Crown Prosecutors must be satisfied that there is enough evidence to provide a 'realistic prospect of conviction' . . . [that is] that a jury or a bench of magistrates, properly directed in accordance with the law, will be more likely than not to convict the defendant of the charge alleged.[41]

The conviction rate for doctors charged with manslaughter in England over the past two decades is about thirty per cent. Ferner and McDowell therefore conclude that: 'The Crown Prosecution Service charges too many doctors, even by its own standards.'[42]

What, then, is the appropriate legal response to the accidental harming of a patient in the course of medical treatment?

---

[40] This is discussed in The New Zealand Medical Law Reform Group, Crimes Amendment Bill (No 5) 1996, 'Medical Manslaughter', Submission (1997), 11.

[41] Ferner and McDowell, 'Doctors charged with manslaughter in the course of medical practice', 314.

[42] Ibid.

## 6. The ideal legal response to an episode in which a patient is harmed

Many patients who have been harmed say they want some or all of the following things:

(1)  an acknowledgement that something has gone wrong;
(2)  an apology;
(3)  an assurance that steps will be taken to avoid the same harm to someone else;
(4)  compensation;
(5)  punishment of the doctor.[43]

The immediate priority when a patient has been harmed is to look after him or her. It is also important to take care of the staff involved with the incident, if only to ensure that they do not compound the harm, or cause harm to someone else while distressed by the primary event. These aspects of responding to harm are very important, and may go a long way to reducing the subsequent need and/or likelihood for legal action, but they are beyond the scope of this chapter and have been discussed elsewhere.[44] Apologies are very important. They must come from the heart if they are to be meaningful, and many doctors do genuinely feel the need to apologize when a patient has been harmed. Unfortunately, perceived liability for criminal prosecution may well inhibit them from doing so at once, or from acknowledging error.

### 6.1 Punishment

People who have been hurt often express a desire for retribution. The punishment of wrongdoing is a long-established part of most cultures. However, vengeance alone is not seen as appropriate in legal systems such as those of England and New Zealand, where it is usually accepted that punishment should be reserved for actions that are blameworthy. The fact that a person has been harmed is not in itself evidence of blameworthiness. Furthermore, a high value is placed on the notion that the innocent must not be punished.

The fundamental issue in deciding whether or not punishment is called for is behaviour. It is not the profession of the accused. For example, Harold Shipman was found guilty of murdering over 200 of his patients;[45] on this basis he deserved to go to jail, whatever his profession. It is also not the outcome of the

---

[43]  C. Vincent, A. Phillips and M. Young, 'Why do people sue doctors? A study of patients and relatives taking legal action', *The Lancet*, 343 (1994), 1609–13.

[44]  W. Runciman, A. Merry and M. Walton, *Safety and Ethics in Healthcare: A Guide to Getting it Right* (Aldershot: Ashgate, 2007).

[45]  See, for example, O. Dyer, 'Shipman murdered more than 200 patients, inquiry finds', *British Medical Journal*, 325 (2002), 181.

behaviour. For example, the administration of a drug to which a patient with no previous history of allergy may result in an anaphylactic reaction and death. This death would clearly have been caused by the person administering the drug, but few people would suggest that punishment was called for. These examples are straightforward. It is in less obvious circumstances that difficulty arises. Furthermore, culpability is not dichotomous. Often it is a matter of degree; some punishment may be warranted, but the severity of the punishment in some cases should be less than in others. The NZMLRG faced the argument that this latter point was a matter to be dealt with in sentencing.[46] This approach overlooks the substantial impact of criminal charges discussed above: even in the event of acquittal, let alone a conviction followed by a lenient sentence, doctors charged with manslaughter have been punished severely. In fact, the leniency of the sentencing (for example, Dr Yogasakaran was convicted and discharged) brings into question the fundamental basis of the conviction. It can be said that one of the general difficulties with manslaughter as a charge is that it encompasses a very wide range of culpability, but manslaughter is generally seen as a very serious matter. Therefore, if this charge is being used in case after case in circumstances where acquittal is more likely than conviction, and conviction if obtained is usually followed by very lenient sentencing, then it is surely the wrong charge for the type of circumstance.

## 6.2 Compensation

Injury usually involves some form of loss. It may not be possible to replace this loss in kind. For example, there is no way to replace a child who has died. On the other hand, injury may involve loss of ability to earn a living or of the dead person's support for those left behind. The adjustment of loss, so that all of it does not fall on the shoulders of the injured person, is a major objective of civil litigation. There is no need to evoke moral culpability for this; the person causing the injury may not be to blame in a moral sense, but neither is the person who has been injured. In no-fault systems of compensation, such as that in New Zealand, the loss is distributed through the community via taxation (by another name). In this situation, it is not even necessary to demonstrate fault.[47] Nevertheless, it is not thought appropriate to compensate all losses. It is generally accepted that some forms of harm are inevitable and must be borne by the harmed person. For example, surgery causes scars, people on certain types of chemotherapy will lose their hair, and anaesthesia predictably evokes nausea in a proportion of those anaesthetized. These are simply the inevitable concomitants of health care, and must be accepted

---

[46] This is discussed in The New Zealand Medical Law Reform Group Submission to Social Services Select Committee on Medical Practitioners Bill 1995, 18, citing Law Commission, *Involuntary Manslaughter* (Law Com CP No 135, 1994), para 5.44.

[47] In fact, the New Zealand legislation has varied from time to time, and this founding principle of the system has not always been adhered to, but it is at present.

by those who agree to have surgery, receive drugs, or undergo anaesthesia. Compensation is reserved for situations in which there is an element of the unexpected. In tort, however, fault is an essential prerequisite for compensation. A tort is a civil wrong, and so there is some element of blameworthiness implied by the award of damages. In practice, most doctors who are sued find the process damaging, emotionally as well as financially. Furthermore, indirect financial effects through loss of reputation may exceed the sum paid in compensation. In effect, suing does punish, but that is not the primary objective of the civil law (although it may be that of a litigant).

If fault does not necessarily mean that that person's behaviour was morally blameworthy, can a simple error justify the award of damages? In reality, reasonable people make errors (see below). However, loss adjustment is important, and even if a doctor's error is understandable, perhaps even reasonable, the injured patient has (usually) done nothing wrong at all. Therefore, compensation does seem to be called for. A civil action is probably an acceptable means to that end under these circumstances.[48] The provision for exemplary damages in cases where punishment is explicitly intended by the courts makes explicit the distinction between the objective of punishment and that of compensation. However, this distinction is even clearer with no fault compensation, which is therefore preferable for true errors. Where violation is involved, there can be no objection to tort. One drawback of the criminal law is that it does not usually provide for compensation at all.

## 6.3 Accountability

Accountability starts with admitting that something has gone wrong. It includes taking responsibility for compensation when appropriate, but it also implies ensuring that the same accident does not happen again, to someone else. This is often cited by patients as their main reason for suing, or laying a complaint. No episode of harm to a patient has been properly resolved until appropriate steps have been taken to understand why it happened and to prevent it happening again. This applies whether punishment is warranted or not. There is little point in punishing a doctor for an error (such as injecting vincristine into the spinal cord), or even in compensating that patient's family, only to have another doctor repeat the same error with another patient a few months later. The criminal law tends to hone down on the aspect of care thought negligent, and is very focused on whether that aspect caused the patient's death. This often means that wider issues relevant to the standard of care overall, and to aspects of the system which predisposed to the accident, are neglected.

A recurrent theme of this chapter has been the tragic nature of many of the deaths which have been associated with manslaughter prosecutions. The fact that

---

[48] See the discussion of the 'Granny Test' above.

terrible consequences can follow simple mistakes is justification for the major investment of time, design, and resources into making health care safer. This relates to duty of care, in that it creates a duty to observe a higher standard of care than might be needed if such risk did not exist. It says little about the standard of care actually observed.

This duty of care lies not only with the practitioner, but also with those who administer and fund health care, and therefore with society. We definitely need to make health care safer. This means a change in a culture which still places greater emphasis on productivity and efficiency than on safety. Safety comes at a price, and society needs to accept that the transition from the status quo to a safer health care system will require substantial investment. However, improving the system will be a better use of resources than spending money on expensive trials in the criminal courts. The best medico-legal response to patient harm is to stop harming patients. Actually, that is what everyone wants.[49] There is no need to motivate the workforce in this regard, nor any need to threaten them with draconian punishment—these people are trying to do the right thing. What is needed is improvements in the system to make those efforts more successful.

It can be seen that the only element of this ideal response reliably provided by the criminal law is that of punishment. Compensation is usually a matter for the civil courts. If we are to be effective in reducing the likelihood of harm from error in health care, we need to look elsewhere. The first step is to understand the nature of human error.

## 6.4 Science—the nature of error and violation

There is a substantial body of theoretical and empirical information concerning the nature of error.[50] Space permits only the briefest discussion of certain key characteristics of error and violation. An example will be useful. On 28 November 1979, Flight 901, an Air New Zealand McDonnel Douglas DC-10-30 on a sight-seeing trip to the Antarctic, crashed into Mount Erebus, a 3,794 metre-high active volcano, with the loss of 257 lives. This was the result of a series of events which can readily be presented using the well-known Swiss Cheese model of accident causation described by James Reason.[51] Factors contributing to this disaster included the following (amongst others): an alteration was made to the coordinates in the navigational computer without informing the crew; the crew were not experienced in Antarctic conditions; flat light prevailed, making it difficult to distinguish geographical features (such as a mountain); these tourist flights over the Antarctic routinely broke a rule concerning minimum altitude, in

---

[49] Or almost everyone—Shipman was an exception.
[50] J. Reason, *Human Error* (New York: Cambridge University Press, 1990). See also Merry and McCall Smith, *Errors, Medicine and the Law.*
[51] J. Reason, 'Human error: models and management', *British Medical Journal*, 320 (2000), 768–70.

order to provide good views of the terrain to the passengers (who, after all, were paying for exactly this).

Errors are not random events. The circumstances which promote error are well understood. Errors can be classified, and certain types of error can be predicted under particular circumstances. In this case, for example, the pilot believed himself to be in one place (descending over the flat ground of McMurdo Sound) but was actually in another (over Lewis Sound, heading directly for Mount Erebus). He was making decisions on the basis of a mental representation of the world. This is what people do. Our experience of reality is, in the end, subjective and interpretive. On this occasion, the mental schema was flawed. The pilot's decisions were (presumably) rational on the basis of his understanding of the situation, but that understanding was wrong. This is a perfect example of what Reason calls a *knowledge based error*,[52] and McCall Smith and I have suggested would be more usefully called *a deliberative error*.[53] It is an error based on a failure to work out a problem from first principles (that is, by deliberation) because of incomplete or inaccurate information.

This story graphically illustrates certain facts about errors (mistakes are one type of error):[54]

(1) errors are unintentional (there is no suggestion that this crash was intentional);

(2) experts make errors (both the captain and the co-pilot were very experienced, albeit not experienced in Antarctic conditions); actually, experts make different types of errors from those made by novices, but they still make errors;

(3) errors do not imply carelessness in the normal sense of the word (the pilots clearly would have cared very much about getting their flight path right);

(4) the corollary of this is that deterrence is ineffective in preventing error: if the thought of crashing one's aircraft and dying as a consequence will not deter pilots from error, draconian laws certainly will not do so either;

(5) the consequences of an error may be entirely out of proportion with the magnitude of the error itself: in this case, the key error was a single failure in communication—the pilots had not been told that the coordinates in the computer had been changed—but the consequences were catastrophic;

(6) good people make errors—there is no reason to believe that these pilots were other than well motivated and competent;

(7) in part, errors can have these disproportionate consequences because of the nature of the activities involved: many medical procedures, like Antarctic flights, are inherently complex, difficult, and risky;

---

[52] Reason, 'Human Error' 55–61.
[53] Merry and McCall Smith, *Errors, Medicine and the Law*, 86–8.
[54] Reason, 'Human Error', 53.

(8) in the end, the consequences of error are highly dependent on luck; exactly the same error would have been without consequence if its effect had been to locate the place over some other area of land which was flat;

(9) the tendency is to punish outcome; had the same error been without consequence, it is unlikely that any punitive action would have followed, even though the culpability of the action would have been identical (this phenomenon is sometimes called 'moral luck').

The story also illustrates some points about violations (in this case, the key violation involved the decision to descend below the recognized minimum height for safe flying):

(1) violations involve choice, so it is possible to choose not to violate;

(2) the corollary is that it may be possible to deter violations (for example, after this event it was decided not to continue flying to the Antarctic, so the need to violate was obviated);

(3) violations may predispose to error and may make serious consequences more likely if error does occur (both true in this case);

(4) some violations are routine, and are tolerated as normal;

(5) violations may be encouraged by those in authority, implicitly or explicitly, and employees may find themselves in a double-bind: in this case, low flying was an explicit expectation, and in medical practice getting through the work is often the implicit priority, even if this means cutting corners;

(6) it follows from points (4) and (5) that not all violations are equally culpable.

In legal terms, violations may be thought of as equating to recklessness, and errors to negligence. Violations are characterized, at least to some extent, by *mens rea* (literally, a guilty state of mind), which, by definition, is entirely absent from errors.

Punishing the pilot (posthumously) would not, in itself, have produced a change in policy on the part of the airline, but, one way or another, this disaster did punish the senior management of Air New Zealand, and a change in policy did occur. There may be justice in punishing an operational person for a violation, but there is still little to be gained in terms of improving standards if that person cannot alter policy; more may be gained by punishing senior people who can. This is highly relevant to the vincristine disasters—punishing the junior doctors seems to have provided little incentive to senior doctors or hospital administrators to fix the deficiencies in the system which predisposed to the mistakes.

The medical profession is trained to analyse situations on the basis of evidence, and the emphasis on 'evidence based medicine' has increased in recent years. It is perplexing to doctors to see the law ignore scientific evidence concerning human error. In order to understand this evidence, the court will need an expert witness.

## 6.5 The need for expert evidence

Expert evidence is not allowable in relation to matters of normal human experience—things about which the judge and jury may be expected to have first hand knowledge from everyday life. Judges and barristers may view human error as simply a matter of common knowledge. By now it should be clear that this is quite wrong. There is a substantial body of knowledge about human error, and this information is not always intuitive. The courts need to differentiate blameworthy behaviour from blameless, and this is sometimes not easily done. It is incumbent upon those involved with legal processes to obtain appropriate expert advice in relation to the particulars of any case. It is also important that experts provide their advice objectively: not all harm caused by health care is attributable to error, and the pursuit of justice must be even-handed.

## 7. Justice

The law must be grounded in reality. In the previous section, I discussed certain characteristics of human error. It is clear that the law does not seek to punish all errors, and that to do so would be seen as unjust. In cases of criminal negligence, the notion of reasonableness is often of pivotal importance.[55] Before one can get into a debate about how far an action has departed from what is reasonable, one has to consider the implications of our understanding of error for the concept of reasonableness.

## 7.1 Is error ever reasonable?

There is nothing reasonable about error. For example, how could one argue that it is reasonable to omit the step of reading the label before administering a drug? The failure to do this was a key element in *Yogasakaran*, in which the expert called by the defence had to admit that one *should* always read every label every time.

To ask whether any action is reasonable is to misunderstand the construct at stake. Actions are neither reasonable nor unreasonable. It is the people doing the actions that need to be considered. The empirical evidence shows that there is a difference between what one *should* do, or *would* do if only one managed to get things right, and what *is* done from time to time. Numerous studies have demonstrated that, for one reason or another, doctors regularly administer the wrong drug.[56] One

---

[55] See the relevant sections of the New Zealand Crimes Act, for example, discussed above.

[56] A. F. Merry and D. J. Peck, 'Anaesthetists, errors in drug administration and the law', *New Zealand Medical Journal*, 108 (1995), 185–7. See also C. S. Webster, A. F. Merry, L. Larsson, K. A. McGrath and J Weller, 'The frequency and nature of drug administration error during anaesthesia', *Anaesthesia & Intensive Care*, 29/5 (2001), 494–500.

should ask, therefore, not whether this action is reasonable, but, rather, whether this action is one that *could* be done by a reasonable doctor, trying to do the right thing. This notion was not quite captured in *Bateman*, in which the judge said:

You should only convict a doctor of causing a death by negligence if you think he did something which no reasonably skilled doctor should have done.[57]

However, in *Marshall v Lindsey County Council*, the judge was much clearer; he said:

What is reasonable in a world not wholly composed of wise men and women must depend on what people presumed to be reasonable constantly do.[58]

The explanation, given by Lord Denning in his judgment in *Whitehouse v Jordan*, an obstetric case involving negligence, was also helpful. He said that an error of judgment in a professional context did not amount to negligence. To test this, he said:

I would suggest that you ask the average competent and careful practitioner: 'Is this the sort of mistake that you yourself might have made?' If he says: 'Yes, even doing the best I could, it might have happened to me', then it is not negligent.[59]

It is interesting to note that this passage was 'corrected' in the House of Lords by Lord Fraser, who courteously suggested that what Lord Denning had meant to say was that an error of judgment was not necessarily negligent:

'The true position,' he (Lord Fraser) said, 'is that an error of judgment may, or may not, be negligent; it depends on the nature of the error.'[60]

The matter could be debated further, and hinges on semantics, but there is a nice irony in the notion that an alleged mistake by a judge is courteously corrected, while a mistake by a doctor is prosecuted.

The important point however is this: reasonable people make errors, even when trying their best not to. Indeed, we have seen that they cannot help making errors. Errors are statistically inevitable in any human endeavour. It follows that it is not just to punish errors. Violations may be a different matter, including any that have contributed to the occurrence of an error. For example, if speeding leads to an error in taking a corner; the speeding may well be culpable. I would agree with Lord Fraser, in relation to violations: each must be judged on its merits.

## 7.2 Justice must be seen to be done

There is no outcry in response to the conviction or jailing of those who steal, rape, murder, and commit fraud. One might expect even some of those who do these

---

[57] *R v Bateman* [1925] All ER 45, at 49.
[58] *Marshall v Lindsey County Council* [1935] 1 KB 516.
[59] *Whitehouse v Jordan* [1980] 1 All ER 650, at 658.
[60] *Whitehouse v Jordan* [1981] 1 WLR 246, 263.

things to acknowledge the criminal law as a fair response on the part of society to these activities. Indeed, many who commit crimes would be quick to call the police if they believed themselves to be threatened by the crimes of others.

This is not the case with the criminal prosecution of doctors. Many members of the medical profession are astonished and dismayed by the use of the criminal law as a response to things which go wrong in their day-to-day clinical work. Few doctors look at those who rape and murder and say 'there but for the grace of God go I', but many do in relation to so-called 'medical manslaughter'.

# 8.  Social policy

Social policy should be informed by an analysis of society's needs. At present, there is a very strong argument that the priority for social policy in relation to safe-guarding patients is to improve patient safety and address the current epidemic of iatrogenic harm.[61] This view is consistent with commonly expressed expectations from patients who have been harmed (see above); many rate the prevention of harm to others as their highest priority. One may ask patients to understand one error. It is hard to justify making the same mistake over and over again. However, this is exactly what will happen if the system is not addressed. The primary question, then, is how best to achieve the aim of improving patient safety?

## 8.1  Preventing a recurrence by punishment

Does punishment serve to prevent accidents in health care? If it does, a utilitarian argument can be made along the following lines: it does not matter whether or not the punished doctor deserves to be punished, because by the punishment we prevent bad things from happening and thereby increase the net happiness (or perhaps well-being) of society.

This question has already been answered: because error is unintentional, it cannot simply be prevented by the threat of punishment. However, some thought should also be given to the social value of the activity in question.

## 8.2  The social value of health care

A non-medical case of manslaughter in New Zealand involved a bungee jump operator who failed to tie the bungee cord adequately to a customer's legs, with fatal results. The operator was under the influence of marijuana at the time. If the effect of convicting this operator of manslaughter had been to put the entire bungee jumping industry out of business (because other operators feared a similar

---

[61] Runciman, Merry, and Walton, *Safety and Ethics in Healthcare*, 105 (this theme is central to the whole book).

fate), this would not matter very much. However, an impact on the willingness of practitioners to provide health care is a different matter. The need for health care is not seriously disputed, and society cannot afford to create an environment in which people are unreasonably inhibited from working as doctors or nurses. In certain parts of the world, fear of litigation has led to at least some withdrawal of services by specialists in high-risk fields, acute neurosurgery and obstetrics being two examples. At least one anaesthetist emigrated from New Zealand because of a stated fear of facing manslaughter charges himself.[62]

## 8.3  Defensive medicine

A variation on this theme is that doctors who feel threatened by legal reprisals will practise defensive medicine. This implies that they will seek to avoid criticism by ordering tests or carrying out procedures which might not be in the patient's best interests. In practice, it sometimes turns out to be difficult to assess the claim that these extra steps are unwarranted. The best defensive medicine is probably the best medicine. Perhaps the risk of litigation encourages doctors to be thorough and discourages shortcuts. It is disingenuous to suggest that unwarranted tests cannot be dispensed with simply because they create a legal risk related to the remote possibility that they might unexpectedly identify some rare and unlikely condition. Every test has costs, risks, and potential benefits, and best medicine involves weighing these up. Limitations on cost, and concern that risks outweigh the likely benefits are perfectly defensible justifications for not undertaking a test. It may well be prudent to discuss the issue with the patient, offer choices where choices are reasonable, and document the conversation. This will take some time and may result in increased cost, but might well improve the standard of care. It is very unlikely that an approach of this type would create much risk of litigation, or any risk whatsoever of criminal liability.

## 8.4  The need for open reporting

A slightly different argument concerns the importance of open reporting when things go wrong. If the health care system is to be improved, it is essential that workers report accidents, and also their insights into why the accidents occurred. In New Zealand and England, the legal system is adversarial, and people are not required to incriminate themselves. An opinion on why something went wrong might well be self-incriminating. A doctor who has harmed a patient accidentally might be well advised to take early legal advice, which in such circumstances might be to say nothing. People are less likely to report fully, frankly, and promptly if they fear that the consequences of doing so might include criminal charges.

---

[62] Personal communication, Dr Bruce Rudge.

In New Zealand, before *Yogasakaran*, anaesthetic deaths were reported on a confidential basis to a review committee which analysed the circumstances, gave feedback to those reporting, and published reports containing recommendations for greater safety. In *Yogasakaran*, the police subpoenaed one of these reports. Mortality reporting stopped forthwith, and has not so far been re-established.

## 8.5 The extent of the problem of iatrogenic harm

There are a few genuinely evil doctors like Harold Shipman. Sending Shipman to jail achieved the objective of punishment, and did presumably save the lives of some patients who might otherwise have been murdered. This was essential, but how effective was it in addressing the overall problem of the harm caused by doctors, most of which is entirely unintentional? Not very.

The fact that Shipman murdered over 200 of his patients certainly commands attention. In fact, the harm he caused through creating widespread public anxiety about the possibility that murderers lurk behind every stethoscope probably outweighs that attributable to the murders themselves, terrible though they were. He has done the work of the terrorist, and has created unreasonable fear. Obviously we must be on the alert for others like him, but we must also retain perspective. The empirical data on iatrogenic harm, referred to in the introduction, suggests that this problem is vast.[63] Very little of this harm is due to deliberate crime by bad doctors; most is due to good doctors making mistakes. The astonishing thing is how little attention these data command. Iatrogenic harm is a public health problem the magnitude of which has been equated with the toll of road traffic accidents. Use of the criminal law may be justified in isolated cases, but we cannot very well put the entire medical workforce behind bars. Better ways have to be found to regulate health care if we are to improve safety and reduce the problem of iatrogenic harm.

## 8.6 Regulating health care

How then should we regulate health care? New Zealand has an advanced system for this. The entry point is the office of the Health and Disability Commissioner. The Commissioner, supported by active medical and nursing councils, can initiate various processes to investigate, discipline, or rehabilitate practitioners who have allegedly breached a code of patient rights.[64] Other mechanisms also come into play when things go seriously wrong—the coronial courts for example, and the criminal courts in the rare instances of genuinely culpable behaviour. The

[63] Runciman, Merry, and Walton, *Safety and Ethics in Healthcare*, 41.
[64] The code is set out in the Sch to the Health and Disability Commissioner (Code of Health and Disability Services Consumers' Rights) Regulations 1996. See also: R. Paterson, 'The patients' complaints system in New Zealand', *Health Affairs*, 21 (2002), 70–9.

present system is the result of a number of reforms, and is not perfect, but it does seem to work reasonably well. The Commissioner can investigate any health professionals (including managers), and institutions, and can make recommendations aimed at improving the system rather than punishing an individual. No fault compensation is provided in a parallel process for those harmed by accidents. This process must, of course, go on hold pending the outcome of a criminal prosecution.

There has been no evidence of any loss of worthwhile protection for the public since the Crimes Amendment Act of 1997. There is room for improvement, of course, but there have been no calls for a return to more frequent use of the criminal law.

In England, there has also been reform of the mechanisms for dealing with accidents in health care.[65] These mechanisms may or may not be working adequately. If they are not, this would be an argument for addressing their deficiencies and introducing mechanisms that do work: it would not be a justification for resorting to the criminal law as an alternative.

## 9. Conclusion

Doctors do not go to work with the intention of harming people. There is no need to evoke altruism to justify the assertion that most health care workers are already trying to do the right thing for their patients. It is simply bad for any doctor's own professional advancement, smooth professional life, reputation, and peace of mind to harm patients. Nevertheless, mistakes are made in health care, despite best endeavours, and patients are harmed, and may even die in consequence. The risk of prosecution arising from such a mistake is actually still low in relation to the risk of harming patients, and that of conviction is even lower, but there is no real doubt that the frequency of manslaughter charges arising from alleged negligence by doctors has increased in England recently. The trend identified by Ferner and McDowell (Figure 1) gives reasonable grounds for alarm. In New Zealand, a similar trend emerged during the 1990s.

After extensive debate and a review by a retired judge of the Court of Appeal, it was eventually accepted by Parliament that manslaughter is an inappropriate crime for acts of mere carelessness, as distinct from gross negligence or recklessness, and the Crimes Amendment Act 1997 effectively realigned the New Zealand position with that in Australia, Canada, and most of the USA (at least). The arguments which, in the end, persuaded all political parties, despite marked initial scepticism, to support the Bill that preceded this Act, were based on

---

[65] See Merry, and McCall Smith, *Errors, Medicine and the Law*, 206–8.

considerations of social policy, justice, and the law, informed by science. These arguments have been discussed, and are now summarized:

(1) Criminal prosecution is substantially harsher than either civil actions or disciplinary proceedings: even in the event of an acquittal, the impact on a practitioner is out of proportion with the egregiousness of a simple error.

(2) Some human error is unavoidable and therefore cannot be prevented by deterrence.

(3) The fact that a normal human error may have tragic consequences does justify every effort to reduce recurrence, but does not (of itself) mean that the error was a crime.

(4) The extent of harm due to error in health care is substantial, and its effective reduction is a priority that depends on improving the system as a whole, and requires open reporting.

(5) The overall contribution of criminal prosecution to patient safety is insignificant when the true extent of the problem of iatrogenic harm is contemplated; furthermore, responding to error by means (such as the criminal law) which are inappropriate and counterproductive is to waste resources and impede appropriate and effective initiatives to improve the system.

(6) Punishment does have a place in the regulation of health care, but punishment should be seen as just by everyone, including those being punished (collectively if not in every individual case).

(7) Punishment should ideally also be directed at those who are responsible for the system and can address its deficiencies, as well as those involved in an accident, and the criminal law does not generally lend itself to this.

(8) It is inconsistent and unjust to respond to the same error (for instance, the administration of a wrong drug) with very serious criminal charges when a patient dies, and with no sanction at all when no harm is done.

(9) Criminal prosecution does not achieve the objectives of an appropriate response to unintended harm to a patient; notably it is expensive, it does not reliably identify correctable faults in the system, does not necessarily reduce the likelihood of recurrence, and does not usually address the need for compensation.

(10) If there are deficiencies in the alternative methods for regulating medical practice in England (or anywhere else), this is an argument for addressing those deficiencies; it is not an argument for resorting to the criminal law.

(11) A low threshold for manslaughter prosecutions reflects the values of the 1800s, rather than those of today's society.

(12) Comparable jurisdictions (for example, Australia and Canada) require 'gross negligence' for manslaughter prosecutions; it is desirable that the law should operate in essentially the same way in similar countries.[66]

(13) Inappropriate criminal investigation impedes openness in reporting errors, and also inhibits common sense medical practice, particularly in emergencies.

(14) No 'special deal' for doctors should be sought; the issues at stake concern justice, effectiveness, and science, and the specific circumstances of each individual case, but not the profession of the person who makes an error.

In New Zealand, consideration was given to the suggestion that manslaughter charges for negligence should require the approval of the Solicitor General. The NZMLRG took the view that this suggestion, while possibly useful, would not address the primary problem which resided in the codified law.[67] In England, however, the legal precedents seem to be entirely consistent with the arguments advanced in this chapter, so the solution does appear to lie with prosecution policy. Many years ago, this author was told by a Procurator Fiscal in Edinburgh that his job was to deal with morally culpable behaviour, and not to regulate medical practice. This insight still seems to hold sway in Scotland, as it does in Canada, Australia, New Zealand, and many other jurisdictions. It is time for those responsible for prosecution policy in England to think again.

---

[66] This argument has not been discussed in the present chapter, because of limits on space, but was advanced in, for example, The New Zealand Medical Law Reform Group Submission to Social Services Select Committee on Medical Practitioners Bill 1995, 7–9. At that time, the argument applied to New Zealand. Today it would seem that England is out of kilter with many comparable jusrisdictions in this context, including New Zealand.

[67] The New Zealand Medical Law Reform Group Submission to Social Services Select Committee on Medical Practitioners Bill 1995, 11.

# 6

# Euthanasia and the Defence of Necessity: Advocating a More Appropriate Legal Response*

*Suzanne Ost*

## 1. Introduction

One of the most prominent and controversial examples of the intersection between the criminal justice system and health care must surely be that of medically assisted death. The debate surrounding the question of whether euthanasia should continue to be equated with murder or, at the other end of the spectrum, completely decriminalized, has intensified in recent years following a number of cases that have explored the boundaries of the current legal distinctions drawn between legitimate and non-legitimate instances of ending life.[1] Rather than going over well-trodden ground by examining the case for the decriminalization of euthanasia in the medical context, in this chapter I will consider how the existing criminal law could better respond to the unique characteristics of such instances of ending life through an application of the defence of necessity.[2] I will argue that legal recognition of the fact that the physician is faced with a situation of necessity would ensure a more effective and just response to this particular form of killing with compassion. Additionally, this approach will avoid inherent difficulties caused by the current application of the doctrine of double effect as a means of establishing the physician's primary intention when administering lethal treatment to his patient. Moreover, allowing the availability of the defence

* First published in the *Criminal Law Review*, [2005], 355–70, published by Sweet and Maxwell. Updated and expanded in places for this volume.

[1] See, for example, *R (on the application of Pretty) v DPP* [2001] 1 All ER 1; *Ms B v An NHS Hospital Trust* [2002] EWHC 429 (Fam); *Moor* (2000) Crim LR. 31; *Re A (Children) (Conjoined Twins: Separation)* [2001] Fam 147; and *R (on the application of Burke) v General Medical Council* [2004] EWHC 1879 (ADMIN), [2005] 2 FLR 1223.

[2] I have raised arguments supporting the legalization of euthanasia elsewhere. See S. Ost, *An Analytical Study of the Legal, Moral and Ethical Aspects of the Living Phenomenon of Euthanasia*, (Lewiston, New York: Edwin Mellen Press, 2003).

of necessity to physicians who induce their patients' deaths for compassionate motivations will remove an anomaly in the current law. This anomaly exists due to the possible availability of the defence of diminished responsibility to murder in a case of a mercy killing by a relative or spouse, when this defence is much less likely to be available in a case of euthanasia in the medical context. For the purposes of this chapter, I am utilizing the term 'euthanasia' to refer specifically to the administration of lethal treatment to the patient by the doctor, at the patient's request, in order to relieve severe suffering.

## 2. The problematical application of the doctrine of double effect when the doctor's administration of pain relieving treatment hastens death

There is some protection currently offered to a physician who administers pain-relieving drugs to his patient in a dosage that hastens death. This protection takes the form of the doctrine of double effect, a doctrine that made its first appearance at common law in the case of *R v Adams*.[3] The physician can rely upon this doctrine if criminal charges are brought against him in relation to his patient's death, provided his intention is to cause the positive effect of relieving pain. This effect is deemed to outweigh the deleterious consequence of hastening death, a consequence that the physician who enjoys the protection of the doctrine is deemed not to have intended. Thus, significantly, the physician acts lawfully when he administers a lethal dosage of a pain relieving medication, such as diamorphine, notwithstanding his knowledge that this will hasten the patient's death. Of course, a physician cannot successfully rely upon the doctrine if the drug that he administers is not known to have pain-relieving effects. In such a scenario, convincing the jury that one's primary intent was to relieve suffering would be next to impossible.[4]

It is possible to challenge the legal application of the doctrine of double effect on a number of grounds.[5] First, in respect of a murder charge, it should be noted that if the doctrine is successfully applied then the physician will be acquitted. This is because the requisite *mens rea* for murder will not have been established. However, since the advent of oblique intent, as explicated by the House of Lords in *R v Woollin*,[6] there are surely strong grounds to challenge this position. For

---

[3] [1957] *Criminal Law Review* 365. Lord Devlin commented that: 'If the first purpose of medicine—the restoration of health—can no longer be achieved, there is still much for a doctor to do, and he is entitled to do all that is proper and necessary to relieve pain and suffering, even if measures he takes may incidentally shorten life' at 375.

[4] As demonstrated by the facts of *R v Cox* (1992) 12 BMLR 38.

[5] Persuasive criticism of the doctrine has been raised by David Price in 'Euthanasia, Pain Relief and Double Effect', *Legal Studies*, 17 (1997), 323–42. See also G. Williams, 'The Principle Of Double Effect and Terminal Sedation', *Medical Law Review*, 9 (2001), 41–53, T. Quill, R. Dresser, and D. Brock, 'The Rule of Double Effect: A Critique of its Role in End-of-Life Decision-Making', *New England Journal of Medicine* 337 (1997), 1768–71, and Ost, *Living Phenomenon of Euthanasia*, 165–70.

[6] [1999] 1 AC 82. See also *R v Nedrick* [1986] 3 All ER 1.

example, if a physician administers a lethal dosage of diamorphine with the primary intent of relieving suffering and foresees death or serious bodily harm as a virtual certainty, then following the direction in *Woollin*, the jury is entitled to find the necessary intent for murder. According to Norrie: 'Oblique intention...includes the intention of means necessary to ends and of necessary side consequences to ends.'[7] Following this analysis, the physician intends both the administration of the lethal dosage of diamorphine as the necessary means to the end of relieving suffering *and* intends that the patient's death will be hastened (the necessary side consequence of administering the lethal dosage of the drug).[8] Furthermore, even if the necessary side-effect (Y) was not desired by the actor, it is Norrie's contention that such a side-effect can still be obliquely intended along with the result that the actor directly intended to bring about (X). He comments:

Y was part of my intention in that I was prepared to accept its necessity as a means to my end or as a side-consequence of it. I may not directly have wanted Y to happen, but I wanted X sufficiently to will the existence of Y too. I may be quite happy that X occurs without Y, but that does not mean to say that the bringing about of Y was not part of my initial intention.[9]

For our purposes, we can substitute 'the hastening of the patient's death' for (Y) above, and 'the relief of suffering' for (X). Now let us consider, hypothetically, that the physician administers diamorphine to his patient in a dosage that he believes to be lethal. However, whilst the patient's suffering is alleviated, she does not in fact die. Of course, the physician is delighted that this state of affairs has been effected by his actions without the patient's death. However, does the fact that he is pleased that the patient has not died mean that he could not have intended this side-effect? Although the hastening of the patient's death may not have been the physician's direct intent, given that he accepted it as a necessary (and in the light of *R v Woollin*, as a *virtually certain*) side-effect of his actions, through adopting Norrie's analysis, we can contend that it still forms a part of his intention. Moreover, whilst the physician may not wish the patient's death to occur, he may desire it to the extent that he sees it as an additional means to an end. It could be that through his actions, he believes that the patient's suffering will be alleviated either by the administration of the diamorphine shortly before her death or ultimately, by her consequent death. In such a case, it can then be seen that hastening the patient's death becomes part of the reason for administering the diamorphine, an intentionally brought about, virtually certain foreseen side effect.[10] Furthermore, in cases where the physician does not desire

---

[7] A. Norrie, 'Oblique Intention and Legal Politics', *Criminal Law Review* [1989], 793–807, 795.

[8] It is also possible here to consider the argument that the hastening of the patient's death is so 'intimately connected' with the intended outcome of relieving the patient's suffering that it must have formed a part of the physician's intent. See A. Simester, 'Moral Certainty and the Boundaries of Intention', *Oxford Journal of Legal Studies* 16/3 (1996), 445–69, 456.

[9] See Norrie, 'Oblique Intention and Legal Politics', 796.

[10] See also V. Tadros, 'Practical Reasoning and Intentional Action', *Legal Studies*, 20 (2000), 104–23, 107.

the patient's death as an additional means to an end, but knowsh it is a virtually certain foreseen consequence of the action he takes to relieve suffering, it can still be argued that he is as morally culpable as if he had the direct intent to hasten death. Kugler maintains that in cases of oblique intent, although the actor may not have directly intended the foreseen side effect of his actions, he has still *chosen* to cause it. This is because he proceeds to act despite the knowledge that this side effect will occur. Thus, he possesses the same degree of blameworthiness as if he did in fact have direct intention.[11]

In the light of my arguments here, it is interesting to note that the Law Commission does not consider the doctrine of double effect to be an aspect of the law relating to intention for murder.[12] Rather, the Commission favours Kennedy and Grubb's analysis that the law treats the doctor who administers a lethal dose of medication to relieve suffering knowing that this will cause the patient's death as having a non-culpable intention to cause death.[13] However, Norrie doubts whether the law is actually as straightforward as this:

There are... discussions of double effect in other cases involving medical practitioners, there is the 'primary intention' or purpose rule in some cases, and there is the famous view in the non-murder case of *Gillick* that 'The bona fide exercise by a doctor of his clinical judgment must be a complete negation of the guilty mind' in relation to aiding and abetting unlawful sexual intercourse. These point in the direction of double effect and intention, even if it is hardly articulated in explicit legal rules.[14]

Further, although the Commission notes that in *Re A*[15] 'Walker LJ pointed out that *Woollin* has nothing to say about cases where an individual acts for a good purpose that cannot be achieved without also having bad consequences',[16] this does not mean to say that the *Woollin* direction cannot apply in the medical scenario we have been examining.

The preceding analysis of the way in which the necessary side effect of hastening the patient's death may in fact be intended by the physician should serve to demonstrate that the current application of the doctrine of double effect as a means of legitimating the physician's actions creates something of an inconsistency and irregularity within the criminal law.[17] Indeed, according to Otlowski, 'there is clearly a wide gulf between strict criminal principles on the one hand, and on the

[11] I. Kugler, 'Conditional Oblique Intent', Crim LR [2004], 284–90, 287.
[12] Law Commission, *A New Homicide Act for England and Wales* (Law Com Cp No 177, 2006) paras 4.72–4.90.
[13] Ibid, paras 4.87 and 4.90. The Law Commission cites I. Kennedy and A. Grubb, *Medical Law: Texts and Materials*, (2nd edn, London: Butterworths, 1994) 1207.
[14] A. Norrie, 'Between Orthodox Subjectivism and Moral Contextualism: Intention and the Consultation Paper', *Criminal Law Review* [2006], 486–501, 500.
[15] *Re A (Children) (Conjoined Twins: Medical Treatment) (No 1)* [2001] Fam 147.
[16] Law Commission, *A New Homicide Act*, para 4.89.
[17] See also M. Watson, 'A Case of Medical Necessity?', *New Law Journal*, 149/6891 (1999), 863–4. Watson argues that 'The doctrine of double effect is irrational, impossible to reconcile with other aspects of criminal law, and produces inconsistent decisions' (at 863).

other, the law as presently interpreted in the *Adams* case'.[18] In order to assess why such an inconsistency has come to exist within the criminal law, it is pertinent to consider the moral content of a judicial finding of intention. According to Norrie,[19] as the history of English law has progressed, there has been a firm move away from the use of legal terms that are indicative of moral opinion in order to invest the law with an objective truth and to prevent the judiciary from deciding cases on the basis of subjective moral judgements. Consequently, judges are set the task of reaching judgements in descriptive legal terminology, unaffected by moral concerns. However, it remains the case that 'Judges... participate in a moral community and make moral judgments'.[20] Thus, Norrie argues that whilst legal terms such as 'intention' and 'foresight' may appear to be morally neutral factual terms, they really relate to inherently moral issues. By way of example, Norrie claims that the legal test of intention can in fact be moulded to lead to the appropriate moral conclusion in each case, by adopting either a narrow[21] or broad[22] approach to the law regarding oblique intent.[23] It is possible to apply Norrie's analysis of the judicial usage of factual legal tests to the utilization of the doctrine of double effect. Thus, it is my contention that the doctrine is being used as a curtain behind which judges can allow moral judgements to influence the conclusion as to the physician's intention and legal culpability. The underlying moral judgement may be to the effect that the physician's motivation is morally commendable, or that he was simply performing his duty to relieve his patient's suffering by the only remaining means available.[24] Indeed, Norrie has recently commented that:

Double effect identifies, in the case of two consequences and their attendant intentions, a moral threshold, wherein the good effect is permitted to override the bad by a moral accounting, which is then cast in terms of intention. Put another way, intentions, treated in their form as abstract cognitive mental states, are enriched through moral

---

[18] M. Otlowski, *Euthanasia and the Common Law* (Oxford: Oxford University Press, 1997) 182. Price raises a similar argument, commenting that there is 'little congruence between mainstream judicial interpretation and application of the concept of intention (notably in the context of murder) and the notion of intention as embedded within the double effect doctrine (and as applied in the pain relief sphere)' in Price, 'Euthanasia, Pain Relief and Double Effect', at 329.

[19] A. Norrie, 'After Woollin', *Criminal Law Review* [1999], 532–44.

[20] Ibid, 542.

[21] That is, the judges could require foresight of a virtually foreseen consequence in order for the jury to be 'entitled to find' intent, as in *Woollin*.

[22] That is, the judges could require foresight of a highly probable consequence in order to make it possible to find intention, as in *R v Hyam* [1974] 2 All ER 41.

[23] See also Tadros, 'Practical Reasoning and Intentional Action'. Tadros states that there appears to be a good argument that in normal usage, the correct utilization of the adverb 'intentionally' is 'determined by whether or not we wish to hold the agent morally responsible for a particular advertent side effect' (at 113).

[24] cf Norrie's discussion of a teacher who gives a student a poor mark in the knowledge that this will cause the student to be upset. Norrie argues that one can morally assess the teacher's actions on the basis that she was performing her duty to grade student work in the proper way. See Norrie, 'Oblique Intention and Legal Politics', at 797.

double effect doctrine by a substantive moral judgment of what the intention in its content was.[25]

Thus, the doctrine of double effect continues to operate, notwithstanding the advent of oblique intent, in order to conceal a judicial perception that there is a moral characteristic to the physician's actions that means we should be very slow to infer the necessary intent that would make his actions legally culpable.

Leaving aside the discrepancies caused by the reliance upon the doctrine of double effect to exonerate the physician's actions in the light of the legal test for oblique intent, a further objection to the legal usage of the doctrine is that the crucial issue of what the physician's primary intent actually is cannot be easily resolved. Undoubtedly, the physician is likely to know what his primary intent was in administering the drug in question, yet how can the jury truly know whether the intent was to relieve suffering rather than cause death? When a certain act can be carried out with more than one intent, perhaps the most we can ascertain as objective actors is what these different intents could be, rather than what the primary intent actually *is*. As Price comments:

The task of the courts in attempting to determine whether death was part of the defendant's chosen *plan* in administering life-shortening pain relief is especially problematic... It may be impossible for a jury to apply the distinction between intended and merely foreseen side-effects, particularly where the evidence is equivocal, eg where only analgesia is administered.[26]

Significantly, in the light of such concerns, the question of whether the doctrine provides an effective means of establishing the physician's intent has been addressed by a recent study involving 683 Australian general surgeons. 247 of these surgeons stated that when administering drugs in order to relieve a patient's suffering, they had administered a greater dosage than they felt necessary to relieve symptoms *with the intention of hastening death*. Interestingly, the authors of the study raise the question of whether the only distinction between these surgeons and the other participants in the study is that they reported their own mental state differently.[27] This leads to a further related criticism of the utilization of the doctrine of double effect in English law. The legal application of the doctrine undoubtedly requires reliance upon physicians to truthfully report their primary intent. Yet, if a physician did administer lethal treatment with a primary

---

[25] See Norrie, 'Between Orthodox Subjectivism and Moral Contextualism', at 499–500.

[26] D. Price, 'Euthanasia, Pain Relief and Double Effect', at 337. In the following chapter, 'Criminal Law is the Problem, Not the Solution', John Griffiths discusses the problems posed by a legal approach that focuses upon the doctor's subjective intention.

[27] C. Douglas, I. Kerridge, K. Rainbird, J. McPhee, L. Hancock, and A. Spigelman, 'The Intention to Hasten Death: A Survey of Attitudes and Practices of Surgeons in Australia', *Medical Journal of Australia*, 175/10 (2001), 511–18.

intent to cause death, can we really expect him to reveal this truth, given the legal consequences of this revelation?[28]

As a final point here, by utilizing the doctrine and thereby circumventing the criminal law regarding *mens rea*, are we not skating around the issue of the intent behind administering lethal doses of pain alleviating treatment towards the end of life instead of tackling it head on? In related areas, the courts have adopted a more realistic legal approach that recognizes the actual intention behind an act leading to death, yet still allows for such acts to be deemed lawful. For example, in *Airedale NHS Trust v Bland*,[29] the House of Lords sanctioned the withdrawal of Anthony Bland's feeding tube through an application of the best interests test, notwithstanding the acknowledged intention of bringing about his death.[30] Thus, rather than trying to draw distinctions between what the physician actually intends and the 'unintended' effects of his act in order to legitimate certain acts and prohibit others, I would submit that the law needs to focus more upon the *circumstances surrounding* the intention to end life in a case of euthanasia. It is therefore significant that in a case of a mercy killing carried out by a relative, such considerations *are* taken into account.

## 3. The potential availability of the defence of diminished responsibility to a relative or spouse who carries out a mercy killing

The legal consequences for a physician who commits euthanasia in circumstances where the doctrine of double effect is unavailable could well differ from the consequences faced by a relative or spouse who carries out a mercy killing. This is due to the fact that there is a greater possibility that the defence of diminished responsibility to a charge of murder may be available in the latter case, thereby reducing the charge to one of voluntary manslaughter.[31] Thus, for example, in 2001, James Lawson was able to successfully rely on the defence of diminished responsibility having given a cocktail of drugs to his mentally unstable daughter and suffocated

---

[28] See also on this point, H. Biggs, *Euthanasia: Death With Dignity and the Law* (Oxford: Hart Publishing, 2001) 57 and Williams, 'The Principle Of Double Effect and Terminal Sedation', 47–8.

[29] [1993] 1 All ER 821.

[30] Lord Browne-Wilkinson stated: 'As to the element of intention, or *mens rea*, in my judgement...the whole purpose of stopping artificial feeding is to bring about the death of Anthony Bland' (ibid, at 880). This statement of intention in cases of withdrawing life-sustaining treatment has since been reaffirmed by Dame Butler-Sloss in *An NHS Trust A v M, An NHS Trust B v H* [2001] Fam 348, at 356.

[31] Ashworth also notes that it is the defence of diminished responsibility that is usually deemed appropriate in cases where a non-professional carries out a mercy killing. See A. Ashworth, *Principles of Criminal Law* (5th edn, Oxford: Oxford University Press, 2006) 283 and J. Smith, *Justification and Excuse in the Criminal Law* (London: Stevens and Sons, 1989). For an early mercy killing case in which the defence was utilized, see *R v Johnson* (1961) 1 Med Sci Law 192.

her with a pillow.[32] His own depression and the effect that his daughter's mental health problems had been having upon the family were sufficient to convince the jury that he was suffering from an abnormality of the mind which was such as to substantially impair his mental responsibility for the killing.

In another case, a husband killed his dependent wife primarily because she had been moved between different care homes and he did not want to her to go through the stress of being moved again. The Crown Court judge, Mr Justice Leveson, described the killing as 'an act of love'. The defendant was a 100-year-old man whom the judge had no doubt had been suffering from a mental disorder at the time and consequently he accepted his guilty plea of manslaughter through diminished responsibility.[33] In December 2005, a verdict in the much-publicized case of Andrew Wragg was finally reached,[34] with Wragg being found not guilty of murder, but given a two-year suspended sentence following his plea of guilty to manslaughter on the grounds of diminished responsibility. Wragg smothered his son, who suffered from Hunter Syndrome, with a pillow.[35] Such decisions illustrate the reality that although the courts have to work within the constraints of the criminal law, they are willing to invest the defence of diminished responsibility with a certain amount of elasticity in order to encompass situations where it appears that a spouse or relative faces tremendous emotional pressure and kills their loved one to relieve suffering.[36] Furthermore, the courts appear to recognize that in these circumstances, the suffering in question is felt by both the person who kills and the person who is killed.[37]

---

[32] *R v Lawson*, The Times 9 June 2001.

[33] The defendant, Bernard Heginbotham, was given a 12-month community rehabilitation order in 2004. See Anon, 'Wife killer, 100, spared prison', BBC News Online (8 July 2004) at <http://news.bbc.co.uk/1/hi/england/lancashire/3876615.stm>. In another recent case, Daniel Gardner killed his elderly parents in order to end their suffering. His father was terminally ill and his mother suffered from Alzheimer's Disease. Gardner also relied successfully upon the defence of diminished responsibility at his trial at the Old Bailey in 2003. See Anon, ' "Loving son" kills parents', BBC News Online (4 April 2003) at <http://news.bbc.co.uk/1/hi/england/2916731.stm>. In 2005, Wendolyn Markcrow also pleaded guilty to manslaughter on the grounds of diminished responsibility after smothering her son, who had Down's Syndrome and autistic traits. See Anon, 'Mother who killed son avoids jail', BBC News Online (2 November 2005) at <http://news.bbc.co.uk/1/hi/england/beds/bucks/herts/4399832.stm>.

[34] The case was initially tried in March 2005, but the jury was discharged after failing to reach a verdict.

[35] The judge in the case stated that she was prepared to be lenient in terms of the sentence given to Wragg because she had no doubt that his former wife had complicit knowledge of what had taken place. See Anon, 'Father cleared of murdering son', BBC News Online (12 December 2005) at <http://news.bbc.co.uk/1/hi/england/southern_counties/4350153.stm>.

[36] See also on this point, B. Mitchell, 'Homicide and Criminal Injustice', *New Law Journal*, 139/6429 (1989), 1450–51.

[37] In passing sentence in the Heginbotham case, Mr Justice Leveson stated that the killing 'was carried out in an effort to end her suffering while [the defendant was] under intolerable pressure'. Similarly, the judge referred to the unbearable pressure that the defendant had been under as a result of being the sole carer for her son in the Markcrow case. See Anon, 'Mother who killed son avoids jail'. Given the apparent willingness of the courts to entertain the defence of diminished responsibility in such cases, it is perhaps surprising that the defence was not pleaded in *R v Cocker*

In a case of euthanasia in the medical context, it is much less likely that a physician would similarly be able to plead diminished responsibility. The lack of a close familial relationship means that the patient's suffering is unlikely to have the kind of severe emotional and psychological impact that could satisfy the requirements of diminished responsibility.[38] This is particularly the case given that the defence of diminished responsibility provides an *excuse* for the defendant's actions. As excuses are personal to the particular actor, it is highly improbable that the physician would be able to claim diminished responsibility on the basis of emotional trauma. Indeed, if this were the case, he would not be deemed fit to practise. As I will argue in the following section, it is more appropriate to view the doctor as being *justified* in acting as he did, rather than being excused for so acting. Thus, given the character of the diminished responsibility defence and its consequent probable unavailability to the physician, depending upon the nature of the drug he administers, he is left either with the protection offered by the doctrine of double effect or a conviction for murder.[39] This must at least raise the possibility that in cases of mercy killings, a relative or spouse can receive more lenient treatment from the law than the physician, not perhaps in terms of the sentence imposed following conviction (as will be noted below), but in terms of the categorization of their offence.

Perhaps one of the main reasons why a relative or spouse who causes the death of a loved one is not branded with the label of murderer and does not suffer the normal penalty for killing another relates to the fact that this would not further one of the main purposes behind the criminal law, that of protecting the public from harm.[40] Such an individual is not thought to pose a threat to society. Indeed, in the *Lawson* case, Mr Justice Nelson emphasized the fact that the case was unique, out of the norm in terms of 'usual' manslaughter cases and that it would serve no purpose to send Lawson to prison, statements echoed by Mrs Justice Anne Rafferty in the Wragg case.[41] It is also significant that Mr Justice Nelson decided that it was inappropriate to send Lawson to prison despite

---

(1989) *Criminal Law Review* 740. Here, a husband killed his incurably ill wife at her request by suffocating her with a pillow. On the night in question, she had repeatedly woken him up and pleaded with him to end her suffering. Rather than diminished responsibility, he relied unsuccessfully upon the defence of provocation. See further Mitchell, ibid.

[38] See also Watson, 'A Case of Medical Necessity?', on this point. The Law Commission also appears to recognize this, noting in its recent consultation paper that carers acting in a professional capacity are unlikely to end life due to overwhelming emotional distress. See Law Commission, *A New Homicide Act*, para 8.55. The Commission considers that relatives or spouses who end life in a mercy killing scenario will be able to rely upon its proposed version of the defence of diminished responsibility. See paras 8. 51–8.57.

[39] As evidenced by the decision in *R v Cox*, where the physician was convicted for attempted murder.

[40] For a summary of the main aims of the criminal law, such as protecting the public, see Ashworth, *Principles of Criminal Law*, 15–17. See also s 142 of the Criminal Justice Act 2003, which requires judges to consider the protection of the public as one of the purposes of sentencing.

[41] See Anon, 'Father cleared of murdering son'.

another purpose of criminal law, that of punishment.[42] Indeed, statutory law now requires judges to have regard to the punishment of offenders as being one of the main purposes of sentencing.[43] If we apply a weaker form of retributivism here, as explicated by Duff, Lawson's guilt is a positive reason for punishing him for his crime, but is not in itself a sufficient reason for punishment.[44] In addition, punishing Lawson would need to bring about some consequential good. Perhaps the reason for the apparent lack of punishment in cases such as that involving Lawson is in part because the judge believes that punishment can only have a negative consequence. He may be of the opinion that a relative or spouse who commits a mercy killing has already gone through enough, having endured the suffering and death—the latter at their own hands—of their loved one.[45] Could the same policy considerations apply in a case of a physician who carries out an instance of euthanasia? In the light of the Harold Shipman case, there may well be a fear that such a physician could pose a threat to the public because of the relationship of power he holds over other vulnerable patients. Moreover, as a strong emotional bond between the physician and his patient is less likely to exist, judges might be less sympathetic to the argument that the physician has 'suffered enough'.

Whilst the potential availability of the defence of diminished responsibility means that a case of a mercy killing carried out by a relative or spouse may be treated differently than a case of euthanasia in the medical context, it is important to note that the sentences passed following conviction may not differ substantially. Justice Nelson's decision was to give Lawson a two-year suspended sentence, a sentence that to some degree reflects that given to Dr Cox, a doctor who administered a lethal dosage of medication to an elderly patient suffering from the incredibly painful condition of rheumatoid arthritis. Dr Cox received a one-year suspended sentence, later replaced by twelve months probation by the Court of Appeal.[46] However, this parity in the punishments imposed does not

---

[42] Similarly, in a recent case, a husband entered into a suicide pact with his wife who was terminally ill with cancer. The defendant pleaded guilty to manslaughter under s 4 of the Homicide Act 1957. The judge stated that he was not going to send him to prison because of the exceptional circumstances of the case and gave him a nine months suspended sentence. See Anon, 'Suicide pact husband spared jail, BBC News Online (14 January 2005) at <http://news.bbc.co.uk/1/hi/england/4174155.stm>.

[43] Under s 142 of the Criminal Justice Act 2003. Antony Duff has written extensively upon the philosophy of punishment and the criminal law. See, for example, R. A. Duff, *Punishment, Communication and Community* (Oxford: Oxford University Press, 2000); 'Crime, Prohibition and Punishment', *Journal of Applied Philosophy*, 19/2 (2002), 97–108; and 'Probation, Punishment and Restorative Justice' (2003) 42 *Howard Journal of Criminal Justice* 181–97. See also H. L. A. Hart, *Punishment and Responsibility: Essays in the Philosophy of Law* (Oxford: Clarendon Press, 1968).

[44] See Duff, *Punishment, Communication and Community*, 19.

[45] Ibid, 20.

[46] *R v Cox*. At the sentencing stage then, at least, the courts appear to take into account the compassionate motivations behind an instance of euthanasia. Alan Norrie in *Crime, Reason and History* (London: Butterworths, 2001), ch 10, discusses the influence that the particular circumstances surrounding the crime can have at the sentencing stage.

alter the fact that physicians such as Dr Cox receive convictions for murder or attempted murder whilst a relative who carries out a mercy killing, such as James Lawson, escapes the label of a murderer because he is deemed to be a person who does not possess the same mental culpability for his actions.[47]

## 4. The potential applicability of the defence of necessity in cases of euthanasia in the medical context

If English law did allow necessity to be utilized in cases of euthanasia in the medical context, ours would not be the first jurisdiction to respond to such instances of ending life in this way. In the Netherlands, prior to the current statutory law governing the practise of euthanasia,[48] the courts effectively legalized voluntary euthanasia by holding that such an act could be justified by the defence of necessity under Article 40 of the Dutch Criminal Code. This was provided the physician complied with certain guidelines. The defence of necessity was available when a physician was under a 'psychological compulsion' to commit the offence of euthanasia or committed the offence of euthanasia in an emergency situation, where she faced a conflict of duties and decided to break the law in order to promote a higher good. Thus, for example, in the case of *Alkmaar*,[49] where a physician administered a series of lethal injections to an elderly patient who was seriously ill with no prospects of an improvement in her condition, it was decided that he had faced a conflict of duties—on the one hand, the duty to preserve life and on the other, the duty to alleviate suffering—due to the emergency situation in the case. Thus, the defence of necessity was available and the physician was acquitted of the offence of taking the life of another at his express and earnest request under Article 293 of the Dutch Criminal Code. It is interesting to note here that under Dutch law, the defence of necessity can be available in cases where an individual takes another person's life, an issue I will return to later.

In terms of the current form that the defence of necessity takes under English law, it was stated by Simon-Brown J in *R v Martin* that in extreme circumstances, a defence of necessity will be available as a result of there being 'duress of circumstances'. This defence will only be available if the defendant acted reasonably and proportionately in order to avoid a threat of death or serious injury, an objective test. The jury has then to decide whether the defendant was impelled

---

[47] Unless there are grounds to suggest that the physician who commits a mercy killing has committed a greater wrong than the relative or spouse who carries out the same act, the current legal position could well violate the principle of fair labelling. As Ashworth comments: 'Fairness demands that offenders be labelled and punished in proportion to their wrongdoing' (Ashworth, *Principles of Criminal Law*, 88–9).

[48] To be found in the Termination of Life on Request and Assisted Suicide (Review Procedures) Act 2001. See further Ost, *Living Phenomenon of Euthanasia*, 216–18.

[49] (1985) Nederlandse Jurisprudentie, 106, 451.

to act because, as a consequence of what he reasonably believed the situation to be, he had good cause to fear that otherwise death or serious injury would result. Finally, the jury must consider whether a sober person of reasonable firmness, sharing the characteristics of the accused would have responded to that situation by acting as the accused acted.[50] The result of the successful utilization of the defence is an acquittal. In a subsequent case, the House of Lords confirmed and upheld the existing common law position that the defence of duress is available to a defendant in respect of any offence other than murder and treason.[51]

The defences of duress of circumstances and necessity are often viewed as being part of the same defence and as really 'nothing more than different labels for essentially the same thing'.[52] However, the defence of duress of circumstances can also be seen as being one of two forms of necessity.[53] Wilson explains duress of circumstances as 'necessity as an excuse'—the defendant commits a criminal offence, but we can excuse his actions because he did so in order to escape death or serious injury to himself or someone else. In such circumstances, we do not hold the defendant culpable for the criminal act he has committed because, given the circumstances, it would be unreasonable for us to expect him not to have acted in this way. Wilson argues that 'justificatory necessity' extends beyond duress of circumstances. Here, although the defendant commits a criminal act, his actions are justified because they are carried out in defence of his own or another's interests.[54] Alternatively, Ashworth identifies the argument that the defendant's actions are seen as justified because they are effectively a 'lesser evil' than the evil which would have occurred had he not acted as he did.[55]

That the defence of necessity as justification may be available in a medical context is demonstrated by *R v Bourne*,[56] a case where a doctor carried out an abortion on a young girl who had been raped, as he believed that she would be unable to cope psychologically with being pregnant. Macnaughten J directed the jury

---

[50] [1989] 1 All ER 652, 653–4.

[51] *R v Gotts* [1992] 2 AC 412.

[52] Per Lord Woolf CJ in *R v Shayler* [2002] HRLR 3 40, 61. The Court of Appeal in *Shayler* supported the decision by the same court in *R v Abdul-Hussain* [1999] *Criminal Law Review* 570 that the defence of duress and necessity are part of the same defence. Given this judicial approach, it is perhaps unfortunate that in its recent consultation paper which focuses upon reforming the law surrounding murder, the Law Commission has chosen to look at duress, but not necessity (or indeed, any other justificatory defence). See Law Commission, *A New Homicide Act*, paras 1.3 and 4.91.

[53] See Smith, *Justification and Excuse in the Criminal Law*, 83–4. According to the judgment of Lord Simon in *Lynch v DPP* [1975] AC 653, 692, cited by Smith, the main difference between the two is that in duress of circumstances, the circumstances relate to a human threat that causes the defendant to act, whereas in necessity, it can be any circumstances that pose a threat to life.

[54] W. Wilson, *Criminal Law: Doctrine and Theory* (London: Longman, 2003) 278.

[55] See Ashworth, *Principles of Criminal Law*, 223.

[56] [1939] 1 KB 687. Other more recent cases where the issue of medical necessity is discussed include *F v West Berkshire Area Health Authority* [1990] 2 AC 1 (Lord Goff's judgment in particular) and *Bournewood Community and Mental Health Trust* [1999] 1 AC 458, 490. Indeed, Wilson considers that currently, the law *primarily* recognizes the availability of necessity as justification in the medical treatment context. See Wilson, *Criminal Law*, 284.

that Dr Bourne had only *unlawfully* procured a miscarriage under section 58 of the Offences Against the Person Act 1861 if, in their judgment, he had not acted for the purpose of preserving the girl's life, in good faith and in the exercise of his clinical judgement, The jury duly acquitted the defendant. In the light of Lord Goff's judgment in *F v West Berkshire Area Health Authority*,[57] a further basis for invoking necessity in the context of medical treatment could be to argue that the physician's actions are justified because he acted in order to resolve a conflict of duties owed to the same patient through the utilization of the best interests test.

Significantly, case law dating back to *R v Dudley and Stephens*[58] reveals that the courts have not allowed the defence of necessity in a situation where the defendant takes the life of another. The decision in this case provided the authority that, even in the desperate situation of a shipwreck, where the defendants had no means of knowing when (and if) they would be rescued and thus killed, and ate the already ill cabin-boy in order to ensure their survival, it was not possible for the defendants' actions to be justified on the basis of necessity. According to Lord Coleridge CJ, to allow the killing to be justified on the basis of necessity would absolutely divorce the law from morality.[59] More recently, the House of Lords in *R v Howe*[60] affirmed the ratio decidendi of *Dudley and Stephens*, Lord Hailsham commenting that a law would be neither 'just nor humane which withdraws the protection of the criminal law from the innocent victim and casts the cloak of its protection upon the coward and the poltroon in the name of a concession to human frailty'.[61] It should be noted however, that this was a case involving the defence of duress specifically. Moreover, the question of whether the defence of necessity may be available to a charge of murder must now be reassessed in the light of the Court of Appeal decision in the much publicized conjoined twins case, *Re A*.[62]

Although the judges in *Re A* emphasized that the case was unique and should not set a precedent,[63] the judgment of Lord Justice Brooke in particular does indicate that the defence of necessity may be available in a case where a defendant takes another's life. Crucially, Lord Justice Brooke considered that important policy considerations lying behind the decision in *Dudley and Stephens* did not exist in the case before him and that it was only in cases where these policy considerations did exist that the defence of necessity would not be available. The first policy consideration was that a person should not be the judge in their own

---

[57] Ibid, at 77–8. I believe that it would be difficult to take such an approach to necessity in the context of euthanasia. See below, n 65.

[58] (1884) 14 QBD 273.

[59] Ibid, at 287.

[60] [1987] AC 417.

[61] Ibid, at 432.

[62] *Re A (Children) (Conjoined Twins: Medical Treatment) (No 1)* [2001] Fam 147. For an interesting examination of the judicial application of the defence of necessity in *Re A*, see J. Rogers, 'Necessity, Private Defence and the Killing of Mary', *Criminal Law Review*, [2001], 515–26.

[63] An issue that will be discussed further later in this section.

cause of the value of their life. This consideration did not apply in *Re A*, given that the doctors and the courts were making the decision to save the stronger twin's life by separating the weaker twin (who was destined for death) from her, rather than this being a scenario where the actual defendant makes a choice to sacrifice another's life to save her own. Furthermore, it was not a case of the doctors and the courts valuing Jodie's life over Mary's, but giving the strongest twin the best chance of survival. Circumstances, or nature, had already selected Mary for death. The second policy consideration was that allowing the defence of necessity in a case where an innocent life was taken would cause there to be an absolute divorce of law from morality. In the case before him, Lord Justice Brooke felt that the unique circumstances of Mary being fated for death and, in the future, being the cause of her sister Jodie's death, meant that this policy consideration did not apply either. Much reference was made throughout the judgment to the separation of the twins leading to Mary's death being the 'lesser of two evils', the worst evil being of course, the death of both the twins. It is thus somewhat inevitable that Lord Justice Brooke's consideration of necessity was based upon utilitarian concerns.[64]

An arguable case for rejecting the applicability of both of these policy considerations can equally be made in terms of euthanasia. With regards to the first policy concern, the physician is not valuing his life above the patient's. Indeed, he is not acting to serve his own interests at all, but rather, those of his patient. In terms of the second policy concern, the physician is faced with unique circumstances where morally, he may feel compelled to end his patient's life in order to achieve a 'greater good', the relief of unbearable pain and suffering when all other means of achieving such relief have failed. In such circumstances, can inducing the patient's death not be considered the lesser of two evils?[65] Moreover, it is certainly arguable that the three main elements of the defence of necessity, as outlined by Brooke LJ in *Re A*[66] are present in instances of euthanasia. First, the act is needed to avoid inevitable and irreparable evil. The obvious 'evil' in the

---

[64] A point also noted by S. Gardner, 'Direct Action and the Defence of Necessity', *Criminal Law Review* [2005], 371–80, 375. For a discerning theoretical consideration of whether necessity is a theory of excuse, justification, or a theory based upon utilitarian concerns, see A. Brudner, 'A Theory of Necessity', *Oxford Journal of Legal Studies*, 7 (1987), 339–68.

[65] I believe that it would be more difficult to claim necessity on the basis that the physician would be resolving a conflict of duties owed to the same patient (the duty to relieve suffering versus the duty to not take life) by the utilization of the best interests test. This is because the best interests test is generally applied only in the case of an incompetent patient, as its application in the case of a competent patient would be inconsistent with the current legal approach that attaches great significance to the principle of patient autonomy (see, for example, Lord Mustill in *Airedale Trust v Bland*, at 889). Further, the judiciary has refused to go so far as to say that death can ever be in a patient's best interests. Consider, for example, Lord Goff's choice of wording in *Airedale Trust v Bland* to the effect that it was no longer in Anthony Bland's best interests to continue to receive treatment (as opposed to it actually being in his best interests to die), at 868.

[66] In stating these three elements (*Re A*, at 225), Brooke LJ was alluding to Sir James Stephen's interpretation of the defence, as found in his *Digest of the Criminal Law* (4th edn, London: MacMillan, 1887), 24–5. Walker LJ also considered that necessity might be applicable to the

circumstances surrounding the instance of euthanasia is the patient's severe pain and suffering, and if the patient's condition is incurable or terminal, then this evil is indeed irreparable. Secondly, no more should be done than is reasonably necessary for the purpose to be achieved. Provided that the patient's pain and suffering cannot be sufficiently alleviated by any available treatment, then this element can also be established, as death provides the only remaining means to relieve the patient's distress. Finally, the evil inflicted must not be disproportionate to the evil avoided. Undoubtedly, this may seem to be the most difficult element to prove in a case of euthanasia.

The question of whether causing death could ever be a proportionate response to allay the evil of a person's suffering has been addressed by the Canadian Supreme Court in a recent case of mercy killing, *R v Latimer*.[67] This case involved an appeal by a father against his conviction for the second-degree murder of his 12-year-old daughter. His daughter suffered from a severe form of cerebral palsy, was quadriplegic, and frequently experienced a great amount of pain and suffering. Having been informed that doctors wished to perform surgery upon her, Latimer decided to take her life. He placed her in his pick-up truck and inserted a hose from the truck's exhaust pipe into the cab. She died as a result of carbon monoxide poisoning. At Latimer's trial for murder, the judge held that the defence of necessity was unavailable and this was the ground for appeal to the Supreme Court. The leading Canadian authority upon the applicability of the defence of necessity is *R v Perka*,[68] in which three elements to the defence of necessity were outlined. First, there is a requirement of imminent peril or danger. In addition, the accused must have had no reasonable legal alternative to the course of action he or she undertook. Finally, there must be proportionality between the harm inflicted and the harm avoided. Having considered each of these elements, the Supreme Court in *Latimer* held that the defence of necessity was not applicable. Specifically, with regards to the question of proportionality, it was held that: 'Killing a person—in order to relieve the suffering produced by a medically manageable physical or mental condition—is not a proportionate response to the harm represented by the non-life-threatening suffering resulting from that condition.'[69]

As noted by the Supreme Court, however, Latimer's daughter's suffering, although severe, was not life-threatening and her condition was medically manageable. This begs the question of whether the Supreme Court's decision that the harm inflicted was not proportionate to the harm avoided would have been the same if the suffering had been life-threatening. And whilst this decision may be persuasive authority, it is still open to English courts to consider whether in certain circumstances, death can be perceived to be a proportionate or lesser evil

circumstances of *Re A*, at 255. Ward LJ favoured the application of a defence he termed 'quasi-self defence', at 205.

[67]  [2001] 1 SCR 3.
[68]  [1984] 2 SCR 232.
[69]  *R v Latimer*, at para 41.

than a life lacking in quality because of severe pain and suffering.[70] The fact that the application of necessity in *Re A* led to Lord Justice Brooke's decision that causing Mary's death was a lesser evil than losing both twins is surely indicative of the fact that the courts are willing to consider the possibility that death can be proportionate to other evils.[71]

There is, however, one important aspect of the facts in *Re A* that is not reflected in an instance of euthanasia and that is that the surgical operation was necessary to *preserve* a life, namely that of Jodie's. Wicks has argued that as applied in *Re A*, the defence of necessity can be seen to require an action to preserve life and this provides an explanation for the general legal reluctance to allow necessity as a defence to murder. For her, such an interpretation of the defence avoids the 'undesirable outcome' that ending a person's life for a compassionate motivation could ever be justified.[72] Yet, whilst in his judgment in *Re A*, Brooke emphasized the great value we attach to life, he also chose to cite a 'powerful' section from Professor Glanville Williams's *Textbook on Criminal Law* in which Williams states that 'it is very unlikely that anyone would be held to be justified in killing for any purpose except the saving of other life ... *or perhaps the saving of great pain or distress*'.[73] The argument could thus be made that an instance of euthanasia fits within the second category, given that the primary purpose behind the physician's actions is to alleviate the patient's severe pain and suffering. Even if this

[70] There is a persuasive philosophical argument that death *can* be perceived not to be an evil, an argument that can be traced back as far as Socrates: 'Socrates long ago ... maintained that we can easily imagine forms of physical or spiritual degeneration that would make life not worth living. If he is right, death is preferable to some possible lives. Death would be a misfortune only when it deprived one of a life that is worth living, and this is, arguably, not always the case'in I. Soll, 'On the Purported Insignificance of Death; Whistling Before the Dark?' in J. Malpas and R. Soloman (eds.), *Death and Philosophy* (London: Routledge, 1998) 22–38, at 31. The issue of proportionality generally in the context of the defences such as necessity, self-defence, and duress is discussed in C. Clarkson, 'Necessary Action: A New Defence', *Criminal Law Review*, [2004], 81–95, at 88–90.

[71] Significantly, commentators have discussed two real examples of situations where death could be deemed a lesser evil and a killing thus justified under the defence of necessity. In *Justification and Excuse in the Criminal* Law, at 73–4, Sir John Smith discusses evidence given at an inquest into the Zeebrugge disaster that an army corporal was helping people to escape up a rope ladder. This ladder offered the only route to safety, but a man was already on the ladder, unable to move because he was frozen with fear or cold. After many attempts to persuade him off the ladder, the corporal ordered another passenger to push him off and he was not seen again. Smith states the coroner's view that a reasonable act carried out to save the lives of others was not necessarily murder. A further example is that of shooting down a hijacked plane and thereby killing all the passengers and crew to prevent an even greater disaster in the light of the September 11 terrorist attack. See D. Ormerod, *Smith and Hogan Criminal Law\** (11th edn, Oxford: Oxford University Press, 2005), 322. See also M. Bohlander, 'In Extremis—Hijacked Airplanes, "Collateral Damage" and the Limits of Criminal Law', *Criminal Law Review* [2006], 579–92.

[72] E. Wicks, 'The Greater Good? Issues of Proportionality and Democracy in the Doctrine of Necessity as Applied in Re A', *Common Law World Review*, 32/1 (2003), 15–34, at 22. Consider also the emphasis placed upon the doctor's belief that an abortion was necessary to preserve the mother's life in *Bourne*, although Macnaughten directed the jury to adopt a reasonable interpretation of 'preserving the mother's life', at 692 and 694.

[73] *Re A*, at 227 (emphasis added). Brooke quoted from G. Williams, *Textbook of Criminal Law* (2nd edn, London: Stevens & Sons, 1983) 604.

argument is not accepted, inroads into the value attached to the sanctity of life principle by the law have been made in a number of cases over recent years.[74]

Perhaps the greatest challenge to arguments that the ratio of *Re A* could apply in cases of euthanasia can be found in Ward LJ's limitation of the potential authority of the judgment in cases beyond the specific situation where it is: 'impossible to preserve the life of X, without bringing about the death of Y, that Y by his or her very continued existence will inevitably bring about the death of X within a short period of time, and that X is capable of living an independent life but Y is incapable under any circumstances... of viable independent existence.'[75]

Despite this attempt to reduce the scope for the judgment to be used as authority, McEwan has argued that by reinterpreting the common law upon the availability of the defence of necessity to a charge of murder, the Court of Appeal in *Re A* has inevitably paved the way for the successful utilization of necessity in cases of euthanasia.[76] And, as I have argued, the *broader* ratio decidendi of the judgment certainly does not seem to preclude the finding that the circumstances of euthanasia may meet the requirements of necessity. Moreover, Brooke LJ's statement in *Re A* that the defence of necessity is not limited to emergency situations only strengthens the argument that a physician who carries out an instance of euthanasia should be able to rely on the defence.[77]

As Bohlander has recently asserted, English law already allows the taking of life in circumstances of duress and necessity.[78] The defence of necessity, as currently understood, would require a certain amount of restructuring in order to encapsulate the situation where a physician commits euthanasia. Thus, a physician could rely upon the defence of necessity if he acts both reasonably and proportionately and ends the patient's life because he believes that it is immediately necessary to prevent the continuation of severe pain and suffering of the patient,

---

[74] See, for example, *Airedale NHS Trust v Bland*, and *Ms B v An NHS Hospital Trust*. It was stated by Munby J in the High Court in the case of *R (Burke) v GMC*, that despite the legal importance attached to the sanctity of life, it could take second place to human dignity, at paras 51 and 79. Given the steady attrition of the sanctity of life value, and the increasing legal importance attached to individual autonomy in medical cases particularly, it may also be possible to argue that the law could adopt an approach to necessity involving rights based justification in the context of euthanasia. Gardner argues that the principle behind such an approach would justify an otherwise unlawful action 'where observing the original rule would infringe some human value more important than the interest protected by the rule'. See S. Gardner, 'Necessity's Newest Inventions', *Oxford Journal of Legal Studies*, 11 (1991), 125–35, 130. Abiding by the rule that it is always unlawful to take another's life could be deemed to seriously infringe the value of autonomy if a competent patient (suffering from a condition that causes his life to have no real quality), wishes to die.

[75] *Re A*, at 205.

[76] J. McEwan, 'Murder by Design: The "Feel-Good Factor" and the Criminal Law', *Medical Law Review*, 9 (2001), 246–258.

[77] Brooke LJ commented that: 'There are sound reasons for holding that the existence of an emergency in the normal sense of the word is not an essential prerequisite for the application of the doctrine of necessity. The principle is one of necessity, not emergency.' (*Re A*, at 239.)

[78] M. Bohlander, 'Of Shipwrecked Sailors, Unborn Children, Conjoined Twins and Hijacked Airplanes—Taking Human Life and the Defence of Necessity', *Journal of Criminal Law*, 70/2 (2006), 147–61.

this belief being reasonable and held in good faith. An issue that could particularly be relevant to ascertaining whether the physician acts reasonably and proportionately is the level of pain the patient is experiencing. I have suggested above that the suffering be 'severe', although if a higher level is required, it may be that the suffering should be able to be described as 'unbearable'.[79] The nature of the patient's request for death could also be a significant issue—has this request been made repeatedly over a period of time and is the patient fully competent when making this request?

There is evidence to suggest that the common law does take into account the unique characteristics of euthanasia, at least to some degree. The Lord Chief Justice has issued guidelines to judges stating that in cases of 'mercy killings', a person is only required to spend eight years in prison.[80] However, this does not adequately take into account the true reality of the situation that causes the physician to take his patient's life. The utilization of the defence of necessity in instances of euthanasia in the medical context will remove the current criminal status of the ending of life motivated by compassion and the desire to offer a relief from unbearable suffering in appropriate cases.

## 5. Conclusion

It is now almost fifty years since Glanville Williams proffered that the criminal law might best deal with euthanasia through the utilization of the defence of necessity.[81] With the subsequent passage of time, this suggestion seems to have fallen along the wayside. Whilst the introduction of the doctrine of double effect has offered some protection to physicians who administer lethal treatment with the *stated* primary intent of relieving pain, I have argued that the legal application of this doctrine fails to provide an effective means of revealing the physician's true intent. Furthermore, the physician who openly acknowledges a primary intent to cause death or who administers drugs with no pain alleviating effect is left facing a conviction for murder. I have sought to demonstrate that the argument

---

[79] Dutch law requires that the patient's suffering be 'unbearable' under the criteria that the physician must meet in order to carry out a lawful instance of euthanasia. See Ch 2, s 2 of the Termination of Life on Request and Assisted Suicide (Review Procedures) Act 2001.

[80] Practice Statement (Crime: Life Sentences) [2002] 1 WLR 1789 (Sup Ct). For an interesting analysis of these guidelines in the light of the principles of desert-based sentencing, see C. Valier, 'Minimum Terms of Imprisonment in Murder, Just Deserts and the Sentencing Guidelines', *Criminal Law Review* [2003], 326–35. Under the Criminal Justice Act 2003, Sch 21, Part 11, 'a belief by the offender that the murder was an act of mercy' is listed as a mitigating factor that may be considered when the court is deciding on an appropriate sentence.

[81] G. Williams, *The Sanctity of Life in the Criminal Law* (London: Faber, 1958) 286–8. In referring to a situation where the patient's pain can no longer be alleviated by anything other than a lethal dosage of drugs, he states that: 'The excuse rests upon the doctrine of necessity, there being at this juncture no way of relieving pain without ending life.' (at 288). See also Otlowski, *Euthanasia*, 173–4.

that euthanasia be viewed as a situation of necessity remains a compelling one that demands serious consideration. Just as the Court of Appeal recognized the uniqueness of the circumstances that led to the case of *Re A*, the law should also recognize the particular characteristics of euthanasia. This could be achieved by redefining the defence of necessity in order to justify the physician's actions as has been argued here, by creating a special defence of mercy killing,[82] or by the more radical legalization of euthanasia.[83]

In arguing for the utilization of the defence of necessity in cases of euthanasia in the medical context, I am in part seeking to address the current anomaly in the law that allows relatives or spouses who commit mercy killings a defence that is less likely to be available to physicians who carry out euthanasia. Yet, given that I have called for recognition of circumstances of necessity where euthanasia occurs in a medical situation, I am aware that the legal approach I am advocating here would inevitably create its own anomaly; a defendant physician could be completely acquitted whilst a defendant relative or spouse who successfully relies upon the defence of diminished responsibility would only find his murder charge reduced to one of manslaughter. It is my view, however, that the law should continue to specifically recognize the impact of emotional suffering experienced by relatives or spouses who carry out mercy killings and in this context, the defence of diminished responsibility does seem to be the most appropriate defence.[84] The decision to take a loved one's life is likely to be less reasoned and guided more by emotion than the decision to take life in a case of euthanasia in the medical context, where the physician will, in all probability, act more objectively and will be better able to ascertain whether the situation is truly one of necessity. Moreover, the anomaly can be addressed to some degree if the courts continue to both allow a flexible interpretation and application of the defence of diminished responsibility and adopt a compassionate approach to sentencing in mercy killing cases where the defendant is a relative or spouse.

---

[82] The introduction of such a defence has been favoured by the Criminal Law Revision Committee as a more appropriate means of dealing with mercy killings. See the Committee's 14th Report, *Offences Against the Person* (HMSO, 1980), para 115. James Rachels has also advocated such a defence, see *The End of Life: The Morality of Euthanasia*, (Oxford: Oxford University Press, 1986) 185.

[83] As would have occurred had Lord Joffe's *Assisted Dying for the Terminally Ill* Bill, HL Bill 36 (2005–6), become law.

[84] Otlowski discusses the alternative argument that euthanasia in the medical context should be treated differently at law than mercy killings carried out by relatives or spouses because there are greater concerns in relation to the existence of mixed motives in the case of the latter. She notes the possibility that such a killing is 'partly motivated by compassion for the patient, but also, in part, driven by a desire to put an end to a difficult family situation or to gain some material benefit from the patient's death'. Otlowski, *Euthanasia*, 463.

# 7

# Criminal Law is the Problem, Not the Solution

*John Griffiths*

## 1. Introduction

Public debate about the possibility of legalizing some forms of medical behaviour that intentionally ends the life of the patient often exhibits passionate disagreement on a whole range of issues. But there is one matter on which everyone seems to be agreed: the behaviour concerned is so fraught with danger that whether it is prohibited, or allowed under strict conditions, it certainly has to be controlled in an effective way. And the only sort of control that is powerful enough is supposed to be the criminal law. Such behaviour, one often hears pronounced as if it were a self-evident fact, is too dangerous to be left to any lesser sort of control. It is the assumption latent in this sort of truism that I shall challenge. I hope to convince the reader that as far as effective control is concerned, criminal law is not the solution but the problem. If we really want effective control, we will have to look for some other way of accomplishing it.

I will not address questions as to why control of this sort of behaviour is necessary, nor what the specific content of the rules governing it should be. I want to focus instead on the problem of control itself. In order to illustrate and support my argument, I shall rely primarily on data from the Netherlands, since this is the only reasonably systematic and reliable information we have. On the matters that will be important to my argument, I am not aware of any significant legal or factual differences between the Netherlands and other Western countries. I therefore take my argument to be a general one, not bound to a particular place or legal system.

## 2. The structural limitations of the criminal control of medical behaviour that potentially shortens life (MBPSL)

Criminal control of behaviour that leads to death is generally reactive: it relies on information coming into the system from outside to set further investigation in motion. Police and prosecutors have their attention called to suspicious deaths, mysterious disappearances, and the like. In general, reactive mobilization of the criminal law seems to be regarded as adequate. The alternative to waiting for reports of suspicious deaths would be to have an independent coroner's investigation of every death. Proposals to that effect founder at once because of the immensity of the control apparatus that would be required to look for what is generally assumed to be a needle in a haystack. There are also other reasons that argue against the whole idea, such as the interference in family privacy and disruption of the mourning process that would be entailed.

As far as I know, no legal system has seriously contemplated universal proactive control. Instead, it is left mostly to doctors to make an initial judgment whether further investigation is warranted. In the Netherlands the doctor attending a patient who dies reports the death as 'natural' or 'not natural'—that is, roughly speaking, one which does or does not call for further investigation. A report that the death was a 'natural' one permits burial or cremation without further ado, whereas a report that it was 'not natural' leads to further investigation by a coroner and by the prosecutorial authorities.[1]

Roughly a third of all deaths are sudden and unexpected; nothing a doctor has done or not done is arguably responsible.[2] In these cases, entrusting the initial decision whether further investigation is required to doctors, seems a reasonable compromise between accuracy on the one side, and speed and efficiency on the other. But roughly two-thirds of all deaths are of patients who are currently being treated by a doctor,[3] and here there can always be some question whether the doctor himself was responsible for the death. Leaving initial control of these cases in the hands of doctors entails some obvious risks. The doctor might be a murderer—like Dr Shipman—or some negligence on his part might have caused the death. In such a case, reporting the death as a 'natural' one is an obvious and usually quite effective way for a doctor to avoid calling attention to what he has done. Medical murderers are presumably rare and seem often to betray themselves sooner or later; even a small amount of official attention to what is going on could undoubtedly greatly increase the risk for doctors like Shipman. Perhaps this is enough as far as murder is concerned. As far as medical mistakes are concerned the magnitude of the problem is considerable—for the Netherlands, for example, the frequency of 'iatrogenic death' is estimated at about 4,000 cases per year.[4] But no one seems to think criminal law affords a promising way of dealing with the problem. I leave these matters for what they are.

---

[1] For a detailed description of the reporting requirement in Dutch law up to 2002, see J. Griffiths, A. Bood, and H. Weyers, *Euthanasia and Law in the Netherlands* (Amsterdam: Amsterdam University Press, 1998), 114–118. For the changes, as far as cases of euthanasia are concerned, under the euthanasia law of 2002, see J. Griffiths, H. Weyers, and M. Adams, *Euthanasia and Law in Europe* (forthcoming in 2007, Oxford: Hart Publishing), ch 4.

[2] See Griffiths, Bood, and Weyers, *Euthanasia and Law in the Netherlands*, 210.

[3] Ibid, 210, n 37.

[4] See T. Zelders, 'Patient risks: an underdeveloped area', *Journal of Clinical Monitoring*, 12 (1996), 237–41; the author supposes such a figure to be characteristic of modern health care systems.

**Table 1:** Estimates of frequencies of death due to MBPSL, 2001/2002 (percentages of all deaths).

| | |
|---|---|
| Euthanasia: | |
| Termination of life on request | 2.6% |
| Assistance with suicide | 0.2% |
| Termination of life without request | 0.7% |
| Pain relief | 20.1% |
| Abstinence (withholding/withdrawing treatment) | 20.2% |
| Total MBPSL | 43.8% |
| Total deaths in the Netherlands | 140,377 |

The question on which I want to focus is whether the initial classification of a death by the attending physician as 'natural' or 'not natural' is a sufficient way of mobilizing control by the criminal law authorities in a different sort of case, one in which the doctor *expects his treatment of the patient to lead to the latter's earlier death*: Medical Behaviour that Potentially Shortens Life (MBPSL). The numbers of deaths due to various sorts of MBPSL are huge. I give the most recent Dutch data in Table 1.[5] Except for euthanasia and assisted suicide—which from here on I will refer to jointly as 'euthanasia'—the numbers elsewhere are roughly the same.[6]

As we have seen, examination of a case of MBPSL by the criminal law authorities to make sure the death is not one that requires further attention depends on the doctor who performed it reporting it as a non-natural death. Proactive control in every case of MBPSL would founder on the numbers alone, but on top of that there is the lack of expertise of the police and prosecutorial authorities.[7]

---

[5] Source: G. van der Wal, A. van der Heide, B. D. Ontwuteaka-Philipsen, and P. J. van der Maas, *Medische Besluitvorming aan het Einde van het Leven: De Praktijk en de Toetsingsprocedure Euthanasie*. [*Medical Decision-making at the End of Life: Euthanasia Practice and the Review Procedure*] (Utrecht: Uitgeverij De Tijdstroom, 2003) 67, Table 7.1.

[6] See Griffiths, Bood, and Weyers, *Euthanasia and Law in the Netherlands*, 27, n 23; A. van der Heide, L. Deliens, K. Faisst, T. Nilstun, M. Norup, E. Paci, G. van der Wal, and P. J. van der Maas, 'End-of-life decision-making in six European countries: descriptive study.' *The Lancet*, 361 (2003) 345–50.

[7] Before the establishment of the Regional Review Committees (see below), the Dutch prosecutorial authorities had their hands full with the relatively small number of euthanasia cases that were reported. Between 1991 and 1995, 6,324 cases were reported, of which only 120 received full consideration; indictments were ultimately brought against 13 doctors (see Griffiths, Bood, and Weyers, *Euthanasia and Law in the Netherlands*, 241–3); between 1996 and 2002, over 14,000 cases were reported, 119 received full consideration, and indictments were brought in two cases (Van der Wal, et al, *Medische Besluitvorming aan het Einde van het Leven*, 154). Really effective criminal enforcement would involve, at a minimum, annual examination of many more cases: in 2001, there were 2,054 reported cases (ibid, 140), an equivalent number of non-reported cases, plus a large number of cases currently classified as pain relief or abstention. Many of the latter will be more problematic than the rather routine cases of euthanasia which are currently being reported. Evaluating them will require considerable medical expertise to penetrate self-serving accounts of what took place.

In practice, enforcement of criminal prohibitions of, or restrictions on particular sorts of MBPSL—for example, euthanasia—is, in all countries, almost entirely dependent on self-reporting by doctors. A doctor who wants to conceal what he has done has to be very careless to give the authorities reason to doubt his version of what happened. Other sources of information—complaints by other doctors or nurses, or by family members of a deceased person—do exist, but such complaints are very sporadic for a number of reasons, of which lack of relevant information, and the strong professional norms against informing on a colleague, are probably the most important. In practice, complaints against doctors for any sort of MBPSL are rare events.

One consequence of such a situation is that prosecutions of doctors for illegal MBPSL, such as euthanasia, are few and far between. The Netherlands is deviant in this respect: there have been quite a few such prosecutions, most of them based neither on proactive control nor on complaints by others, but on self-reporting by the doctor himself.[8] We seem to be faced here with a paradox: the only system of control that works at all depends on self-reporting by the subjects of control. A priori, I do not suppose that many people would put much faith in such a system.

### 3. The Dutch experience with reliance on self-reporting

From the perspective just sketched, the Dutch experience with criminal control of euthanasia seems remarkable. Figure 1 shows the development of the rate of self-reporting of euthanasia, from the early 1990s, when a formal reporting procedure was established, to the present.[9] Reading this graph requires some care, since the reporting rate shown is not the ratio of reported cases to the total number of cases of euthanasia; making such a graph would be impossible, since we only know the amount of euthanasia at three discrete points when national research took place: 1990, 1995, and 2001. At those points, the rate of accurate reporting was 18 per cent, 41 per cent, and 54 per cent respectively.[10] The graph uses, instead, the *total of all deaths*, which we know for every year, as a proxy. If we assume that the ratio of euthanasia to total death is fairly stable, we can therefore assume that Figure 1 roughly parallels the reporting rate on a yearly basis. Doing so obviously has its limitations,[11] but it does permit some interesting observations to be made.

---

[8] This is true, for example, of most leading cases: *Schoonheim*, *Chabot* and *Kadijk* (translated in Griffiths, Bood, Weyers, *Euthanasia and Law in the Netherlands*, 322 ff), and *Brongersma* (Supreme Court, *Nederlands Jurisprudentie* 2003/167).The situation is similar where euthanasia is illegal. In the United States, for example, the prosecution of Quill took place after he 'reported' what he had done in the famous article in the *New England Journal of Medicine* (T. Quill, 'Death and dignity. A case of individualized decision making,' NEJM 324 (1991), 691–5). Kevorkian, too, publicly and repeatedly provoked the prosecutorial authorities.
[9] I am grateful to my colleague Albert Klijn for the conception and execution of this graph.
[10] See Van der Wal, et al, *Medische Besluitvorming aan het Einde van het Leven*, 140.
[11] For example, interpretation of the stagnation beginning in about 1998 is difficult. The most likely interpretation seems to lie in the possibility that the assumption of a constant ratio of

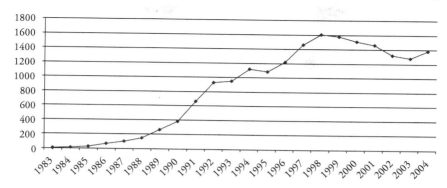

**Figure 1:** Reporting Frequency Euthanasia, 1983–2004 *(per 100,000 deaths)*

Regarded as a summary of the results of an experiment in legal control, such a graph is little short of astonishing. A new policy concerning behaviour that the government cannot observe directly, and that requires the people concerned to run the risk of external criticism or even legal sanctions, started with an effectiveness of about zero, as one would expect. But within little more than a decade, this policy was producing the desired effects in about half of all cases. We must not lose sight of the enormous success of the reporting requirement— nor of the fact that the reporting rate is zero everywhere else in the world except Oregon and Belgium—when we focus attention on the unpleasant fact that legal control can hardly be considered adequate, given that only half of the cases to which it is supposed to be applied ever come to the attention of the legal authorities.

The situation is actually worse than this, since it is known that the problematic behaviour which we would like the authorities to look at more carefully— for example, failure properly to consult a second doctor—is far more common among unreported cases than among reported ones.[12] In other words, we have a control system that, from the point of view of influencing behaviour by legal rules, is an impressive success, one that puts the Netherlands in a class by itself as far as criminal control of euthanasia is concerned, but which nevertheless deals with only half of all cases, and then in particular with legally unproblematic ones. And if we look beyond 'euthanasia' to the other sorts of MBPSL, the situation is worse still, since among the vast number of cases of withholding or withdrawing treatment (henceforth, 'abstention'), and of pain relief, all of which get reported

euthanasia to total deaths broke down at about this time, that the frequency of euthanasia levelled off, and then began to decline. If so, the upward trend up to about 1995 may well have continued at more or less the same rate until 2001, and perhaps beyond.

[12] See Griffiths, Bood, and Weyers, *Euthanasia and Law in the Netherlands*, 238.

as 'natural deaths', there is a completely unknown number that require attention. For example, as the head of the Dutch Prosecution Service recently observed, 'terminal sedation' is too similar to euthanasia to be left outside the arrangements for control.[13] The same argument applies to many cases of death due to pain relief or abstention, especially when the patient is no longer competent. I will devote no further attention to these questions here, because the case of euthanasia permits me to make my argument, and affords a far richer body of data. What we can say about euthanasia applies a fortiori to the rest of MBPSL.

## 4. Two reasons for not reporting

Why does the doctor concerned still not report so many cases of euthanasia? There are basically two sorts of answer to this question. The first has completely dominated the public and political discussion of the reporting rate. What it comes down to is that non-reporting doctors are simply lying: knowing that they performed euthanasia, which for purposes of control is considered to give rise to a 'non-natural death', they prefer nevertheless to report the death as a 'natural' one. The other possible explanation for non-reporting has received, until recently, very little attention. It is that the doctor concerned does not consider what he did to be 'euthanasia'. Let us look briefly at these two explanations.

Why might a doctor lie about what he has done? Doctors are keenly aware of the costs to themselves, and to the families of the deceased, of accurate reporting. These have to do with three matters: first, breach of the relationship of trust with the patient and his family; secondly, the bureaucratic hassle and unpleasantness of the reporting procedure itself (having to fill out forms; having the coroner visit the scene shortly after death; disrupting the privacy of the home at a particularly delicate time; and so on); and, thirdly, the risk that reporting will attract prosecutorial attention (confrontation with police and prosecutors; a fairly long period of uncertainty; the risk of actual investigation or prosecution, with the attendant costs in time, money, and emotional strain). Since the creation of the Regional Review Committees in 1998—specifically intended to increase the reporting rate by creating a 'buffer' between doctors and the criminal law authorities— the perceived risk of a criminal investigation may have declined somewhat, but in its place has come the rather more expert and critical inquiry by a Review Committee. One should also not lose sight, in this connection, of the fact that, since cases in which the doctor may not perfectly have followed the applicable rules are heavily concentrated in the group of non-reported cases, the doctors involved may well have at least some minor unpleasantness to fear should they report.

---

[13]  J. de Wijkerslooth, 'Twee lacunes in de euthanasieregeling', *Opportuun*, 9/10 (2003).

If we return for a moment to Figure 1, which shows the development of the reporting frequency over twenty years, some peculiarities in the pattern of steadily increasing willingness to report seem to lend support to the idea that non-reporting is a matter of lying, resulting from apprehension concerning the reaction of the authorities. In 1992 to 1993, and again in 1994 to 1995, one sees a temporary pause in the increasing frequency of proper reporting. These are years in which highly publicized prosecutions took place of doctors who had accurately reported what they had done.[14] At the time, it was predicted that these prosecutions, by increasing the perceived costs of accurate reporting, would adversely affect the willingness of doctors to report, and Figure 1 appears to confirm these predictions. The same can be said of the period after 1998, which saw three new and highly controversial prosecutions,[15] and also the introduction of the Regional Review Committees. While these Committees were intended to increase doctors' sense of security in reporting, the immediate result of a major change in the existing reporting procedure to which doctors had become accustomed may well have been precisely the opposite.[16] After about 2000, Figure 1 becomes more difficult to interpret, for reasons to do with the way in which the graph is constructed.[17] And it seems from more recent data that the current level of disingenuous reporting may by now actually be very low.[18]

What about the other explanation for not reporting? I have previously argued that conceptions of 'intentionality' and 'causality' among doctors may be quite different from those used by lawyers and latent in the official definitions of 'euthanasia' and other sorts of MBPSL.[19] If this is right, doctors may well apply their own conceptions to their behaviour in a way that leads them to report deaths as 'natural' which, according to the official definitions, should be classified as 'unnatural'. Den Hartogh[20] uses a similar idea as a basis for reinterpreting the reporting rate. He observes that the 'euthanasia' measured in the Dutch

---

[14] In 1992–1993, the *Chabot* case; in 1994–1995 the *Prins* and *Kadijk* cases (discussed in Griffiths, Bood, and Weyers, *Euthanasia and Law in the Netherlands*, 80–4).

[15] The *Brongersma* and *Van Ooijen* cases (Supreme Court, *Nederlands Jurisprudentie* 2003/167 and 2005/17) and the *Vencken* case (Court of Appeal, 's-Hertogenbosch, 19 July 2005, LJN: AU0211).

[16] At least in the beginning, the careful scrutiny that the Committees gave to reported cases led to negative reactions from some doctors. See, for example, B. Crul, 'Melding en toetsing vooraf, daar had ik wat aan gehad' ['Reporting and review in advance, that would have been useful'], *Medisch Contact,* 54 (1999), 1038–9.

[17] See the discussion of Figure 1, above.

[18] See Griffiths, Weyers, and Adams, *Euthanasia and Law in Europe*, ch 5.4.3.

[19] See J. Griffiths, 'Legal knowledge and the social working of law: the case of euthanasia' in H. van Schooten (ed.), *Semiotics and Legislation: Jurisprudential, Institutional and Sociological Perspectives* (Liverpool: Deborah Charles Publications, 1999) 81–108; Griffiths, Bood, and Weyers, *Euthanasia and Law in the Netherlands*, 269–73.

[20] G. Den Hartogh, 'Mysterieuze cijfers' ['Mysterious numbers'], *Medisch Contact,* 58 (2003), 1063–6.

national studies is not based on classification of their behaviour by doctors themselves. Instead, the researchers asked doctors a number of questions about what they had done and what their intention had been. Classification of the death in one or another of the categories of MBPSL was done by the researchers on the basis of the information supplied by doctors. Den Hartogh argues that the researchers seem in this way to have classified as 'euthanasia' many cases that the doctor involved did not regard as euthanasia at all. When Den Hartogh recalculated the reporting rate based upon an estimate of what doctors themselves considered to be euthanasia, he came to the conclusion that the rate of honest—if perhaps mistaken—non-reporting is not 50 per cent but only about 10 per cent. The difference lies in a different classification of behaviour. This, unknowing falsification by doctors, is the problem of the reporting system.

Until very recently, Den Hartogh's and my arguments were a matter of hypothesis. Hypothesis well-grounded in a variety of indications in the available empirical data,[21] but nonetheless hypothesis. However, in research which has recently been published,[22] Van Tol shows that Den Hartogh and I were right in hypothesizing that doctors classify various situations of MBPSL in a way quite different from that of lawyers. He did this by confronting family doctors (who are responsible for the lion's share of all euthanasia in the Netherlands) and prosecutors with short descriptions of concrete deathbed situations and asking them to classify what the doctor had done, and to say whether the death of the patient was 'natural' or 'non-natural'. His results show that doctors and prosecutors consistently classify in remarkably different ways: a very large number of deaths that prosecutors consider to be 'non-natural,' and therefore to require reporting, are classified by doctors as 'natural' deaths. The differences confirm Den Hartogh's idea that the reporting rate for cases that doctors consider to be 'euthanasia' must be far higher than the 'official' reporting rate based on classification by the national researchers.

Van Tol's research is complex and sophisticated, and I am afraid those who cannot read Dutch will have to wait until his book is translated to be able to fully appreciate it. I will give just an illustrative taste: some global results of one of the situations he asked his respondents to classify. Case Report 1[23] is based on a

---

[21] An example of indirect support provided by the data is the fact that in 1995, 75 per cent, and in 2001, 91 per cent of the doctors interviewed in national surveys claimed that they always report (Van der Wal, et al, *Medische Besluitvorming aan het Einde van het Leven*, 143). Examined from the point of view of the traditional interpretation of the reporting rate, this claim can hardly be true. Examined from the point of view of Den Hartogh's and my hypothesis, however, the claim seems quite plausible.

[22] D. G. Van Tol, *Grensgeschillen: Een rechtssociologische onderzoek naar het classificeren van euthanasie en ander medisch handelen rond het levenseinde* [*Boundary Disputes: A Study of the Classification of Euthanasia and other Medical Behaviour*]. Dissertation, University of Groningen, 2005.

[23] Source: Van Tol, ibid, 133, Case 8.

---

### Case Report 1

---

A man of 75 with a weak heart contracts a severe case of pneumonia. From that time on he is regularly admitted to hospital because of difficulty breathing. Each time his condition improves, and he remains optimistic. On his most recent admission, he asks the doctor whether he will ever get better. The answer is negative: he is already on maximum medication. Having learned this, the patient decides to go home. His family doctor, who has known the man for years, takes over the responsibility for treatment. The man becomes increasingly invalided and can hardly get out of bed. He asks the doctor to make a house call and expresses the view that his life has become meaningless, he can't do anything anymore. He wants to die and he wants the doctor to help him. He has a written and signed request for euthanasia. The doctor is in doubt—the man could live for months more—and he asks for time to think about the request. After some days the man's situation takes a sudden turn for the worse. The doctor makes a house call and finds the man in a very bad condition: his complexion is blue, and it is almost impossible to communicate with him. His wife tells the doctor that her husband has stopped taking his medicine, that when, from time to time, he regains awareness, he asks 'when is it going to happen?' The doctor agrees to come again the next morning, at which time he gives a morphine suppository and Valium to alleviate the man's feeling of suffocation and his restlessness. In the course of the day, he comes back several times to repeat this treatment. At four in the afternoon the family tells him that the man frequently wakes up, needs to urinate, and goes back to sleep. It is then impossible to awaken him and he seems very far gone. The family members can hardly endure the situation any longer. The doctor decides to give the man a higher dose of morphine subcutaneously, partly in order to hasten his death. Early in the evening the man dies.

---

newspaper article[24] in which a doctor described a case which had occurred in his practice. In the article, he confesses that he does not think his behaviour 'deserves a beauty prize'; he reported the death as a 'natural' one.

Table 2,[25] and Figure 2 which derives from it give the results when doctors and prosecutors were asked to classify the man's death (coroners were included in the study and tended to occupy a middle position between doctors and prosecutors, but for the sake of simplicity I am not discussing them here). The differences are

[24] *NRC/Handelsblad*, 23 November 2000.

[25] Source: Van Tol, *Grensgeschillen*, 264. The number of prosecutors is very small, but amounts to half of all prosecutors in the Netherlands who deal with medical cases, including prosecutors attached to the national 'expertise centre' for such cases. The level of agreement among the prosecutors was high over the eight cases put to them. The classifications used by Van Tol are derived from the Dutch literature and intended to correspond to the way doctors and lawyers think about this sort of behaviour; only some of them (such as 'euthanasia' and 'murder') are formal 'legal' classifications (it is clear from the results of Van Tol's research that neither doctors nor lawyers always use the latter in the legally 'correct' way). Note that the slight deviations from 100 per cent and due to rounding off the percentages in the table.

**Table 2:** Classifications of Case Report 1 (percentages)

| | Family doctors (N=110) | Coroners (N=25) | Prosecutors (N=9) |
|---|---|---|---|
| Palliative care | 34 | 12 | - |
| Abstention | - | - | - |
| Help in dying | 27 | 20 | - |
| Terminal sedation | 14 | 28 | - |
| Euthanasia | 19 | 20 | 89 |
| Termination w/o request | 2 | 12 | - |
| Murder/manslaughter | 1 | - | - |
| Other | 4 | 7 | 11 |
| Total | 100 | 100 | 100 |

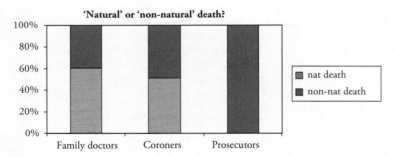

**Figure 2:** Classifications of Case Report 1

striking, and the implications for a system of control based on self-reporting are too obvious to require further belabouring.

Let me give another example of the difficulties of classification involved in a system of self-reporting, this time qualitative, and based on my own direct observation. The case derives from a meeting of a working group on medical ethics in a Dutch hospital to which I was invited. I have reason to believe that discussions very much like it could be heard in many other Dutch hospitals and probably in British ones as well. Case Report 2 involves not 'euthanasia', but 'termination of life without request', but both of these classifications require a doctor to report the death as a 'non-natural' one, so the classificatory problem, and hence the implications for the efficacy of criminal control over life-terminating behaviour by doctors, are the same.

---

### Case Report 2:  Baby with spina bifida

A baby was born with severe spina bifida. According to the professional norms applicable in the Netherlands to this sort of situation, any of the various surgical measures that might have been taken were considered 'medically futile,' so the decision was taken to abstain from any life-prolonging treatment. The parents agreed with this decision, but were insistent that the baby must not suffer as a result.

The decision to abstain necessarily entailed the death of the baby. However, it might have taken some weeks before this would occur. In the meantime, the baby would experience pain if nothing were done to prevent this. A heavy dose of a drug used for pain relief was administered and the baby died shortly thereafter. The doctors reported the baby's death as a 'natural' one.

In the discussion in the medical ethics working group, the responsible doctors consistently described what they had done as 'pain relief'. There was some discussion about changing medical opinion on the question of whether newborn babies experience much pain—apparently, in the past, it was believed that this was not the case, and nothing much was done by way of pain relief. Over time, opinion had changed, and spina bifida was taken to involve acute pain which was aggressively treated. But, said the doctors, they were having increasing doubts about the actual level of pain experienced by such babies. When someone in the working group asked what sort of pain relief would have been necessary just to deal with the baby's pain, the answer was that Tylenol[26] would probably have sufficed.

This answer was completely unexpected. It led immediately to the question: 'I thought you said you administered [whatever the drug was] to relieve the baby's pain?' To which the answer was: 'Yes, we did. But we also wanted the baby to die as quickly, and humanely as possible.' And to this the response was: 'How can you call it pain relief when you yourself say Tylenol would have been enough?' Answer: 'But it *was* pain relief: we used [drug X], which is considered very appropriate for relieving pain, but we just gave rather more than we otherwise would have done.' And so forth.

---

What were these doctors doing and why were they doing it? Were they lying when they reported the death as a 'natural' one, when they 'knew' it was not really due to pain relief? I think that would be a facile interpretation of what was going on. 'Pain relief' was not just a characterization they used to avoid having to account for what they had done, it was the characterization they themselves used in thinking and talking about their behaviour. It seemed, for them, the natural way to look at what had happened. Were they, then, confused about what had happened? There seems to me to be no evidence for this. They knew exactly what they had done, and why and how the baby had died. I think the point is that the idea of 'intent' is subject to very different interpretations, and that the classification of their behaviour by doctors, based upon what they take themselves to have

---

[26] A popular, over-the-counter, pain relieving drug, called Paracetamol in the Netherlands.

'intended' (which in their view is almost always in the first place the prevention of suffering), is quite different from the way a lawyer would classify it.

It is important to realize in this connection that if the doctors had called what they did 'termination of life without request', it would probably have been deemed justifiable under current Dutch law; it is unlikely that there would have been a prosecution, and, if there had been, the doctors would probably have been acquitted.[27] Over the past eight years, twenty-two such cases have been reported, and not one has been prosecuted.[28] Given the way the doctors classified what they did in the case I just described, however, they saw no reason to report the death as a non-natural one, so it, and presumably many others like it, escaped every form of external control.

Over the past few years, I have written repeatedly on the way that our reliance on the subjective intentions of the doctor to distinguish between cases of MBPSL that must be reported as 'non-natural deaths', and those that need not be, frustrates every possibility of effective control over the 'not natural' cases.[29] The line between euthanasia and termination of life without a request—both of them potentially very serious criminal offences—on the one hand, and pain relief on the other, is supposed to depend on the doctor's intention: to relieve pain, or to shorten life. And Keown wants us to apply the same logic to abstention.[30] Like Otlowski[31] before him, he argues that the action/omission analysis of withdrawing or withholding treatment does not work. But where Otlowski argues that we should deal with these cases not in terms of subtle differences in 'intentionality', but rather in terms of the justifiability of the doctor's behaviour, Keown wants, here too, to base everything on the doctor's subjective intention: if the 'intention' is to refrain from futile treatment, then all is well, but if it is to shorten the patient's life, then the doctor is a murderer.

I will not here dwell upon all the arguments that can be made against such an approach: the difficulty of proving subjective intentions (except if there is a confession), the fact that Keown's approach comes awfully close to wanting to punish people not for what they do but for their bad motives, the philosophical impossibility of separating intentions from behaviour in the way his approach requires, and so forth. The point I want to make is that *people do not necessarily know what*

---

[27] Griffiths, Bood, and Weyers, *Euthanasia and Law in the Netherlands*, 123–6.

[28] A. A. E. Verhagen, J. J. Sol, O. F. Brouwer, and P. J. Sauer, 'Actieve levensbeëindiging bij pasgeborenen in Nederland; analyse van alle 22 meldingen uit 1997–2004' ['Deliberate termination of life in newborns in the Netherlands; review of all 22 reported cases between 1997 and 2004'], *Nederlands Tijdschrift voor Geneeskunde*, 149 (2005), 183–8.

[29] See, for example, Griffiths, Bood, and Weyers, *Euthanasia and Law in the Netherlands*, 254–7, 270–3; Griffiths, 'Legal knowledge and the social working of law', 81–108. 'Intent' is, by the way, not the only problematic concept involved in the classification of MBPSL. Doctors and lawyers seem also to differ in their use of the concept of 'causation'.

[30] J. Keown, *Euthanasia, Ethics and Public Policy. An Argument Against Legalisation* (Cambridge: Cambridge University Press, 2002) 9–17.

[31] M. Otlowski, *Voluntary Euthanasia and the Common Law* (Oxford: Clarendon Press, 1997) 152–69.

*their own intentions are*—more precisely, they can think about their behaviour in terms of a variety of different intentions without experiencing any difficulty. And professional groups such as doctors and lawyers can differ radically and systematically in the intentions that they attribute to the very same behaviour.

To sum up: basing a system of control on self-reports, especially if these depend on classifications of behaviour in terms of subjective intentions, is to base it upon quicksand.

## 5. Are the Regional Review Committees a real alternative?

Euthanasia became legal in the Netherlands in the mid-1980s as a result of court decisions recognizing a justification of necessity.[32] An institutionalized reporting procedure for euthanasia cases was created in the early 1990s, but the assessment of reported cases remained in the hands of the prosecutorial authorities. In 1998, the Government created, by decree, five Regional Review Committees to examine reported cases of euthanasia; the Committees consist of a lawyer, a doctor, and an ethicist. The Committees were at first supposed to advise the prosecutorial authorities whether a reporting doctor had abided by the rules governing legal euthanasia. The most important reason given for creating the Committees was that doctors would have more confidence in the Committees' judgment than in that of prosecutors, and would therefore be more willing to report cases of euthanasia. In 2002, as part of the ultimate legislative legalization of euthanasia, the Committees were given a statutory status, and their judgment that a doctor has abided by the rules was made final.[33] Only if a Committee decides that a doctor has not kept to the rules is the case passed along to the prosecutorial authorities for a decision whether or not to prosecute. In practice, the Committees do not pass along every case in which some minor departure from the rules has taken place; their further investigation of such cases, and confrontation of the doctor concerned with their criticisms of what took place, seem to be experienced by doctors as serious sanctions.[34]

Figure 1 has already revealed that neither the original advisory Committees, nor the later Committees with final authority, led to the anticipated increase in the reporting frequency. As I have argued, this may be due to the fact that knowingly false reporting was not a serious part of the problem anyway.

Table 3[35] gives a quantitative overview of the work of the Committees and prosecutorial authorities between 1999 and 2005. As far as the formal treatment

[32] See Griffiths, Bood, and Weyers, *Euthanasia and Law in the Netherlands*, 98–100.
[33] See the Termination of Life on Request and Assisted Suicide (Review Procedure) Act [Wet toetsing levensbeëindiging op verzoek en hulp bij zelfdoding, (*Staatsblad* 194, 2001); effective 1 April 2002 (*Staatsblad* 165, 2002)]; available online at <http://www.minbuza.nl/binaries/en-pdf/pdf/euth-amendedbill-en.pdf> (accessed 7 February 2007).
[34] See n 16 above.
[35] Source: Annual Reports 1998–1999 through 2005, Regional Review Committees.

of reported cases is concerned, not very much seems to have changed. The prosecutorial authorities were very lenient with doctors in the past, and the new system of legal control has continued that tradition. In their treatment of doctors, the Committees seem, if anything, to be rather more critical than prosecutors were in the past, although this is not reflected in their final judgments.[36]As for the prosecutors, they have yet to prosecute a doctor found 'not careful' by the Review Committees (there have, however, been two medical disciplinary cases leading to warnings or reprimands).[37]I leave aside the question of whether such a system can be considered an adequate way of dealing with reported cases. I suspect the answer is 'yes', but, in the absence of more detailed study, this remains a matter of informed guesswork. The main point is that the importance of the Committees is not limited to the way that they dispose of cases. The whole system has become far more transparent as a result of the way the Committees have interpreted their responsibility to report on their activities. Their annual reports offer qualitative and quantitative insight into euthanasia practice—at least, in reported cases—of a sort that did not exist before. The discussion in their annual reports of recurring problems encountered in reported cases, and the Committees' reasons for dealing with them as they do, are slowly building up a sort of case law that never existed when most final decisions were taken within the opaque prosecutorial system. In short, the Committees have contributed a great deal to the level and quality of publicly available information about what doctors are doing and how the system

**Table 3:** Disposition of cases by the Regional Assessment Committees, 1999–2005

| Year | Reports | No jurisdiction | 'Careful' but referred to Medical Inspector | 'Not careful' |
|---|---|---|---|---|
| 1999 | 2,216 | 5 | 5 | 0 |
| 2000 | 2,123 | 11 | 12 | 3 |
| 2001 | 2,054 | 8 | 4 | 1 |
| 2002 | 1,882 | 5 | 0 | 5 |
| 2003 | 1,815 | 2 | 0 | 8 |
| 2004 | 1,886 | 0 | 0 | 4 |
| 2005 | 1,933 | 1 | 0 | 3 |

[36] In the two years for which we have information (1999 and 2005), the Committees asked the doctor to supply additional information in close to 10 per cent of all cases (information received from the General Secretary of the Regional Review Committees).

[37] See J. Griffiths, H. Weyers, and M. Adams, *Euthanasia and Law in Europe*, ch 5, Appendix. It should be noted that the majority of all cases of a 'not careful' judgment involve inadequacies connected with consultation. It is the policy of the prosecutorial authorities not to prosecute in such cases unless other failures of due care are also involved (*Aanwijzing vervolgingsbeslissing inzake levensbeëindiging op verzoek (euthanasie en hulp bij zelfdoding. Staatscourant* nr 46, 6 March 2007, 14.

is reacting. This is obviously a significant improvement over the way the system of criminal control normally works.

But of course, my real interest lies elsewhere: in the problem of *unreported* cases. And as far as that problem is concerned, as we have seen, the Committees do not appear to have made much difference.

## 6. How might a genuinely decriminalized system of control work?

Any realistic system of control over medical behaviour that potentially shortens life will have to be based on self-reporting by doctors—as I argued at the beginning of this chapter. To make such a system reasonably effective, two things are required: first, all MBPSL must be covered, and secondly, control must be organized outside the criminal law. These propositions are not dependent on whether especially problematic forms of MBPSL such as euthanasia are legalized or not, a fundamental point conveniently ignored by many critics of Dutch euthanasia policy.

Coverage not just of those MBPSL currently considered problematic, but of all MBPSL, is necessary for two reasons: first (a point I have not argued here), because abstention and pain relief (and, more recently, terminal sedation) include a considerable amount of behaviour that is more or less questionable, and needs to be subjected to some sort of organized scrutiny; and, secondly (a point I have particularly emphasized), because the classifications of different sorts of MBPSL on which the current system of control directly or indirectly tied to the criminal law depends, are not, and cannot be applied in a reliable way by those supposed to report their own behaviour. Even if all doctors were always scrupulously honest about what they have done, the use in a self-reporting system of a criminal law concept like intention will make the system intrinsically ineffective.

A comprehensive control system implies devoting attention to all cases in which something the doctor did or did not do probably influenced the time or the manner of the patient's death. This is, as we have seen, almost half of all deaths. Examining so many reports would far exceed the capacity and expertise of the prosecutorial authorities, or even of a 'buffer' system such as the Regional Review Committees. We seem to be caught on the horns of a dilemma: if we give the criminal control system sufficient scope, the number of cases will be beyond its capacity and it will be ineffective; if we retain a system of limited scope, it will miss a great many cases that deserve examination, and hence be ineffective.

A comprehensive control system would probably also be objectionable for another reason: it would promote 'defensive medicine'. Just as many Dutch doctors currently do not perform euthanasia because they do not want to have to report, so might many doctors under a comprehensive system fail to give adequate pain relief, or fail to abstain from futile treatment, for the same reason. To deal with this risk, one must be sure that doctors will have so much confidence in the control system that the necessity of reporting all cases of MBPSL will not prevent them from engaging in desirable behaviour.

The only apparent escape from this situation is to decriminalize the control system entirely; to make it conceptually, and in operation, entirely independent from the criminal law, so that a doctor reporting the death of a patient as an instance of MBPSL[38] could not be prosecuted. But this begs the question of what to put in the place of the current, ineffective system of criminal control. My intention in this chapter has been destructive rather than constructive, so I will not go into any detail here. The essence of the system I have in mind is professional self-control, backed up by monitoring by the Health Inspectorate. Roughly, it would consist of the following elements:

(1) The medical profession would be encouraged to continue the work on self-regulation of MBPSL that has been underway in the Netherlands for many years.[39] This began with the self-regulation of euthanasia practice that forms the basis of the current system of legal control. More recently the profession has dealt particularly thoughtfully and thoroughly with MBPSL in neonatology.[40] At both the local and the national level, professional protocols dealing with substantive and procedural requirements for various sorts of MBPSL would be worked out. The Government would be involved in the process leading to national protocols, as it is now.

(2) Reporting would be to a *local* assessment committee, either of the hospital or nursing home involved, or of a regional group of family doctors. Reports would be on forms that cover all points relevant to an assessment of what the doctor did.[41] The required information would be requested in terms familiar to doctors (the situation of the patient, the drugs used and the doses, estimated time to death, and so on) and not in criminal law terms such as intention. In most cases, assessment—and possible corrective measures—would be taken at the local level, and the case would stop there. Serious violations would be referred to the medical disciplinary authorities. Each local committee would submit an annual report to a national office responsible for general

---

[38] The concept of 'acting as a doctor' will require some attention, so that a murderer who happens to be a doctor is not covered by the decriminalization. The problem of medical gross negligence may have to be dealt with separately too.

[39] See J. Griffiths, 'Self-regulation by the Dutch medical profession of medical behaviour that potentially shortens life', in H. Krabbendam, H.-M. ten Napel (eds.), *Regulating Morality: A Comparison of the Role of the State in Mastering the Mores in the Netherlands and the United States* (Antwerp/Apeldoorn: Maklu, 2000) 173–90.

[40] See Griffiths, Bood, and Weyers, *Euthanasia and Law in the Netherlands*, 123–7. For the most recent instalment of this process of legal development, see E. Verhagen, and P. J. J. Sauer, 'The Groningen Protocol—Euthanasia in Severely Ill Newborns', NEJM 352 (2005), 959–62.

[41] Such a form would have not only a function in control after the fact, but also a preventive function in advance by keeping the doctor aware, as he acts, of everything for which he will have to account afterward.

supervision of the control system and for calling attention to possible problems arising in medical practice.

(3) The Medical Inspectorate would make unannounced, random checks of the files of local assessment committees to make sure they are doing their work properly.

This, in rough outline, is the sort of non-criminal regulation and control of MBPSL that I have in mind. I think there is every reason to believe that such a system would achieve far more effective control of this sort of socially problematic behaviour than does our current reliance on the criminal law.

# 8

# Lessons in Legal and Judicial Ethics From *Schiavo*: The Special Responsibilities of Lawyers and Judges in Cases Involving Persons with Severe Cognitive Disabilities

*Robert A. Destro*

## 1. Introduction

In earlier chapters of this book, doubts have been expressed about the role of the criminal justice process in regulating questions of health care, practice, and ethics. In this chapter, I shall explore the tragic case of Terri Schiavo, a severely incapacitated woman who, according to the courts and the media, was 'allowed to die' after the Florida courts ordered her guardian to remove all nutrition and hydration.[1] I will argue here that the criminal justice process provides an excellent reference point by which to judge the adequacy of the *civil* justice process in cases where severely incapacitated persons are alleged to be in need of medical or rehabilitative services. Had Theresa Marie Schindler Schiavo (commonly known as 'Terri') been a criminal facing either the death penalty or a lengthy term of incarceration in any state or federal court in the United States, the ethical and legal norms built into the process by which criminal charges are proved, defended, and appealed would have required the federal appellate courts to order the State of Florida to conduct a new trial in strict conformity to the civil guardianship and medical neglect process mandated by Florida and federal law. This chapter explores the legal and ethical reasons why the civil justice system failed so badly, and asserts, finally, that the *Schiavo* case, and others like it, demonstrate that both law *and* medicine are often far too willing to relax civil, criminal, *and*

---

[1] I argued *Schiavo v Bush*, No SC 04-925, on behalf of Governor Jeb Bush in the Florida Supreme Court. I was the primary author of the Petitions for *Certiorari* filed on behalf of Governor Bush in December 2004, and on behalf of Terri Schiavo's parents in 2005. I also worked on the first draft of, and wrote the initial justification for, the bill that was later to become Public Law 109–3. See n 63 below.

professional ethics standards for severely incapacitated persons who should, in the judgment of some at least, be 'allowed to die.'

## 2. What happened to Terri Schiavo?

*In re: The Guardianship of Theresa Marie Schiavo, Incapacitated*[2] (hereafter the *Schiavo* case) is one of the most notable, complex, and cautionary controversies in American legal and political history. It began as the private tragedy of a young woman who suffered a traumatic brain injury. It ended as a legal and political power struggle between the Florida and federal courts and the elected branches of the Florida and federal Governments. During the fifteen year period between Terri's injury and the entry of the final decree ordering the removal of nutrition and hydration, the state of her health and actual cognitive abilities became increasingly irrelevant. By the time the *Schiavo* case finally reached the Florida Supreme Court, the federal courts, and Congress, Terri Schiavo had become irrelevant.

### 2.1 The medical case and initial court proceedings

The medical facts of the *Schiavo* case are fairly straightforward. Sometime before 05:00 am on 25 February 1990, Theresa Marie (Terri) Schindler Schiavo, then 26 years–old, suffered cardio-respiratory arrest. According to court documents, her husband, Michael Schiavo, found her lying face-down on the floor at 05:00, and he placed a call to Terri's father, Robert Schindler, at around 05:40. Mr Schindler told him to hang up and call for emergency medical assistance. According to logs kept by the St Petersburg, Florida police, the emergency call was received at 05:40. Emergency medical services personnel arrived approximately twelve minutes later (at 05:52) and began resuscitation immediately. According to the Report of the Pinellas County Medical Examiner: 'Although a pulse was documented at 06:32hrs, a measurable systolic blood pressure was not recorded until 06:46hrs[,] almost one hour after resuscitation began.'[3] The result was a massive brain injury.[4] Intensive rehabilitation efforts and the first set of legal proceedings—medical malpractice cases against her primary care physician and the gynaecologist who had been treating her for infertility—began shortly thereafter.

---

[2] *In Re Guardianship of Theresa Marie Schiavo*: *Schindler v Schiavo* 780 So 2d 176, 177 (Fla Dist Ct App, 2001), aff'd without opinion *In re Guardianship of Schiavo* 789 So 2d 348 (Fla, 2001) (Table).

[3] The post-mortem examination of Mrs Schiavo showed 'marked, global anoxic, ischemic encephalopathy resulting in massive cerebral atrophy', but was unable to draw any conclusions concerning the condition and function of her brain at any point during her life post-trauma. Report of the Pinellas County Medical Examiner on Medical Examiner's Case No ME-5050439, 13 June 2005, at 39.

[4] Ibid, at 8.

## 2.2 The guardianship case

At the root of the legal case was an intra-familial dispute over the nature, quality, and extent of the rehabilitation and medical care provided to Terri Schiavo after she was released from the hospital. Because Terri had left no advance directive of any kind, her husband, Michael Schiavo, became her legal guardian by operation of Florida law. Her parents, Robert and Mary Schindler, believed him to be unfit to serve in that role, and mounted several attempts (all unsuccessful) to have the court remove him as guardian, and to assert their right as parents under Florida law to undertake that role themselves.

Review of the extensive, verbatim trial record developed over more than fifteen years discloses that there were significant, and unresolved, disputes between Terri's husband and her parents over brain function, including visual and auditory abilities, and the physical response of her brain to stimulation.[5] These disputes led to an ongoing battle over the value of continued rehabilitation, basic medical care, and complaints by Terri's parents that Michael had abandoned her, first by refusing to continue rehabilitation, and later, through his relationship with another woman, with whom he had two children.[6]

Money also played a role in this dispute. The medical malpractice case against the gynaecologist resulted in a 1993 award of $750,000 in economic damages[7] to Terri Schiavo, and $300,000 in damages for loss of consortium and non-economic damages to Michael,[8] who had testified in 1992 that his incapacitated wife was expected to live out her normal life span and that he would provide for her health care.[9] By early 1994, however, his position had changed. When Terri developed a urinary tract infection, he elected not to treat it, and requested a 'Do Not Resuscitate' order in the event she suffered another cardiac arrest.[10] When the nursing facility resisted the order, he cancelled it and transferred her to another facility,[11] and, in 2000, to the hospice in which she spent the last five years of her life.[12] From that point forward, her parents alleged, he would not permit routine medical and dental care, or any form of physical stimulation, including physical

---

[5] See generally the Transcript of Proceedings in the Circuit Court for Pinellas County, Florida, *In re: The Guardianship of Theresa Marie Schiavo, Incapacitated* Case No 90-2908-GD-003, Vol IV (15, 16, 17, 20, 22 October 2002).

[6] Second Amended Petition to Remove Guardian, 3–8, *In re: The Guardianship of Theresa Marie Schiavo, Incapacitated* Case No 90-2908-GD-003 (10 January 2005).

[7] J. Wolfson, Guardian *ad litem* for Theresa Marie Schiavo, 'A Report to Governor Jeb Bush and the Sixth Judicial Circuit in the Matter of Theresa Marie Schiavo' (1 December 2003) 7.

[8] Ibid, 9 and *In re Guardianship of Theresa Marie Schiavo*, 780 So 2d 176, 177–178 (Fla App 2d Dist, 2001) (hereafter *Schiavo* I).

[9] See, for example, Jurisdiction Brief of Petitioners, Robert and Mary Schindler, 1, *Schindler v Schiavo*, 855 So 2d 621 (Fla, 2003), 2003 WL 22400860.

[10] Wolfson, Guardian ad Litem Report, 10.

[11] Ibid.

[12] See Second Amended Petition to Remove Guardian, 15–16.

therapy or rehabilitation, the use of a wheelchair to take her outside, natural light from the window, or music in her room.[13]

All of these factors led the Florida District Court of Appeal to recognize that 'both Michael and the Schindlers [were] suspicious that the other party is assessing Theresa's wishes based upon their own monetary self-interest',[14] but that it saw 'no evidence in this record that either Michael or the Schindlers seek monetary gain from their actions. [They] simply cannot agree on what decision Theresa would make today if she were able to assess her own condition and make her own decision.'[15] It did hold, however, that Michael could not be permitted to make the decision to continue or refuse life-sustaining treatment. 'Because Michael Schiavo and the Schindlers could not agree on the proper decision and the inheritance issue created the appearance of conflict', the Court of Appeal permitted 'Michael Schiavo, as the guardian of Theresa, to invoke...the trial court's jurisdiction to allow the trial court to serve as the surrogate decision-maker.'[16] As we shall see in the discussion below, it is my contention that this ruling was legally and ethically erroneous on several grounds.[17]

## 2.3 The role of the courts in a disputed guardianship case

Properly understood, the law provides a framework within which those who are empowered to decide difficult medical questions can do so without fear of criminal or civil liability. In the Anglo-American common law tradition that prevails in the United Kingdom, the Commonwealth countries, and the United States, the courts provide a forum for the formal *and final* resolution of public and private disputes, including those involving medical care.

In an ideal world, disputes among family members, between physicians and their patients, or among partisans in the field of medical or biological research would be rare. Unfortunately, they are all too common, and when one of the parties to such a dispute invokes the power of the court to resolve it, the 'justice' of

---

[13] Ibid, 17–21.

[14] *In re Guardianship of Theresa Marie Schiavo, Incapacitated* 780 So 2d 176, 178 (Fla App 2d Dist, 2001):

This lawsuit is affected by an earlier lawsuit. In the early 1990s, Michael Schiavo, as Theresa's guardian, filed a medical malpractice lawsuit. That case resulted in a sizable award of money for Theresa. This fund remains sufficient to care for Theresa for many years. If she were to die today, her husband would inherit the money under the laws of intestacy. If Michael eventually divorced Theresa in order to have a more normal family life, the fund remaining at the end of Theresa's life would presumably go to her parents.

[15] Ibid.          [16] Ibid.

[17] The Court of Appeal was correct in its view that Florida law does not automatically compel the appointment of a guardian *ad litem* when a surrogate decision-maker may ultimately inherit from the patient, because it recognized that 'there may be occasions when an inheritance could be a reason to question a surrogate's ability to make an objective decision'. Ibid. Its mistake, discussed below in sections 6.4 to 6.5, was that Florida law expressly forbids the appointment of a guardian when there is a potential conflict of interest.

the outcome will depend not only on the strength of their respective medical and legal positions, but also on the quality of the legal process itself.

This point cannot be over-emphasized. The role of the judge is to preside over an adversarial hearing in which the parties and their counsel, not the court, must shoulder the burden of presenting enough facts to permit either the judge or a jury to resolve the factual issues in dispute. Where cases involve difficult questions relating to diagnosis or treatment, the law will often defer, but judicial deference cannot be assumed. The parties must prove, to the satisfaction of the judge, that the law provides a remedy (including deference) under the circumstances. As a result, the duty of a legal guardian, guardian *ad litem*, prosecutor, or counsel for one of the parties is to get as many of the relevant facts on the table as possible. If there is a default by any one of the parties to a case, the quality of justice will suffer.

This chapter proposes that enquiries of this type are best conducted in the language of professional ethics. The professional norms common to criminal and civil cases provide not only a set of readily accessible and commonly accepted definitions of the rights and obligations of those having an interest in the outcome, they also provide a powerful lens through which we can analyse the often-erroneous factual assumptions that drive the 'conventional wisdom'.

## 2.4 Characterizing the Schiavo case

To Terri's husband, Michael, and groups that traditionally support the 'right to die', the *Schiavo* case was little more than a heavy handed attempt by Terri's parents and their supporters to utilize state and Congressional political power to interdict Terri's *own* very personal, and intensely private, choice to forego life-sustaining medical care. To her parents, Robert and Mary Schindler, the *Schiavo* case involved criminal medical and rehabilitative neglect, in which those charged with the responsibility to care for her (her husband, the Florida judiciary, and the State of Florida's Department of Children and Families) lined up to support a factually and legally questionable finding that Terri would have preferred death by dehydration to rehabilitation and life as a person with severely impaired cognitive abilities. To the Florida and federal judiciaries, the case had two, inter-related aspects: (1) the separation of powers; and (2) the right of Terri's proxy to control her medical care. In this view, once the Florida judiciary had determined that Terri would not want to live in such a cognitively impaired state, the Florida Legislature had no authority to authorize the Governor to inquire regarding the adequacy of the judicial process or the continued protection of her rights.[18] To those who supported the Schindler family, including Governor Jeb Bush, a majority of the Florida Legislature, a majority of those voting in the United States

---

[18] Chapter 2003–418, Laws of Florida.

Congress,[19] and President George W. Bush, the *Schiavo* case was the functional equivalent of a death penalty case in which procedural and substantive errors at the trial level rendered the verdict inherently unreliable.

My goal in this chapter is to explain why the *Schiavo* case provides an excellent example of the dangers that arise for both law and medicine when policy disputes over the proper boundaries of law and medicine are resolved by 'characterization' rather than an analysis that carefully seeks to examine and balance all relevant interests. Kathleen Sullivan describes the difference between the two approaches as follows:

> Categorization and balancing each employ quite different rhetoric. Categorization is the taxonomist's style—a job of classification and labeling. When categorical formulas operate, all the important work in litigation is done at the outset. Once the relevant right and mode of infringement have been described, the outcome follows, without any explicit judicial balancing of the claimed right against the government's justification for the infringement. Balancing is more like grocer's work (or Justice's)—the judge's job is to place competing rights and interests on a scale and weigh them against each other. Here the outcome is not determined at the outset, but depends on the relative strength of a multitude of factors. These two styles have competed endlessly in contemporary constitutional law; neither has ever entirely eclipsed the other.[20]

I argue here that the *Schiavo* case fits comfortably within the intersecting boundaries of civil and criminal procedure; the law of homicide; family, guardianship, and disability law; the art and science of medicine; neuroscience; professional ethics; constitutional law; politics; and morals. The case was not controversial because it was complex; it was controversial because advocates oversimplified it. The lesson of the *Schiavo* case for the readers of this book is that 'hard cases make bad law'. Working together, legal and medical professionals must find both a common point of departure from which we can analyse our differences, and a common language in which to discuss them.


## 3. Starting at the beginning: A model of ethical professionalism

Doctors, nurses, allied health care professionals, and researchers from every profession have weighty professional responsibilities. These duties do not exist in the abstract. They arise from and govern the relationships formed with those who need, and rely upon their knowledge, expertise, good judgment, and artistry.[21]

---

[19] While this allocution might seem a bit strange, it is, in fact, an accurate description of the process by which Congress adopted the statute authorizing the federal courts to grant Terri Schiavo a new trial. The debate in the United States House of Representatives was televised live, worldwide. There was no debate in the Senate. The bill was adopted by unanimous consent.

[20] K. M. Sullivan, 'Post-Liberal Judging: The Roles of Categorization and Balancing', *U Colo L Rev* 63 (1992) 293–4.

[21] See, for example, M. D. Bayless, *Professional Ethics*\* (2nd edn, Belmont, Calif.: Wadsworth, 1989); M. Davis and A. Stark (eds.), *Conflict of Interest in the Professions* (Oxford; New York: Oxford

The same holds true for lawyers and judges. At the centre of all of our respective professional endeavours is a human person—a patient, a client, a research subject, or a party who has an interest in the outcome of our efforts. We must be free, we argue, to perform our respective duties as professionals because both 'skill' and 'judgment' are a uniquely personal combination of art and science:

Every science touches art at some points—every art has its scientific side; the worst man of science is he who is never an artist, and the worst artist is he who is never a man of science. In early times, medicine was an art, which took its place at the side of poetry and painting; today they try to make a science of it, placing it beside mathematics, astronomy, and physics.[22]

A similar combination of art and science explains the profoundly important role that lawyers and judges play in the regulation of health care. By law and the ethics of their profession, lawyers are the gatekeepers and administrators of the justice system. We serve as the civil and criminal investigators, evaluators, and 'judges' of first instance. It is our responsibility to ensure that no case under our control proceeds to a judge, or to a grand or petit jury, unless the evidence supporting the alleged grievance, crime, or defence is both admissible in court and strong enough to withstand the rigours of cross-examination.[23] As the 'arbiter of facts and law for the resolution of disputes and a highly visible symbol of government under the rule of law',[24] the judge is legally and ethically obligated to 'administer justice without respect to persons, and do equal right to the poor and to the rich'.[25]

Read together, the ethics of both law and medicine thus lead inexorably to the conclusion that the boundary between law and medicine is defined by the consistent application of a rule of reason to the facts and circumstances of each case.[26] Because duty is our common calling, a 'professional responsibility'

University Press, 2001); S. S. Phillips and P. Benner (eds.), *The Crisis of Care: Affirming and Restoring Caring Practices in the Helping Professions* (Washington, D.C.: Georgetown University Press, 1994).

[22] A. Trousseau, *Lectures on Clinical Medicine, Vol. 2* (The New Sydenham Society, 1869), submitted to the *British Medical Journal* by A. L. Wyman, retired physician, London, quoted in 'Endpiece—Medicine: Art or science', *British Medical Journal*, 320 (13 May, 2000) 1322.

[23] See American Bar Association [ABA] Model Rules of Professional Responsibility, 3.1, quoted in the text at n 73 below.

[24] American Bar Association [ABA] Model Code of Judicial Conduct, Preamble, available online at <http://www.abanet.org/cpr/mcjc/pream_term.html#PREAMBLE>.

[25] The material quoted in the text is drawn from 28 USC §453 (2007), which prescribes the Oath of Office for each judge or justice of the USA. The United States Code is available online at <http://uscode.house.gov/>. See American Bar Association [ABA] Model Code of Judicial Conduct, Canon 3, available online at <http://www.abanet.org/cpr/mcjc/canon_3.html>.

[26] *Bolitho v City and Hackney Health Authority* [1998] AC 232, [1997] 4 All ER 771, (1998) 39 BMLR 1, [1998] Lloyd's Rep Med 26, [1998] PIQR 10 (holding that 'there are cases where, despite a body of professional opinion sanctioning the defendants' conduct, the defendant can properly be held liable for negligence... [when] it cannot be demonstrated to the judge's satisfaction that the body of opinion relied upon is reasonable or responsible'.) Justice Farquharson made much the same point in the jury instructions delivered in *R v Arthur* [1981] 12 BMLR 1 ('There is no special law in this country that places doctors in a separate category and gives them extra protection over the rest of us.').

(or 'duty') model provides a powerful and precision-crafted lens through which to examine *any* decision, act, or omission by a legal or medical professional.

Viewed through this lens rather than the 'real-time' glare of the twenty-four hour news cycle, the *Schiavo* case is a textbook example of questionable behaviour *across-the-board*.

## 4. The ethics of due process and equal protection in disputed proceedings to withdraw nutrition and hydration

### 4.1 The Relevance of the Law of Homicide

'Homicide' is defined by the common law as 'the killing of one human being by another'.[27] It has two purposes: (1) to protect the living from homicidal acts or omissions; and (2) to protect those who become parties to a post-mortem inquiry into the reasons why a specific death occurred. Florida law does not expressly define the term homicide,[28] but it does impose criminal liability for specific acts or omissions.[29] In most cases, the physician's role is limited to making the initial determination that the patient has died and filing the appropriate death certificate.[30] If the cause of death is extraordinary in any way, such as by violence or under unusual circumstances, the medical examiner or coroner has the authority 'to perform, or have performed, whatever autopsies or laboratory examinations he or she deems necessary and in the public interest to determine the identification of or cause or manner of death of the deceased or to obtain evidence necessary for forensic examination', and, thereafter, to make it available to the appropriate legal authorities.[31]

There are only two situations in American law in which the execution of a judicial decree authorizes acts taken with the *express* intention of *causing* death. The first is the death penalty;[32] the other is a judicial decree authorizing families,

---

[27]  See <http://dictionary.reference.com/browse/homicide>.

[28]  Florida Statutes, § 775.01 provides that: 'The common law of England in relation to crimes, except so far as the same relates to the modes and degrees of punishment, shall be of full force in this state where there is no existing provision by statute on the subject.'

[29]  See, for example, Florida Statutes, §§ 782.03 (excusable homicide); 782.04 (murder); 782.07 (manslaughter); 782.071 (vehicular homicide); 782.08 (assisting in self-murder, defined in § 781.081(1)(b) as 'the voluntary and intentional taking of one's own life. As used in this section, the term includes attempted self-murder').

[30]  See, for example, Florida Statutes, § 382.008 (2007).

[31]  See, for example, Florida Statutes, § 406.11 (2007).

[32]  See, for example, Florida Statutes, § 922.105(1) ('A death sentence shall be executed by lethal injection, unless the person sentenced to death affirmatively elects to be executed by electrocution. The sentence shall be executed under the direction of the Secretary of Corrections or the secretary's designee.').

physicians, or medical facilities to withhold or terminate life-sustaining care from an incompetent person.[33]

Laws authorizing the execution of a death sentence make it clear that capital punishment is an exception to the general rule prohibiting acts or omissions 'perpetrated from a premeditated design to effect the death of the person killed or any human being'.[34] Because death is a sentencing option in these cases, the law requires effective representation of counsel[35] and other procedural safeguards that are supposed to ensure that the trial, appeals, and sentencing are conducted fairly.[36] If the sentence is actually carried out, the law also requires that the method of execution be neither cruel nor unusual.[37]

A judicial decree authorizing acts or omissions that will inevitably result in the death of an incompetent person presents equally difficult legal and judicial ethics issues.[38] Death is not only the inevitable consequence of such decrees; it is, in many cases, the *intended* result. Even though the law and many commentators draw a distinction in such cases between acts or omissions, or between direct and indirect effects, the fact remains that:

... in many termination of treatment cases, it is specious to say that death is unintended. That explanation makes sense in administration of pain medication that is foreseeably lethal. It is also true where the decision to terminate life support is genuinely directed to the treatment, independent of its role in keeping the patient alive... But this reasoning does not apply to many decisions to cease a life-sustaining procedure. Often what the patients or the families want to end are lives so impoverished and hopeless that they are judged not worth living. Despite repeated rejection of suicide and euthanasia, judicial decisions approving the right to such terminations make clear the judges' own sympathies with this judgment. The miserable existence

---

[33] Laws expressly authorizing euthanasia at the request of a patient are distinguishable because there is no pretence of judicial process.

[34] Florida Statutes, § 782.04 (defining 'murder'). cf Florida Statutes, § 922.105( 5–8) (creating exceptions from the general rules prohibiting for the acts or omissions necessary to execute a death sentence).

[35] K. Cunningham-Parmeter, 'Dreaming of effective assistance: The awakening of *Cronic's* call to presume prejudice from representational absence', *Temple L Rev* 76 (2003) 827.

[36] See, generally, R. Warden, 'Illinois death penalty reform: How it happened, what it promises', in *Symposium: Innocence in Capital Sentencing, J Crim L & Criminology* 95 (2005) 381.

[37] cf Florida Statutes, § 922.105(8) ('In any case in which an execution method is declared unconstitutional, the death sentence shall remain in force until the sentence can be lawfully executed by any valid method of execution.') with Florida Statutes, § 782.03 ('Homicide is excusable when committed by accident and misfortune in doing any lawful act by lawful means with usual ordinary caution, and without any unlawful intent... and not done in a cruel or unusual manner.'). See, generally, P. R. Nugent, 'Pulling the plug on the electric chair: The unconstitutionality of electrocution', *Wm & Mary Bill of Rights J.* 2 (1993) 185.

[38] American Bar Association [ABA] Model Code of Professional Responsibility, available online at <http://www.abanet.org/cpr/mrpc/mrpc_toc.html>; ABA Model Code of Judicial Conduct, available online at <http://www.abanet.org/cpr/mcjc/>.

suffered by the patient (apart from the procedure to be ended) is often described in heart-breaking detail.[39]

It is clear from an examination of the record and published opinions in the *Schiavo* case that the stated justification for the orders entered by the Probate Court was that Terri had told her husband's relatives that she would not want to be maintained in a severely incapacitated condition. It is also clear that this alleged desire was the one that the Probate Court of Pinellas County Florida sought to effectuate in Terri Schiavo's case.[40] Consider the sequence of the orders entered by the court:[41]

(1) The decree of 11 February 2000 authorized the guardian, Michael Schiavo, to 'proceed with the discontinuance of said *artificial life support* for Theresa Marie Schiavo'.[42] Such a decree is not, by its terms, an order authorizing acts or omissions that will inevitably result in the death of the incompetent ward. Although death may well result from the discontinuance of artificial life support, it is always *possible* that a person sustained by artificial nutrition and hydration can survive by ingesting food and water by mouth. Whether, and at what point, oral ingestion would have been possible for Terri Schiavo in late 2003 and in 2005 is a matter of some dispute.[43]

---

[39] R. S. Kay, 'Causing Death for Compassionate Reasons in American Law' 54 *Am J Comp L* 693, 714–15 (2006) (footnotes omitted). The Florida courts provided just such detail in *Schiavo*:

The evidence is overwhelming that Theresa is in a permanent or persistent vegetative state. It is important to understand that a persistent vegetative state is not simply a coma. She is not asleep. She has cycles of apparent wakefulness and apparent sleep without any cognition or awareness. As she breathes, she often makes moaning sounds. Theresa has severe contractures of her hands, elbows, knees, and feet. Over the span of this last decade, Theresa's brain has deteriorated because of the lack of oxygen it suffered at the time of the heart attack. By mid 1996, the CAT scans of her brain showed a severely abnormal structure. At this point, much of her cerebral cortex is simply gone and has been replaced by cerebral spinal fluid. Medicine cannot cure this condition. Unless an act of God, a true miracle, were to recreate her brain, Theresa will always remain in an unconscious, reflexive state, totally dependent upon others to feed her and care for her most private needs. She could remain in this state for many years.

*In re Guardianship of Schiavo* 780 So 2d 176, 177 (Fla App 2d Dist, 2001) (*Schiavo* I) (footnotes omitted).

[40] Ibid, 780 So 2d at 180 ('Her statements to her friends and family about the dying process were few and they were oral. Nevertheless, those statements, along with other evidence about Theresa, gave the trial court a sufficient basis to make this decision for her.').

[41] All references to court orders are to the guardianship case: *In re: The Guardianship of Theresa Marie Schiavo, Incapacitated—Michael Schiavo v Robert Schindler and Mary Schindler* No 90-2908GD-003.

[42] Order of 11 February 2000. [emphasis added].

[43] The autopsy takes the position that oral nutrition and hydration would have been impossible given the condition of Terri's throat musculature. Report of the Pinellas County Medical Examiner, 13 June 2005, 7, Question 3. The family, by contrast, argues that, with proper rehabilitation and training, Terri could have been taught to swallow, and there were indications in the medical records that she had, in the early 1990s, both taken liquids and responded on one occasion to a question.

In this regard, the Medical Examiner and the family are talking past each other. The Medical Examiner's Report describes only the condition of the body after death, and draws a careful

(2) The decree dated 17 September 2003, by contrast, directed that the guardian, Michael Schiavo, 'shall cause the *removal of the* nutrition and hydration *tube* from the Ward, Theresa Marie Schiavo'.[44] That particular tube was removed pursuant to the court's order. In accordance with the Executive Order authorized by 'Terri's Law', another tube was inserted later. The Governor's action precipitated the litigation in *Schiavo v Bush*.

(3) The final decree, issued by Judge Greer on 25 February 2005, directed 'that the guardian, Michael Schiavo, shall cause the removal *of nutrition and hydration* from the ward, Theresa Schiavo'.[45] This order was unquestionably designed to ensure that Terri Schiavo's life would end—a point underscored by his ruling on the 'Emergency Expedited Motion to Provide Theresa Schiavo with Food and Water by Natural Means' filed on 28 February 2005 by Terri's parents, Robert and Mary Schindler. In that motion, Terri's parents asked that they be permitted to provide food and water to their daughter by mouth. Judge Greer denied that motion on 8 March 2005 because, in his view, their request was the medical equivalent of 'asking for an experimental procedure'.[46] A police guard was then posted outside Terri's room in order to ensure that no fluids were provided.

Because Section 782.03 of the Florida Statutes excuses only acts taken 'by lawful means with usual ordinary caution, and without any unlawful intent...and not done in a cruel or unusual manner', the timing and manner of death is relevant. In Terri Schiavo's case, '[p]ostmortem findings, including the state of the body and laboratory testing, show that she died of marked dehydration (a direct complication of the electrolyte disturbances brought about by the lack of hydration)'.[47] Were the patient capable of experiencing the pain and mental anguish that would attend such a horrible demise, there would be no doubt that utilizing such a method for ending the person's life would be 'cruel and

---

distinction between a medical diagnosis and a post-mortem examination. The family's position, by contrast, focuses on their longstanding argument that the failure to provide rehabilitation services after the diagnosis of PVS was medical neglect. This argument may well be supported by advances in rehabilitation medicine and the scientific community's increasing awareness that the neuroplasticity of the brain makes it possible to regain physical and mental functions that were once thought to be irreversibly lost due to trauma or disease. See, for example, S. Begley, *Train Your Mind, Change Your Brain: How a New Science Reveals Our Extraordinary Potential to Transform Ourselves* (New York: Ballantine Books, 2006); J. M. Schwartz and S. Begley, *The Mind and the Brain: Neuroplasticity and the Power of Mental Force* (New York: Regan Books/Harper Collins, 2002).

[44] Order of 17 September 2003 [emphasis added].

[45] Order of 25 February 2005 [emphasis added]. But see Joshua Perry's discussion in text at n 54 below.

[46] Order dated 8 March 2005.

[47] Report of the Pinellas County Medical Examiner, 13 June 2005, 8, Question 7 ('By what mechanism did Theresa Schiavo die?'). Because the Medical Examiner could not determine the cause of the 'severe anoxic brain injury...with reasonable medical certainty[, the] manner of death will therefore be certified as undetermined'. Ibid, 9, Question 8 ('What was the cause and manner of death?').

unusual'—if not barbaric. Theresa Schiavo's *actual* cognitive abilities at the time of her death were thus a critically important—but unknown—fact.[48]

## 4.2  Comparing the substantive and procedural requirements in capital punishment and disputed withdrawal of treatment cases

In *State v Davis*,[49] the Florida Supreme Court made the following statement concerning the unique nature of cases in which a judicial decree will result in death:

As the United States Supreme Court first stated more than twenty-five years ago, 'death is different in kind from any other punishment imposed under our system of criminal justice.'[50] We have acknowledged that 'death is different' in recognizing the need for effective counsel in capital proceedings 'from the perspective of both the sovereign state and the defending citizen'.[51]

Terri Schiavo was not dead when these orders were entered. She was incapacitated and uniquely vulnerable, but also entitled as a matter of Florida constitutional law to have a surrogate exercise her right to decide whether to continue further nutrition and hydration.[52] Florida lawmakers responded to the problems created by the concept of 'substituted judgment' by creating a conditional immunity for those involved in the inquiry. As long as health care facilities, providers, surrogates, and proxies follow the procedures prescribed in Chapter 765 of the Florida Statutes, and there is a finding, based on clear and convincing evidence, that the incapacitated person had given some indication that he or she would have refused life-sustaining treatment under the circumstances, the surrogate may act. That immunity, however, is expressly conditioned on two factors. The first is compliance with specific due process requirements. The second is the development of factual findings concerning the incapacitated person's physical, mental, and cognitive condition.[53]

Careful examination of the procedural requirements in capital cases and disputed withdrawal of treatment cases leaves little doubt that the law of Florida

---

[48]  Ibid, 8, Questions 5 ('Was Mrs Schiavo in a persistent vegetative state?') and 6 ('What diagnoses can be made in regards to the brain of Mrs Schiavo?').

[49]  *State v Davis* 872 So 2d 250, 254 (Fla, 2004).

[50]  *Gregg v Georgia* 428 US 153, 188, 96 S Ct 2909, 49 L Ed 2d 859 (1976); see *also State v Dixon* 283 So 2d 1, 7 (Fla, 1973) (stating that because '[d]eath is a unique punishment in its finality and in its total rejection of the possibility of rehabilitation ... the Legislature has chosen to reserve its application to only the most aggravated and unmitigated of most serious crimes').

[51]  The latter part of the quotation in *State v Davis* is taken from *Sheppard & White, PA v City of Jacksonville* 827 So 2d 925, 932 (Fla, 2002).

[52]  *In re Guardianship of Browning* 568 So 2d 4 (Fla,1990).

[53]  Florida Statutes, § 765.401(3) (2007) requires that substituted judgment proceedings comply with § 765.205, which defines the powers of the surrogate decision-maker, and § 765.305, which deals with procedure where there is no advance directive. Both statutes contemplate compliance with Chapter 744 (governing guardians and their powers), as well as the possibility that life-sustaining treatment can be withdrawn even in the absence of evidence concerning the patient's wishes in cases where the patient is in a persistent vegetative state. See Florida Statutes, § 765.404 (2007).

treats all cases in which judges are asked to authorize actions or omissions that would otherwise be subject to prosecution under the laws governing homicide as 'death cases'. There are, however, important differences.

In a capital punishment case, the defendant is usually competent to stand trial and can participate in the defence of his or her case. There is an extensive body of constitutional and statutory law that mandates 'effective assistance of counsel', and a vocal—and growing—group of individuals and organizations who are willing and able to delay process up for years in order to ensure that the trial was conducted fairly and that the court's findings of fact are *objectively* verifiable (ie that the defendant is actually guilty).

The *Schiavo* case proves that precisely the opposite can be true in a disputed 'substituted judgment' case. The client is under a severe 'disability' as that term is understood in both civil rights law and legal ethics. The disability that gives rise to the claim that treatment should not continue makes it impossible for the incapacitated person to participate in a trial or to indicate his or her present preferences in any way. Although Florida prescribed almost exactly the same procedural safeguards for such cases as it does in capital punishment cases, the courts were willing either to dispense with them, or to view them as impediments standing in the way of effectuating the court's decision that the incapacitated ward's would have chosen to refuse life-sustaining care under the circumstances. When Terri's parents and pro-life activists stepped forward to question the procedural fairness of the trial, they were described, not as zealous guardians of the right to a fair trial and the rights of the accused, but as 'those who wanted to keep [Terri] alive indefinitely—including her elderly parents' and 'politicized religious forces [who] were responsible for the international attention garnered by Mrs Schiavo's plight and the escalation of her cause to a culture war flashpoint'.[54] And when Terri's family asked that state-of-the-art diagnostics, such as functional magnetic resonance imaging (fMRI), be used to test her actual, as opposed to assumed, cognitive state, the court refused the request.

As *Wall Street Journal* science reporter, Sharon Begley, points out in the quotation below, there is a 'conventional wisdom' concerning the ability of the brain to adapt to experience, including injury. 'Neuroplasticity' (which can also be referred to as 'cortical plasticity' or 'brain plasticity') is the ability of the brain to adapt *physically* in response to stimuli, and to shift the locus brain function.[55] It should come as no surprise that the Florida courts were just as sceptical about the utility, reliability, and feasibility of fMRI testing for Terri Schiavo[56] as they were

---

[54] J. E. Perry, 'Biblical bio-politics: Judicial process, religious rhetoric, Terri Schiavo and beyond', *Health Matrix* 16/2 (Spring, 2006) Available at SSRN <http://ssrn.com/abstract=775587>.

[55] See, for example, J. Doyon and H. Benali, 'Reorganization and plasticity in the adult brain during learning of motor skills', *Curr Opin Neurobiol* 15/2 (2005) 161–7; B. Draganski, C. Gaser, V. Busch, G. Schuierer, U. Bogdahn, and A. May, 'Neuroplasticity: changes in grey matter induced by training', *Nature* 427/6972 (22 January 2004) 311–2.

[56] See Letter of Stephen J. Nelson, MA, MD, FCAP, Chief Medical Examiner, 10th Judicial Circuit of Florida, to Jon R. Thogmorton, MD, District 6 Medical Examiner, 8 June 2005, 9 ('Neuropathology Report').

when presented in death penalty proceedings with issues involving the reliability of DNA testing.[57] As Begley comments:

If you are attacking the dogma [of neuroscience], you don't make a lot of friends... [The rejection of neuroplasticity is] yet another dogma that is now in the dustbin of history... This was yet another case where science has deemed something impossible without really ruling it out empirically.[58]

To understand the claims made on Terri's behalf by her parents, and the lengths to which the political branches of both the State of Florida and the United States Government went to in the attempts to vindicate this young woman's right to a fair trial, one must first consider not only their substantive claims, but also the procedural and historical context in which they were considered.

The following were the main issues pressed by the Schindler family on Terri's behalf:

(1) Terri's physical and cognitive abilities;

(2) the efficacy of treatment and rehabilitation services, and whether the decision to stop rehabilitation services was medical neglect;

(3) the duration of the dying process after nutrition and hydration have been removed;

(4) the physical, psychological, and emotional condition of a patient dying from lack of nutrition or hydration;

(5) the patient's beliefs and wishes concerning treatment options (including no treatment at all) in the event she became incompetent to make such decisions on her own; and

(6) the need for due process in the guardianship proceeding, including effective assistance of counsel assigned to represent the patient's interests *alone*; and

(7) a hearing before an unbiased judge.

I will deal briefly with the substantive ethical and constitutional issues presented by these claims in Parts 6 and 7.

---

[57] See B. P. Kuehne, *Criminal Law and Procedure: 1993 Survey of Florida Law*, 18 *Nova L Rev* 235, 259 (1993) noting the discrepancy between 'general acceptance' test for the admission of scientific evidence applied in *Robinson v State* 610 So 2d 1288 (Fla, 1992) (admissibility of DNA testing in capital case) and the approach taken by the Supreme Court of the United States under Rule 702 of the Federal Rules of Evidence:

Faced with a proffer of expert scientific testimony, then, the trial judge must determine at the outset, pursuant to Rule 104(a), whether the expert is proposing to testify to (1) scientific knowledge that (2) will assist the trier of fact to understand or determine a fact in issue. This entails a preliminary assessment of whether the reasoning or methodology underlying the testimony is scientifically valid and of whether that reasoning or methodology properly can be applied to the facts in issue.

[58] Interview with Sharon Begley, science reporter for *The Wall Street Journal* and author of, *Train Your Mind, Change Your Brain* (New York: Ballantine Books, 2006), National Public Radio, *Science Friday*, 2 February 2007 (hour 2). The mp3 file can be accessed at <http://www.sciencefriday.com/pages/2007/Feb/hour2_020207.html>, (accessed 3 February 2007).

## 5. Distinguishing between the facts of a case and the 'Record of its Proceedings'

I joined the Terri Schiavo case as appellate co-counsel in the Florida Supreme Court[59] for Florida Governor Jeb Bush in early August 2004. Later that month, after having immersed myself in the trial record and all of the briefs filed to that point, I argued the case for the constitutionality of 'Terri's Law',[60] and of the Governor's October 2003 Executive Order restoring the nutrition and hydration tube sustaining Terri Schiavo's life[61] after Judge Greer's 17 September 2003 order that it be withdrawn.[62] From that review of the record, it became clear to me that the *Schiavo* case had all of the characteristics of a problematic death penalty case: serious procedural errors, ineffective assistance from her guardian, no assistance of counsel, and a judge who had overstepped the proper boundaries of his judicial role. Whatever the actual facts were in the *Schiavo* case, neither I nor the appellate courts who would be asked to review the record would ever know them. It is my contention that the record in the case had been developed in a seriously flawed judicial proceeding.

Throughout the later proceedings, including the federal habeas corpus and civil rights litigation that occurred in early 2005 and the flurry of legislative activity in Congress on legislation 'For the relief of the parents of Theresa Marie Schiavo',[63] it was clear that the Schindler family was litigating against a 'conventional wisdom' rooted in attitudes about the 'right to die'. In *Schiavo*, it took the form of a series of presumptions about disputed facts, including:

(1) *Terri's condition.* In her husband, Michael Schiavo's view, 'Terri was beyond any meaningful rescue' after suffering a massive brain injury in 1990, and 'she never had any hope of recovery'.[64] The medical record, however, contained some

---

[59] The case was argued in the Florida Supreme Court on 31 August 2004. The transcript of the oral argument is available online at <http://www.wfsu.org/gavel2gavel/transcript/04-925.htm>. The video is available at <http://www.wfsu.org/gavel2gavel/archives/04-08.html> (31 August 2004).

[60] HB 35-E, Chapter 2003-418, Laws of Florida, available online at <http://election.dos.state.fl.us/laws/03laws/ch_ 2003-418.pdf> (accessed 4 February 2007).

[61] Executive Order No 03-201, available online at <http://sun6.dms.state.fl.us/eog_new/eog/orders/2003/october/eo 2003-201-10-22-03.html> (accessed, 4 February 2007).

[62] See discussion at Section 4.1.

[63] Public Law 109-3 119 Stat 15 (21 March 2005) at <http://frwebgate.access.gpo.gov/cgi-bin/getdoc.cgi?dbname=109_cong_public_laws&docid=f:publ003.109.pdf>. The original draft of the legislation was an amendment to the federal habeas corpus statute, 28 USC § 2241 (2007). That amendment would have made it clear that persons enmeshed in disputed guardianship proceedings can be considered a 'person in custody'. As finally adopted, Public Law 109-3 granted specific subject matter jurisdiction to the United States District Court for the Middle District of Florida:

... to hear, determine, and render judgment on a suit or claim *by or on behalf of Theresa Marie Schiavo for the alleged violation of any right of Theresa Marie Schiavo under the Constitution or laws of the United States* relating to the withholding or withdrawal of food, fluids, or medical treatment necessary to sustain her life [emphasis added].

[64] M. Shelden, 'Her soul had gone, her body was ready' (interview with Michael Schiavo) *The Telegraph Online*, 30 October 2006. See <http://www.telegraph.co.uk>.

evidence of cognitive function, including a reference to a situation in which Terri had responded verbally to a question posed by a physical therapist.

(2) *The rejection of neuroplasticity.* We will never know for certain whether the cessation of rehabilitation harmed Terri Schiavo's chances of recovery, but recent advances in neuroscience support her parents' claim that aggressive rehabilitation would have been helpful. These advances also support the contention that the condition of Terri's brain at death was attributable, at least in part, to lack of stimulation, rather than the initial injury. Both human and animal studies have shown that 'the primary motor cortex (M1) can reorganize after a focal vascular lesion if there is motor skill retraining. In animals not trained after a stroke, there is a further reduction in the size of the hand representation in M1.'[65]

(3) *Lack of medical and neuroscientific understanding of the minimally conscious state.* At the time the *Schiavo* case was tried in the guardianship court, it was widely assumed that the brain, once injured, could not recover. Today, there is a far more extensive literature on these subjects, and a far greater understanding of the organization and functioning of the brain. At the time of the habeas corpus proceeding in February 2005, this literature was available, and neuroplasticity was 'generally accepted' in the scientific community. It is unclear why the courts rejected the family's attempt to utilize state-of-the-art imaging to get an accurate picture of Terri's brain functions, but it is safe to assume from the 'heart-breaking detail' and empathy expressed by the judges in the various proceedings in early 2005 that, like Michael, they had concluded that Terri's life was 'so impoverished and hopeless that [it was] judged not worth living'.[66]

(4) *The unfairness of her trial.* Both the federal courts and many post-mortem commentaries on the *Schiavo* case focused on the 'proceedings' in the guardianship case. One writer even went so far as to state that:

A thorough examination of the Terri Schiavo guardianship proceedings reveals that the judicial process, both substantively and procedurally, achieved a decision that was consistent with the specific facts of Mrs Schiavo's case and Florida's established legal framework. This conclusion is important because it challenges the claims of those religious forces that attempted to undermine the credibility and legitimacy of the Florida judiciary.[67]

Each of these points assumes (a) that the 'specific facts of Mrs Schiavo's case' were fully litigated; (b) that the *conduct* of the trial was consistent with 'Florida's established legal framework'; and (c) that a habeas corpus attack on the proceedings of a guardianship court was little more than an 'attempt . . . to

---

[65] R. M. Bracewell, Editorial Commentary, 'Neuroplasticity and Rehabilitation, Stroke: Neuroplasticity and Recent Approaches to Rehabilitation,' *Journal of Neurology Neurosurgery & Psychiatry* 74 (2003)1465.

[66] R. S. Kay, 'Causing death for compassionate reasons in American law', *Am J Comp L* 54 (2006) 693, 714–15 [footnotes omitted]. The Florida courts provided just such detail in *Schiavo*— see quoted passage at n 39 above.

[67] Perry, 'Biblical bio-politics'.

undermine the credibility and legitimacy of the Florida judiciary'.[68] The goal of the Schindler family, by contrast, was to raise enough doubts about the fairness of the proceeding to make a plausible case for a new trial.[69] This would have been the outcome had a federal court granted the family's petition for a writ of habeas corpus[70] or, in the alternative, granted the new trial authorized by Congress in Public Law 109–3.[71]

## 6. 'Thinking like a (good) lawyer': The Code of Professional Responsibility and the lawyer's obligation to investigate the factual and legal predicates on which the 'conventional wisdom' is based

A number of commentators have argued, in the words of Joshua Perry for example, that criticism of the Florida courts was 'imprecise and irresponsible because it fails to distinguish between the quality of the judicial process and the outcome of the judicial process'.[72]

This is a rather strange criticism. The professional responsibility (or lack thereof) of any lawyer who serves as advocate or advisor (or both) in any civil or criminal case, including one as high-profile as *Schiavo*, is—and, ethically, must be—the starting point for an analysis of the lawyer's behaviour.

### 6.1 The duty to make only good faith claims

The first duty of the lawyer is to make an *independent, professional* judgment[73] concerning the merits of the case. This is so because Rule 3.1 of the American Bar Association's Model Rules of Professional Conduct provides that:

A lawyer shall not bring or defend a proceeding, or assert or controvert an issue therein, unless there is a basis in law and fact for doing so that is not frivolous, which includes a good faith argument for an extension, modification or reversal of existing law. A lawyer

---

[68] Ibid, assuming that *Bush v Schiavo* 885 So 2d 321 (Fla, 2004), *certiorari denied*, 543 US 1121 (2005), was correctly decided.

[69] See Petition for *Certiorari, Bush v Schiavo* No 04-757, October Term 2004, *certiorari denied* 543 US 1121 (2005).

[70] *Schiavo v Greer* 2005 WL 754121, 18 Fla L Weekly Fed D 361 (MD Fla, 18 March 2005) (No 8:05-CV-522-T-30TGW), *vacated by* Schiavo *ex rel Schiavo v Greer* 2005 WL 2240351 (MD. Fla, 21 March, 2005) (No 8:05CV522T30TGW).

[71] See n 63.

[72] See, for example, Perry, 'Biblical bio-politics', 51. See also Perry at 28–29 and n 161 and 168 (recounting allegedly inflammatory comments by counsel for the Schindler family and Governor Bush).

[73] American Bar Association, Model Rules of Professional Conduct (2006) [hereafter ABA Model Rules], Rule 2.1 'Advisor' ('In representing a client, a lawyer shall exercise independent professional judgment and render candid advice. In rendering advice, a lawyer may refer not only to law but to other considerations such as moral, economic, social and political factors, that may be relevant to the client's situation.'). Available online at <http://www.abanet.org/cpr/mrpc/rule_2_1.html>.

for the defendant in a criminal proceeding, or the respondent in a proceeding that could result in incarceration, may nevertheless so defend the proceeding as to require that every element of the case be established.[74]

For many readers, and indeed for many of the judges assigned to hear Terri's case, the claim that Terri did not get a fair trial is somewhat counter-intuitive. The case did, after all, take nearly fifteen years to work its way through the courts. Nevertheless, the fact remains that *none* of the courts that actually considered the case was willing to consider the fair trial issue. Consider the following extract from the transcript of the oral argument in *Schiavo v Bush*:

CHIEF JUSTICE: Good morning, ladies and gentlemen, and welcome to the Florida Supreme Court. The first case this morning is Bush versus Schiavo. Are the parties ready? . . .
[MR DESTRO:] Yes, Your Honor. . . .
[CHIEF JUSTICE:] Before you get into your argument, the court would appreciate it if . . . you would address the separation of powers, first, with the privacy argument, and with whatever free time you have, you can argue the other issues.
[MR DESTRO:] Thank you, Your Honor. May it please the Court. Terri Schiavo did not have [a fair trial or the benefit of] an independent [guardian *ad litem* represented by counsel].
JUSTICE WELLS: Let's try to get into the argument on separation of powers . . .[75]

From my perspective as appellate counsel, this was an extraordinary (albeit expected) exchange. Lack of procedural due process during the trial was one of the only plausible legal theories on which a claim for relief could have been granted. Once the guardianship court had made its initial finding that Terri was in a 'persistent vegetative state' and that she would not want to be maintained in that condition, the only way to attack those findings of fact was to attack the process by which they were found. Viewed from that perspective, 'Terri's Law' and the Governor's Executive Order are similar to the non-judicial proceedings that are the last hope of condemned criminals seeking to avoid the death penalty.

## 6.2 The lawyer's duty to a client with diminished capacity

Representing an incompetent person is, even in the 'best' of times, a difficult proposition. Rule 1.14(a) of the American Bar Association's Model Rules of Professional Responsibility recognizes this problem when it advises that 'the lawyer shall, as far as reasonably possible, maintain a normal client-lawyer relationship

[74] Rule 3.1 'Meritorious Claims and Contentions.' Available online at <http://www.abanet.org/cpr/mrpc/rule_3_1.html> (accessed 5 February 2007). The two states in which I am admitted to the Bar, California and Ohio, have similar rules, as does the Florida State Bar, whose rules govern in all legal proceedings before the courts of the State of Florida.
[75] Transcript of oral argument, *Bush v Schiavo*, supra, n 59, at 1. The bracketed material was omitted from the transcript, which appears to have been developed from the recording referenced in n 59. Obvious misspellings of names have been corrected without making note of the change.

with the client', even in cases where 'a client's capacity to make adequately considered decisions in connection with a representation is diminished, whether because of minority, mental impairment or for some other reason'.

In the case of an incompetent, laws governing guardianship, such as Florida Statutes Chapter 744, are the foundation of the lawyer's duty to seek the appointment of a guardian. Rule 1.14(b) provides:

(b) When the lawyer reasonably believes that the client has diminished capacity, is at risk of substantial physical, financial or other harm unless action is taken and cannot adequately act in the client's own interest, the lawyer may take reasonably necessary protective action, including consulting with individuals or entities that have the ability to take action to protect the client and, in appropriate cases, seeking the appointment of a guardian *ad litem*, conservator or guardian.

Once that step is taken, the ethical terrain becomes treacherous indeed.

## 6.3 Who is the client? The incompetent ward or the guardian?

Perhaps the most basic question in all of legal ethics is: *Who is the client?* In the case of an incompetent ward, the answer is clear: the client is the *ward*, not the guardian. Because the guardian is competent and usually a close relation of the ward, the attorney must take great care to distinguish their respective interests.[76]

## 6.4 May an attorney represent a guardian who has a concurrent conflict of interest with the interests of his or her ward?

The answer to this question is an unequivocal 'no'. In order to understand its significance, however, it is necessary to describe the interests of the parties in the *Schiavo* case. Terri Schiavo was the incapacitated ward, and was supposed to be the focus of the guardian's lawyer's duty of loyalty. In *Schiavo* I, decided in 2001, Florida's Second District Court of Appeal had held that the difference of opinion concerning treatment 'and the inheritance issue created the appearance of conflict' of interest between Michael, the guardian, and Terri, his ward.[77] In early 2005, Terri's parents renewed this charge in their 'Second Amended Petition to Remove Guardian', alleging that Michael Schiavo, her husband and guardian, effectively controlled Terri's representation, that he was represented by counsel throughout the proceeding, but that she was not, and that he had personal and financial interests adverse to Terri's.[78]

---

[76] ABA Model Rules, Rules 1.6, 1.7(f) (conflict of interest). See Restatement (3d) of the Law Governing Lawyers, § 24.

[77] *In re Guardianship of Theresa Marie Schiavo, Incapacitated* 780 So 2d 176, 178 (Fla App 2d Dist, 2001).

[78] Second Amended Petition to Remove Guardian, 37–50.

A recent filing in the Supreme Court of the United States, *Nault v Mainor*,[79] presented the following question for review:

Whether a court violates due process when it appoints a guardian *ad litem* who has a clear conflict of interest and when it subsequently approves a settlement without considering the conflict of interest between the guardian and the incompetent person.

It is somewhat surprising that there is a difference of opinion among the courts that have considered the due process implications of a conflict of interest between a guardian and his or her ward. In Delaware, Hawaii, Mississippi, and Washington State, the absence of an adequate guardian is a denial of due process, but in Alabama, Florida, and Minnesota it is not.[80] The Rules of Professional Responsibility, however, leave no doubt as to the answer to this question. Rules 1.7(a) and 1.8(g) prohibit representation in any case involving a 'concurrent conflict of interest'. Rule 1.7(a) provides:

(a) Except as provided in paragraph (b),[81] a lawyer shall not represent a client if the representation involves a concurrent conflict of interest. A concurrent conflict of interest exists if:
   (1) the representation of one client will be directly adverse to another client; or
   (2) there is a significant risk that the representation of one or more clients will be materially limited by the lawyer's responsibilities to another client, a former client or a third person or by a personal interest of the lawyer.

Rule 1.8(g) deals directly with the 'Question Presented' in *Nault v Mainor*, and would not permit a lawyer to represent both the guardian and the ward if there is any sort of conflict of interest between them:

(g) A lawyer who represents two or more clients shall not participate in making an aggregate settlement of the claims of or against the clients, or in a criminal case an aggregated agreement as to guilty or *nolo contendere pleas*, unless each client gives informed

---

[79] *Nault v Mainor* 101 P 3d 308 (Nov 2004), *certiorari denied* 126 S Ct 380 (No 05–82, October Term, 2005). The Petition for Writ of *Certiorari* to the Supreme Court of Nevada appears at 2005 WL 1660295.

[80] cf, for example, *Wilmington Medical Center v Severns*, 433 A 2d 1047, 1049 (Del, 1981); *Leslie v Estate of Tavares* 984 P 2d 1220, 1231 (Haw, 1999); *Interest of RD and BD, Minors v Linda D* 658 So 2d 1378, 1383 (Miss, 1995); *In re MC* 2001 Wash App Lexis 364, at 4 with, for example, *In re EF* 639 So 2d 639, 644 (Fla, 1994) (due process does not require appointment of a guardian *ad litem*); *In re Frederickson* 388 N W 2d 717, 721 (Minn, 1986) (no due process violation from the failure to appoint a guardian); *Leigh v Aiken* 311 So 2d 444, 446 (Ala Civ App, 1975) (due process does not require appointment of a guardian *ad litem*).

[81] ABA Model Rules, Rule 1.7(b) provides:
   (b) Notwithstanding the existence of a concurrent conflict of interest under paragraph (a), a lawyer may represent a client if:
      (1) the lawyer reasonably believes that the lawyer will be able to provide competent and diligent representation to each affected client;
      (2) the representation is not prohibited by law;
      (3) the representation does not involve the assertion of a claim by one client against another client represented by the lawyer in the same litigation or other proceeding before a tribunal; and
      (4) each affected client gives informed consent, confirmed in writing.

consent, in a writing signed by the client. The lawyer's disclosure shall include the existence and nature of all the claims or pleas involved and of the participation of each person in the settlement.

## 6.5  Does Florida statute law prohibit conflicts of interest between guardians and wards even if Florida courts refuse to hold as a matter of Florida constitutional law that a conflict of interest between guardian and ward creates a due process violation?

Notwithstanding the Florida courts' willingness to permit conflicts of interest between guardians and wards, and, as we shall see, conflicts of duty between judges and litigants, the Florida Legislature has expressly forbidden such conflicts. Section 744.309 of the Florida Statutes governs 'who may be appointed guardian of a resident ward'. It provides, in relevant part:

(b) No judge shall act as guardian after this law becomes effective, except when he or she is related to the ward by blood, marriage, or adoption, or has maintained a close relationship with the ward or the ward's family, and serves without compensation.

. . .

(3) Disqualified persons—No person who has been convicted of a felony or who, from any incapacity or illness, is incapable of discharging the duties of a guardian, or who is otherwise unsuitable to perform the duties of a guardian, shall be appointed to act as guardian... *The court may not appoint a guardian in any other circumstance in which a conflict of interest may occur.*[82]

## 7.  Applying the rules: Can a 'colourable' case be made that Terri Schiavo was denied a fair trial in the 'substituted judgment' case in which the nature of her condition and her intent to refuse treatment were litigated?

It is axiomatic that '[a] fair trial in a fair tribunal is a basic requirement of due process',[83] and the adversarial nature of common law trials requires not only that the proceeding *be* fair, but also that 'justice must [also] satisfy the *appearance* of justice'.[84]

In civil or criminal cases involving severely incapacitated individuals like Terri Schiavo, the law, the rules of legal ethics, and simple respect for the equal rights and human dignity of the individual require that all of the lawyers and judges involved in the proceeding satisfy themselves that there is no bias on the basis of

---

[82] Emphasis added.
[83] *In re Murchison* 349 US 133, 136 (1955).
[84] *Offutt v United States* 348 US 11, 14 (1954) [emphasis added].

'disability'.[85] It should also be apparent by this point that any breach of ethics in the decision-making *process* will cast doubt on the effectiveness of the representation, the reliability of the fact-finding process, and the integrity of the judicial proceeding as a whole.

Florida courts have held that Florida's explicit right to privacy[86] guarantees the right of both competent and incompetent patients to make fully informed decisions to refuse medical treatments, including the assisted provision of food and water.[87] If the family members agree about the incompetent patient's wishes, and there is no dissent, the decision to discontinue artificial life support is a private medical decision that needs no court oversight. If there are questions about the oral instructions of the incapacitated person, however, or if an interested party disagrees with the decision, 'the surrogate or proxy may choose to present the question to the court for resolution' or 'interested parties may challenge the decision of the proxy or surrogate'.[88] When a dispute arose between Michael Schiavo and Terri's parents over cessation of treatment, Robert and Mary Schindler, acting on behalf of their daughter, presented the question to Judge Greer for review pursuant to section 765.401 of the Florida Statutes.

A guardianship trial that contemplates an order to withhold or withdraw life-sustaining treatment will necessarily consider the evidence concerning the patient's condition, as well as evidence about the patient's attitudes about life and death, her beliefs, aspirations, relationships, and fears. Effective representation necessarily includes careful fact investigation, presentation of credible witnesses, active cross-examination and presentation of direct medical evidence. Without it, the incompetent person's right to privacy can easily fall prey to imbalances in the relative experience, knowledge, or time commitment of the counsel who appear in the case.

Because of the nature of the conflicting interests involved when a family splits into warring camps in a contested proceeding over the termination of life-sustaining treatment, there are only two real ways to understand the dangers that ineffective assistance of counsel can pose to the interests of the incompetent ward. The first is to consult the voluminous case law on 'ineffective assistance' that has arisen in the context of criminal law and procedure. The other is to determine whether, and to what extent, it is possible under the facts of the specific case to make a colourable assertion that there is, in fact, a conflict of interest between the incompetent ward and those who purport to represent their interests.

---

[85] See American Bar Association [ABA] Model Code of Professional Responsibility, Rule 1.14 [Client with Diminished Capacity], available online at <http://www.abanet.org/cpr/mrpc/rule_1_14.html> and ABA Model Code of Judicial Conduct, Canon 2(B)(5, (6) requiring special attention to elimination of bias on, among other grounds, 'disability', available online at <http://www.abanet.org/cpr/mcjc/canon_3.html>.

[86] Fla Const Art I, § 23 (2007). See also Bar Standards Board (UK), Part III, 305.1.

[87] *In re Guardianship of Browning; Satz v Perlmutter* 379 So 2d 359 (Fla, 1980) (competent patients).

[88] Ibid.

An incompetent person is, by definition, incapable of contributing *in any way* to the preparation or presentation of the case, and cannot possibly observe, or complain about, any conflict of interest. That duty falls to others, namely the lawyers who seek to represent any party to the proceeding, or the judge who must decide the case.

Terri Schiavo did not have *any* legal representation in Judge Greer's courtroom. Michael Schiavo was represented by experienced counsel in both his individual capacity and in his capacity as guardian. Various attorneys represented the Schindlers during the nearly fifteen years of litigation over this guardianship. Which of these counsel represented Terri?

The record shows that Terri was not officially noticed to appear for the proceedings, she was not provided with a guardian *ad litem*[89] assisted by legal counsel. She had no way to confront witnesses against her, or to present her own evidence. In Terri's case, only those who I have argued were *disqualified* to act on her behalf presented evidence and were represented by counsel.

The record also shows that the court considered explicit allegations of conflict of interest between and among the parties: specifically, disputes over inheritance and over the proper course of treatment. Because Terri had not left an advance directive, the first issue for the Florida courts to decide *should have been* the need for a guardian *ad litem* who would be represented by counsel. Instead, the Second District Court of Appeal held that 'there may be occasions when an inheritance could be a reason to question a surrogate's ability to make an objective decision'. As noted earlier, due to disagreement between Michael Schiavo and the Schindlers and an appearance of conflict regarding the inheritance issue, the court held that 'Michael Schiavo, as the guardian of Theresa, invoked *the trial court's jurisdiction to allow the trial court to serve as the surrogate decision-maker*'.[90]

The importance of the italicized words above may not be immediately apparent, so a bit of 'unpacking' may be in order.[91] Both the Probate Court and the District Court of Appeal agreed that *neither* Michael Schiavo *nor* the Schindlers could serve as Terri's surrogate because both stood to inherit from her estate, *and* there was a conflict between them regarding, among other things, the utility of rehabilitation, the quality of medical care, and Terri's attitudes toward cessation

---

[89] The term 'guardian *ad litem*' is defined in Florida Statutes, § 39.820(1) (2007) in cases involving children as an attorney or other 'responsible adult who is appointed by the court to represent the best interests of a child in a proceeding as provided for by law, including, but not limited to, this chapter, who is a party to any judicial proceeding as a representative of the child, and who serves until discharged by the court'. Florida Probate Rule 5.120 provides a similar rule for probate proceedings.

[90] *In re Guardianship of Theresa Marie Schiavo: Schindler v Schiavo* 780 So 2d 176, 177–178 (Fla App 2d Dist, 2001), aff'd without opinion *In re Guardianship of Schiavo* 789 So 2d 348 (Fla, 2001) (Table) [emphasis added].

[91] A useful chart explaining the organization of the Florida court system can be found on the website of the National Center for State Courts, available at <http://www.ncsconline.org/D_Research/csp/2003_Files/2003_SCCS_Charts1.pdf> (accessed 12 March 2007).

of life-sustaining treatment. The Court of Appeal did, however, approve Michael's request as guardian *on Terri's behalf* 'to allow the trial court to serve as the surrogate decision-maker'. This made the problem worse, not only for the Schindlers, who objected strenuously, but for Terri herself.

Neither Michael nor the Schindlers could serve as Terri's surrogate. There was no guardian *ad litem* at this point. Counsel for Michael and the Schindlers were also disqualified by virtue of their respective clients' conflicting interests. Who, then, acted on Terri's behalf? The record makes it clear that the Probate Court *itself*, undertook the role of 'surrogate decision-maker'. As 'surrogate decision-maker', Judge Greer became the *alter ego*, and legal representative, of Terri Schiavo.[92]

This, I contend, was clearly improper. A judge must serve as a dispassionate trier of fact, and may not participate as a representative of any party. If the court undertakes such a role, the trial becomes an advisory process, rather than an adversary proceeding. This is why Section 744.309(b) of the Florida Statutes expressly prohibits such a conflict of roles.[93] When a judge serves as either the advocate or surrogate for any of the parties who have an interest in a case pending before the court, he or she is no longer serving as a judge. In *Re TW*, the Florida Supreme Court held that:

Under no circumstances is a trial judge permitted to argue one side of a case as though he were a litigant in the proceedings. The survival of our system of justice depends on the maintenance of the judge as an independent and impartial decision maker. A judge who becomes an advocate cannot claim even the pretense of impartiality.[94]

For the Schindlers, the judge's conflict of interest made an already difficult case even harder to litigate. But the most serious impact of all fell upon Terri herself. She had *no* representation, legal or otherwise.

In *Sandstrom v Butterworth*,[95] the United States Court of Appeals for the Eleventh Circuit (which includes Florida) recognized that an attorney's allegation that the judge has compromised his judicial independence 'are among the most perplexing challenges that this Court encounters' and noted:

This habeas corpus appeal presents just such a challenge. It involves one manifestation of the tension that exists between the courts' criminal contempt power and various tenets of constitutional due process. In the case at bar, petitioner's conviction for criminal contempt stands in conflict with an important principle of due process—the right to an impartial tribunal. To uphold the state court's adjudication of contempt would necessarily

---

[92] Compare Canon 3(E)(1)(d)(iii) of the Florida Code of Judicial Conduct (requiring disqualification in any case in which a family member 'within the third degree of relationship' to either the judge or his or her spouse has anything more than a '*de minimus* interest that could be substantially affected by the proceeding').

[93] See § 744.309(b) of the Florida Statutes, discussed at n 53 above.

[94] *In re TW*, 551 So 2d 1186, 1190 n 3 (Fla S Ct, 1989).

[95] 738 F 2d 1200, 1201 (11 Cir, 1984).

and significantly intrude upon that fundamental due process value. Alternatively, to vindicate the petitioner's right to an impartial tribunal would require imposing some limitation upon courts' traditionally broad contempt authority. Under the circumstances here, however, the potential impairment of the court's power is outweighed by unfairness to the petitioner. We, therefore, resolve the instant conflict of values in favor of due process.[96]

The Florida courts apply precisely the same rule in other cases. In *Scott v Anderson*,[97] the First District Court of Appeal noted:

The familiar axiom 'a man should not be judge of his own case' is of ancient origin, but it has apparently not yet found its way into Florida law to the extent necessary to provide distinct guidelines for deciding under what circumstances a judge must disqualify himself to adjudicate direct criminal contempt charges involving disrespect or criticism directed to that judge. Since the question is ultimately one of federal constitutional import, we must turn to, and be guided by the federal decisions.

Because '[a]djudication before a neutral and unbiased tribunal stands as one of the most fundamental of due process rights',[98] raising questions of bias is, under the code of ethics, one of the most fundamental obligations of the first attorney to recognize the problem. Even then, allegations of bias, even those that are, as in Terri's case, founded on questions of law, are 'highly personal aspersions'[99] leveled at the trial judge that carry 'such a *potential* for bias as to require disqualification.'[100]

Counsel for the Schindlers did move to have Judge Greer recuse himself. They also moved to have Michael Schiavo removed as guardian. In both cases, the allegation that Terri Schiavo and her parents were litigating before a tribunal whose process was irretrievably tainted was factually and legally supportable. In *Mayberry v Pennsylvania*, the Supreme Court of the United States addressed precisely this situation when it noted that '[n]o one so cruelly slandered is likely to maintain that calm detachment necessary for fair adjudication',[101] and its decision has been read by the Eleventh Circuit as not 'turn[ing] on proof of actual bias, but instead [it was] centered around a "presumption" of bias'.[102]

These facts, we argued, were sufficient to raise a colourable claim that Terri had been denied a fair trial in the original guardianship proceeding, and that she and her family were entitled to a new trial in which both her condition, and her intent, would be fully and fairly litigated.

---

[96] Ibid, at 1201.

[97] 405 So 2d 228, 233 (Fla 1st DCA, 1981).

[98] *Sandstrom* 738 F 2d (11 Cir, 1984) at 1210.

[99] *Mayberry v Pennsylvania* 400 US 455, 466–467 (1971)

[100] Ibid (emphasis supplied), quoting from *Ungar v Sarafite* 376 US 575, 84 S Ct 841 (1964) at 847 (distinguishing *Mayberry* from that case, in which comments to the judge did not rise to the level of a claim of bias).

[101] 400 US at 465, 91 S Ct at 505.

[102] *Sandstrom* 738 F 2d at 1210, citing *United States v Meyer* 462 F 2d 827, 842 (D C Cir, 1972).

## 8. Conclusion

The burden of this chapter was not to disprove any of the points made by either Michael Schiavo or critics of those who sought, however unsuccessfully, to defend Terri Schiavo's interests. It is, rather, to argue a point that is taken for granted in all criminal cases in which the 'Great Writ' of habeas corpus might be employed. A proceeding seeking habeas corpus in a guardianship case would (or should) not need to question any of the specific findings in order to state a claim for a new trial. It need only make a showing that the 'process errors' in the guardianship case were so serious that the record *and the proceeding itself* were tainted by a denial of due process.

Like an involuntary commitment or a capital punishment case, the discontinuation of assisted feeding constitutes a deprivation of life, liberty, and property interests requiring scrupulous attention to the preservation of procedural due process rights.[103] The incapacitated person whose life and liberty interests are being curtailed with state approval has 'a right to the effective assistance of counsel at all judicial proceedings which could result in a limitation on the subject's liberty'.[104]

Not surprisingly, the conventional wisdom is (once again) wrong. Terri Schiavo's case was never about 'politicized religious forces' or nefarious attempts by the religious right to create a 'culture war flashpoint'. It was about whether a person with a severe brain injury could get a fair trial in a Florida court. Had she been a condemned criminal, the outcome—and the tenor of the discussion—would have been very different.

And thus, this chapter ends with the observation with which it began. Read together, the ethics of both law and medicine thus lead inexorably to the conclusion that the boundary between law and medicine is defined by the consistent application of a rule of reason to the facts and circumstances of each case. Because duty is our common calling, a 'professional responsibility' (or 'duty') model provides a powerful and precision-crafted lens through which to examine *any* decision, act, or omission by a legal or medical professional.

A good lawyer investigates the facts before drawing a conclusion, addressing the court or a witness, or making a legal argument. A good physician, neuroscientist, or allied health professional does precisely the same thing in the medical or research setting. Neither profession need worry about intrusion into the respective spheres of the other unless there is some professional, ethical, or process lapse that creates probable cause to proceed.

There were several such lapses in the *Schiavo* case. Public Law 109–3, 'For the relief of the parents of Theresa Marie Schiavo' shows that Congress viewed the

---

[103] *Chalk v State of Florida* 443 So 2d 421, 422 (Fla 2d DCA, 1984).
[104] Ibid.

*Schiavo* case as one involving *process*. Like Lord Browne-Wilkinson in *Bolitho v City and Hackney Health Authority*, Congress and the President were not bound to hold that the parties to a state court proceeding can escape judgment for acts that were not reasonable 'just because [of] evidence from a number of medical [and legal] experts who are genuinely of opinion that the defendants' [legal procedures,] treatment or diagnosis accorded with sound medical [or legal] practice'.[105]

And so, I close this chapter with an admonition for both legal and medical professionals. Ethics requires taking personal responsibility for one's actions. If one can do that, and can prove that those actions are reasonable under the circumstances, neither has anything to fear from the criminal or civil law.

---

[105] See *Bolitho*. Bracketed material indicates the author's changes from Lord Browne-Wilkinson's original text and meaning.

# 9

# Medical Treatment at the End of Life—A British Doctor's Perspective

## *Michael Wilks*

Ethical medical practice is based on a code that expresses what is 'right' in a particular circumstance, a position reached through consideration of moral, ethical, and cultural norms, filtered through clinical decision-making. These considerations need to embrace what is legal, but are not concerned that the 'right' decision is necessarily consistent with the law. It is also likely to be a more nuanced approach than that based on a legal approach, where the basis of a decision is anchored in both primary legislation and case law.

Reaching a solution by reference to case law has considerable drawbacks, and may not always provide a good and consistent reference in dealing with similar cases. Courts have reached what appear to health care professionals to be confusing and conflicting conclusions in deliberations about what are inaccurately portrayed as 'right to life' cases.[1] These judgments are often applicable to the individual case, rather than forging a new legal framework for similar dilemmas.

Arguably, ethical consideration is a more flexible instrument than legal argument played out in the confines of a court, contained as it is by legal process and procedural argument. Ethicists have the freedom to debate, while the courts have the duty to decide, but clinicians charged with a responsibility to resolve ethical issues often bear a heavy responsibility. This burden is both lightened and more focused because the patient, being at the centre of all decisions, is either present to play this crucial role through the expression of his or her autonomy, or others are charged with fulfilling this function as a representative of the patient's wishes.

While there are many influences on the way that ethical principles in clinical practice have been shaped in relatively recent times, the most important in terms of treatment at the end of life are:

- greater demand, and respect for 'patients' rights';
- advances in medical practice that prolong life; and
- the Human Rights Act 1998.

---

[1] For example, *R (on the application of Burke) v GMC* [2005] 2 FLR 1223.

When applied to treatment at the end of life, these influences come to bear on the following areas, which require wide debate:

- greater patient autonomy in decisions about the timing and mode of death;
- an increasing perception that what patients want in this regard is being denied by doctors; and
- the view that laws on assisted dying are restrictive of autonomous patient choice.

There is a paradox in the ethics of end-of-life treatment. The time at which, by virtue of the terminal, or life-threatening nature of the disease, patient autonomy should be at greatest influence, it may be at a low ebb. It is the duty of health care professionals caring for the patient to do their best to respect this vulnerability, to help the patient express his or her wishes, and, as far as possible, follow these wishes in treatment, or non-treatment decisions.

Recent cases relating to patient refusal of treatment have commonly been taken under the umbrella of the Human Rights Act 1998. Many will see the application of the Act to medical decision-making as inappropriate, given its origins in the European Convention on Human Rights of 1950, which was itself a response to gross abuses in pre-war and wartime Germany and elsewhere. The two central Articles are the 'right to life' (Article 2), and the right not to be subjected to inhumane or degrading treatment (Article 3). Article 2, in fact, provides no such thing as a right to life in all circumstances. At the very least, to do so would imply that the law delivers protection from the inevitability of death. The medical profession's settled view is that this clause should be interpreted as placing a responsibility on the doctor to respect human life, and to seek to preserve it, except when to do so comes at the price of a level of suffering that is unacceptable to the patients. This suffering may be physical, mental, or both.

'Treatment', in the general context of Article 3, is not a direct reference to medical care, and the attempted application of the Act to health care issues (such as rationing) dilutes the concept of 'degrading' or 'inhumane' treatment to a questionable and unhelpful degree.

When applied to decisions at the end of life, a tension is immediately created between the concept of a right to continuing life, and the right not to be treated inhumanely. In medical terms, inhumane or degrading treatment is that which has no possibility of achieving a net benefit, and whose continuation therefore represents a net harm. Cases in which autonomy has been expressed in terms of the right to refuse treatment (which is a different context than the right to remain alive) have almost always been decided in favour of the right of a patient to expect an autonomously expressed refusal of treatment to be followed and respected, even if that will lead to the likely or certain death of the patient.[2]

---

[2] For example, *Ms B v An NHS Hospital Trust* [2002] EWHC 429 (Fam).

It is important to stress that these judgments have been delivered in spite of, rather than because of the Human Rights Act, since they are based on the common law. Any doctor who overrules a competent refusal of treatment (see below) commits a trespass or assault.[3] The Human Rights Act does not need to be employed. Where it does have (some) relevance is in its application to end-of-life decisions by the patient in which current laws preventing the doctor acting upon patient requests for assisted dying are restrictive of patient rights.[4]

Where courts have been asked to arbitrate between Articles 2 and 3, judgment has usually been given in support of a patient's right to refuse treatment. If pressed, one would have to argue that, in these cases, the respect for patient autonomy reflects a superiority of Article 3 over Article 2, since autonomy is reflected in support for a decision not to be subjected to inhumane treatment. The only circumstances in which courts have effectively found in favour of a clinical decision to continue life-supporting treatment have been in cases where uncertainty exists regarding the capacity of a patient to make decisions, or where there is evidence of clinical uncertainty.

At a simple level, respect for the principles of beneficence and non-maleficence reflects the idea of a health care professional seeking to do good. In terms of clinical outcome, the linked concepts of net benefit and best interests come into focus. All medical procedures carry risk, and many have negative, as well as positive outcomes. The short term outcome of the risk, and the pain of a Caesarean section carries an extremely positive net benefit in the delivery of a healthy baby. Similarly, the brief pain of an injection or venepuncture is justified by the associated immunization, medication, or blood test.

In all therapeutic encounters, it is a fundamental principle that the doctor approaches these from a clinical perspective. That is both the primary duty of a doctor, and the job for which he or she has been trained. Every encounter starts from this point, and from it flow the completion of a diagnosis, a decision about management, and the weighing up of alternative therapeutic plans. This last stage also includes a choice between treatment and non-treatment, although a decision not to treat does not automatically terminate the doctor/patient relationship, but transfers its content to one of palliative, or supportive care.

The weighing up of different therapeutic decisions under the rubric of net benefit is therefore a clinical process that is familiar to the doctor at every step. What has changed, and arguably only in the last thirty years, has been the additional concept, the required next step, in framing these decisions in a new context, that of the best interest of the patient; it is only relatively recently that both the legal and ethical duties to view the clinical decision through the eyes of the patient have become a feature of good practice.[5] In many cases, this is a decision inseparable from that

---

[3] *F v West Berkshire AHA* [1990] 2 AC 1.

[4] *R (on the application of Pretty) v DPP* [2001] 1 All ER 1.

[5] Here, I am arguing that it is in the best interests of a *competent* patient to act in accordance with her wishes, even if the result will be less 'good' in clinical terms than the doctor

of net clinical benefit. One fits the other like a glove. The careful control of the blood sugar in a diabetic patient reduces the risk of both short-term and long-term problems, and compliance with treatment is clearly in the patient's best interest.

However, at the end of a life characterized by disability, physical restriction or pain due to multiple pathology, a doctor should pause before assuming that a chest infection should be treated, even if the outcome will be the (probable) control of the illness, and the preservation of life. In this type of scenario, how the patient views the probable outcome of a successful resolution of bronchitis or pneumonia, beyond the purely clinical, is central to the decision-making process. Doctors have had difficulty in seeing their responsibility as being to respect this aspect as much as the need to achieve net benefit, and the influence of patient demand and expectation has been a strong driver in changing attitudes.

How can best interests be assessed? Often, with great difficulty. Even if a patient is fully competent, informed, and engaged, there may be communication problems. These will not just relate to language, but also to the circumstances in which the patient is communicating with doctors. A feeling of vulnerability may exacerbate a reluctance to openly express wishes and fears, for example. The doctor needs to understand this, and be open to the variations of expression that often reveal underlying fears and anxieties.

In the case of an incapacitated patient, the problem of identifying best interests assumes a new difficulty. The opinions and wishes of others close to the patient may be extremely helpful in understanding a patient's wishes, expressed prior to the onset of incapacity, but they are not determinative.[6] Many family members find this confusing and difficult, feeling that they should have more control over the outcome, but an explanation of the legal limits of their involvement, combined with an approach that stresses the importance of their contribution, will usually improve their feeling of involvement.

How the autonomy of an incapacitated patient can be respected is obviously particular to the case, and absolute certainty that treatment will follow a patient's wishes is never complete, but a careful assessment of evidence from family, friends, and other health care staff involved in their care, and an approach based on teamwork and consensus, will almost always produce a decision that *feels* appropriate and 'right'. It will, at least often, be the case that such an approach will also provide the health care team with protection from the attentions of the criminal law.

---

intended/expected/wished. This was exactly the situation in the case of *Ms B*, where the doctors behaved both unethically and illegally in denying her wish to cease ventilation. The overriding condition, of course, is that the patient makes that decision with full knowledge of the (likely) outcome of her decision, as well as understanding all the available other options.

[6] Although the Mental Capacity Act 2005 enables Lasting Powers of Attorney (LPA) to be conferred by a person. Under an LPA, the person confers authority upon another to make decisions that can include decisions about his or her personal welfare relating to the carrying out or continuing medical treatment when he or she lacks capacity (s 9–11).

The advent of the Mental Capacity Act 2005 offers a more precise instrument by which autonomy can be respected, providing, as it does, the legal protection of the advance directive.[7] Although uncertainty as to the purpose of these instruments caused much parliamentary confusion during the passage of the then Mental Incapacity Bill, their importance in end-of-life treatment lies in the fact that they are now legally binding.

A contemporaneous *refusal* of treatment, given by an informed and competent patient, must be respected. As already mentioned, cases have confirmed that a refusal to honour such a refusal places the doctor in a position of assault or trespass. The force of a relevant advance refusal is no different, but an assessment of its relevance to a particular clinical situation demands some work.

In general, an advance refusal should determine medical treatment if:

- it was completed with a full understanding of the context in which it could be applied; and
- it is relevant to the situation the patient is now in.

It must be the case that patients who complete an advanced directive can never fully anticipate the circumstances in which it might be operative. A common experience is that the factors we might believe would influence choices of care or treatment become less certain once that situation is reached. Many of us, seeing a dependent, elderly relative suffering under the weight of ill-health, deteriorating capacity, and limited opportunities, are quick to make the assumption that we would reject living a life so constrained, on the basis that it would have little value or meaning. It is the experience of many who work in such clinical environments that different perspectives come to bear when we reach such situations, and absolute certainties become more nuanced.

These considerations are of less importance when applied to an advance statement that outlines general requirements and expectations of care. It should be emphasized, that, in spite of the judgment in the case of *R (on the application of Burke) v GMC*, there is no specific legal requirement for a doctor to provide treatment that is demanded in an advance statement, but good advice, based on ensuring patient trust, must be to take such a requirement into account, even if there is a potential 'waste' of resources in so doing.

Where the advance statement requires more careful interpretation is when it becomes an advance *refusal* of treatment. This will usually refer to a refusal of life-supporting treatment in which the outcome may (refusal of antibiotics, refusal of dialysis), or almost certainly will (refusal of CPR, ventilation, or artificial nutrition and hydration (ANH)), lead to death.

Here, the imperative is to ensure, as far as possible, that the patient, when completing an advance refusal, understood and foresaw the circumstances in which it might apply. As we have seen, neither this, nor the absolute certainty that a

---

[7] See ss 24–6 of the Mental Capacity Act 2005.

patient had full information and capacity at the time of completion, can be achieved, and the advance refusal, while a significantly useful new instrument, needs to be applied with care, and with a proportionate approach. This approach demands that some weight is given to the patient's previously expressed wishes, as evidenced by family and friends, as well as an assessment of the relevance of the document to the clinical situation now presenting.

Debates around end-of-life treatment are always passionate, and frequently polarized. They also tend to be further muddled by a number of confounding factors. These include a confusion between what is assisted dying, and what is palliation, a problem with the ethical and legal distinctions between euthanasia and withdrawal of treatment, a poor understanding of the 'double-effect' doctrine, and a substantial level of ignorance about what actually occurs when treatment, particularly ANH, is withdrawn.

In the course of a final illness, there is usually clarity for doctors, and for many of our patients, about when it is no longer appropriate to persist with treatment, and when that treatment itself has no further purpose, and therefore becomes a burden. The doctor's duty in these cases is the relief of suffering, both physical and mental. This will nearly always bring into consideration whether 'active' treatment—treatment to preserve life and to *act* to treat a condition—should be withheld or withdrawn. For some, often driven by strong religious belief, there is an acceptance that while palliation is a central obligation, treatment should never be refocused on assisting the patient to die. This is one area of continuing difficulty since, for such people, a decision to withdraw treatment is tantamount to assisting dying, because the doctor cannot separate foreseeing the likely consequence of the decision from an intention to assist the patient's death. This was at the heart of opposition at the final stages of the passage of the Mental Capacity Bill, when a passionate debate ensued on whether patients who took advantage of an advance refusal of life-supporting treatment were effectively creating a legally enforceable suicide request.

This leads us into considering the ethical and legal distinctions between euthanasia and withdrawal. It is both an ethical and legal dilemma because, although many doctors would claim to be able, in all cases, to separate an intention to relieve suffering from an intention to end life, these thoughts cannot in reality be distinguished in the doctor's mind. Physicians are driven by a fundamental imperative to reduce pain and suffering. When faced with a patient who is suffering both physically and mentally, the primary effort will be to give whatever treatment is appropriate to achieve this aim, providing net benefit in terms of best interest. It is unrealistic to think that the doctor at all times keeps from his mind the thought that part of that benefit includes death. Obviously, whether the doctor acts on this thought will define whether he or she remains within accepted ethical and legal practice, but that these thoughts will arise must be simply a natural part of a doctor's professionalism. They are particularly difficult to deal with when the patient also articulates a wish to discuss assisted dying.

The principle, or doctrine of double effect has long been a convenient protection, used (often with some sleight of hand) to avoid conviction for murder. It is a relic of a time before doctors developed palliative skills, and when the relief of pain depended on the use of powerful drugs given in sufficiently high doses to threaten the patient's life. With the development of good, although far from universal palliative care, in which careful attention is paid to dosage and outcome, the double effect concept is not only irrelevant, but a positive barrier to informed and honest debate on end-of-life care. Nowadays, a major ethical requirement of doctors is to provide evidence-based care, and practice, and evidence confirms that, for the majority of patients, the appropriate use of pain-relieving drugs involves prescribing them at a level that does not, in itself, threaten life, although, of course, the primary threat to life remains the terminal nature of the illness.

We are therefore now at a point at which this outdated 'principle' has become harmful to rational debate. It also acts as a protection for an outdated paternalistic attitude to terminal care, in which the 'doctor knows best' approach prevents further involvement, both of the patient, in expressing his or her wishes about treatment, and of those close to a patient who has lost capacity, in advising the doctor on what the patient's known wishes might be.

Finally, there is the wide level of ignorance amongst patients, politicians, and, unfortunately, many health care professionals, about the processes involved in the withdrawal of ANH. Ending treatment that involves the provision of intravenous fluid and nutrition via a nasogastric tube carries profound implications, since the consequence of so doing will be the certain death of the patient, over a number of days. The period between the withdrawal and death is often uncertain, but the relationship between the two is absolute. There is a less strong link between the withdrawal of, say, antibiotics for a chest infection in a patient with advanced dementia and the patient's death, as a number of other factors will influence the course of the illness.

There are, of course, as many scenarios as there are patients. Let us consider the case of a patient with a terminal malignancy. In this case there is a reasonable predictability about the course of the final illness. Experience suggests that when there is a strong likelihood that death will occur within one month, then artificial feeding makes no difference to the course of the illness. If that is the case, it follows that withdrawal of ANH will also not influence the outcome, and therefore that doing so cannot reliably be predicted to accelerate the dying process, and therefore be the primary cause of death.

In cases which are very familiar to doctors, where the course of the disease, although inevitably terminal, is less predictable, the place of ANH is also unclear in terms of whether the outcome ('outcome' here being delaying dying) is helped by instituting feeding, or harmed by withdrawing it. If the final course of the illness is likely to last less than a month, again the provision, or non-provision of ANH appears to have little effect in terms of predictable outcome. If the terminal phase extends beyond a month, the removal of ANH may accelerate the dying process, but a direct causal relationship is hard to identify.

In an increasingly common group of patients, those suffering from long-term, debilitating, but not immediately life-threatening illness, the contribution of ANH to the final outcome is also debatable, but for different reasons. A patient suffering from advanced dementia will be prey to a variety of potentially life-threatening conditions, each of which may individually cause death (whether treated or not) in an already vulnerable, and weakened patient. It is, therefore, impossible to say with any certainty what contribution the withdrawal of feeding makes to the final outcome, although, of course, it may feel to the health care professionals involved that a decision to withdraw ANH, after a long period of its provision to the patient, will create a strong association between the act and the outcome, even if the causal relationship is absent or weak.

These difficult and unpredictable scenarios cause discomfort to those who want more certainty in medical treatment and outcome, where it often does not exist. The debate is further polarized by the habit of those opposed to the withdrawal of ANH as describing its effect as death by starvation. As well as being wrong, this view also overlooks the fact that good palliative care must be provided to all patients in which a non-treatment decision has been reached.

What has been missing from the debate is an ethical approach that provides the same rights to patients, and which respects their autonomy in the way the law already allows. There is a strong, and well-tested legal protection for the principle that a competent patient can decide to refuse life-supporting treatment, even if the likely consequence of that decision will be death. There is a clear disjunction between the law and ethics in these cases, and ethics needs to catch up with what the law already permits.

Euthanasia is a minority issue, in the sense that the vast majority of decisions about end-of-life treatment will be ones involving withdrawing and withholding treatment, rather than whether to actively end life. As more of us approach old age, with a greater certainty that our life-ending cancers and vascular diseases will be successfully treated, we—or, very often, those close to us—will be making decisions about the circumstances in which we would wish to be treated, or not treated.

In this context, the opposition of many doctors, and some politicians and pressure groups to opening up legal opportunities for patients to be provided with assisted dying, has an impact beyond the particular issue. The debate around euthanasia may not appear very important in terms of the small number of patients who would wish to benefit from a relaxation of the law of murder, but as a symbol of the current gap between what our patients want, and what we doctors think they want, it is extremely potent.

Whether the medical profession maintains its curiously paternalistic need to control patient wishes on the most important area of care we will all eventually face is not that significant when applied to assisted dying. But it carries strong implications for the way in which we approach the care of our patients at the end of their lives. Doctors do need to be more sensitive to the autonomy of their patients if they are to be effective partners for them and their families when making decisions about withdrawal and withholding life-supporting care.

# 10

# Dignity: The Difference Between Abortion and Neonaticide for Severe Disability

*Stephen W. Smith*

## 1. Introduction

One of the biggest concerns—quite possibly the biggest concern—in any field of ethics, including medical ethics, is to make sure that ethical decisions are consistent. That is, one must make sure that the ethical foundations used to make a particular decision are utilized in the same manner to make other decisions or that there are convincing reasons for the difference in the treatment of the particular cases. This consistency is seen as a laudable goal as it allows us to be able to test the foundational concepts of particular ethical systems, to be able to find a logical basis for any extension or refinements of the principles used in a particular ethical system, to be able to predict future ethical decisions, and to provide one reason to suppose that our own ethical decisions are fair, just, or equitable.

However, consistency by itself does not alleviate all difficult questions in ethics. In fact, it may create certain ethical problems. One particular problem that arises is when foundational ethical principles tested in a specific case result in a decision that seems counter-intuitive or invalid within the larger ethical framework that has been constructed. In such a case, there appear to be only a limited number of options, particularly if that intuition about the 'right' decision in such cases is to be given any credible weight.[1] We might, in these situations, be forced to re-examine the foundational concepts which anchor a particular ethical system. We might also assume we have somehow misunderstood, or misapplied the ethical concepts of the ethical system. Finally, we may attempt to find a way to distinguish the current case from the normal result of the ethical system.

One particular ethical problem that falls within the general difficulty mentioned above is the disparate, acceptable treatments of severely disabled fetuses

---

[1] It is, of course, possible to simply dismiss the intuitive wrongness of the result as being incorrect. In other words, the result is not wrong; it is the intuition that says differently which is in fact wrong. This paper will assume, however, that there is merit in at least presuming these intuitions have validity.

and severely disabled newborns, particularly as it relates to intentional termination of life through either abortion or neonaticide.[2] A pregnant woman carrying a severely disabled fetus can terminate her pregnancy and, in so doing, act
consistently with many ethical systems, and in accordance with law.[3] It is also
consistent with many ethical systems that the fetus' disability is the reason for
doing so. However, it is less likely that ethical systems would accept the killing of
a newborn after birth on the grounds of severe disability, and the current law does
not allow for such a practice.[4] This appears to be true even if it would have been
consistent with one's ethical system for the newborn to be terminated for the
same disability while still within the womb of the mother. As this creates at least a
facial inconsistency within many ethical systems, it is worth examining in detail
whether it is possible to distinguish between these two practices.

It is also worth examining this particular question for the legal ramifications
which would result. As noted above, a mother is well within her legal rights to
seek an abortion for severe disability. Consistent with this, a doctor performing an
abortion on a severely disabled fetus will avoid legal sanction provided the doctor
acts in compliance with the Abortion Act 1967. The same, however, is not true for
cases of neonaticide. A mother cannot request that a severely disabled newborn be

---

[2] For the purposes of this paper, most of the terms used will be taken to have non-technical
meanings. Thus, by 'severe disability', I mean any disability which is likely (or perceived to be
likely) to have a significant impact on quality of life. Under the current law, this would include disabilities such as Down's syndrome, spina bifida, and even cleft palates (the latter given the Crown
Prosecution Service's decision in the light of the case of *Jepson v The Chief Constable of West Mercia
Police Constabulary* [2003] EWHC 3318 not to bring a prosecution against doctors who performed
an abortion under s 1(1)(d) of the Abortion Act 1967 on the grounds that a cleft lip and palate constituted a serious handicap, as they had acted in good faith that a substantial risk existed that the
child would be seriously disabled). Likewise, 'newborn' will be taken to mean any infant within the
first 28 days after birth. Finally, 'intentional termination of life' shall include only those practices
which would involve any overt acts with the purpose of terminating life, such as the injection of
a lethal substance. It will not include the withdrawal or withholding of life-sustaining treatment
as this treatment is dealt with differently under the law. According to the law of the UK, parents
may request that treatment be withdrawn from a severely disabled newborn and doctors may act in
compliance with this request. See *R v Arthur* (1981) BMLR 1. Additionally, even if the parents do
not agree, doctors may seek a court order to withdraw treatment should it not be in the best interests of the child. See, for example, *Re Wyatt (a child)(medical treatment: parents' consent)* [2004] Fam
Law 866. However, it should be noted that doctors cannot withdraw treatment of a child without
parental consent or prior court approval in non-emergency cases. See *Glass v United Kingdom*
[2004] 1 FCR 533, [2004] 1 FLR 1019, (2004) BMLR 120.

[3] See Abortion Act 1967, s 1(1)(d) (as amended by the Human Fertilisation and Embryology
Act 1990). For a clear discussion of the ethical viewpoints, see Nuffield Council on Bioethics,
*Clinical care decisions in fetal and neonatal medicine: ethical issues* (2006) at <http://www.nuffield-
bioethics.org/fileLibrary/pdf/CCD_web_version_8_November.pdf>, paras 2.17–2.20 (accessed
27 February 2007).

[4] As shown below, the fact that it is less likely does not mean that all ethical systems hold that
the killing of a newborn after birth for severe disability is unacceptable. For examples of ethical
systems where the killing of a newborn after birth for severe disability would be acceptable, see
J. Harris, *The Value of Life: An Introduction To Medical Ethics* (London: Routledge and Kegan Paul,
1985); J. Glover, *Causing Death and Saving Lives* (Harmondsworth: Penguin Books, 1977);
H. Kuhse and P. Singer, *Should the Baby Live?: The Problem of Handicapped Infants* (Oxford: Oxford
University Press, 1985).

intentionally terminated. Nor, if the doctor complies with such a request, would the doctor be able to escape legal liability. Instead the doctor, like any other individual, would be charged with murder.[5] The law's stance, then, is similar to the standard ethical intuition about these practices and provides another reason why it is useful to attempt to distinguish between these two practices.

Thus, in this chapter, I will consider whether there is any way to create a logical, ethical distinction between allowing the termination of a fetus for severe disability prior to birth while maintaining that the intentional killing of a newborn after birth for the same severe disability is not acceptable. In order to accomplish this goal, I will begin by examining two of the more common ethical theories used in debates involving either abortion or neonaticide. It will be shown that neither of these viewpoints as commonly understood can provide a basis for the distinction between abortion and neonaticide. I will then put forth an alternative argument based upon the dignitarian approach utilized by Deryck Beyleveld and Roger Brownsword.[6] It will be shown that this approach can create the necessary distinction between abortion and neonaticide for severe disabilities. Finally, the chapter will consider some of the lingering difficulties that may exist even if we adopt the dignitarian approach to the problem.

## 2. Current approaches

Before considering the dignitarian approach outlined by Beyleveld and Brownsword, it is important to assess whether one of the common ethical approaches to these issues can deal adequately with the problem of the difference between the termination of severely disabled fetuses and killing severely disabled infants. If one of the current approaches can deal with the issue, there is less reason to look for an alternative justification.

The first approach to consider is the position, generally referred to as the 'pro-life' argument, that life begins at conception. In such an approach, it is necessary to understand that the moral relevance of life beginning at conception is that all life with a specific genetic makeup is considered to be part of a larger group, members of which are all subject to the same ethical considerations. Thus, an entity with human genes is a human being and therefore is entitled to all of the rights and interests given to humans.[7] So, the species to which one belongs dictates the

---

[5] Nuffied Council, *Clinical care decisions in fetal and neonatal medicine*, paras 8.13, 9.20, 9.22.

[6] D. Beyleveld, and R. Brownsword, *Human Dignity in Bioethics and Biolaw* (Oxford: Oxford University Press, 2001).

[7] See, for example, R. Dworkin, *Life's Dominion: An Argument About Abortion, Euthanasia, and Individual Freedom* (New York: Vintage Books, 1993) 11. Dworkin actually splits pro-life claims into two different statements in relation to abortion claims. First, there is the derivative view, which holds that abortion is wrong because it violates someone's right not to be killed. Secondly is the detached view, which holds that abortion is wrong because it interferes with the intrinsic innate

set of general rights and duties which apply to the specific entity. As such, there is a certain minimum level of rights which all members of the same species must receive. Primary among those rights afforded to human beings (particularly for the purposes of this chapter) is the right to life.[8] Since conception creates a new and unique organism which does not exist previously, and that organism contains human genetic material, it is classified as human and is, therefore, entitled to all of the rights and interests afforded to human beings.

One of the specific problems associated with this particular theory is that it does not appear to be factually accurate. While conception creates a new organism, this is only one of its consequences, and it therefore appears inaccurate to consider each fertilized egg to be a human being.[9] This has led some to suggest a more complex version of the 'life begins at conception' argument. In this version, the fertilized egg is not considered to be a human being at the point of conception. However, it is considered to have the potential to be a human being. In other words, given the right circumstances (for example, adequate nutrition) and time, the fertilized egg will become at least one human being. Since it has that potential, the argument is that we ought to protect it, and allow it to reach that potential. Therefore, even if the fertilized egg is not technically a human being, we ought to treat it as such. Thus, we arrive at the same conclusion regarding the rights and interests that we afford the fetus as if we considered life to actually begin at conception, while accepting the scientific viewpoint which suggests that that position is not completely accurate.[10]

It is not important for the purposes of this chapter to consider which version of the argument is stronger, because neither version of this argument provides a satisfactory solution to the issue being addressed. They will both provide a satisfactory answer to why we consider it to be unacceptable to kill a severely disabled newborn. Under both versions, the newborn falls within the category of human being. It is therefore entitled to the necessary rights and interests applicable to human beings. Foremost among those is the right to life, and thus we cannot kill the severely disabled newborn. Unfortunately, though, neither version can explain why it is often considered acceptable to allow the termination of severely disabled fetuses. Since a fetus would also be a human being (or have the potential

---

value inherent in human life. It does not appear to be necessary for our purposes to distinguish between the detached view and the derivative view.

[8] Broadly speaking, the 'right to life' argued by those taking a pro-life position is that every entity, particularly a human entity, has the right to a normal chance of life.

[9] For example, only part of the zygote created at conception goes on to form the human embryo. The other part forms the trophoblast which attaches to the uterine wall and provides nutrition for the embryo. It is also possible that the fertilized egg will form two embryos, in the case of identical twins, or fail to form an embryo at all, in the case of hydatidiform moles. See Harris, *The Value Of Life*, 10.

[10] Whether this 'potentiality' argument, as it is commonly known, adequately addresses the scientific evidence which undermines the 'life begins at conception' argument is one we need not consider specifically in this chapter. We also need not consider whether it is a good idea to use potential states of being to determine current rights. See Harris, *The Value Of Life*, 11–12.

to be a human being), it would likewise be entitled to be protected as any other human being, and thus have the right to life. As such, the life begins at conception approach would require that we do not kill the fetus. This viewpoint cannot provide an adequate justification for the current state of the law and the intuitive belief many individuals hold about the acceptability of the different practices.

Due to the inability of the pro-life argument to adequately deal with the issue being considered, we must look towards another ethical theory. One sort of ethical theory worth considering starts from a very different ethical point. As noted above, the pro-life arguments presume that we can determine, at least in part, the moral worth of an individual entity based upon the species to which it belongs.[11] However, many have argued that belonging to a particular biological species is not a morally relevant criterion for determining rights and duties.[12] According to these theories, rights and duties cannot flow from species membership because those things that must count as morally relevant criteria do not occur equally in all members of the same species. Instead, each individual member of a particular species must be considered separately, and accorded those rights to which they are entitled based upon their individual criteria.

One such version of this kind of ethical theory involves the concept of personhood.[13] While, at first blush, this may appear to amount to the same thing as being a human being, it is not. The notion of personhood gives rise to a special category of beings which possess criteria that we think are morally relevant. For a large number of these types of ethical theories, the morally relevant criteria are developmental and (primarily) cognitive ones. These include such capacities as self-awareness, self-control, a sense of the future, a sense of the past, and so forth.[14] If a being possesses these qualities, then it is considered to be a person with all of the necessary rights and interests associated with that status. If a being does not have these particular qualities, then it is not a person, and does not have the associated rights and interests. We may therefore have two beings within the same species who are treated differently if one has the requisite criteria for personhood and another does not. Moreover, there may be beings that are not humans which are classified as persons and there may also be humans who are not classified as persons. Thus, the category of persons is both broader and narrower than the category of human beings, and the personhood theory is significantly different from the pro-life theories we have considered.

---

[11] See, for example, J. Finnis, 'The fragile case for euthanasia: a reply to John Harris' in J. Keown (ed.), *Euthanasia Examined* (Cambridge: Cambridge University Press, 1995) 46–55.

[12] P. Singer, *Rethinking Life and Death: The Collapse of Our Traditional Values* (Oxford: Oxford University Press, 1995) 202–6.

[13] The idea of personhood as being a morally relevant criterion different from simply belonging to the species of human beings has its roots in enlightment thinkers such as Kant and Locke, and has continued to be utilized by authors such as Peter Singer and John Harris. See Harris, *The Value Of Life*, 14–15, and Singer, *Rethinking Life and Death*, 168, 180–3.

[14] Kuhse and Singer, *Should the Baby Live?*, 130–1.

However, even though the theory is significantly different, it provides no better answer to the issue of a difference in treatment between abortion and neonaticide. This is particularly true in the case of late term abortions for severe disabilities. It is important to note that, under the current state of the law, it is permissible to have an abortion for fetal disability very late in pregnancy. In fact, it appears that it would be possible to have an abortion for fetal abnormality up to the point of birth, as section (11)(d) of the Abortion Act 1967 does not include any time limit. With this being the case, there is no developmental criteria that would differentiate a newborn from a fetus in the latter stages of pregnancy. It may be possible to make a distinction earlier in pregnancy, but not the closer the fetus gets to birth.

Under this theory, then, we cannot create a relevant difference between a fetus before birth and a newborn after birth. A fetus does not appear to have things like self-awareness or control, or a sense of the past or future. This, therefore, means it is not entitled to the rights and interests given to persons. Thus, the fetus prior to birth may be terminated, under the personhood theory, because it does not have the relevant criteria necessary for personhood. However, there is no significant change in the morally relevant criteria used in the theory which would protect the newborn. The newborn also does not appear to have self-awareness or control, nor does it have a sense of the past or future. It, therefore, would not qualify as a person either, and, consequently, would not be entitled to the rights and interests associated with personhood. Thus, while the personhood theory may provide an explanation as to why it is acceptable to terminate the severely disabled fetus, it cannot explain why we do not allow the killing of the severely disabled newborn.[15]

It should be noted that, while none of the theories discussed thus far have been useful in solving the particular issue in question, this does not mean those who propose these theories are being intellectually inconsistent. Those who take the position that life begins at conception, or that the potential for human life begins at conception, do not normally argue that the termination of severely disabled fetuses is acceptable. In fact, one of the reasons for this particular ethical theory is to argue against abortion in most, if not all, circumstances. Thus, these individuals are arguing that, in order to be consistent with ethical theory, we ought not to allow either practice. Conversely, those who utilize the personhood approach noted above are more likely to view certain instances of neonaticide as ethically justifiable, yet they still voice a consistent argument. Authors such as Peter Singer and John Harris, both of whom are closely connected with the personhood theory, readily accept that the consequences of the position they hold is that neonaticide is not necessarily unethical.[16]

The fact that proponents of these theories may not take the position articulated in the introduction, however, does not solve the problem. The position articulated that the abortion of severely disabled fetuses is acceptable while the deliberate killing of severely disabled newborns is unacceptable is a common intuitive

---

[15] Kuhse and Singer, *Should the Baby Live?*.
[16] Ibid; Harris, *The Value of Life*.

position held by many people and it is, as previously noted, the current status of the law in the UK. The problem, therefore, of finding a logical, ethical basis for that intuitive position needs to be addressed on those particular terms. The only other alternative is to find that many individuals holding that intuitive position are being ethically inconsistent, and that conclusion should only be accepted if there is no reason to justify the difference in treatment.

There is, of course, one important distinction between a fetus and a newborn that has not been previously considered in this chapter. That distinction is that the fetus is still physically connected to the mother whereas a newborn has ceased to be physically connected to the mother. However, using this distinction as a justification for the differences in the ethical or moral appropriateness of the two particular practices creates its own difficulties. First, if we utilize this criterion to determine moral worth, we are using a criterion that is external to the being in question. We are not deciding the difference in moral worth between a fetus and a newborn based upon criteria intrinsic to that being, but based upon the environment in which the entity happens to find itself. As we do not tend to determine moral worth on that basis (for example, people in the UK are not considered to be different from people in the USA as far as moral worth is concerned), it seems a difficult way to provide an ethical distinction in this case.

More importantly, though, this seems to make an individual's necessary moral rights subject to the moral rights of someone else. Furthermore, that someone else (the mother) is actually the stronger member of the pair. Once again, the tendency is for necessary moral rights to be independent of the moral rights we owe other parties. For example, the owing of a right to life for you does not normally depend on my granting or not granting a right to life to someone else.[17] However, in this case, it appears that is exactly what is required. This will then create further problems in determining what extent such a principle would have. So, if we grant the mother rights over a fetus, does that mean that parents ought to have rights over their children? Since the right in question is the right to life, this could lead to some very worrying results. It is therefore imperative that if the physical separation from the mother is going to create the ethical difference, there needs to be a way to deal with the problems associated with this point of view.

## 3. The dignitarian approach

Since none of the previous theories mentioned appear sufficient to untangle this particular problem, it is necessary to find an alternative theory. The theory which will next be considered is the dignitarian approach utilized by Beyleveld

---

[17] This is not to challenge the universality of rights. The general tendency is to only grant those rights that we can grant to all individuals. See, for example, J. Rawls, *A Theory of Justice* (Oxford: Oxford University Press, 1971). What we do not tend to do is to grant moral rights contingent on other rights that are bestowed upon other people.

and Brownsword in *Human Dignity in Bioethics and Biolaw*.[18] This approach
bears some similarity to the personhood approach. However, there are differences which will prove to be significant when attempting to justify the difference
in treatment between severely disabled fetuses and severely disabled newborns.
Before discussing that, it is imperative to set out the dignitarian approach.

The dignitarian approach used by Beyleveld and Brownsword is based upon the
work of the American philosopher Alan Gewirth.[19] Gewirth attempted to create
a moral theory which contained some of the benefits of Kantian ethics without as
many of the problems associated with it. To do this, Gewirth focused on the idea
of agency. Agency requires a degree of rationality because agents must be able to
rationally decide on life goals and the means for achieving those goals.[20] Thus,
agency is not species-based, but based upon the abilities of individual agents. So,
in this way, agency is similar to personhood.

This idea of agency, in and of itself, is not enough to form an ethical theory
and Gewirth needs to expand on this idea in order to generate a moral theory. He
does so in the following way. He argues that agents ought to have what he terms
the generic rights of agency. These are 'pre-requisites of an ability to act at all or
with any general chance of success, regardless of the purposes being pursued'.[21]
They are thus necessary for any agent to have any chance of satisfying their goals
or in putting life plans into action. These generic rights, therefore, will include
the right to life since (as far are we know) it is impossible to act while not alive.[22]
Gewirth argues that all agents ought to be entitled to having these generic rights
respected by others. Just as importantly, though, Gewirth argues that agents
ought to respect the generic rights of others in addition to ensuring that their own
generic rights are respected. The reason it is necessary for agents to respect the
generic rights of others is that the consequence of not respecting those rights is to
deny one's own agency.[23] This complex assessment about how agency influences
the generic rights (and how agents respect other's generic rights) is referred to as
the Principle of Generic Consistency (PGC).[24]

Once again, as stated, the PGC provides little reason to justify the difference
in treatment between fetuses and newborns. The concept of agency is not substantially different from the idea of personhood and will still rely on criteria that
a fetus and newborn are unlikely to satisfy. Since neither fetuses nor newborns

[18] Beyleveld and Brownsword, *Human Dignity*.
[19] A. Gewirth, *Reason and Morality* (Chicago, Illinois: University of Chicago Press, 1978).
[20] Ibid, 120.
[21] D. Dwyer, 'Beyond Autonomy: The Role of Dignity in "Biolaw"', *Oxford J Legal Studies*, 23
(2003), 319, 322–3.
[22] Beyleveld and Brownsword, *Human Dignity*, 70.
[23] There is a complex logical argument associated with this conclusion that we need not consider
now. Those interested in the supporting argument should consult Beyleveld and Brownsword,
*Human Dignity*, 72–9.
[24] Ibid, 70–2.

qualify as agents, the PGC will not provide any support for the granting of generic rights to either fetuses or newborns.

However, it is at this stage that Beyleveld and Brownsword differ from Gewirth and do so in an important way. Gewirth argues that while beings such as fetuses and newborns are not agents, they are quite likely to be partial or potential agents.[25] As such, while they are not entitled to the full rights applicable to full agents, they would be entitled to partial rights equivalent to their status. Beyleveld and Brownsword disagree, and the reason they do so is that they believe that agency is not something one can possess only in part. Instead, agency is an all-or-nothing proposition. Either you are an agent and thus the PGC requires you be extended the full rights of agency, or you are not an agent and the PGC does not entitle you to those rights.[26] This highlights the important concern of determining who is and who is not an agent.

The determination of who is and who is not an agent, while vital, is also extremely difficult. The reason it is so difficult is that we, as individual agents, have imperfect knowledge. This is especially true about our knowledge of other people. Thus, an agent can only really be sure about his or her own agency.[27] The agency of anyone is subject to the imperfect knowledge of the agent making the determination and it is therefore possible to get it wrong. I, as an agent, may think that someone else is an agent when they are not, or I may think that the other individual is not an agent when they are, in fact, an agent. The second possibility is particularly a problem for the PGC. As stated above, if we do not extend the generic rights of agency to other agents, then we are denying our own agency with all of the consequences that entails. On the other hand, if we extend the generic rights to non-agents, then, while not required by the PGC, it does no harm to the principle itself. It is therefore better, from the basis of the PGC, to err on the side of caution and assume things to be agents if we are unsure.[28]

This leads to what Beyleveld and Brownsword term the precautionary principle. Under the precautionary principle, if something has the possibility of being an agent, we ought to treat it as if it is an agent. This then means that, as far as possible, agents ought to extend the generic rights to anything that is even conceivably an agent.[29] Even a cursory examination of this principle, though, will show that it is unworkable in that form. The number of things which are theoretically possible agents is infinite. It would include not only all adults but many other things as well. It would include fetuses, newborns, higher primates, dogs, cats, birds, fish, and perhaps even plants, or even single-celled organisms. As it stands, the agent cannot rely entirely on what he or she knows about the world because it has already been stated that such knowledge is imperfect. This,

[25] Ibid, 117–19.
[26] Ibid, 118.
[27] Ibid, 120.
[28] Ibid, 121.
[29] Ibid.

then, opens the door to considering everything as an agent. However, it would be impossible to include all things within the concept of agent. The PGC, and thus the generic rights, would have to be extended to almost anything. Extending the generic rights would not be possible because there is likely to be a significant increase in the number of conflicts between possible agents. For example, if all animals are considered agents under the precautionary principle, then they would be entitled to the right to life. This means we would be unable to kill animals for food. While this may please vegetarians, it should be noted that plants might also fall under this category, and thus the eating of plants would likewise violate the PGC. Agents would then be unable to function at all, which would defeat the concept of the PGC in the first place.

One possible response to this problem is to refuse to accept the precautionary principle. However, Beyleveld and Brownsword instead choose to clarify the 'as far as possible' part of the principle. What they suggest is, in essence, a probability exercise. While it is possible that everything in the world is an agent, it is not likely to be the case. Considering what we know about the world, there are beings which are highly likely to be agents, such as other competent adults. There are also things which are extremely unlikely to be agents, such as plants. So, in cases where we have conflicts between the generic rights of possible or potential agents, and there is no way to resolve the conflict without breaking the generic rights of one of the beings in question, we ought to respect the rights of those things which are more likely agents than those that are less likely agents.[30] This will provide us with a practical way to resolve the issue which, while perhaps not perfect, would greatly increase the probability that agents will not violate the PGC.

## 4. Application of the dignitarian approach to abortion and neonaticide

In light of this explanation of the dignitarian approach, it is possible to explore the issue of allowing an abortion of a severely disabled fetus but not allowing the intentional killing of a severely disabled newborn. As will be shown, the dignitarian approach can provide a justifiable basis for the intuitive position that has been proposed.

Starting with the abortion of a severely disabled fetus, under the dignitarian approach it is necessary to determine whether the fetus is an agent or not. As previously stated, the fetus does not appear to be an agent. Fetuses, as far as we are aware, do not have goals or life plans. However, assuming normal development, a fetus would become an agent. It is therefore a potential agent under

---

[30] Ibid, 124.

Beyleveld and Brownsword's terminology.[31] Since it is a potential agent, using the precautionary principle, we ought to treat the fetus as if it were an agent, provided those interests do not conflict with other more likely agents. It should be noted that the fetus should still be considered a potential agent even if the severe disability at issue involves significant mental impairment that would put into question the ability of the fetus to ever develop goals. In such a case, while the probability of the fetus being an agent may be reduced, it is still a possibility, and the precautionary principle would require we continue to treat the fetus as an agent. The fetus, however, is not the only being at issue in a case of abortion. The mother is also an important consideration and her status as potential agent must also be considered. Unlike the fetus, the mother does appear to have the ability to form goals and plans to achieve those goals. She is thus an ostensible agent.[32]

The issue of abortion is likely to involve a dispute between the mother's generic rights and the generic rights of the fetus. It is also very unlikely, due to the physical connection between the mother and the fetus (at least with current medical science), that the conflict between the mother's rights and the fetus' rights can be resolved by respecting the rights of both parties. In other words, the likelihood is that any resolution of the case will require that either the mother's or the fetus's rights be given priority over the other. The prioritization part of the precautionary principle must then be applied. Since the mother is an ostensible agent while the fetus is only a potential agent, the mother is more likely to be an agent than the fetus. Her rights would therefore be given priority over the rights of the fetus. This should increase the probability that all agents involved have their rights respected and the PGC has not been broken. It is also illuminating to note that this type of logical analysis can help to resolve other problems involving the termination of a fetus where the mother did not want an abortion, as occurred in the *Vo* case.[33] In such a case, the generic rights of the mother would not be in conflict with the generic rights of the fetus. It is possible, then, to respect the generic rights of both parties. This would allow scope for granting the fetus rights in a situation such as the *Vo* case without abortion becoming more suspect.

Neonaticide, however, must be examined differently. Using the dignitarian approach, the mother would still be an ostensible agent.[34] The newborn, like the

[31] Beyleveld, and Brownsword, *Human Dignity*, 122–34. Of course, part of the determination of the likelihood of agency for a fetus depends on how far along the fetus is in its development. However, even if the discussion involves a fetus the moment before the birthing process begins, it would still only seem to be at best a potential agent.

[32] The only reason this is phrased in non-definite terms is because, as noted previously, the only agent one can be completely sure about is oneself.

[33] *Vo v France* (2005) 10 EHRR 12, where a mother went into the hospital and, through the negligence of hospital staff, the fetus she was carrying was terminated. The mother did not wish a termination. The European Court of Human Rights decided that France had not violated the rights of the mother and declined to decide whether the fetus would have had rights under Article 2 of the European Convention on Human Rights.

[34] It would also be possible to bring in other ostensible agents at this point such as the father. Of course, it is also possible to bring in the interests of other ostensible agents such as the father in the

fetus, would only be a potential agent, since the process of being born would not seem to cause any change as to whether the being in question is capable of being an agent. Consequently, both the mother and the newborn, while perhaps not agents, should be considered as such because of our imperfect knowledge. Thus, we should, as far as possible, find ways to resolve any conflict that respects the generic rights of both parties. While that is not possible in a case of termination prior to birth, we now have a situation where the newborn is physically separate from the mother. This makes a significant difference, as there now exists the possibility of respecting both parties' generic rights. If the mother, for example, no longer felt capable of providing for the severely disabled child, there are additional options such as adoption, care by the father, or state care that enable us to respect the rights of both parties, options which were not available in the case of termination prior to birth. Since it is possible to respect the generic rights of both parties, we ought to do so, as it will increase our chances of satisfying the PGC by respecting the rights of all possible agents.[35]

Thus, using the dignitarian approach outlined above, it is possible to provide a logically consistent ethical reason for allowing the abortion of severely disabled fetuses while not allowing the killing of severely disabled newborns. However, there are concerns with this approach that should be identified when considering whether it provides a firm grounding for the intuitive belief in the result reached.

First, there is something slightly messy about the precautionary principle. The reason we need the principle in the first place is because our knowledge of the world is imperfect. However, having admitted that, by applying the precautionary principle the way out under the dignitarian approach is to use that imperfect knowledge to then make the same distinctions. In other words, in some sense, it appears that Beyleveld and Brownsword appear to be trying to have their cake and eat it too. They admit imperfect knowledge of the world, but then continue to use that knowledge to make ethical decisions. Having said that, it is not as contradictory as it may at first appear. One method of testing the validity of our knowledge about the world is to see if it is coherent. If we have two options when considering which fact about the world to believe, the one which is more consistent with the information we already possess is the one we are likely to accept.

---

case of abortion. However, it seems unlikely that under Beyleveld and Brownsword's approach, the interests of the father would ever outweigh the interests of the mother. The reason for this is that while both would be ostensible agents, the impact on the mother's generic rights (due to her physical connection with the fetus) would be much greater than any impact on the father's generic rights. As such, the rights of the mother would prevail over the rights of the father. Thus, any attempt to prevent an abortion based upon the generic rights of the father would appear to be doomed to fail. Additionally, if one looks at the issue from a legal point of view, there need not be any consideration of the father's rights as they do not take precedence over the mother's right to bodily autonomy. See *Paton v British Pregnancy Advisory Service Trustees* [1979] QB 276.

[35] It is possible that the mother could argue that this resolution would still violate her generic rights because the child's mere existence, whether she cares for it or not, interferes with her goals and life plan. However, this argument is not required by the PGC and, in fact, may be in violation of the PGC. It is therefore an argument we need not consider further.

This does not hold true in all cases, but, generally, we assume things to be true when they coincide with our general views about the world.[36] Such an approach provides some reason to accept that the precautionary principle is valid, despite the apparent discontinuity of the principle.

A second concern with the dignitarian solution to allowing abortions of severely disabled fetuses but not allowing the killing of severely disabled newborns is that there is still the hint of preference for the stronger party. As noted, in the case of abortion, we prefer the rights of the mother to the rights of the fetus, and the mother is the stronger party (in a legal sense at least).[37] However, while this is true in the case of abortion, it is not necessarily the case when considering neonaticide. As noted above, the mother may still feel her rights are being infringed if a severely disabled child survives whom she does not want. Yet, in such a case, the newborn's generic rights would still be protected even if the mother's interests are frustrated as a result. Thus, the stronger party is not always to be preferred under the dignitarian approach. It is only in circumstances where there is no other way to resolve the dispute other than to place the rights of one possible agent over the rights of another possible agent that this becomes an issue. Even then, though, the party that wins is not necessarily the stronger party, but the one which has the greatest likelihood of being an agent.

A final concern with the dignitarian approach outlined above is that it actually proves too much. Since non-disabled fetuses would also not classify as agents, the dignitarian approach can provide a basis to argue for abortion generally, and is not specific to severe disability. Additionally, since the mother's generic rights take precedence over the generic rights of the fetus, this would seem to justify abortion on 'social grounds' up until the moment of birth, instead of the time limits in use in the UK at the present time.[38] There are several possible solutions to this particular problem. We may decide to accept the truth of that assertion and change the current law on abortion. Alternatively, we might change the criteria for agency, meaning that fetuses after a certain age would qualify as agents. Finally, we could re-examine the impact of abortion on the mother's generic rights in the case of late term abortion. Of these, the second option appears to be the least appealing of the three, as it would invariably change most of the dignitarian approach as it is currently stated. Thus, either the first or third approach seems to be preferable. Whilst it is beyond the scope of this chapter to determine which of the two remaining approaches best sits within the dignitarian approach, this problem warrants future research and investigation.

---

[36] Such approaches are referred to as coherence theories of truth. For a more complete discussion on coherence theories, see R. Kirkham, *Theories of Truth* (Cambridge, MA: MIT Press, 1992) 104–12.

[37] See, for example, *Paton v Trustees of British Pregnancy Advisory Services* [1979] QB 276.

[38] Under the Abortion Act 1967, s 1(1)(a).

## 5. Conclusion

In conclusion, the current law allows for the late term abortion of a severely disabled fetus, but does not allow the intentional killing of the same being once it has become a severely disabled newborn after birth. Additionally, such a legal situation appears to attract much intuitive support from the general public. However, under either of the pro-life stances mentioned above, or under the personhood stance, this difference between late term abortion and the killing of newborns appears to be logically inconsistent. Utilizing the dignitarian approach of Beyleveld and Brownsword, however, provides a logically consistent ethical justification for the continued support of this legal position. While the approach does not solve all of the problems associated with end-of-life treatment at the beginning of life, it does provide an answer to the general perceived inconsistency between allowing the abortion of severely disabled fetuses and prohibiting the intentional killing of severely disabled newborns.

# 11

# Terminating Life and Human Rights: The Fetus and the Neonate

*Elizabeth Wicks*

## 1. Introduction

A severely disabled child is vulnerable to decisions to terminate his or her life both before and after birth. However, the fetus and the neonate are treated very differently by the criminal law because of the predominance of birth as a starting point for legal rights and interests. While both abortion and neonaticide are prima facie criminal offences, the former's wide-ranging statutory defences mean that the criminality of a termination of pregnancy is tempered by an appreciation of the relevance of the fetus's condition (as well as maternal health) to decisions about continuance of the pregnancy. The same entity is therefore treated in different ways before and after its journey down the birth canal and, while serious handicap (and, more broadly, an actual or potential poor quality of life) opens doors to a termination of life throughout this process, the means, justifications, and implications of the ending of life vary to such an extent that we might wonder whether it is the same entity in question at all. This chapter will consider the significance of birth as a key point in the criminal law's treatment of a fetus/neonate (and specifically one who is suffering from a serious handicap) and will evaluate the significance of human rights law to the issue.

## 2. The legal significance of birth

### 2.1 Termination of pregnancy for fetal abnormality

A severely disabled fetus can be actively killed, by means of a termination of pregnancy for fetal abnormality under section 1(1)(d) of the Abortion Act 1967, at any stage of gestation, including, in theory, the day before full term. Three legal conditions must be satisfied in order for this active killing to be legal. First, the mother of the fetus must consent. A termination of pregnancy is a form of (albeit controversial) medical treatment and English law prioritizes the need for consent to all treatment as a means of enforcing the ethical principle of autonomy which underlies all medical law.[1] The need for consent is subject to the requirement of capacity and therefore both minors and mentally incompetent mothers may find that a refusal of consent to a termination of pregnancy is not effective.[2]

The second requirement for a legal termination is that two doctors are willing to certify in good faith that there is 'a substantial risk of serious handicap' if the child is born. The terms 'substantial' and 'serious' are both open to (mis-)interpretation.[3] This issue was brought into the public eye by a judicial review application concerning a late termination on a fetus diagnosed as suffering from a cleft palate. A trainee vicar, Joanna Jepson, alleged that a cleft palate could never be regarded as a 'serious' handicap and sought a judicial review of the decision not to prosecute the doctors who performed this termination. The case was stayed in order for the police to conduct an inquiry into the matter. Public and media debate ensued on the question of whether a cleft palate is or can be (or is indicative of) a serious handicap and more broadly on the appropriateness of a twenty-four week time limit on most terminations and the permissibility of later terminations. Much of the discussion missed the crucial point that the Abortion Act does not require an objectively 'serious handicap' (or 'substantial risk') but merely a certification by two doctors in good faith that both aspects exist. The requirement of good faith is notoriously difficult to disprove and probably explains the failure to prosecute in this case.[4] The final requirement for a legal termination is that it be performed by a registered practitioner. If these three requirements are satisfied, a disabled fetus can be actively killed *in utero*.

---

[1] For an eloquent explanation of the connection between consent and autonomy, see Judge LJ's comments in *St George's Healthcare NHS Trust v Strasbourg; R v Collins, ex Strasbourg* [1998] 3 All ER 673, at 688: 'how can a forced invasion of a competent adult's body against his will even for the most laudable of motives (the preservation of life) be ordered without immediately damaging the principle of self-determination? When human life is at stake the pressure to provide an affirmative answer authorising unwanted medical intervention is very powerful. Nevertheless, the autonomy of each individual requires continuing protection even, perhaps particularly, when the motive for interfering with it is readily understandable, and indeed to many would appear commendable . . .'

[2] In *Re SS* (2001) 1 FLR 445, however, Wall J refused to authorize a termination of pregnancy for a mental patient on the basis that it had not been proved that a termination would be any less distressing for the patient than carrying the child to full term. The fact that the application to the court was only received a day before the statutory 24-week limit (in s 1(1)(a) of the Abortion Act 1967, as amended) was criticized by the judge and was probably crucial to the decision.

[3] The vagueness of the terms is deliberate. As the then Lord Chancellor, Lord Mackay of Clashfern, explained in the parliamentary debates on the 1990 amendment to the 1967 Act: 'It is surely impossible to take an absolutely certain view of these cases. It is a matter of opinion, and the requirement is that the opinion should be formed in good faith.' (*Hansard*, vol 522, col 1098)

[4] Only one case has been brought against a doctor under the Abortion Act 1967, *R v Smith* [1973] 1 WLR 1510, and here the facts were quite extreme. The doctor in this case had failed to make any genuine medical assessment of the woman seeking an abortion and this, coupled with other actions characteristic of a lack of good faith such as a failure to inform the patient of the need for a second opinion and excessive fees, led the court to convict him of unlawfully procuring a miscarriage.

## 2.2 Post-natal termination of life

By contrast, once that same child is delivered, the possibility of a legal active kill-ing vanishes. This is because the law treats the newborn as a full human being, equal to all others, and thus protected from any act causing death by the homi-cide laws. The personhood argument, as advocated by Harris, takes a different view, arguing for a distinction between human beings and 'persons'.[5] In Harris' view, persons are human beings capable of valuing their own lives.[6] The lives of those humans (and non-humans) who lack such capacity, do not have value and thus do not require legal protection. He argues that '[t]he reason it is wrong to kill a person is that to do so robs that individual of something they value, and of the very thing that makes possible valuing anything at all... Creatures that cannot value their own existence cannot be wronged in this way, for their death deprives them of nothing that they can value'.[7] There is no doubt that the judicial attitude to those Harris would regard as non-persons—Anthony Bland, the conjoined twin Mary, for example—could suggest that their lives are less valuable than the typical competent, healthy adult. Bland's life could legally be ended by the with-drawal of artificial hydration and nutrition, apparently without any violation of the right to life.[8] Mary was the first living human being to be killed by an inten-tional act without any legal liability ensuing to the perpetuators.[9] Harris's theory would justify such a difference in treatment, as he has explained in the context of the conjoined twins case.[10] However, the personhood theory is open to criti-cism because it creates inequality between human beings, fundamentally at odds with the equality underlying modern human rights law. Within the European Convention on Human Rights (ECHR), for example, it is explicitly required under Article 14 that the enjoyment of the rights and freedoms set forth in the Convention shall be secured without discrimination on any ground. This will include discrimination on the basis of disability, illness, and life expectancy. The importance of securing rights without discrimination rests not only in ensuring

---

[5] See J. Harris, *The Value of Life: An Introduction to Medical Ethics* (London: Routledge, 1985).

[6] This view draws support from both Kant, who regarded personhood as rational moral agency, and Locke, who emphasized reflective consciousness. For a recent discussion of varying views on personhood against a medical ethics background, see M. Ford, 'The Personhood Paradox and the "Right to Die"', *Medical Law Review*, 13/1 (2005), 80–101.

[7] Harris, *The Value of Life*, 18–19.

[8] *Airedale NHS Trust v Bland* [1993] 1 All ER 831. In *NHS Trust A v M; NHS Trust B v H* [2001] 2 WLR 942, Dame Butler-Sloss, the President of the Family Division, confirmed that withdrawing artificial nutrition and hydration from a patient in PVS was not a violation of his or her right to life, provided that the continuation of the treatment was no longer in the patient's best interests.

[9] *Re A (Children) (Conjoined Twins: Surgical Separation)* [2000] 4 All ER 961. The doctrine of necessity was expanded to provide a justification for the doctors' actions. See E. Wicks, 'The Greater Good? Issues of Proportionality and Democracy in the Doctrine of Necessity as Applied in *Re A*', *Common Law World Review*, 32 (2003), 15–34 for criticism of this use of the necessity doctrine.

[10] J. Harris, 'Human Beings, Persons and Conjoined Twins: An Ethical Analysis of the Judgment in *Re A*', *Medical Law Review*, 9/3 (2001), 221–36, 235–6.

equality for all persons but also in preserving the integrity of the rights themselves. If some living human beings are not protected in law from an intentional deprivation of their life, the fundamental right to life is irretrievably undermined. English law has reassuringly always taken the unambiguous view that all human beings are protected by the homicide laws, regardless of whether their lives have either objective, or subjective, value. However severely disabled an infant may be, and however lacking in capacity to value its life, the law itself regards it as of some value and prohibits any intentional taking of it by means of an unlawful act.

It is possible, however, that treatment of a severely disabled neonate can cease, or not commence, and that death may ensue in this way. The only legal condition for this is that treatment would not be in the best interests of the neonate, as judged by a doctor acting in accordance with a responsible body of medical opinion.[11] The issue of treating severely disabled neonates was clarified by the Court of Appeal in the case of *Re J*.[12] The patient in this case was a premature baby born at 27 weeks who was suffering from convulsions and breathing difficulties, as well as severe brain damage due to a shortage of oxygen and impaired blood supply at the time of birth. Even the most optimistic prognosis included paralysis of the arms and legs, blindness and deafness, an inability to sit up or hold the head upright, unlikely to speak or have any intellectual abilities, and a likelihood of feeling pain. The question for the court was whether the child should be placed on a ventilator if this became necessary due to breathing difficulties. The Court of Appeal confirmed that this issue must be decided solely on the basis of the patient's best interests which must be determined by a balancing exercise performed by the doctors. The baby's quality of life was recognized as relevant to a determination of medical best interests[13] and the Court of Appeal concluded that it would not be in the baby's best interests to reventilate if his breathing should cease again.

More recently in *Wyatt v Portsmouth NHS Trust*,[14] the Court of Appeal again confirmed that best interests remains the only test for the determination

---

[11] This is based upon the infamous *Bolam* test, derived from *Bolam v Friern Hospital Management Committee* [1957] 2 All ER 118 and extended into the treatment of incompetent patients arena by the House of Lords in *Re F (Mental Patient: Sterilisation)* [1990] 2 AC 51. Its suitability in this context has been doubted by both academics and senior members of the judiciary. In *Re S (Adult Patient: Sterilisation)* [2000] 3 WLR 1288, the Court of Appeal emphasized that the final decision on best interests must rest with the judge and yet medical evidence as to the patient's interests remains crucial.

[12] *Re J (a minor) (medical treatment)* [1992] 4 All ER 614.

[13] The relevance of quality of life can also require that treatment continue. This was first apparent in the Court of Appeal decision in *Re B (a minor)* [1990] 3 All ER 927, a case involving a baby born with Down's syndrome and also suffering from an intestinal blockage which would be fatal without an operation. The parents refused to consent to the operation as they regarded the additional complications as nature's way of allowing the Down's baby to die. Medical evidence made clear that without the operation the baby would die within days but with the operation it was possible that she may live a normal Down's lifespan of 20–30 years. On the basis of this evidence, the Court of Appeal made the child a ward of court and authorized the operation.

[14] [2005] 1 WLR 3995.

of treatment of a severely ill baby and that this test does not necessarily require that the child is suffering intolerably because broader quality of life judgments are relevant. Charlotte Wyatt was born prematurely at 26 weeks. She suffered from chronic respiratory and kidney problems and severe brain damage. Her doctors believed that ventilation in the event of an infection which leads, or might lead, to a collapsed lung would not be in her best interests. This view was based on the doctors' belief that such ventilation might kill Charlotte or, if she survived, it would merely be a painful process which would bring no improvement to her condition.[15] A disagreement between Charlotte's parents and her doctors led the hospital to seek and obtain a court declaration that ventilation would not be in the patient's best interests. The parents subsequently applied for the discharge of the declarations on the basis that their daughter's condition had improved significantly. A pessimistic conclusion by Hedley J, based on medical evidence, that there was a high probability that Charlotte would die within a few months, had proven to be in error and there was no doubt that some positive improvements in Charlotte's condition had occurred. The judge noted that she was no longer wholly unresponsive, nor in such discomfort as to require sedation. In other words, her condition was regarded as no longer 'intolerable' by the judge.[16] Nevertheless, the judge accepted the majority medical evidence that invasive methods would still not be in the baby's best interests.[17] Permission to appeal on the best interests question was refused but an appeal on other issues only led to confirmation of the judge's approach. In particular, the Court of Appeal confirmed Hedley J's approach that the issue of intolerability of suffering is not a supplementary test to, or even a gloss on, the best interests test but merely a factor that may be relevant amongst others.[18]

## 2.3 Comparison of the legal position pre- and post-birth

A number of interesting points arise from the above comparison between the options for treating a severely disabled fetus and neonate. First, the mother is cast in a curious position. As the person most intimately connected with the child, we might expect her to play a significant role in protecting the interests of the child. However, she is only legally empowered to do so before birth. By refusing consent to a termination of pregnancy, the mother is legally empowered to preserve the life of her unborn child but once that child is born, the mother's (and indeed the

---

[15]  Ibid, at para 13.       [16]  Ibid, at para 32.
[17]  Ibid, at para 37.
[18]  In justifying the decision in *Re B*, Templeman LJ had described the issue for the court as 'whether the life of this child is demonstrably going to be so awful that in effect the child must be condemned to die.' (at 929). This wording was subsequently criticized in *Re J (a minor) (wardship: medical treatment)* [1990] 3 All ER 930, where Taylor LJ regarded it as 'more emotive than accurate' (at 944). *Wyatt* now makes even more clear that intolerability of suffering is not required in order for life-sustaining treatment to be withdrawn.

father's) view will no longer be conclusive. Cases such as the 1992 case of *Re J (a minor)*[19] have demonstrated that, if the doctors do not regard continued treatment to be in the child's best interests, the mother's wish to save her child will be ineffective.[20] This was also indicated in the conjoined twins case of *Re A*, where the mother was able to validly refuse an abortion of the weaker twin, Mary, but was unable to prevent the killing of Mary after birth,[21] even though her views remained unchanged. It seems that at this stage (that is after birth) society, in the form of the medical profession and the courts, acquire a legitimate interest in the life (and death) of the child. Thus, once the child is born, the mother is no longer regarded by the law as the primary determinator of the child's best interests. The mother is surely best placed to protect the child's interests, but her ability to do so becomes significantly weaker once the child is born.

The second interesting point to emerge from the comparison of the handicapped fetus and neonate is that the death of a severely handicapped fetus is always optional because it is dependent upon the doctors' assessment and the mother's choice. By contrast, in some limited cases, the severely handicapped neonate's death is effectively mandatory, because treatment cannot legally be imposed if it is not regarded as in the child's best interests.

Thirdly, the legal conditions for a termination of pregnancy for fetal abnormality omit three key factors which become relevant once the child is born. First, the best interests of the fetus, which is the only relevant factor after birth, is not expressly relevant to the legality of a termination of pregnancy. This is not to imply that fetal interests are not taken into account both by the mother and by the doctors (and, indeed, the fetal abnormality ground for a legal termination, section 1(1)(d), is sometimes, controversially, regarded as existing for the benefit of the future child as well as for the benefit of the parents and wider family[22]) but there is no legal obligation upon either party to have regard to the interests of the

[19] In this case, the mother tried to ensure intensive care for her child who had suffered severe brain damage but the court refused to force the doctors to provide treatment against their clinical judgement.

[20] This is also apparent in the *Wyatt* case, discussed above, in which the parents' desire to continue treatment in all circumstances has repeatedly been overruled in light of the medical evidence that treatment is not in the child's best interests.

[21] Unusually, in this case, the post-natal killing was by means of an act rather than an omission to treat because of the unique conflict between Mary's rights and that of her stronger twin sister, Jodie. The Court of Appeal's sanctioning of what would normally amount to murder by the doctors was expressly limited to the unique situation of conjoined twins and should not be used as a precedent for the active killing of any other severely disabled infant with a comparable poor quality of life.

[22] Morgan argues that ground (d) is 'primarily a fetal interests ground and not a parental interests ground, nor a state (eugenic) interest provision'. (D. Morgan, 'Abortion: The Unexamined Ground', *Criminal Law Review* [1990] 687–94, 692.) The justification for this view is that the mother's interests are adequately served by the other grounds in s 1, that is, through the harm to mental health or existing children grounds. However, Morgan's view carries with it the difficulty that, if a termination of pregnancy for fetal abnormality is in the fetal interest, surely it should be compulsory once a substantial risk of a serious handicap has been identified?

fetus when making a decision. Secondly, the method of death, which is crucial once the child is born, due to the act/omission distinction in English criminal law, apparently has little application before birth. The offence of procuring a miscarriage can be committed by administering 'any poison or other noxious thing' or by the use of 'any instrument or other means whatsoever'[23] and the Abortion Act 1967 (as amended) provides defences to this offence howsoever committed.[24] If the method of death *in utero* were to be regarded as of legal importance, the question would be raised whether it is potential for physical distress to the fetus or mental distress to the mother which is of prime concern. Finally, once the child is born alive, the issue of the human rights of that child becomes crucial, whereas in respect of the fetus the issue of rights is much more ambiguous. It is to this issue of human rights law that we must now turn.

## 3. The right to life of the child: Before and after birth

### 3.1 The right to life after birth

Article 2 of the ECHR, now incorporated into domestic law by means of the Human Rights Act 1998, protects the right to life. It declares that 'everyone's right to life shall be protected by law'. It may be noted that the Article does not declare that everyone is entitled to a right to life but, rather, that this pre-existing right must be given legal protection. This suggests that the Convention is merely recognizing that this fundamental human right must be protected by law within the contracting European states. After requiring that everyone's right to life shall be protected by law, Article 2 of the ECHR continues by declaring that 'No one shall be deprived of his life intentionally'. This requirement has been interpreted in domestic cases as not requiring the continuation of life-sustaining treatment if it is futile. For example, in *A National Health Service Trust v D*,[25] Cazalet J granted a declaration that it would be lawful not to resuscitate a child suffering from irreversible lung disease and multi-organ failure in the event of a further cardio-respiratory arrest. The judge held that this was in the best interests of the child and that, therefore, Article 2's protection of the right to life was not infringed. The judge also suggested that Article 3's prohibition on inhuman and degrading treatment incorporated the idea of dying with dignity. The judgment contains little reasoning on either point, however.

---

[23] Offences Against the Persons Act 1861, s 58. The *actus reus* of child destruction is similarly satisfied by 'any wilful act' causing the death of a child capable of being born alive (Infant Life (Preservation) Act 1929, s 1).

[24] Section 1(1) states that: 'Subject to the provisions of this section, a person shall not be guilty of an offence under the law relating to abortion . . .'

[25] (2000) 55 BMLR 19.

In *NHS Trust A v M; NHS Trust B v H*[26] in 2001, Dame Butler-Sloss, the President of the Family Division, confirmed that incompetent patients (in this case, adult patients in a persistent vegetative state (PVS)) do not have their human rights violated when life-sustaining treatment is withdrawn. Dame Butler-Sloss considered in some detail whether Article 2 was consistent with the withdrawal of artificial nutrition and hydration from a patient in PVS. She divided the issue into two parts reflecting the two aspects of Article 2: a negative and a positive obligation. First, she queried whether an omission to provide life-sustaining treatment was an 'intentional deprivation of life', which is prohibited in Article 2, and concluded that it was not because the phrase requires a deliberate act, as opposed to an omission. This conclusion has been subject to some justified criticism.[27] There is no obvious reason why a person cannot be deprived of his or her life by an omission to act just as easily as by a positive act.

Dame Butler-Sloss then proceeded to consider the other obligation under Article 2, namely the positive obligation to preserve life. This was first identified by the European Court of Human Rights in *Osman v United Kingdom*,[28] when it held that public authorities (the police in that case) must do all that is reasonable to avoid a real and immediate risk to life. In certain situations this could require the continuation of life-sustaining medical treatment. However, Dame Butler-Sloss sought, in an extremely unsatisfactory manner, to superimpose the domestic best interests test onto the requirements of Article 2:

Article 2...imposes a positive obligation to give life-sustaining treatment in circumstances where, according to responsible medical opinion, such treatment is in the best interests of the patient but does not impose an absolute obligation to treat if such treatment would be futile.[29]

The *NHS Trusts* case therefore holds that a state's (and an NHS Trust's) positive obligation to preserve life is discharged if a decision to withdraw life-sustaining treatment is taken in the patient's best interests and supported by a responsible body of medical opinion. On this basis, the withdrawal of treatment from a severely handicapped neonate will not necessarily involve a violation of that child's right to life. However, this reasoning is open to question as it overlooks the fact that the best interests test is not evident in the text of Article 2 and has never been expressly read into it by the Strasbourg institutions. Article 2 does not say that everyone's right to life must be protected by law until the continuation of that life is no longer in the person's own interests. Such an interpretation casts

[26] [2001] 2 WLR 942.
[27] For example, see A. Maclean, 'Crossing the Rubicon on the Human Rights Ferry', *Modern Law Review*, 64 (2001), 775–94, 780, where Maclean argues that both acts and omissions are capable of 'depriving' someone of his life, although he concedes that the omitted act would need to be one that would have been efficacious if performed, and the actor would need to be both capable of performing the act and under an obligation to do so.
[28] (2000) 29 EHRR 245.
[29] *NHS Trust A v M; NHS Trust B v H*, at para 811.

significant doubt upon the applicability of the ethical principle of sanctity of life within Article 2. The domestic cases have so far failed to grapple with the question of whether the right to life under Article 2 seeks to uphold the sanctity of life in a relatively strict form or whether it admits the idea that life has mainly instrumental value. This latter argument may be regarded as garnering some support from the location of Article 2 in a convention primarily concerned with upholding an individual's right to self-determination and freedoms within a democratic society. But domestic judges, including most strikingly Dame Butler-Sloss, have failed to make this argument, or even acknowledge the question, and therefore the *NHS Trusts* case's reconciliation of the domestic best interest principle with Article 2 remains entirely unconvincing.

## 3.2 The right to life before birth

English law has consistently and unambiguously declared that a fetus has no rights or interests until born. For example, in *Paton v British Pregnancy Advisory Service Trustees*, Sir George Baker P held that: 'The fetus cannot, in English law...have a right of its own at least until it is born and has a separate existence from its mother.'[30] This rejection of any rights or interests for the fetus holds good even though (or perhaps because) it has been acknowledged that the fetus is a 'unique organism'.[31] But if English law is clear, the Strasbourg Court has been more ambiguous on the issue. With the incorporation of the Convention rights into English law in the Human Rights Act and the requirement in section 2(1) of that Act that domestic courts 'take account' of the judgments of the Strasbourg institutions, the view of the Strasbourg Court is increasingly vital and yet it has repeatedly refused to decide whether a fetus has any protection under Article 2. The most recent and explicit refusal to decide occurred in the *Vo v France* case.[32]

In this case, a mix-up at a French hospital involving mistaken identity, led to a doctor attempting to remove a coil from the applicant who was in the sixth month of a pregnancy. In doing so, he pierced the amniotic sac, causing substantial loss of amniotic fluid. Owing to this injury, the fetus was damaged and a termination of pregnancy was subsequently necessary. The applicant lodged a criminal complaint alleging, inter alia, the unintentional homicide of her child but the French criminal courts held that a fetus could not be a victim of homicide. The applicant thus complained of a violation of Article 2 ECHR due to the lack of protection for the unborn child under French criminal law.

The crucial part of the judgment is contained in paragraph 85: a few short sentences in which the Strasbourg Court refuses to decide whether the fetus has any protection under Article 2. The Court reaches dual conclusions. First, it concludes that it would be neither desirable nor possible to answer in the abstract

---

[30] [1979] 1 QB 276, 279.  [31] *AG's Reference (No 3 of 1994)* [1997] 3 All ER 936.
[32] (2005) 10 EHRR 12.

whether an unborn child is given protection under Article 2. Secondly, the Court concludes that it is also unnecessary to decide the issue on the facts of the case because, even if the fetus had a right to life, it was not violated here. The basis for this second argument is that a criminal sanction was held not to be required under Article 2 for unintentional homicides. Other legal options, such as negligence, were held to be available under French law and sufficient to satisfy the requirements of Article 2. This refusal to decide the key issue is surely an unacceptable abdication of judicial responsibility. It is not clear how the court feels able to discuss the requirements of the right to life in this case without actually deciding whether such a right even exists. Previous decisions of the Strasbourg institutions such as *Paton v United Kingdom*,[33] had made clear that a right to life for the fetus is, at most, a limited right and yet in this case the Court felt able to conclude that there had been no infringement of the right without clarifying the boundaries of this limited right.

The decision of the Court was not unanimous and the individual judgments reveal some complexity in the division of the Court. Officially there was a fourteen to three majority for the decision that Article 2 had not been violated in this case. The three officially dissenting judges all thought that a fetus has a right to life and that it had been violated in this case. One other judge also agreed that a fetus has a right to life under Article 2 but held that it had not been violated in this case.[34] Five other judges wrote a separate opinion in which they concluded that the fetus does not have any protection under the right to life. In the view of these judges, Article 2 was inapplicable to this case. This leaves eight judges who refused to decide whether the fetus has a right to life or not (with four saying 'yes' and five saying 'no'). What, if anything, can be implied from that refusal?

The unwillingness of the majority to exclude the fetus from Article 2 implies that it does have some protection. Indeed, individual judges who held that either the fetus did or did not have a right to life, all agreed upon this point: discussing the procedural requirements of Article 2, as the majority judgment does, presupposes the applicability of that Article. But, if this is so, the *Vo* judgment leaves us without any guidance as to the boundaries of that limited right to life. What factors might be relevant to forming the boundaries of fetal protection under Article 2? An obvious factor, which is entirely ignored by the majority judgment in *Vo*, is the age of the fetus. If a fetus has a limited, rather than an absolute, right to life, surely its gestation would be a crucial factor in determining the limits of its protection?[35] The Court's failure to explicitly recognize protection for the fetus under Article 2 means that the factors which will limit that protection remain unknown.

[33] (1980) 3 EHRR 408.
[34] The judge in question was Judge Costa and it could be argued that he was actually expressing what the majority of the Court really thought, but for whatever reason did not dare say.
[35] Two of the dissenting judges do mention this issue and conclude that there was a violation in this case because the fetus in question was aged between 20 and 24 weeks and therefore was viable.

One of the opportunities provided by the *Vo* case was the determination of the issue of fetal rights in the absence of the conflicting issue of the rights of the mother. Rarely, in a case on fetal rights, are the mother and the fetus on the same side. In *Vo* they were and thus a decision in principle on the inclusion of the fetus within Article 2 could have been made without the need to resolve the narrower question of conflicting rights, which could really only be dealt with in specific cases where a conflict arises. But, assuming that the Court's failure to rule out any human rights protection for the fetus means that we can imply some such protection, the question of the reconciliation of these rights with those of the mother, should they conflict, must be addressed. This is the key distinguishing factor between the fetus and the neonate: only the former resides within another human being who is also entitled to the full protection of the Convention rights.

## 3.3 The dilemma of conflicting rights: a question of geography?

Some limited guidance on the issue of conflicting rights is available within Article 2 because it is clear from this Article that the right to life is not absolute. A number of situations are specified in this Article in which a life can be intentionally taken without legal consequences and which will not amount to a violation of the fundamental right to life. These situations include the death penalty (subject to more recent moves in international law to prevent the re-introduction of this form of punishment) and acting in self-defence or to effect a lawful arrest. This recognition that the right is not absolute opens the door to consideration of when, and in what circumstances, a person's life can be sacrificed. It should be noted, however, that the idea of a limited right to life is not without conceptual difficulties. There is nothing in the wording of Article 2 to suggest a hierarchy of rights to life. Indeed, the entire concept of human rights is based upon the idea of equality which suggests that all entities that are entitled to a right to life should have an equal right. To give a fetus a right to life but one of a lower order than a living human being is not reconcilable with the ethos of human rights within the ECHR. But it is clearly established in the Convention that many (indeed, the overwhelming majority of) rights are not absolute in all circumstances. Thus a fetus' right to life may be limited by external factors such as, most obviously, its residence within another's body. The fetus is, under this argument, entitled to an equal, but limited, right to life. While this may appear to be semantics, it is vital that any extension of Article 2 to incorporate the unborn does not violate the general principle that no category of persons should be singled out for a lesser right. It is the fetus' location rather than its categorization as a fetus which necessitates reconciliation with other conflicting rights. Similarly, it is the criminal's actions rather than his categorization as a criminal which justifies a restriction of his right to life under Article 2's wording.

The European Court of Human Rights has made clear that if the fetus does have a right to life, it is not a right which can overrule the rights of the mother in the case of a maternal-fetal conflict. In *Paton v United Kingdom*,[36] for example, the possibility of an absolute right to life was ruled out because the mother's rights, as a pre-existing living human being, would have to be prioritized over those of the fetus in situations where the fetus was putting the mother's life at risk. It appears well-established that a fetus' right to life (assuming that it has one) is subject to the overriding right to life of the mother, but what of the other rights of the mother? Can a fetus' right to life be overruled by the mother's right to health? A right to health is not a concept which is specified in the Convention but it is one which could, perhaps, be implied in two ways. First, the prohibition on degrading and inhuman treatment in Article 3 could be relevant if protecting the fetus' right to life entails the woman being forced to continue a pregnancy which is endangering her health. Secondly, the old 'life depends upon health' argument from the case of *R v Bourne* could be used to imply a right to health into the right to life. In *Bourne*,[37] Macnaghten J took two intellectual leaps by concluding, first, that the proviso 'unlawfully' in the offence of procuring a miscarriage[38] incorporated a defence of acting to preserve the life of the mother and, secondly, that life depends upon health and thus that the offence also incorporated a defence of acting to preserve the physical and mental health of the mother. Such intellectual leaps could conceivably be used to imply a right to health into Article 2's protection of the right to life. However, this would ultimately be undesirable because it would inevitably undermine the fundamental nature of the right to life. Other than in the context of law enforcement, the legal protection for everyone's right to life is required to be absolute. In the context of the ECHR, it is unusual in that characteristic. Any interpretation of the right to life which extends it beyond the protection of life itself threatens to weaken the right, and to do so is unnecessary when the ECHR already protects human dignity (in Article 3) and self-determination (in Article 8).

The English law on abortion unambiguously elevates the mother's health interests over those of her unborn child. But this emphasis on the woman's physical and mental health frequently serves merely as a camouflage for the woman's wish to exercise her reproductive autonomy. Such a concept has roots in a number of sources, including academic theory,[39] the right to found a family in Article 12 ECHR,[40] and Article 8's protection for a right to respect for private life. Reproduction self-evidently falls within the category of 'private' matters which

---

[36] (1980) 3 EHRR 408.     [37] *R v Bourne* [1939] 1 KB 687.

[38] Offences Against the Persons Act 1861, s 58.

[39] See R. Dworkin, *Life's Dominion: An Argument about Abortion and Euthanasia* (London: HarperCollins, 1993); J. Harris, 'Rights and Reproductive Choice' in J. Harris, and S. Holm, (eds.), *The Future of Human Reproduction: Ethics, Choice, and Regulation* (Oxford: Clarendon Press, 1998); J. A. Robertson, *Children of Choice: Freedom and the New Reproductive Technologies* (Princeton: Princeton University Press, 1994).

[40] This is not an absolute right and contains potentially the most wide-ranging limitation of any of the Convention rights: the right is expressed as subject to 'the national law governing the exercise of this right'.

find protection in Article 8 and could easily have been used to establish a right to choose in respect of abortion[41] but the European Commission of Human Rights has declined to do so, holding in *Bruggemann and Scheuten* that pregnancy is not solely a private issue.[42] The Commission's reluctance to acknowledge the right to an abortion is probably due to the potential implications across Europe if all limitations upon access to legal abortion were regarded as a violations of the mother's rights. However, this is an exaggerated concern because admitting a prima facie right to choose in respect of terminating a pregnancy need not prevent all state limitations on abortion. Article 8 protects individual self-determination in many different contexts but simultaneously permits a wide range of limitations upon that freedom. Restrictions upon abortion in terms of gestation, or method, or the need for reasons (health or otherwise) could comfortably be accommodated within the permissible limitations which are 'in accordance with the law' and 'necessary in a democratic society' for the protection of health or morals, or the protection of the rights and freedoms of others. Or, at the very least, it may be within a state's margin of appreciation (that is area of discretion) to regard these as justifiable limitations.

The discussion has so far assumed that the conflicting right is that of the mother. However, it is conceivable that the mother may choose a termination of pregnancy for reason of fetal abnormality because she regards this as in the interests of the fetus. Could such a decision overrule the fetus' right to life? Would it then be comparable to a decision that continuing to treat a handicapped neonate is not in its best interests? As discussed above, the difficulty with this conception of a termination of pregnancy for fetal anomaly is that it would require the procedure to be compulsory in situations where it is not in the fetus' best interests to be born alive. In the context of the right to life, assuming that the fetus has the protection of Article 2, the reasoning from the *NHS Trusts* case could perhaps be applied to prevent a violation of the right to life when life is no longer in the fetus' best interests. However, this presents two problems. First, a termination of pregnancy is an act rather than omission and thus the reasoning in the *NHS Trusts* case cannot be directly applied and, secondly, that reasoning is extremely unconvincing even in its original context. The best view, therefore, is that, although the fetal right to life can be overruled by the mother's rights, a violation of it cannot be justified on the basis of post-natal suffering for the disabled child.

[41] In Canada, a right to choose has been implied into the right to security of the person. Section 7 of the Canadian Charter of Rights and Freedoms declares that: 'Everyone has the right to life, liberty and security of the person and the right not to be deprived thereof except in accordance with the principles of fundamental justice.' The Canadian Supreme Court held in *R v Morgentaler* [1988] 1 SCR 30 that: 'Forcing a woman, by threat of criminal sanction, to carry a fetus to term unless she meets certain criteria unrelated to her own priorities and aspirations, is a profound interference with a woman's body and thus a violation of security of the person' (per Dickson CJ, at 56).

[42] (1977) 10 DR 100. The applicants in this case complained that a change in the criminal law on abortion in the Federal Republic of Germany, which meant that abortion was no longer available on demand in the first 12 weeks of pregnancy, amounted to an interference with their right to respect for private life. The Commission rejected this argument, holding that 'pregnancy cannot be said to pertain uniquely to the sphere of private life' (at para 59).

## 3.4 The development of human life: the significance of gestation and/or birth

Finally, an obvious factor which will be relevant to establishing the boundaries of fetal protection under Article 2 is the age of the fetus. If a fetus has a limited, rather than absolute, right to life, and this much is clear, then its gestation will be a crucial factor in determining the limits of its protection. This brings us back to the issue of the protection offered to a human entity as it develops from a fetus to a baby. It is a truism to describe the beginning of life as a process and, ultimately, this assists little in determining the appropriate way to treat a fetus and/or neonate suffering from a severe disability other than justifying the obvious conclusion that an eight-week-old baby should be given greater legal protection than an eight-week-old fetus. Two questions remain unanswered: is birth the most suitable stage at which to transform the legal protection; and does legal protection necessarily require the preservation of life, regardless of suffering?

The stage at which legal protection for human life should begin is an issue of constant disagreement. Conception, implantation, viability, and birth all have individual merits but choosing any one of these is ultimately an arbitrary decision.[43] If a conventional line is drawn, conception is the earliest candidate for the location of such a line and has some religious support but is unrealistic as it would require not only all abortions but also some contraceptive methods to be prohibited. The pill, for example, not only works to prevent fertilization but also changes the womb lining to make it reject fertilized eggs and thus prevent implantation. Is this murder? If so, we should, as Mason has noted, also regard each menstrual period as a potential for mourning as 'untold numbers of zygotes are lost daily on a worldwide basis'.[44] The inappropriateness, not to mention the futility, of seeking to legally protect all human life from conception, particularly when such protection will inevitably involve legal restraints upon the mother's freedom, is what leads many to reject this early starting point for legal protection. A slightly later starting point—implantation of the fertilized egg into the womb—suffers from similar criticisms, although it is to some extent the starting point for legal protection of the fetus in the UK due to the criminal offence of procuring a miscarriage.[45]

---

[43] Glover explains that any boundary between a person and non (or pre) person is man-made: 'To ask "When does one start to be a person?" is like asking "when does middle age begin?" Conventional lines for social or legal purposes could always be drawn, but we would be mistaken if we took the shadows cast by these lines for boundaries in biological reality' (J. Glover, *Causing Death and Saving Lives* (London: Penguin, 1977), 127).

[44] J. K. Mason, *Medico-Legal Aspects of Reproduction and Parenthood* (2nd edn, Aldershot: Dartmouth Publishing, 1998), 109–10.

[45] Section 58 of the Offences Against the Person Act 1861 contains the criminal offence of procuring a miscarriage. In *R (application of Smeaton) v Secretary of State for Health* [2002] 2 FLR 146, the court had to consider whether the effect of the 'morning after' pill, which serves to prevent implantation of a fertilized egg, amounts to procuring a miscarriage and thus is a criminal

Viability is a far more realistic point at which an unborn life is entitled to protection of the law. Once a fetus is capable of being born alive and has the potential to survive independently of its mother's body, there is a strong argument that the issue is no longer one internal to the mother but rather one which the state and its laws should regulate. However, as convincing as this argument is, viability remains an incomplete solution to the problem because it is a shifting boundary dependent upon the state of modern technology and its availability to a particular fetus. As Glover argues: 'There seems to be something absurd about a moving boundary, so that we might say "last year this fetus would not have been a person at this stage, but since they re-equipped the intensive care unit, it is one." This just does not seem to be the morally significant boundary people are looking for.'[46] This returns us to birth: a clear and unambiguous point in time and thus the most appropriate stage in the continuous development of a human being at which to transform the legal protection of life from a right subject to another's rights into a right equal to that of all others.

The second unanswered question raised above is whether legal *protection* for life necessarily requires the *preservation* of life, regardless of suffering. This question depends upon one's view of the sanctity of life. Keown helpfully outlines three different approaches to the issue of the valuation of human life.[47] First, there is the 'vitalism' approach which regards human life as an absolute moral value and considers it to always be wrong to either shorten life or fail to lengthen it, regardless of considerations of pain, suffering, or expense. As Keown sensibly notes, this approach is 'as ethically untenable as its attempt to maintain life indefinitely is physically impossible'.[48] At the other extreme of the valuation of human life outlined by Keown is the 'Quality of life'. This approach assesses the worthwhileness of the patient's life (rather than the proposed treatment) and regards certain lives as not worth living and therefore susceptible to intentional termination. Keown criticizes this approach for denying 'the ineliminable value of each patient' and for engaging in potentially discriminatory judgments.[49] It certainly poses seemingly insurmountable problems for a right to life based upon the inherent equality of all human lives. Finally, Keown outlines the 'sanctity of life' approach which holds that we ought never to intentionally kill an innocent human being, but does not regard life as an absolute good and therefore there is no moral obligation to preserve life by imposing treatment which is not worthwhile 'either because it offers no reasonable hope of benefit or because, even

---

offence under the 1861 Act. Munby J held that the prevention of implantation does not amount to procuring a miscarriage (because, inter alia, there has as yet been no 'carriage'). The 1861 offence, therefore, applies only to post-implantation. Some commentators strongly disagree with this conclusion. See J. Keown, ' "Morning After" Pills, "Miscarriage" and Muddle', *Legal Studies*, 25 (2005), 296–319.

[46] Glover, *Causing Death and Saving Lives*, 125.

[47] J. Keown, 'Restoring Moral and Intellectual Shape to the Law after Bland', *Law Quarterly Review*, 113 (1997), 481–503.

[48] Ibid, 482.    [49] Ibid, 487.

though it does, the expected benefit would be outweighed by burdens which the treatment would impose, such as excessive pain'.[50] This approach is the one most in line with Article 2's protection for the right to life because the Article prohibits the intentional deprivation of life and imposes some limited positive obligations upon the state to preserve life. If we accept Keown's sanctity of life approach as the one most consistent with the right to life, and one which has gained some judicial support,[51] human life has value regardless of its quality but the state will not face an absolute obligation to preserve it at all costs.[52] This is the only realistic interpretation of Article 2 which, while imposing positive obligations to preserve life where there is a real and immediate risk to life, has been interpreted by the Strasbourg Court as incorporating a need for the state to balance resources in doing so.[53] Such a limited right to state preservation of life leaves room for the withdrawal of life-sustaining treatment if it is futile or counter-productive. When dealing with a living human being, however, the assumption must always be to preserve life in line with his or her fundamental right to life, regardless of the interests or rights of others. It is this strong assumption which most starkly distinguishes the handicapped fetus from the neonate.

## 4. Conclusion

The criminal law's involvement at the beginning of human life is extensive. The fetus is protected by the criminal law prohibition on the procurement of a miscarriage, although this protection is significantly tempered nowadays by the existence of broad defences. Once born alive, the neonate is included within the general criminal law prohibition on homicide, although this is also tempered somewhat by the controversial application of an act/omission distinction to issues of criminal liability. The approach of the criminal law in these two contexts reflects the status of fetal and neonatal life in human rights law, specifically the application of the right to life to these two entities. The idea of a fetal right to life, but one which is subject to the mother's rights until birth, ties in well with the idea mentioned earlier of the mother as the most appropriate protector of her child's rights: she can ensure that the fetus' limited rights are not violated by a third party but can also feel safe in the knowledge that her rights, as an already living human being entitled to the full protection of Article 2 and other human rights, will be

---

[50] Ibid, 485.

[51] Ward LJ in *Re A* quoted Keown's definition of sanctity of life with approval and confirmed that 'each life has inherent value in itself and the right to life, being universal, is equal for all of us. The sanctity of life doctrine does, however, acknowledge that it may be proper to withhold or withdraw treatment' (at 1000).

[52] The Court of Appeal's decision in *R (on the application of Burke) v General Medical Council* [2005] 2 FLR 1223 is consistent with this approach.

[53] *Osman v United Kingdom* (2000) 29 EHRR 245.

prioritized by the law. Once the fetus is born alive, the question of a mother's conflicting rights no longer arises. The neonate is a human being, entitled to the full and equal protection of his or her human rights, including both a right to life and a right to be free from degrading treatment. It is impossible to escape the problem of conflicting rights, therefore, but post-birth the conflict is between the child's differing rights and not between the mother and child. The treatment of severely handicapped neonates is a perennially difficult dilemma for doctors, parents, and the judiciary. General rules, particularly drawn from an academic paper, will ultimately be unhelpful. The key, however, is that the neonate is treated as a full human being entitled to legal protection for its fundamental rights. We are concerned, after all, with human rights, not 'person' rights. Once a human is born alive, regardless of disability, prognosis, potential lifespan, or pain and suffering, the entity becomes a beneficiary of human rights law. This, in itself, is the underlying reason for the difference in treatment which occurs at birth.

# 12

# Non-treatment of Severely Disabled Newborns and Criminal Liability Under Spanish Law[1]

*Sergio Romeo-Malanda*

## 1. Introduction: The issue from the Spanish perspective

Developments in medical technology and medical science have revolutionized modern medical practice over the past two decades, and have created novel ethical and legal dilemmas for medical practitioners. A particularly difficult dilemma in paediatric medical practice involves the decision whether to implement or omit a life-sustaining treatment[2] for a newborn baby who is severely disabled, when it is thought that such a condition will bring him or her a very poor quality of life, a life that will be, on many occasions, full of suffering. In fact, one might justifiably claim that the decision to start or not, or to discontinue techniques intended to keep neonates alive is one of the most complex and distressing issues in medical ethics (indeed, in medical law) in our time.[3]

In this chapter, I will discuss, from the Spanish perspective, one of the most contentious legal issues associated with withdrawal of life sustaining treatment

---

[1] I would like to thank the editors of this volume, Margaret Otlowski, and Dianne Nicol for their insightful comments on earlier drafts of this chapter. Responsibility for ignoring their best advice, and making mistakes is, of course, mine alone.

[2] When I speak about 'omission of a life-sustaining treatment', I mean: (a) not to initiate medical treatment (understanding treatment in a broad sense, including resuscitation, operation, intensive care, etc); or (b) to withdraw the existing medical measures that are ensuring the continuation of life.

The Nuffield Council on Bioethics, Critical care decisions in fetal and neonatal medicine: ethical issues (Working Party chaired by Professor Margaret Brazier), 2006, also concludes (at 155) that 'there is no reason to distinguish between withdrawing treatment and deciding not to start it, provided the decision is made in the best interest of a baby'.

[3] F. Abel, and F. J. Cambra, 'Neonatology and severe handicap', in Institut Borja de Bioética, *Diagnóstico prenatal, neonatología y discapacidad severa: problemas éticos/Intervention in perinatology and the birth of severely handicapped children* (Madrid: Institut Borja de Bioética and Fundación MAPFRE Medicina, 2001) 84.

from severely disabled newborn babies, where such discontinuance will inevitably bring about death, namely, the question of criminal responsibility of doctors
who decide to undertake such termination. I will describe the limits placed by the
criminal law on parents' power to refuse treatment for their child, or to request
that their child be allowed to die rather than face a life of pain and distress, and
also the potential criminal liability of doctors who allow a child to die, even where
that is what the parents want.

In the field of paediatric medicine, and especially in neonatology, in Spain,
unlike other countries, there is a distinct lack of legislation, case law,[4] and literature dealing with the issue of whether to omit or withdraw life-sustaining treatment for neonates.[5] This does not mean, of course, that it is not a daily problem
in Spanish hospitals, but what happens is that the decision adopted in each case is
not publicized. The decisions are taken between doctors and families, sometimes,
perhaps, at the limits of legality. Nevertheless, the limited knowledge about these
practices in Spain has impeded a public debate about them, and the lack of any
court cases means that there are no judgments to provide assistance in determining the ambit of lawful activity. Therefore, in Spain, we currently do not have
clear guidelines that might help to resolve this question.

In other countries, like the UK, the USA, Canada, or Australia,[6] the situation
is different. In these countries, it is possible to find many cases that have been
the object of judicial decisions. According to the system of legal precedent in
these countries, such decisions are very important in establishing the basis of the
legal treatment of the issue.[7] This does not happen in Spain, where a decision of
a judge, or of a court is not binding on another judge or court in a similar case,
without prejudice to the significant influence of prior legal decisions, especially
the rulings of the Supreme Court, in interpreting the law.[8]

---

[4] A case may come before the courts in two different ways: on the one hand, for guidance on the
appropriate treatment for a living child; on the other hand, when the lawfulness of a doctor's conduct is examined after the event in a criminal prosecution.

[5] Actually, I have not been able to find any court judgment dealing with this issue. Similarly,
most of the available literature deals with ethical and medical questions, but not with the legal
implications. In the very rare cases in which legal aspects are addressed, they are always pushed into
the background, and not considered as the main issue of the work in question.

[6] See L. Skene, *Law & Medical Practice: Rights, Duties, Claims & Defences* (2nd edn, Australia:
Butterworths, 2004) 330 ff.

[7] However, even in these cases, this issue is far from being solved. Recently, for example, one
could read in an Australian newspaper an article in which it is reported that 'neonatal specialists fear they are breaking the law by withdrawing life support and administering pain-relieving
drugs that may hasten the death of newborn babies with severe disabilities'. These specialists complained that 'the legal status of withdrawing life support and/or administering pain relief, which
may hasten death, was unclear and neonatal teams were forced to make decisions in the absence
of clear guidelines'. K. Grube, 'Clarity call on baby deaths' *The Mercury* (8 February 2007) at
<http://www.news.com.au/mercury/story/0,22884,21190257–5007221,00.html> (accessed 9
March 2007).

[8] See E. Merino-Blanco, *Spanish Law and Legal System* (2nd edn, London: Sweet & Maxwell,
2006) 45 ff.

The Spanish criminal law system is based upon a very complex dogmatic construction.[9] Therefore, it is usually necessary to go through elaborate legal reasoning to give a response to a particular case, and normally such reasoning is beyond the layperson's reach. For this reason, the real problem is that doctors move within an area that is far from clearly determined from a legal point of view. In this complex area, they can take a decision that is probably correct from a humanitarian point of view, but which can nevertheless be punished according to the criminal law.[10]

In relation to the situation in Spain, while we are awaiting a clear legal solution to this problem, I submit that it is necessary to distinguish two different cases in order to analyse the question of whether medical treatment can be omitted: on the one hand, it is necessary to consider the case of the non-viable human being, outside the uterus of a woman; and, on the other hand, it is also essential to consider the viable human being,[11] also outside the uterus of a woman, as a separate case.[12]

---

[9] In Spain, criminal law is divided into two parts: the general part, and the special part. The general part consist of the main principles and theoretical concepts of crime and punishment, and it provides a framework for the special part, which consists of details of particular crimes, and the rules relevant to those specific offences. The general part has a philosophical nature since it is constructed around a series of principles or theories which constitute the axioms of criminal law in a democratic system. It contains the broad principles which accommodate the rules of the specific crimes.

For an overview of the Spanish criminal system in English, see C. Villiers, The Spanish Legal Tradition: An introduction to the Spanish Law and Legal System (Aldershot: Ashgate, 1999) 99 ff.

[10] F. J. Caballero Harriet, 'Reflexiones acerca de la eutanasia (especial referencia a la eutanasia infantil)', *Anuario de Sociología del Derecho* (1990) 79.

[11] When I use the term 'human being', I include both 'viable' human beings and 'non-viable' human beings (unless specified otherwise). Both (viable or non-viable) fetuses and persons are human beings, but their respective legal status is different under Spanish Law.

[12] We are here dealing exclusively with living human beings, because, if such a subject does not meet the conditions to be considered a living human being, the omission of medical treatment does not present any legal problem, even where some of the subject's organs actually function.

*In utero* human beings also remain beyond the scope of this work. In these cases, the possibility of producing death may be sanctioned by the law if it is foreseen that the fetus will be born severely physically or mentally disabled, provided some legal conditions are satisfied. I am referring here to so-called 'embryopathic' or 'eugenic' abortion, regulated by (the still applicable) Article 417 bis of the former Spanish Criminal Code. (Article 417 bis was added by Organic Law 9/1985, of 5 July 1985, amending Article 417, Criminal Code, introducing a new Article between Articles 417 and 418 numbered 417 bis, in which three abortion indications were included.)

Abortion is a crime when it is practised without the woman's consent, and outside the cases permitted by the law. There are three situations in which abortion is expressly declared nonpunishable. All are foreseen in Article 417 bis of the former Criminal Code. According to this Article, abortion is not a punishable offence if carried out by a medical practitioner in a public or private clinic with the express consent of the pregnant woman under the following circumstances: (a) to avoid physical or mental harm to the mother (in this case two specialists must consent to the abortion going ahead); (b) if the pregnancy is the result of rape—the abortion must, however, be carried out within the first 12 weeks of pregnancy; and (c) if the baby is severely physically or mentally handicapped. The abortion must again take place within the first 22 weeks. In this instance, two specialists from an approved health centre plus the doctor in charge must certify that the fetus will suffer from severe defects if allowed to be born.

## 2. The concepts of birth and viability

Before proceeding, it is important to define two concepts which share a very important relationship: birth and viability.

### 2.1 The concept of birth

To be clear, and to correctly focus the subject of this chapter, we are analysing the question of the legal consequences, especially those under the criminal law, of behaviour (actions and omissions) directed towards bringing about the death of a severely disabled newborn baby. The starting point is, therefore, to determine the precise point of time when we are faced with a living newborn human being. If there is no newborn human being, or if life does not exist, the problems disappear.

The determination of the moment of birth (from a legal perspective) is extremely important, because Article 29 of the Spanish Civil Code states that *personality*, namely the condition necessary for the subject to be the holder of rights and obligations, is obtained at that moment. Thus, in Spanish law, as in English law, the fetus does not acquire legal personality until it is born alive. This fact will determine, among other questions, the application of the criminal offences of homicide or injuries to a person, or the offences of abortion or injuries to a fetus.[13]

Strictly speaking, to be born means 'to come out from the uterus of the mother'.[14] Although the Spanish legislation does not offer a legal concept of birth, we can state that the term 'birth' used by the Civil Code does not correspond exactly with the usual meaning. On the contrary, the concept refers to a circumstance in which a human being acquires the legal status of 'personhood'. The exact moment, and the conditions that must be satisfied to acquire that status, have to be established by legal scholarship and the courts, taking into account that they must pay attention to the whole legislation and the society in which the law is applied in order to interpret it correctly.[15]

Article 29 of the Civil Code states that the status of personhood is acquired at the moment of birth, but it says nothing about the moment at which a human being is considered to be born, and the conditions that this human being must satisfy to be considered to be born. In relation to the *moment* of birth, the literature offers several possibilities: complete separation between the fetus and the mother (with or without the severance of the umbilical cord); beginning of autonomous lung respiration; and so on.[16] The fact is that the Supreme Court has

---

[13]  See Criminal Code, Articles 138–143 (homicide), 144–146 (abortion), 147–156 (injuries to a person), and 157–158 (injuries to a fetus).

[14]  According to the definition given by the Spanish Academy of the Language.

[15]  Civil Code, Article 3.1.

[16]  For a statement of the different stances, see C. M. Romeo Casabona, *El Derecho y la Bioética ante los límites de la vida humana* (Madrid: Centro de Estudios Ramón Areces, 1994) 156 ff;

dealt only a few times with this question. In recent times, this Court has considered that the moment of birth corresponds to the beginning of 'contractions' and the 'opening' of the uterus.[17]

The question of the requirements that a human being must fulfil to be considered a newborn presents more problems, notwithstanding the fact that it is outside the uterus of the mother. The main opinion voiced in the literature is that whether the human being is viable or not is irrelevant to the understanding of a legal concept of birth.[18] In my opinion, however, the fetus outside the uterus that is alive but is non-viable cannot be considered a newborn baby (from a legal point of view) and, for that reason, it is not a person.[19] I explore this notion in more detail below.

With no agreement between the social, or usual meaning, and the legal meaning of the term 'birth', it is thus possible to speak of a 'newborn baby' or a 'neonate' from a legal point of view when the subject is inside the uterus (the 'contractions' have begun), at a point at which we would not, in normal usage, apply these terms. Further, according to my position, a newborn baby does not exist from a legal point of view when we are faced with a non-viable human being outside the uterus of the mother, although, in normal usage, it is considered as a newborn or a neonate, and not a fetus anymore.[20] Likewise, there is no newborn human being when a fetus is clinically dead.

In effect, Article 32 of the Civil Code states that the civil personality extinguishes with the death of the person; only living human beings can have the legal status of person. Although the Spanish legislation does not expressly provide for when a human being is to be considered alive,[21] it does provide guidance on the conditions for determining the death of a person. In this way, it is possible to establish whether the human being at issue is dead or is not.

The relevant provision is contained in the First Appendix of the Royal Decree 2070/1999, of 30 December 1999, relating to the obtaining and transplantation

---

J. T. Salas Darrochoa, 'El concepto de feto en el Código penal español', *Derecho y Salud*, 1 (2005), 125.

[17] Rulings of the Supreme Court (Criminal Division) of 22 January 1999 and 29 November 2001.

[18] C. M. Romeo Casabona, *Los delitos contra la vida y la integridad personal y los relativos a la manipulación genética* (Granada: Comares, 2004) 17; J.L. Lacruz Berdejo, F. de A. Sancho Rebullida, A. Luna Serrano, J. Delgado Echeverría, F. Rivero Hernández, and J. Rams Albesa, *Elementos de Derecho civil. Parte General. II. Personas* (Madrid: Dykinson, 1999) 13.

[19] Law 42/1988, of 28 November 1988, regulating the donation and use of human embryos and fetuses or the cells, tissues or organs thereof, expressly uses the term 'foetuses outside the uterus' even when they are alive, so it is a term of art in Spain. This term is used to refer to human beings outside the womb, when they are non-viable, so they cannot be considered to be born from a legal point of view, that is, they are not 'persons'.

[20] However, at the level of strict legal terminology, according to the wording used by Law 42/1988, we will have to refer to them as (non-viable) 'foetuses outside the uterus' and not neonates or newborns.

[21] Actually, the problem exists beyond the Spanish jurisdiction. According to the Nuffield Council on Bioethics (*Critical care decisions in fetal and neonatal medicine: ethical issues*, 153), 'there exists no single precise definition in use as to what constitutes "born alive"'.

of organs and tissues. This appendix regulates the 'Protocols of Diagnosis and Certification of Death in order to Perform Organ Extraction from Deceased Donors'. It begins by stating that 'the diagnosis and certification of death in a person is based on the confirmation of the irreversible cessation of cardiorespiratory functions (death from cardiorespiratory arrest) or encephalic function (encephalic death)'.[22] Thus, those human beings for which the criteria established in this regulation about the lack of encephalic or cardio-respiratory functions can be detected will be considered as deceased human beings, whether or not it is possible to observe any kind of organic activity. This activity is necessary in some cases to ensure that certain organs remain viable for transplantation.

In the legal and medical literature, it is possible to find opinions that affirm that 'life' does not exist in the absence of encephalic function in the case of anencephalic babies.[23] In any case, it is important to distinguish between lack of life (death) and lack of the possibility of survival (non-viability).[24] As a result, anencephalics are actually dead fetuses, which have never obtained the status of personhood. Thus, according to Article 6, Law 42/1988, of 28 November 1988, regulating the donation and use of human embryos and fetuses or the cells, tissues, or organs thereof, it is permissible to obtain and use biological samples from dead embryos and fetuses for different purposes: diagnostic, therapeutic, pharmacological, clinical, or surgical. Moreover, their donation is possible to achieve these purposes.

## 2.2 The concept of viability

It is necessary to clarify the concept of viability, because, as I asserted above, a non-viable 'newborn baby' will not become a person, and this has very important consequences. However, a definition of viability is not to be found in the Spanish legislation.

The concept of viability is really very important in relation to prenatal life, because the aforementioned Law 42/1988, refers to this question to establish a different legal status for embryos and fetuses. According to two Rulings of the Spanish Constitutional Court,[25] ' "viable" ... denotes something capable of life. In the case of a human embryo or foetus, "non-viable" denotes specifically that it is incapable of developing into a human being, a "person" in the fundamental sense of Article 10.1 of the Constitution'.[26]

---

[22] My translation. See J. L. Trueba Gutiérrez, 'La muerte cerebral como evidencia clínica (ocho preguntas fundamentales)' in J. J. Ferrer and J. L. Martínez (eds.), *Bioética: un diálogo plural: Homenaje a Javier Gafo Fernández, SJ* (Madrid: Universidad Pontificia Comillas, 2002) 201 ff.

[23] cf Romeo Casabona, *El Derecho y la Bioética ante los límites de la vida humana*, 174 ff; Romeo Casabona, *Los delitos contra la vida y la integridad personal y los relativos a la manipulación genética*, 17; F. Abel i Fabre, *Bioética: orígenes, presente y futuro* (Madrid: Institut Borja de Bioética, 2001) 155 ff.

[24] Romeo Casabona, *El Derecho y la Bioética ante los límites de la vida humana*, 180.

[25] No 212/1996, of 19 December 1996, and No 116/1999, of 17 June 1999.

[26] See the complete text of the Rulings of the Spanish Constitutional Court No 212/1996, and No 116/1999, in *Revista de Derecho y Genoma Humano/Law and Human Genome Review*, 8 (1998),

This concept of viability cannot be applied directly in our case, because we are referring to a human being outside the uterus of the mother. In fact, the legislature is conscious of the different senses of the term 'viability' when it is applied to fetuses inside the uterus and outside the uterus respectively. For this reason, Law 42/1988 provides that the Government must establish the criteria of viability and non-viability of fetuses outside the uterus.[27] At this point in time, these criteria have yet to be established. However, according to the aforementioned interpretation of the term viability given by the Constitutional Court, viable means 'capable of life'. As such, in the case of living human beings outside the uterus, a 'viable human being' can be defined as the individual who is able to continue a process of living development. So a human being is non-viable when it suffers from such serious defects that it is not expected to live, even with aggressive and sophisticated medical intervention.

Having explained the terms 'birth' and 'viability', I will now address the legal status of non-viable and viable fetuses outside the uterus. Here, the problems will be significantly more difficult.

## 3. Legal status of the non-viable human being outside the uterus

A first reading of the Civil Code could give the impression that all living human beings outside the uterus are persons. However, Article 30 of the Civil Code and Law 42/1988 require us to make this assertion more precise, because it can be seen to base ascription of the status of person upon viability.

On the one hand, according to Article 30 of the Civil Code, to be considered a newborn (a person), it is necessary to have a 'human figure'.[28] Again, we must pay attention to the whole legislation and the society in which the law is applied in order to interpret this article correctly.[29] Although there are presently different opinions in the literature about the meaning of this requirement, I agree with those authors who consider that it must be interpreted in the sense that the fetus must be viable to be considered a newborn from the legal point of view, that is, a person.[30]

---

119–33 (in English), and *Revista de Derecho y Genoma Humano/Law and Human Genome Review*, 11 (1999), 97–117 (in Spanish), respectively.

Article 10.1 of the Spanish Constitution states that 'the dignity of the person, the inviolable rights which are inherent, the free development of the personality, the respect for the law and for the rights of others are the foundation of political order and social peace'.

[27] First Additional Provision.

[28] The Spanish Civil Code was passed in 1888, and this article clearly denotes the influence of Roman law upon it.

[29] cf Civil Code, Article 3.1.

[30] cf L. Puig i Ferriol, M. C. Gete-Alonso y Calera, J. Gil Rodríguez, and J. J. Hualde Sánchez, *Manual de Derecho Civil. I. (Introducción y derecho de la persona)* (Madrid: Marcial Pons, 2000) 115; L. Diez-Picazo and A. Gullón, *Sistema de Derecho Civil. Vol I*, 8th edn.

On the other hand, according to Article 5.4 of Law 42/1988, 'foetuses expelled prematurely and spontaneously, and considered biologically viable, will be treated with the sole aim of favouring their development and autonomy of life'.[31] Therefore, if the 'prematurely and spontaneously expelled foetuses' in question are non-viable, they can be used for any other purpose, and on this basis it would be permissible to omit any treatment directed to favour their development and autonomy of life. That is, they may be left to die. Moreover, Article 9.2(B) of Law 42/1988 considers it a very serious infraction 'to research with live embryos or foetuses, viable or non-viable, *unless they are non-viable and are located outside the uterus*', provided that the experimentation has been approved by the relevant public authorities.[32]

In addition, Law 42/1988 equates the legal status of embryos and fetuses when they are non-viable, although they are outside the uterus. If Article 29 of the Civil Code was interpreted to deem the living human fetus outside the uterus to be a newborn baby, then it is clear that, as a person, it would require a different legal treatment than those other living human beings that cannot be considered 'a person'.

In conclusion, a fetus outside the uterus, if non-viable (for any reason), is not a person in the Spanish legal system, although it is a living human being outside the uterus.[33] However, this thesis is not an obstacle to admitting a presumption of viability for all living human beings outside the uterus and, with it, the legal status of person. I would argue that those interested in declaring a human being as non-viable must demonstrate why this should be the case.

## 4. Legal status of the viable human being outside the uterus

Recall that, according to Article 5.4 of Law 42/1988, 'foetuses expelled prematurely and spontaneously, and considered biologically viable, will be treated with the sole aim of favouring their development and autonomy of life'. Although this

---

(Madrid: Tecnos, 1992) 226; M. Albaladejo, *Derecho Civil. I. Introducción y Parte General. Vol. I*, 14th edn. (Barcelona: José María Bosch Editor, 1996) 214; L. Puig Ferriol, *Fundamentos de Derecho Civil. Tomo I. Vol. I. Primera Parte. Parte General: sujeto y objeto del derecho* (Barcelona: Bosch, 1979) 25 ff; B. Pérez González, 'El requisito de la viabilidad', *Revista de Derecho Privado*, 28 (1944), 290, 298.

[31] My translation.

[32] Emphasis added. On resolving the appeal of unconstitutionality against this law (the aforementioned Ruling No 212/1996), the Constitutional Court did not consider that Article 5.4 of Law 42/1988 was unconstitutional, that is to say, they did not find that it was contrary to the right to life protected by Article 15 of the Spanish Constitution.

[33] cf E. Ramón Ribas, *El delito de lesiones al feto. Incidencia en el sistema de tutela penal de la vida y la salud* (Granada: Comares, 2002) 316, n 239; S. Huerta Tocildo, 'De ciertas incongruencias y aparentes paradojas en los delitos de lesiones al feto' in G. Quintero Olivares and F. Morales Prats (coords), *El Nuevo Derecho Penal Español. Estudios Penales en Memoria del Profesor José Manuel Valle Muñiz* (Pamplona: Aranzadi, 2001) 1430.

article refers to a preterm birth, this is a general rule. As a consequence, when dealing with viable human beings outside the uterus, we can speak of newborn human beings or neonates, so all the measures existing in the Spanish legislation to protect the person become relevant, especially, in this case, the offences of homicide and injuries to a person, as well as the offence of omission of a medical duty to rescue.

## 4.1 Omission of medical treatment producing death

The most usual scenario relating to omission of medical treatment producing the death of a human being outside the womb arises when a doctor decides voluntarily and consciously to omit any kind of treatment or medical care in respect of a newborn baby with the intention of producing his or her death, regardless of whether he takes any measure to avoid the suffering of the newborn baby while death comes about. In such a case, the doctor clearly commits the offence of homicide. According to Article 138 of the Criminal Code, 'a person who kills another person is guilty of an offence of homicide and shall be punished with imprisonment for a term between 10 and 15 years'.[34]

## 4.2 Omission of medical treatment that does not produce the death of the newborn baby, but aggravates the disability or disease

If there is an omission of medical treatment or medical care directed at producing the death of the newborn baby, and this omission does not achieve that result, but, in fact, makes worse the disability of the newborn baby, then, apart from the offence of attempted homicide, it is possible to find the doctor guilty of an offence of injuries to the person.[35]

## 4.3 Omission of medical treatment or medical care that jeopardizes the life and integrity of the newborn baby, but does not cause him or her damage

Another possibility is the omission of medical treatment or medical care that jeopardizes the life and integrity of the newborn baby, but he or she is not damaged, perhaps due to the intervention of a third person. In this case, Article 196 of the Criminal Code punishes the 'doctor who, having an obligation, denies medical care to a patient or who does not make him or herself available to treat the patient, if such refusal or abandonment jeopardises the health of a person'[36] (with a penalty of imprisonment for between 12 and 18 months and professional disqualification).

---

[34] My translation.    [35] Criminal Code, Articles 147 and 617.
[36] My translation. Thus, Article 196 effectively imposes a medical duty to rescue.

## 5. Severely disabled newborns outside the uterus: Delimitation between viability and non-viability

Until now, I have commented briefly on the legal status of viable and non-viable human beings outside the uterus. In the first case, we are dealing with a person. This is not the legal position in the case of non-viable human beings outside the uterus, and hence the legal protection offered in such circumstances is very different. The next step is to analyse two different circumstances: first, the concrete delimitation between viability and non-viability; and, secondly, the legal effects of the omission of medical treatment of a human being who is alive and viable in very exceptional situations.

### 5.1 Extremely premature (non-viable) human beings

The first situation to consider involving a lack of viability refers to the rate of organic development of the fetus. From a medical point of view, there is scientific evidence establishing the impossibility of any living development of human fetuses outside the uterus, if the gestation period inside the uterus has not been sufficient.[37] The period required for gestation can change, according to the medical knowledge available at that moment. In the last few decades, intensive care has made extraordinary progress, yielding, in the settings of paediatrics and neonatology, a number of achievements which were unthinkable but a short time ago.[38] Today, the vital prognosis of many pathological disorders has improved, allowing children to live who would inevitably have died a few years ago.

---

[37] The limit of viability for premature newborns in the 1970s was around 1,500 grams, increasing to 1,000 grams in the 1980s. Nowadays, we can find in the medical literature surveys that affirm that fetuses outside the uterus with a development of less than 23 weeks and 400 grams of weight are not viable. See, for example, Grupo de Reanimación Cardiopulmonar de la Sociedad Española de Neonatología, 'Recomendaciones en reanimación neonatal', *Anales de Pediatría*, 1 (2004), 74; V. Molina, 'Consideraciones éticas en el periodo neonatal', *Protocolos de la Asociación Española de Pediatría*, at <http://aeped.es/protocolos/neonatologia/index.htm>, 59. See also Nuffield Council on Bioethics, *Critical care decisions in fetal and neonatal medicine: ethical issues*, 155 ff.

With regard to this point, we must analyse the differences in prognosis depending on the quality of the care provided immediately after birth, since the prognosis criteria on viability will vary depending on the socio-cultural standards in different countries, and even within the same health care setting. It would not be the same to be born in a hospital that is perfectly equipped for caring for these children as it would to be born in another centre in which the care provided is different and the child must be transferred, thus involving a clear increase in risks of morbidity and mortality.

[38] Recently, we have witnessed the case of the first baby known to survive after a gestation period of less than 23 weeks. She was just 24 cm long and weighed less than 285 grams when she was born on 24 October 2006. She was delivered in a Hospital in Miami (USA) after just under 22 weeks of pregnancy. The only known premature babies that have survived so young prior to her were all born at 23 weeks. The baby has suffered respiratory and digestive problems, as well as a mild brain haemorrhage, but doctors believe the health concerns will not have major long-term effects. According to the doctors, the 'baby showed signs of being viable at the time of delivery, which means she showed signs that she was mature enough to survive...She made efforts at breathing,

As discussed above, the First Additional Provision of Law 42/1988 states that the Government has to establish the criteria of viability and non-viability of fetuses outside the uterus. When these criteria are established, they will be applied case by case according to the medical knowledge in each.

In a nutshell, a premature baby considered non-viable will not be treated clinically, according to Article 5.4 of Law 42/1988. This means, for example, that doctors must not start resuscitation.

## 5.2 Non-premature newborns that are non-viable due to biological conditions

Another case involving a lack of viability is that in which the malformations or the disabilities of the fetus are so serious that survival is not possible. The existing measures can delay the moment of death, but an effective treatment does not exist. In these cases, it is senseless to use measures directed at artificially extending the life of the fetus outside the uterus. On the contrary, it is necessary to help the fetus die without suffering, unless a research project involving it has been authorized under Law 42/1988. Thus, a fetus outside the uterus will be considered as 'non-viable' when the medical treatment is only able to delay the moment of an unavoidable and imminent death, so it is pointless to guarantee the survival of the fetus.

Non-viability must be determined according to medical and scientific criteria. For example, if, in accordance with the scientific criteria, an anencephalic fetus is not considered dead, this would be a good example of non-viability. Of course, the concept of viability is subject to change, so it is necessary to take into account the latest available medical knowledge in every case.

## 5.3 Viable newborn infants and the 'quality of life'

The most complicated situation arises when the fetus outside the uterus is viable. In principle, once a baby is born alive, the parents and the health care professionals in the hospital where he or she is delivered owe the baby a duty of care.[39] In some such situations, the baby may live if he or she is appropriately treated, even though there is no reasonable expectation that he or she will grow up to enjoy an acceptable quality of life. There again, the impressive advances that are taking place in neonatology make it possible to save the life of a severely disabled newborn baby.[40]

---

[an] attempt to cry at birth. So when she was assessed at the delivery, she showed signs that she may have been mature enough to survive, and she proved us right'. Anon, 'Tiny baby has bright future', ABC News, at <http://abcnews.go.com/GMA/Health/story?id=2888874&page=1> (accessed 9 March 2007).

[39] Nuffield Council on Bioethics, *Critical care decisions in fetal and neonatal medicine: ethical issues*, 153.

[40] Molina, 'Consideraciones éticas en el periodo neonatal', 53.

Here I am concerned with disabilities that will not allow this infant to enjoy a good quality of life, according to the relevant social standards, disabilities that may mean the infant will not be conscious of his or her own life, and will need the continuous support of a third party. The question here is whether the criterion of quality of life can support a decision not to offer medical treatment to these newborn infants. Although these cases have not come before the Courts in Spain, medical professionals must confront this problem.

## 6. Legal basis of the non-punishability of omitting to treat viable but severely disabled human beings

The scenario to be considered is as follows: a doctor (or a medical team) decides to omit to treat a viable human being outside the uterus, with the effect that this 'person' will undoubtedly die. Since we are speaking of a person, this conduct corresponds with the offence of homicide, because an offence can be committed either by a positive action or by an omission (so-called 'commission by omission').[41] In effect, criminal liability may also be imposed for omitting to take steps to preserve life if that is what 'reasonable care' requires in the circumstances. This applies just as much to critically ill newborn infants and children as it does to adult patients at the end of life.[42] A doctor who deliberately causes or hastens a child's death, whether by withdrawing or withholding treatment, or by excessive doses of pain-killing drugs, is liable to criminal prosecution for homicide. If the parents participate in the decision, they can also be prosecuted.

If we were to leave the analysis of the question here, we would have to conclude that such an omission would constitute criminal conduct in every case, so it would be forbidden. However, ignoring the ethical considerations, the reality appears to be that it is not strange in Spanish hospitals to take this measure in extreme cases. That is to say, doctors believe that, in many cases where a viable newborn has very severe disabilities, it is better to let it die. They are approaching the matter in terms of 'quality of life', so it is not strange that they choose to omit some life-saving treatments: they let some newborns die to avoid a life full of suffering. And they take this decision in a transparent way, as the more medically appropriate measure in that situation.[43]

What I will try to clarify now is whether doctors are making a medical decision that is against the law in this situation, and, especially, whether this decision entails criminal liability or, on the contrary, whether this conduct cannot be

[41] cf Criminal Code, Articles 10 and 11.

[42] This seems to be a common legal consequence throughout the world. See, for example, Skene, *Law & Medical Practice*, 327.

[43] cf Grupo de Trabajo sobre limitación del esfuerzo terapéutico y cuidados paliativos en recién nacidos, 'Decisiones de limitación del esfuerzo terapéutico en recién nacidos críticos: estudio multicéntrico', *Anales de Pediatria*, 6 (2002), 547 ff.

punished at law. The solution is by no means easy. In principle, it seems that doctors who let a viable newborn die must be considered guilty of an offence of homicide, even though the baby is severely disabled or handicapped. However, the fact is that the lack of any judicial decision about this question shows that the adoption of this measure does not cause social repulsion, and, what is more interesting for us, it does not attract legal liability. This is despite the fact that, at first glance, this conduct corresponds with the offence of homicide.

In order for an omission of medical treatment producing the death of a person to be punishable, the Spanish criminal law requires a previous obligation of acting, of positive conduct. A person can only be considered guilty of the offence of homicide by an omission with the following requisites, among others:[44] (1) the lack of a positive action directed to avoid the damage (medical treatment); (2) the production of the damage (death); (3) the capability of acting, including the capability of avoiding the damage (the omitted medical treatment could have avoided the death of the patient); and, as I said before, (4) it is necessary that the person who omitted the conduct had an obligation to act to avoid the result, in this case, to avoid the death of the newborn.[45]

In principle, doctors have an obligation to take all possible measures to protect the health and the lives of their patients. However, in relation to this particular situation, we have to determine if doctors really have an obligation to treat a newborn in every case, even though they know that, as a result, the infant will remain alive but with a very poor quality of life. The problem here is to determine what 'quality of life' means.

In 2002, the Working Group of the Spanish Society of Neonatology about End-of-Life Decision-Making (Limitation of Therapeutic Effort) and Palliative Care in Newborns produced a report entitled 'Decisions on limiting treatment in critically-ill neonates: a multicenter study'.[46] The introduction of this report states the following:

Advances in recent years in neonatal medicine have achieved a big increase in the survival of infants who until few years ago died irremediably. In a parallel way, a debate about the use of technology for the care of critical newborns has arisen, because what is technically and medically possible is not always appropriate to the interests of the patient. Frequently doctors are not sure about the benefit for the patient of starting or continuing an intensive treatment or other life-prolonging measures. Sometimes technology allows a doctor to prolong the life of a patient for a variable period of time. On occasion, what really happens is that the process of death is artificially prolonged. At other times, doctors cause a

[44] See J. Cerezo Mir, *Curso de Derecho penal español. Parte General, III. Teoría jurídica del delito/2* (6th edn, Madrid: Tecnos, 1998) 269 ff.

[45] C. M. Romeo Casabona, 'Límites de los delitos de comisión por omisión' in E. Gimbernat, B. Schünemann, and J. Wolter, (eds.), *Omisión e imputación objetiva en Derecho penal* (Madrid: Servicio de Publicaciones de la Universidad Complutense de Madrid, 1994) 33, 45.

[46] Grupo de Trabajo sobre limitación del esfuerzo terapéutico y cuidados paliativos en recién nacidos, 'Decisiones de limitación del esfuerzo terapéutico en recién nacidos críticos: estudio multicéntrico', *Anales de Pediatria*, 6 (2002).

patient to survive with a very serious neurological condition or other sequelae that bring a very poor quality of life as a result. That produces great suffering for the patient, for the family, and for the medical team, apart from drawing on important resources from society. These end-of-life decisions are usually polemical and difficult to take, producing intellectual and emotional stress in the people who must decide.[47]

According to some opinions, medical intervention in the case of a newborn should only be attempted to achieve medical aims.[48] This means that the medical intervention must be directed to improve the newborn's health, or allow the newborn to survive, to keep the child alive as long as possible. But doctors do not have to think in terms of future 'quality of life'.

The main problem related to the omission of medical treatment relates to the conditions and limits for the application, continuation, and interruption of such treatment. The question is how to determine the limits of health care. In the case of newborns, not all the measures directed toward saving life seem to be justified.[49] Therefore, doctors do not have a legal duty to save the life of a newborn in every case, particularly when, as a result of the intervention, the newborn will survive with a very poor quality of life.[50] And this corresponds with day-to-day work in neonatology units in Spanish hospitals, where the prognosis regarding future quality of life is relevant when reaching an end-of-life decision.

In the aforementioned report, 'Decisions on limiting treatment in critically-ill neonates: a multicenter study', we can observe the criteria used by doctors when the decision is made to omit medical treatment in the case of a newborn:

... poor living prognosis of the patient: 136 patients (79.5%); poor present quality of life: 64 patients (37.4%); poor future quality of life: 82 patients (48%); and external factors relevant to the patient, such as their family situation, the expenses of care, etc.: 9 patients (5.3%). If we consider these criteria individually we can see that the low probability of survival of the patient was the only criterion in 50.3% of cases; and considerations about the patient's quality of life were taken into account as the only criterion to omit the medical treatment in 17.6% of the cases analysed. On no occasion were external factors used as the only reason to omit a treatment.[51]

Of course, the decision to omit a medical treatment must be based on reasonable and reasoned medical criteria,[52] and it is necessary to obtain the consent of the parents of the newborn.[53] The parents must evaluate whether the disability

---

[47]  Ibid, 548 (my translation).
[48]  Romeo Casabona, *El Derecho y la Bioética ante los límites de la vida humana*, 466.
[49]  cf A. Couceiro Vidal, '¿Es ético limitar el esfuerzo terapéutico?', *Anales de Pediatría*, 6 (2002), 505.
[50]  J. M. Silva Sánchez, 'La responsabilidad penal del médico por omisión', *La Ley*, 1632 (1987), 5.
[51]  Grupo de Trabajo sobre limitación del esfuerzo terapéutico y cuidados paliativos en recién nacidos, 'Decisiones de limitación del esfuerzo terapéutico en recién nacidos críticos: estudio multicéntrico', 550.
[52]  Couceiro Vidal, '¿Es ético limitar el esfuerzo terapéutico?', 506.
[53]  Silva Sánchez, 'La responsabilidad penal del médico por omisión', 5; M. Gómez Pellico, 'Decisiones difíciles en neonatología. Una aproximación ética', in Ferrer and Martínez, *Bioética: un*

explained by the medical team implies a lack of quality of life for them.[54] Parents are usually the appropriate decision-makers because they are assumed to have the best interests of their children at heart.[55]

The fulfilment of the following two requirements avoids the main problems that could arise:

(a) On the one hand, if we require that identification of a significant disability be based on medical and scientific criteria, we deny that the parents can decide in every case about the continuation of the newborn's life. In addition, we make sure that the decision adopted takes into account only the best interests of the child (although other interests can be taken into account).[56] Admittedly, the parents have the first right or duty to decide in the best interest of the child. However, there may be some situations in which their opinion must be judged with reservation, or even in which they should not take upon themselves the weight of the decision (for instance, when they are unable to understand the most relevant aspects of the case, when they show a high emotional instability, or when they place their own interests before those of the child).[57]

(b) On the other hand, if we require the consent of parents in order to omit medical treatment, broader State purposes for selective treatment of newborns cannot be considered. For instance, treatment cannot be omitted because of the considerable expense that medical care during the life of the handicapped person costs the State.

Obviously, the main problem here is to determine how important the disability must be in order to justify the omission of a treatment. One relevant consideration is whether or not the decision had the approval of an Ethics Committee. An Ethics Committee, depending on its composition and nature, can guarantee the impartiality, coherence, and logical structure of the opinion issued, acting with the necessary emotional stability, which is possibly difficult to achieve for parents or health care staff involved in the decision.[58]

---

*diálogo plural*, 106 ff; Molina, 'Consideraciones éticas en el periodo neonatal', 55; Couceiro Vidal, '¿Es ético limitar el esfuerzo terapéutico?', 506; Abel and Cambra, 'Neonatology and severe handicap', 89. Abel and Cambra affirm that 'it is the parents who have the greatest right to decide what is in the best interest of their child'.

[54] cf Molina, 'Consideraciones éticas en el periodo neonatal', 55; Couceiro Vidal, '¿Es ético limitar el esfuerzo terapéutico?', 506.

[55] After an analysis of case law in different countries, Skene (*Law & Medical Practice: Rights, Duties, Claims & Defences*, 336) concludes that courts and juries are reluctant to find a doctor guilty of a criminal offence if he or she acted in good faith, in what appeared to be the best interest of the child, and with the consent of the parents.

[56] As Abel and Cambra ('Neonatology and severe handicap', 89, 92 ff) note, 'it is not the function of doctors to obey the decisions of parents if they consider them to be mistaken where the best interest of the child is concerned...Parents can be confused by selfishness or a less enlightened love'.

[57] Ibid, 93; Skene (*Law & Medical Practice*, 341) also points out that 'it is not always possible for parents to decide objectively and dispassionately about what is best for their child'.

[58] See Nuffield Council on Bioethics, *Critical care decisions in fetal and neonatal medicine: ethical issues*, 143 ff.

In neonatology, the criterion that accounts for 'quality of life' is known as 'the best interest of the patient'.[59] This criterion involves determining if, for a newborn, death is a better option than life,[60] analysing in each case the benefits and risks of the different medical possibilities available to treat the patient.[61] The concept of quality of life must be understood not only as the question of biological survival, but as a support and basis for living life with a meaningful horizon (that is, in those cases in which the interaction of the child with the environment is non-existent in the present and in the foreseeable future).[62] According to this view, medical treatment could be omitted, with the consent of the parents, if it is foreseen, on the basis of the available medical knowledge, that the child will survive in such conditions that his or her capacity to interact with his or her environment will not exist, or will be seriously limited either because of a physical cause (such as paralysis, a lack of any limbs) or for psychological causes (for example, low capacity to communicate and understand).[63]

Thus, if the omission to treat meets the two indicated requirements, namely, objective medical and scientific criteria, and consent of the parents, this conduct can be considered correct from a medical point of view, and, consequently, a legal obligation to treat does not exist. In other words, not all the treatments that prolong biological life are humanely beneficial for the patient as a person, so the individual is not under any forced obligation to accept disproportionate procedures to preserve life.[64] Consequently, the lack of the medical intervention will not be punished despite the inevitable outcome, the death of the patient.

Of course, if there is any doubt or unresolvable conflict between doctors and the family, it will be necessary to allow a judge to decide.[65] Parents can be confused

[59] Grupo de Trabajo sobre limitación del esfuerzo terapéutico y cuidados paliativos en recién nacidos, 'Decisiones de limitación del esfuerzo terapéutico en recién nacidos críticos: estudio multicéntrico', 551 ff. See also, Abel and Cambra, 'Neonatology and severe handicap', 83 ff, Gómez Pellico, 'Decisiones difíciles en neonatología. Una aproximación ética', 105 ff.

[60] Molina, 'Consideraciones éticas en el periodo neonatal', 54.

[61] See Nuffield Council on Bioethics, *Critical care decisions in fetal and neonatal medicine: ethical issues*, 159 ff.

[62] cf Abel and Cambra, 'Neonatology and severe handicap', 90.

[63] In this regard, the Group of Cardiopulmonary Resuscitation of the Spanish Society of Neonatology believes that there is a big consensus about the non-resuscitation of newborns when they suffer from a Trisomy 13 or 18. See Grupo de Reanimación Cardiopulmonar de la Sociedad Española de Neonatología, 'Recomendaciones en reanimación neonatal', 74.

[64] Abel and Cambra, 'Neonatology and severe handicap', 85. See also, Nuffield Council on Bioethics, *Critical care decisions in fetal and neonatal medicine: ethical issues*, 154: 'there is no legal obligation to provide life-sustaining treatment where parents and professionals are agreed that a baby is unlikely to survive and/or suffers from such severe abnormalities as to render it not in his or her best interests to be offered invasive intensive care'.

[65] M. A. Núñez Paz, *Homicidio consentido, eutanasia y derecho a morir con dignidad* (Madrid: Tecnos, 1999) 95. Skene (*Law & Medical Practice*, 347) states that judges who have been consulted during a child's life in relation to the treatment which is appropriate in such circumstances have traditionally been conservative. They have almost always ordered that even very severely disabled babies should have surgery to preserve their lives and that, in making decisions about treatment, it is not justifiable to take into account the child's likely quality of life if the child survives. However, if it happens, and a prosecution is commenced, a doctor is unlikely to be convicted. Criminal

by selfishness, or a less enlightened love, but physicians may also be too inclined to deploy all the therapeutic armamentarium, with an eye to the technically possible rather than the humanly desirable and beneficial.

The problem is different when the conduct that has been omitted is not a life-prolonging treatment, but any other care that is not strictly medical, and this omission of care produces the death of a severely disabled newborn. In this case, the decision is not the omission of a medical treatment, but the omission of simple welfare care to newborns who are viable (for instance, allowing the newborn to starve to death, or letting the newborn die of cold).

In respect of both types of conduct, we are dealing with a severely disabled or handicapped newborn, and in both cases it is thought that the quality of life will be very poor. However, the difference between these two situations is very clear. While in the first case, the survival of the newborn requires a medical treatment, it is not necessary in the second case. It is not about an end-of-life decision in a strict sense, because therapeutic care is not necessary. The medical obligation of treating a patient can only be legitimately discharged when the conduct that is omitted is really a treatment, as in the situations I have discussed. But this obligation can not be discharged when the conduct that is omitted is a general duty of assistance to a helpless person. Without a doubt, these two obligations are not comparable.

Finally, all those active behaviours directed at relieving the suffering of the child by ending its life as quickly and painlessly as possible are also punishable. Both the doctors and the parents of the baby (if actively involved) can be punished in this case. Such cases of neonatal euthanasia or neonaticide are clearly prohibited in the Spanish Criminal Law,[66] and the offender will be charged with murder.

## 7. Conclusion

In this chapter, I have discussed, from the Spanish perspective, the question of criminal liability of doctors who decide not to initiate medical treatment, or to

charges are difficult to prove. Judges may sum up favourably for an accused doctor; and juries are traditionally sympathetic towards people caring for a critically ill infant.

[66] cf Romeo Casabona, *El Derecho y la Bioética ante los límites de la vida humana*, 468 ff. In Spain, the Law does not permit active steps to cause or hasten a person's death (euthanasia), even if the person is terminally ill, in great pain, and there is a general agreement that an early death would be in the person's best interest. However, if it happens (with the consent of the patient), the penalty will be extenuated compared to that imposed for murder.
Article 143.4 of the Criminal Code states that whoever causes or cooperates with necessary and direct actions in the death of another person, after his or her expressed petition, in the case that the victim suffered from a serious illness that would necessarily lead to his or her death, or that produced serious, permanent, and hard to tolerate suffering, will be punished with a penalty of up to six years in prison if he or she executes the death, and up to two years if he or she only cooperates in it. See M. Navarro-Michel, 'Advance directives: the Spanish perspective', *Medical Law Review* 13 (2005), 142, n 12. cf also, Nuffield Council on Bioethics, *Critical care decisions in fetal and neonatal medicine: ethical issues*, 157 ff.

withdraw existing medical measures that are ensuring the continuation of life of a severely disabled newborn baby. I have distinguished two different situations: on the one hand, the non-viable human being, outside the womb of a woman; and, on the other hand, the viable human being, also outside the womb of a woman. According to Article 30 of the Civil Code and Law 42/1988, I maintain that a newborn baby does not exist from a legal point of view when we are faced with a non-viable human being outside the uterus of the mother. These two legal texts can be seen to base ascription of the status of personhood upon viability. A human being is non-viable when it suffers from such serious defects that it is not expected to live, even with aggressive and sophisticated medical intervention.

However, when dealing with viable human beings outside the uterus, we can speak of newborn human beings or neonates. As a consequence, all the measures existing in the Spanish legislation to protect the person become relevant, namely the offences of homicide, injuries to a person, and omission of a medical duty to rescue. That is to say, a doctor who deliberately causes or hastens a child's death, whether by withdrawing or withholding treatment, or by excessive doses of pain-killing drugs, is liable to criminal prosecution for homicide. And if the parents participate in the decision, they can also be prosecuted.

I have also dealt with the legal effects of the omission of medical treatment of a human being who is alive and viable, but severely disabled, when it is thought that such a condition will bring him or her a very poor quality of life, a life that will be, on many occasions, full of suffering. In the Spanish legal system, a person can only be considered guilty of the offence of homicide by omission if the person who omitted the conduct had an obligation to act to avoid the result, which in this case would be to avoid the death of the newborn. Consequently, it is necessary to determine if doctors really have an obligation to treat a newborn in every case, even though they know that, as a result, the infant will remain alive but with a very poor quality of life. In this respect, I have concluded that, in the case of newborns, not all the measures directed toward saving life seem to be justified. I have argued that doctors do not have a legal duty to save the life of a newborn in every case, particularly when, as a result of the intervention, the newborn will survive with a very poor quality of life. But the decision to omit a medical treatment must be based on reasonable and reasoned medical criteria, and it is necessary to obtain the consent of the parents of the newborn. Thus, if the omission to treat meets the two indicated requirements, namely, objective medical and scientific criteria, and consent of the parents, this conduct can be considered correct from a medical point of view, and, consequently, a legal obligation to provide treatment does not exist, so that the lack of the medical intervention will not be punished despite the death of the child.

# 13

# Should We Criminalize
# HIV Transmission?

*Rebecca Bennett*

## 1. Introduction

2003 witnessed the first prosecutions and convictions in England and Wales for transmitting HIV. These convictions involved HIV transmission during consensual sexual contact and have led to an increasing number of cases being brought on these grounds. It appears that the charge in these cases is one of 'reckless' rather than intentional transmission. That is, it seems that the HIV-positive individuals did not intend to infect their partners, but were aware of their infection and aware that their behaviour might cause the infection of their partner with the virus. This chapter considers whether it is appropriate to criminalize the reckless transmission of HIV via consensual sexual contact in this way.

## 2. Biological grievous bodily harm

In the recent criminal cases concerning HIV transmission in England and Wales, the accused were prosecuted for reckless transmission of HIV under section 20 of the Offences Against the Person Act 1861 (OAPA), which makes the infliction of grievous bodily harm an offence. These cases have resulted in custodial sentences of between two and ten years imprisonment.[1]

Before these prosecutions the position of the law was thought to be that reckless transmission of a sexually transmitted infection was not an offence, even if the infection was concealed from the partner. This was based on precedent established in *R v Clarence*.[2] This case also was brought under section 20 of the OAPA. It concerned a husband who transmitted gonorrhoea to his wife but had

---

[1] See Terrence Higgins Trust, *Criminal prosecutions for transmitting HIV*, at <http://www.tht.org.uk/informationresources/prosecutions/recentcourtcases/> (accessed 27 February 2007).
[2] (1888) 22 QBD 23.

not forewarned her of his infection. His wife argued that she would not have consented to sex with him if she had been aware of his infection. On appeal, he was found not guilty of assault. This case thus established that '[c]onsent to sexual intercourse was not to be regarded as invalid because of the failure to disclose a venereal disease'.[3] *Clarence* established the precedent that an offence under section 20 could only be committed 'where there was a battery, in the sense of a direct infliction of physical force to the body of the victim'.[4] Thus, an individual who attacks someone with an HIV infected syringe, or an HIV-positive person who bites someone could be prosecuted for inflicting grievous bodily harm. However, most instances of HIV transmission do not involve such deliberate and violent 'infliction' of the virus.

Although this position was based on precedent established over 100 years ago, it was echoed by what appeared to be Government policy on this issue in 2000. According to the Government's consultation document on the law relating to manslaughter:

> … we made it clear that the Government proposed that only the intentional transmission of disease should be a criminal offence. This was in part because the Government is determined to ensure that people are not deterred from coming forward for diagnostic tests and treatment and for advice about the prevention of sexually transmitted diseases such as HIV or hepatitis B and that someone with such a disease could have no reason to fear prosecution, unless they deliberately set out to cause serious injury to another by passing on the disease. The Government remains wholly committed to this approach.[5]

Thus, up until these very recent cases, it was assumed that it would not be possible to successfully prosecute an HIV-positive person for transmitting the virus to a consenting sexual partner, even if the infection had been concealed. However, a House of Lords ruling in 1998 that recognized grievous bodily harm can consist of non-violent acts ('stalking', making silent phone calls, and so forth), overturned the principle that only violent (physical) infliction would allow the charge of grievous bodily harm.[6]

This ruling opened the way for prosecutions of reckless transmission of HIV under the OAPA, and in the first of the recent English HIV transmission cases, the Court of Appeal decided that *Clarence* no longer applied with regard to the transmission of infections without forewarning.[7]

---

[3] J. Chalmers, 'The criminalisation of HIV transmission', *Journal of Medical Ethics,* 28 (2002) 160.

[4] M. Weait, 'Criminal Law and the Sexual Transmission of HIV: *R v Dica*', *Modern Law Review*, 68/1 (2005), 122.

[5] Reforming the Law on Involuntary Manslaughter: The Government's Proposals (May 2000), section 4.3, at <http://www.homeoffice.gov.uk/documents/cons-2000-invol-manslaughter/consultation-paper.pdf?view=Binary> (accessed 27 February 2007).

[6] *R v Ireland*; *R v Burstow* [1998] AC 147.

[7] *R v Dica* [EWCA] Crim 1103 (5 May 2004), [2004] 3 All ER 593.

## 3. What does this mean for English law? Do HIV-positive people have to disclose their HIV status to every new sexual partner?

These recent English cases focused on the issue of forewarning. The rulings in these cases established that where 'a person chooses to consent to the risk of HIV transmission (that is, they know that their sexual partner is HIV positive and choose to have unprotected intercourse regardless of the fact), then that will be a valid defence to a criminal prosecution'.[8] These cases, therefore, effectively establish a legal duty upon HIV-positive persons to disclose their HIV status before engaging in activities which are considered to pose a high risk of transmission of the virus. In this chapter, I consider whether imposing such a legal duty to forewarn on HIV positive individuals is justified. Thus, the first question that needs to be addressed is what exactly we hope to achieve by imposing this legal duty.

## 4. What are the goals of criminalization?

### 4.1 Public health goals

One of the clear aims of the criminalization of HIV transmission is the prevention of further infection. It is hoped that criminal penalties imposed on those who transmit the virus will act as a deterrent to others, causing them to modify their high risk behaviour. However, while aiming to reduce the incidence of HIV transmission is a laudable aim, it is not clear that criminalization of transmission will be likely to achieve this goal.

There is a risk that the criminalization of HIV transmission may be counterproductive in terms of public health goals. While there is limited research regarding this issue, there are concerns that criminalization of HIV transmission will increase reluctance to be open about HIV infection, and increase the stigmatization and discrimination associated with HIV; stigmatization and discrimination that we already know deters individuals from being tested for HIV and seeking treatment and advice.[9]

As the Crown Prosecution Service (CPS) has pointed out, establishing recklessness in the transmission of HIV will depend on 'the defendant's awareness of his/her infection at the time when the sexual activity occurred... The greater his/her

[8] J. Chalmers, 'HIV Transmission and the criminal law', Aidsmap, at <http://www.aidsmap.com/cms1044409.asp> (accessed 1 March 2007).
[9] S. C. Kalichman, 'HIV transmission risk behaviors of men and women living with HIV-AIDS: Prevalence, predictors, and emerging clinical interventions', *Clinical Psychology: Science and Practice*, 7/1 (2000), 39.

understanding is of the infection the easier it will be to establish recklessness.'[10] It would be difficult to establish the required recklessness where the individual is unaware of their infection, or ignorant of the risk factors of HIV transmission. It also would seem likely that courts may try and gain access to any health care records that might establish the level of knowledge and understanding of the defendant regarding their HIV infection. Such a position would not seem to encourage individuals to come forward to discuss their risky sexual behaviour with health care professionals, or to be tested, or receive information about HIV. Thus, there is reason to suppose that the result of criminalization of HIV transmission may be to discourage individuals from coming forward for testing and counselling.

Against this, it might be argued that actual knowledge of HIV infection is not necessary for a conviction for transmission of HIV. In one of the recent cases, it seemed that the accused had never been tested for HIV, but the supposition that he *believed he could be* HIV positive appeared sufficient to find this individual guilty of inflicting grievous bodily harm by HIV transmission.[11] If this is the case, then avoiding testing would not provide a defence in such cases. It may also be argued that criminalization of HIV transmission will not significantly deter individuals from being tested, as coming forward for testing is the only way of receiving effective treatment.

Further, while there may be some legitimate concern that criminalizing HIV transmission will discourage HIV testing and effective counselling, it might be argued that removing those who transmit the virus from society will prevent at least some further infections by reducing the dangers of infection posed by those convicted and by deterring those who might otherwise infect their sexual partners. However, it is unlikely that transmission rates will be significantly reduced by the incarceration of a handful of HIV-positive individuals. Also, there is no reason to suppose that incarceration will prevent transmission. Sexual contact and intravenous drug use is common within prisons, and often occurs in an environment where condoms and clean needles are not readily available. It is also unlikely that criminalization of HIV transmission will provide a significant deterrent for others who may transmit the virus. It seems reasonable to assume that HIV transmission during consensual sexual contact often occurs in a situation of reduced rationality as a result of high sexual arousal, inebriation, strong feelings towards the sexual partner, and so on. It is not clear that the threat of prosecution would have a significant impact upon risky behaviour in such circumstances.

---

[10] Crown Prosecution Service, *Prosecuting cases involving the sexual transmission of infections which cause grievous bodily harm: A consultation paper*, (Crown Prosecution Service, September 2006) 6, paras 4.3/4.4, at <http://www.advisorybodies.doh.gov.uk/eaga/pdfs/cpsconsultation-nov2006.pdf> (accessed 16 November 2006).

[11] Anon, 'HIV bigamist jailed for infections', BBC News Online (12 January 2004) at <http://news.bbc.co.uk/1/hi/england/merseyside/3389735.stm> (accessed 27 February 2007).

It may also be the case that the existence of a public perception that HIV transmission has been criminalized will create a false expectation of disclosure from HIV-positive individuals. It might be supposed that as the law requires HIV-positive individuals to disclose their infection, not only is it the responsibility of HIV-positive individuals to do so, but that they are, in fact, *likely* to do so. The reality of the situation may be somewhat different for many reasons, and the most prudent advice to uninfected individuals is to protect themselves from infection regardless of the disclosure or otherwise of their partners.

In summary, there is no clear evidence that taking the bold and controversial step of criminalizing reckless HIV transmission via consensual sexual contact will further public health goals. Until evidence to this effect is available, it will be difficult to prepare a strong case for criminalization of reckless HIV transmission based on public health grounds. However, whilst questions may exist regarding whether criminalization of HIV transmission will actually prevent further transmission, perhaps a greater concern is uncovered when we explore a second major reason for criminalization: the punishment of wrongdoing.

## 4.2 The punishment of wrongdoing

If we choose to go down the practically and ethically problematic route of criminalizing HIV transmission, then we should do so because we believe that this is such a serious moral wrong that these drastic steps must be taken, both to punish, and to send out a strong message that this is morally repugnant behaviour. This is certainly a primary goal of the criminalization of HIV transmission, as is indicated by the CPS's statement that:

We wish to issue a clear statement that the intentional or reckless sexual transmission of infections that cause grievous bodily harm is not acceptable and, where appropriate, will be prosecuted effectively through the criminal courts.[12]

However, in order to be justified in sending out this message of moral repugnancy, we need to be clear about if and when this behaviour deserves such severe reaction.

As we have seen, the recent English cases reveal that consent after being forewarned of one's partner's HIV infection is an adequate defence. Yet, this legal ability to consent to bodily harm appears to go against the precedent established in the case of *R v Brown*,[13] in which defendants who engaged in consensual sadomasochist activity were successfully prosecuted for inflicting bodily harm. The ruling in *Brown* was that 'consent to bodily harm in fact does not constitute a consent recognized in law, other than in certain socially accepted and established activities which are themselves lawful (for example, surgery and

---

[12]  CPS, *Prosecuting cases involving the sexual transmission of infections.*
[13]  *R v Brown* [1994] 1 AC 212 (HL).

organised contact sports)'.[14] As the transmission of HIV was not considered socially acceptable or lawful in the same way that dangerous sports or surgery might be, the courts had to distinguish cases of HIV transmission from cases like *Brown* in order to allow a defence of consent. The distinction was reached on the basis that the case of *Brown* involved the deliberate infliction of injury, whereas sexual contact with an HIV-positive individual involves only the *risk* of harm. As Weait explains:

> In the context of consensual sexual intercourse, such risks are, and have always been, present—whether those be the risk of disease or the risks associated with pregnancy and childbirth. To criminalize the taking of such risks, by denying the defence of consent to those who create them, would not only be impracticable in enforcement terms, but would involve an unwarranted intrusion into the pre-eminently private sphere of adult sexual relations.[15]

Thus, it is claimed that just as we are able to consent to the *risk* of pregnancy and all the dangers and discomfort that this condition entails, so we must be able (after forewarning) to consent to the *risk* of HIV infection. However, in line with the *Brown* ruling, the defence of consent would not be available in instances of intentional or deliberate HIV transmission.[16] So the legal defence of consent *is* available where the HIV-positive individual warns his/her partner of his infection prior to sexual contact and, thus forewarned, his/her partner consents to the risk of infection. Without forewarning, the partner's consent is considered to be uninformed, and thus does not provide a defence for the HIV-positive individual.

In order to be secure in our justification of this newly established legal duty to forewarn and the legal defence of consent, we need to be sure that this legal stance does the job it sets out to do; that is, that it accurately reflects the moral situation in such cases. Only if we can be confident that this is an accurate reflection of morality can criminalization in such cases be deemed a legitimate option if this criminalization is to be justified on the grounds of punishing wrongdoing. The judgments in the recent cases seem to indicate that the morality of such cases is a straightforward issue. The assumptions seem to be that:

- if you forewarn, you have not wronged your partner, and, therefore, you should not be punished by the criminal law; and
- if you do not forewarn sexual partners, you have done wrong, and very serious wrong that warrants punishment by criminal law.

However, as I hope to demonstrate, the reality of cases of HIV transmission shows that the issue of consent is much more complex than this simplistic view suggests.

---

[14] Weait, 'Criminal Law and the Sexual Transmission of HIV', 124.
[15] Ibid.     [16] Ibid, 125.

## 4.3 Self-inflicted harm?

The reason why consent to the risk of HIV infection is seen as a defence for those charged with HIV transmission is that this consent to harm renders the harm self-inflicted. The argument is that these individuals were forewarned about their partner's HIV-positive status, but consented to high-risk activities all the same. Clearly, if we can catagorize the harm as self-inflicted, then it seems inappropriate to prosecute for the transmission of the virus.

For HIV transmission via consensual sexual contact to be categorized as an instance of self-inflicted harm, it would have to be shown that an individual consented to the risk of infection. In cases where an individual was *unaware* of the specific risk involved, a categorization of self-harm could not be confidently applied. Thus, the question that needs to be addressed is how much information must be available for consent to risk of HIV infection to be valid, and whether valid consent would indeed render any resulting harm self-inflicted?

## 4.4 Informed consent

As we have seen, in the recent English cases, the central issue was whether the 'victims' were forewarned of the HIV status of their partners. The assumption being that if the 'victims' had been forewarned of their partner's HIV-positive status and then consented to unprotected sex, the accused would have done no wrong. However, there is a common argument that forewarning is not necessary in order for consent to risk to be valid. Feston Konzani attempted to use this defence in his recent trial.[17] Konzani was jailed for ten years in 2004 for infecting three women with HIV. His lawyers had argued that, even though Konzani had not forewarned his partners of his HIV-positive status, by consenting to unprotected sexual intercourse with him, the women had consented to all the risks associated with sexual intercourse including the risk of HIV infection.[18]

The argument here is that it is not clear that an individual is necessarily being deceived when a sexual partner does not disclose his or her HIV-positive status, because a failure to disclose need not preclude an autonomous choice. With sex education in schools and extensive educational campaigns and media coverage, it is reasonable to suppose that most adults are aware of the existence of HIV, and have some elementary knowledge of its transmission routes. Arguably, then, it can be assumed that any consent given to, say, 'high-risk' sexual activity includes consent to the background risk of HIV infection, without disclosure of specific information about the particular sexual partner in question.

Many reject this line of thought. They argue that consent to sexual contact is invalidated if any information which may cause a potential partner to refuse

---

[17] *R v Konzani* [2005] EWCA Crim 706.
[18] Ibid, para 5.

consent to sexual activity is withheld.[19] But this view does not translate readily to other circumstances. For instance, it would be difficult for a woman who
becomes pregnant to blame her partner for this on the grounds that he did not
warn her of this possibility. It is not unreasonable for men to suppose that women
who are competent to consent to sex are also aware of the risk of pregnancy and it
is not, therefore, morally irresponsible of them to fail to provide a specific warning about this risk.

Against this claim, it can be argued that the risk assessment individuals may
make when they believe that the chances of their sexual partner being HIV
positive is low is very different from the risk assessment after their partner
has told them that he or she is HIV positive. On this view, consent to sexual
contact is invalidated if any information which may cause a sexual partner to
refuse consent to sexual activity is withheld.[20] It is difficult to argue that failure to disclose infection with a potentially fatal sexually transmitted disease
renders an otherwise consensual sexual act as rape, or battery. However, it may
be that while the consent to the sexual contact is valid in such cases, the consent to risk of *infection* is invalid. Consent to the possibility that a partner is
infected may well be significantly different from consent where the partner is
in fact infected, especially where the sexual partner is aware of his or her HIV-
positive status.

Yet, even if we accept that there may be an absolute moral obligation to forewarn sexual partners of one's HIV-positive status, does this mean that not to do
so is always a moral wrong of such magnitude that it deserves punishment by the
criminal law? Consider some hypothetical cases:

---

Early in a committed consensual relationship, an HIV-positive woman does not wish
to disclose her HIV status for fear of frightening away her new partner. She insists on
the use of condoms.

A gay man has sex in saunas, and backrooms of clubs. He is HIV positive, but does
not tell his very casual sexual partners as he assumes that regulars on this scene will be
aware of the risks involved in these activities.

A woman from a high-risk group (for example, from Sub-Saharan Africa, or an
intravenous drug user) has never been tested for HIV, but is aware that she is at a
relatively high risk of being infected. She begins a relationship with a new sexual partner. The new partner is aware of her high-risk affiliations, but does not seem unduly
worried about this. He persuades her to have unprotected sex with him.

A man infects his wife after a string of affairs. As far as she is concerned, they have a
committed monogamous relationship.

---

[19] See, for example, C. A. Erin and J. Harris, 'Is there an ethics of heterosexual AIDS?', in
L. Sherr (ed), *AIDS and the Heterosexual Population* (London: Harwood, 1993) 245.
[20] C. A. Erin, and J. Harris, 'AIDS: Ethics, justice and social policy', *Journal of Applied
Philosophy*, 10/2 (1993) 167.

I would argue that while all of these HIV-positive people probably do have a moral duty to forewarn their sexual partners of their HIV status (in the sense that it would be the right thing to do), if they fail to do so, they are not all 'guilty' to a similar degree.

It seems that the level of moral wrong we feel exists here depends not only on whether the HIV-positive person has forewarned his or her partner, but also on the level of risk involved, and on the kind of relationship in which these individuals are involved. It is clear that, in some instances, a serious moral wrong has been done by failure to forewarn; however, to move from this position to the stance that there is a legal obligation to disclose one's HIV status to sexual partners, with failure to do so punishable by the criminal law, seems to penalize at least some cases far too harshly.

## 4.5 Levels of risk[21]

It might be argued that these differing levels of 'guilt' will be reflected in the legal cases brought. The claim might be that those attempting to protect their partners by, for instance, insisting on condom use, are less likely to face criminal prosecution for the simple reason that it is unlikely that prosecutions will occur where HIV transmission has not occurred. However, there is no such thing as 'safe sex', only 'safer sex'. Sex with an HIV-positive person, even where condoms are used and other precautions taken, always carries some risk of infection. Would it be morally acceptable to prosecute the unlucky person who infected their partner despite taking precautions to protect them?

It is apparent that the CPS recognizes the moral significance of the differing levels of risk to which sexual partners are exposed:

Where there is no evidence showing a failure in use, . . . the use of a condom will be a significant factor that the prosecutor will take into account in deciding whether the defendant was reckless.[22]

However, the evidence of 'failure in use' to which the CPS refers includes considerations of the quality of the condoms, how and when they are put on and taken off, and so forth.[23] While, clearly, the nature and effectiveness of one's condom use is a fundamental moral issue when one partner is infected with HIV (or any other sexually transmitted disease with serious consequences), what is not clear is how the level of effectiveness of condom use is likely to be established in a court of law. It may be possible to establish that condoms were used, or that high-risk activities were avoided in other ways (although this in itself will not be easy), but

---

[21] For a more detailed exploration of the moral obligations of HIV infected individuals towards their sexual partners, see R. Bennett, H. Draper, and L. Frith, 'Ignorance is Bliss?: HIV and moral duties and legal duties to forewarn', *Journal of Medical Ethics*, 26/9 (2000), 9–15.
[22] CPS, *Prosecuting cases involving the sexual transmission of infections*.
[23] Ibid.

would it be possible to confidently establish that a 'gold standard' of condom use was adhered to consistently?

## 4.6 Levels of trust

As well as levels of risk being morally significant in cases of HIV transmission, levels of trust assumed in different relationships are also highly morally significant in such cases. The kind of sexual relationship that we are in determines our expectations of the risk involved. For instance, it seems reasonable to suppose that there might be an expectation of risk involved in very casual contacts, whereas in a committed relationship where there is an assumption of monogamy, it seems reasonable to assume that there is an expectation of very low risk of infection. Thus, someone who knows she is HIV positive and engages in high-risk sexual activity without forewarning her sexual partner of her infection would seem to have committed a more serious moral wrong if her partner is her spouse, or another long-term partner with whom there is an assumption of monogamy, than if the relationship was a casual relationship where no such assumption of monogamy was likely. Given this, it might seem obvious that the kind of relationship people are engaged in should influence the outcome of a legal case in this area. However, ascertaining, with any level of accuracy, the sort of relationship a couple may have had at any moment in time, and assigning moral guilt based on this assessment, would seem to be a very tall order for a court of law. Emotional and sexual relationships are, by their very nature, immensely complex. Partners may have different understandings of the nature and expectations of a relationship, casual relationships may develop into committed ones, committed relationships may become less so, and so on. Thus, while the levels of trust and expectations in a relationship greatly influence our moral obligations, basing convictions for serious offences on an assessment of these levels of trust and expectations is hugely problematic.

## 5. Is informed consent a complete defence in cases of HIV transmission?

Erin and Harris argue that:

If an HIV seropositive individual does inform any sexual partner of his HIV status, and the partner nevertheless indulges in sexual intercourse, whether protected or unprotected, he is a volunteer to the respective risks. This latter individual had made an informed consent and must bear responsibility for any consequences detrimental to himself. The HIV seropositive person who discloses his HIV status has discharged his responsibilities to his partner.[24]

---

[24]  Erin and Harris, 'Is there an ethics of heterosexual AIDS?', 248.

This is in line with the judicial stance that, despite the *Brown* ruling, fully informed consent is a complete defence in cases of HIV transmission. The argument here is that no moral wrong has been done, and, therefore, it is not appropriate to punish this behaviour. But again, does this provide an accurate reflection of the morality of such forewarning?

Consider some cases:

> A couple wish to have children. The male is HIV negative, and the woman is HIV positive. Despite the woman's positive status, they decide to have unprotected sex in order to conceive. They are both aware of the risks this involves.
>
> A young girl is deeply infatuated with an older man who is HIV positive. He tells her about his positive status, but she decides to have unprotected sex with him to prove her love for him.

Assuming an individual has a general obligation to do no harm where he or she has the option of doing no harm, can this obligation to do no harm be nullified by another's consent to be harmed? Can it ever be morally justifiable to harm someone?

Clearly, there are cases where consent to harm makes the infliction of the harm morally justifiable (for example, surgery). Consent to the risk of HIV infection may be given for many reasons, all of which may be very significant in, say, the context of a long-term relationship. It may be that the uninfected partner wants to prove how much he or she cares about his or her partner, or to increase the quality of their sex lives, or even to have a child with his or her partner. However, HIV disease is still potentially fatal. It is arguable that there are few benefits that could outweigh the harm of a potentially fatal disease. One of the strongest moral obligations must be an obligation not to kill others. This obligation is clearly not absolute, but where killing is deemed morally permissible, it is usually as the lesser of two evils, for example, in war, or instances of euthanasia. However, it is difficult to imagine a circumstance which would absolve one of one's obligation not to kill other people by infecting them with a potentially fatal virus like HIV, and it is not clear that gaining their consent to this harm makes a significant moral difference.

I suggest that, while HIV-positive individuals may have a moral obligation to forewarn sexual partners, this is only part of a wider moral obligation to protect others from infection. Whether this moral obligation should be used as the basis for a legal duty is quite another matter.

## 6. Exposure or harm?

One final issue I would like to consider is this: if the moral wrong done is in *exposing* someone to a high-risk of infection without forewarning them of this risk, then it seems that this moral wrong has occurred even where transmission does not occur. As Chalmers points out, 'it seems rather odd that the non-discloser's criminal liability should depend on the chance occurrence of whether HIV is transmitted'.[25] If the moral wrong attaches to the exposure to infection, then, if we are aiming to punish wrongdoing, it is this exposure that should be criminalized. If we accept this, then it follows that 'if criminal sanction is to be applied in this area, it should apply both to transmission and exposure... This view would probably entail the creation of two separate offences—an offence of transmission and a distinct offence of exposure.'[26]

All of this leads to the following *moral* conclusions:

- those who believe themselves to be HIV positive have a moral obligation to forewarn their sexual partners of this;
- however, the strength of this moral obligation depends on the nature of the relationship, and the level of risk involved;
- even where forewarning occurs, and consent to high-risk behavior is given, this may not always absolve the HIV-positive partner from moral 'guilt'; and
- even where transmission does not occur, it seems that, if someone is exposed to a high risk of transmission, the wrong has been done, whether or not the individual becomes infected.

## 7. Conclusion

We have seen that criminalization of HIV transmission is problematic as it risks being counterproductive to efforts to reduce the spread of infection, and may fuel discrimination and stigmatization of those living with HIV. However, this might be a price we are willing to pay if it means we are able to punish serious moral wrongs. Yet, identifying which sort of moral wrongs merit criminal prosecution is not an easy task. We will have to identify and quantify the level of this moral wrong in each case. As I have argued, attempting to do this with regard to sexual relationships is extremely difficult, if not impossible to do with any confidence.

As a result, I suggest that criminalization of HIV infection should only be considered if it can be restricted to the cases where we suspect that serious moral harms are committed. I would suggest that these cases would only be ones where force, or deceit were involved. While it might be true that people have behaved immorally in other cases of HIV transmission, this behaviour is generally not such that it is appropriate to justify a criminal prosecution.

---

[25] Chalmers, 'The criminalisation of HIV transmission', 161.
[26] Ibid.

# 14

# The Rightful Domain of the Criminal Law

*Charles A. Erin*

*The number of laws is constantly growing in all countries and, owing to this, what is called crime is very often not a crime at all, for it contains no element of violence or harm.*

P. D. Ouspensky (1878–1947)[1]

## 1. Preamble

I am not the possessor of a so-called 'legal mind'. This is an admission that, as one who teaches in one of the leading law schools in the UK, I normally find rather embarrassing. However, for the purposes of this essay, I see my lay credentials as positively advantageous, for what I hope to do in this piece is to give a view 'from the outside looking in', so to speak. As I see it, my position as an 'outsider' facilitates my adoption of a lay perspective in addressing the law. While my approach here may, as I openly admit, miss several of the nuances of legal reasoning, it will, I would aver, represent, to some fair degree, the view of the law that many of those subject to it are likely to possess.

One fundamental point I would wish to assert, rather than argue here is that there should be a law narrative that is not only easily accessible by, but easily comprehensible to the Everyman. How else would non-lawyer citizens (including many health care professionals) be expected to know, and understand whether, and why they contravene 'the law', especially when, in certain circumstances that are perplexing to at least one non-legal mind, they fall foul of the *criminal* law?

## 2. Introduction

In essence, this chapter constitutes a plea for consistency in the law, or, at the very least, a plea for reasonable explanation of why the inconsistencies that the lay eye

---

[1] P. D. Ouspenky, *A New Model of the Universe: Principles of the Psychological Method in its Application to Problems of Science, Religion and Art*, trans R. R. Merton (New York: Alfred A. Knopf, 1931).

perceives are not *just that*, inconsistencies. Why is it that that the likes of Laskey, Jaggard, and Brown[2] face grave penalties from the criminal law for harmful but mutually consensual acts, while doctors who perform acts ('operations') with fundamentally similar characteristics, and their willing 'patients' do not? Why is it that mutual consent to certain harmful acts is *not* a defence for private citizens, yet stands in law as such for similar acts involving the clinician and his/her patient? To the *lay* mind, I will argue, consent is clearly the core issue. And the lay person is left wondering why the mutual consent of Messrs Laskey, Jaggard, and Brown to harmful acts is to be seen to be irrelevant in law, while, for example, a woman who does not like the cut of her labial jib,[3] and her attending surgeon, will not face such risks to liberty from the criminal law.

My launching point is *Brown*,[4] simply because this was the case that brought such considerations to my mind. It is fair to say that I was brought up in a generation that felt it safe to take a certain view of liberty, as emblematic of our democracy, for granted, but perhaps we take liberty too much for granted.[5] *Brown* forced me to carefully reconsider my position as a free citizen under the law of England and Wales, not because of any resonance between the acts described in that case and any acts that my somewhat sedentary life has entertained to date, but, more basically, and more frighteningly (from the lay perspective), because of the seemingly broad implications of the legal decisions in *Brown*. I cannot think of any harmful acts to which I have been a party during my life that would not fall under the exceptions to the defence of consent outlined by the Offences Against The Person Act 1861, but that is hardly the point. That we need, and that we have exceptions to the defence of consent is what troubles my lay mind. I am the product of one of those generations that were brought up to believe that we were free, so free that we could do anything, just so long as 'anything' did not extend to acts which caused harm to non-consenting others. Thus, for instance, it would never have occurred to me during my youth that while playing school rugby, I would need an exemption, by way of the defence of consent, under the 1861 Act, in order to deploy the effects of a little too much *hwyl* in tackling a member of an opposing team.[6] Neither here nor

---

[2] *Laskey, Jaggard and Brown v the United Kingdom* 109/1995/615/703-705 (Strasbourg, February 1997), available at <http://194.250.50.200/eng/LASKEY.html>. See also *Laskey v United Kingdom* (1997) 24 EHRR 39 (ECtHR); *Laskey v United Kingdom* The Times, 20 February, 1997 (ECtHR).

[3] See discussion of labiaplasty, below.

[4] *R v Brown* [1993] 2 All ER 75 (HL). See also *R v Brown* [1994] 1 AC 212 (HL); *R v Brown* (1993) 143 NLJ Rep 339 (HL); *R v Brown* [1993] 2 WLR 556 (HL); *R v Brown* [1992] 2 WLR 441 (CA); *R v Brown* (1992) 94 Cr App R 302 (CA).

[5] I am reminded of the words of Allen Buchanan in a discussion of rights ('What's so special about rights?'(1984) 2 *Social Philosophy & Policy* 61):

Unfortunately, that which enjoys our greatest enthusiasm is often that about which we are least critical.

[6] A heart-warming Welsh word, a word of the blood, that I have never seen translated into English with any great success, and I'm not convinced that even the Oxford English Dictionary (<http://dictionary.oed.com>) comes particularly close with: 'An emotional quality which inspires and sustains impassioned eloquence; also, the fervour of emotion characteristic of gatherings of Welsh people.' From my experience, the influence of *hwyl* extends far further than 'impassioned

there, perhaps, but certainly indicative of the broad range of the 1861 Act (if, and when brought to the attention of a lay mind).

My professional field is health care ethics, and it was here that I immediately perceived the possible implications of the rulings in *Brown*. Doctors do harm to their patients every day. From 'jabs' to the removal of organs for transplantation, doctors must do harm in order to do good—good either for their own patient, or, in the case of the removal of an organ from a living donor for transplantation, for another's patient. We are familiar with these kinds of practices, and, just so long as the optimally informed consent of the patient (or donor) has been obtained, we rarely question such practices. But should we not?

## 3. *Brown*

*Brown* is, as I say, my starting point for this analysis. For the facts in the case, I will run, in the main, with the account given in the European Court of Human Rights (ECtHR) judgment.[7] From paragraph 8 of the ECtHR judgment:

In 1987 in the course of routine investigations into other matters, the police came into possession of a number of video films which were made during sado-masochistic encounters involving the applicants and as many as 44 other homosexual men. As a result the applicants, with several other men, were charged with a series of offences, including assault and wounding, relating to sado-masochistic activities that had taken place over a ten-year period.[8]

Apparently, Operation Spanner, as it was named by the police, had its origins in an investigation into a series of raids conducted in 1987 as part of an investigation into child pornography,[9] which, by chance, led to the discovery, by the Greater Manchester Police,[10] of a number of video tapes, on of which was initially thought, mistakenly, to be a 'snuff movie'.[11]

During the course of the police investigation,[12] hundreds of men were interviewed. In September 1989, sixteen men were charged,[13] but it was only Mr Colin

eloquence', and I have certainly experienced *hwyl* (off the pitch) while alone. (I was born, brought up, and, until the end of my undergraduate days, educated in Wales.)

[7] *Laskey, Jaggard and Brown v the United Kingdom*.

[8] *Laskey, Jaggard and Brown v the United Kingdom*, at para 8.

[9] S. Edwards, 'No defence for a sado-masochistic libido', *New Law Journal*, 143 [6592] (1993) 406.

[10] C. Stanley, 'Sins and passions', *Law & Critique*, IV [2] (1993) 212.

[11] C. Stanley, 'Sins and passions', 212, Edwards, 'No defence for a sado-masochistic libido', 406.

[12] According to the Spanner Trust, the investigation lasted four years, involved fourteen of the police forces in England and Wales, and cost an estimated £4m—see the Spanner Trust, 'Response of the Spanner Trust to the Scottish Law Commission Discussion Paper No 131 on Rape and Other Sexual Offences January 2006', available at <http://www.spannertrust.org/documents/Response_of_the_Spanner_Trust_to_the_Scottish_Law_Commission_Dicussion_Paper_No_31_on_Rape_and_other_Sexual_Offences_January_2006.pdf>.

[13] Anon, 'Spanner Time Line', at <http://www.barnsdle.demon.co.uk/span/sp-timel.html> (accessed 8 May 2007). According to this source, a further twenty six men were cautioned.

Laskey, Mr Roland Jaggard, and Mr Anthony Brown who took their cases as far as the ECtHR. The charges included assault, aiding and abetting assault, and/or keeping a disorderly house.[14] I will be focusing on the charges that involve assault and wounding. According to the ECtHR, '[a]lthough the instances of assault were very numerous, the prosecution limited the counts to a small number of exemplary charges'.[15]

What kinds of acts are we talking about? Here, naïfs such as myself are liable to blush, and I am happiest to run with the wording supplied by the ECtHR:

The acts consisted in the main of maltreatment of the genitalia (with, for example, hot wax, sandpaper, fish hooks and needles) and ritualistic beatings either with the assailant's bare hands or a variety of implements, including stinging nettles, spiked belts and a cat-o'-nine tails. There were instances of branding and infliction of injuries which resulted in the flow of blood and which left scarring.[16]

It is important to stress that '[t]hese activities were consensual and were conducted in private for no apparent reason other than the achievement of sexual gratification'.[17]

A layperson may be forgiven for thinking that these activities came to the attention of the police because they necessitated medical attention, and that the health care professionals involved suspected criminal activity as the cause of injury. However:

The infliction of pain was subject to certain rules including the provision of a code word to be used by any 'victim' to stop an 'assault', and did not lead to any instances of infection, permanent injury or the need for medical attention.[18]

The case against the men was based in the content of a large number of videos discovered, by chance,[19] by the police during the raids:

The activities took place at a number of locations, including rooms equipped as torture chambers. Video cameras were used to record events and the tapes copied and distributed amongst members of the group. The prosecution was largely based on the content of those video tapes. There was no suggestion that the tapes had been sold or used other than by members of the group.[20]

## 3.1 The rulings

### Central Criminal Court, Old Bailey, 19 December 1990
As already mentioned, nobody denies that what these men got up to was mutually consensual, and was done in private. However, at the first hearing, in late

---

[14] Ibid.
[15] *Laskey, Jaggard and Brown v the United Kingdom*, at para 8.     [16] Ibid.
[17] Ibid.                                                           [18] Ibid.
[19] Ibid, para 38.                                                  [20] Ibid, para 9.

1990, Rant J ruled that the fact that the 'victims' had consented was ineligible as a defence.[21]

The defendants pleaded guilty to the assault charges, and were convicted. Mr Laskey was sentenced to four and a half years' imprisonment: four years for aiding and abetting keeping a disorderly house,[22] and a consecutive six-month term for possession of an indecent photograph of a child; he also received concurrent sentences of twelve months' imprisonment for various counts of assault occasioning actual bodily harm, and aiding and abetting assault occasioning actual bodily harm.[23] Mr Jaggard was sentenced to three years' imprisonment: two years for aiding and abetting unlawful wounding, and twelve months for assault occasioning actual bodily harm, aiding and abetting assault occasioning actual bodily harm, and unlawful wounding.[24] And Mr Brown was sentenced to two years and nine months' imprisonment: twelve months for aiding and abetting assault occasioning actual bodily harm, nine months for assault occasioning actual bodily harm, and twelve months for further assaults occasioning actual bodily harm.[25]

### Court of Appeal, Criminal Division, 19 February 1992
All three men appealed against their convictions and sentences, and, in early 1992, the appeals against the convictions were dismissed by the Court of Appeal. However, the three men's sentences were reduced[26] on the ground that the appellants 'did not appreciate that their actions in inflicting injuries were criminal'.[27]

### House of Lords, 11 March 1993
The next stage in the saga was the appeal to the House of Lords. In March 1993, that too was dismissed, by a majority, with two of the five Law Lords dissenting.[28]

---

[21] Ibid, para10.

[22] From ibid, para 31:

Keeping a 'disorderly house' is a common law offence. A disorderly house is defined as 'one which is not regulated by the restraints of morality and which is so conducted as to violate law and good order. There must be an element of "open house", but it does not need to be open for the public at large... Where indecent performances or exhibitions are alleged as rendering the premises a disorderly house, it must be proved that matters are there performed or exhibited of such a character that their performance or exhibition in place of common resort (a) amounts to an outrage of public decency, or (b) tends to corrupt or deprave, or (c) is otherwise calculated to injure the public interest so as to call for condemnation and punishment' ([1996] *Archbold's Criminal Pleading, Evidence and Practice* 20, at 224).

[23] Ibid, para 11.        [24] Ibid, para 12.

[25] Ibid, para 13.

[26] Mr Laskey's sentence was reduced to a total of two years' imprisonment (eighteen months on the charge of aiding and abetting keeping a disorderly house, three months to run concurrently in regard of the charges of assault, and six months to run consecutively for the possession of an indecent photograph of a child); Mr Jaggard's to six months' imprisonment; and Mr Brown's to three months' imprisonment. See ibid, paras 16–17.

[27] Ibid, para 15.

[28] Ibid, para 19.

**European Court of Human Rights, 21 October 1996**

In October 1996, the ECtHR heard the application from Laskey, Jaggard, and Brown that the UK had made an unlawful and unjustifiable 'violation of their right to respect for their private lives through their sexual personality',[29] as guaranteed by Article 8 of the European Convention on Human Rights. In its February 1997 ruling, the ECtHR unanimously held that there had been no violation of Article 8 of the Convention.

## 4. Some jurisprudence

### 4.1 Mill On Liberty

I have already hinted at my general philosophical approach. I take autonomy and liberty as central to my worldview, and, perhaps, overarching; thus, put somewhat simplistically, my attitude to the law is this: there is no legitimate ground for State interference with the conduct of citizens that results in no harm to others. The reader will recognize immediately a strong Millian flavour to this. In the introduction to his *On Liberty*, Mill famously asserted that 'the only purpose for which power can be rightfully exercised over any member of a civilized community, against his will, is to prevent harm to others'.[30] This liberty limiting principle has come to be known as the *harm principle*. Typically, that is all one is given of *On Liberty* when the harm principle is referred to in secondary sources,[31] but I think it is instructive, in the current context, to rehearse more of the passage from which this is extracted. Mill writes:

The object of this Essay is to assert one very simple principle, as entitled to govern absolutely the dealings of society with the individual in the way of compulsion and control, whether the means used be physical force in the form of legal penalties, or the moral coercion of public opinion. That principle is, that the sole end for which mankind are warranted, individually or collectively, in interfering with the liberty of action of any of their number, is self-protection. That the only purpose for which power can be rightfully exercised over any member of a civilized community, against his will, is to prevent harm to others. His own good, either physical or moral, is not a sufficient warrant. He cannot rightfully be compelled to do or forbear because it will be better for him to do so, because it will make him happier, because, in the opinions of others, to do so would be wise, or even right. These are good reasons for remonstrating with him, or reasoning with him, or persuading him, or entreating him, but not for compelling him, or visiting him with any evil in case he do otherwise. To justify that, the conduct from which it is desired to deter him, must be calculated to produce evil to some one else. The only part of the conduct of any one, for which he is amenable to society, is that which concerns others. In the part

---

[29] Ibid, para 34.
[30] J. S. Mill, *On Liberty*, in J. Gray and G. W. Smith (eds), *J. S. Mill's On Liberty In Focus* (London: Routledge, 1991) 30.
[31] And in some student essays.

which merely concerns himself, his independence is, of right, absolute. Over himself, over his own body and mind, the individual is sovereign.[32]

As already conceded, prior to my encountering the judgments in *Brown*, I had taken Mill's principle for granted, and assumed, perhaps naively, that in our kind of modern, Western, liberal democracy, harmless offences fell outside the remit of the criminal law.[33]

Note that Mill refers to his principle as 'very simple'.[34] Mill's principle can be seen as controversial, though, in that it maintains that the prevention of harm is the *only* ground for State interference.

Appendix C of the Law Commission's Consultation Paper, *Consent in the Criminal Law*[35] of 1995, is substantial, and is devoted to 'philosophical foundations'[36] and I find it interesting, and somewhat reassuring that the Law Commission saw fit to go to the same authors and texts as I do when discussing Liberalism in this context. It seems *natural* to me to move from Mill to Joel Feinberg, chiefly, I think, because of Feinberg's strong presumption in favour of liberty.[37] The Law Commission do the same, because Feinberg's is the 'most subtle and comprehensive elaboration to date'[38] of Mill's harm principle.

## 4.2 Harm and offence

In his masterful four-volume work, *The Moral Limits of the Criminal Law*,[39] Feinberg takes Mill as his jumping-off point, and develops a less tractable *harm principle*. Succinctly stated, Feinberg's harm principle asserts:

[T]he need to prevent harm (private or public) to parties other than the actor is always an appropriate *reason* for legal coercion.[40]

---

[32] J. S. Mill, *On Liberty*, 30–31.

[33] I find the notion of 'consensual *crime*', or 'victimless *crime*' oxymoronic. From the *Word IQ* at <http://www.wordiq.com/definition/Consensualcrime>:

A *consensual* or *victimless crime* is a crime where all of those involved in the act give consent, and no third parties suffer as a direct result.

[34] When a philosopher refers to anything as 'simple', this is usually a good sign that we are talking about something that is complex, subtle, and complicated.

[35] The Law Commission, *Criminal Law: Consent in the Criminal Law* (Law Com Cp No 139, 1995).

[36] The Law Commission is surely to be congratulated for this.

[37] Consider this, for example (J. Feinberg, *The Moral Limits of the Criminal Law, Volume One: Harm to Others* (New York: Oxford University Press, 1984) 9):

[W]henever a legislator is faced with a choice between imposing a legal duty on citizens or leaving them at liberty, other things being equal, he should leave individuals free to make their own choices. Liberty should be the norm; coercion always needs some special justification.

[38] Law Commission, *Consent in the Criminal Law*, 252, C 26.

[39] Feinberg, *Harm to Others*; J. Feinberg, *The Moral Limits of the Criminal Law, Volume Two: Offense to Others* (New York: Oxford University Press, 1985); J. Feinberg, *The Moral Limits of the Criminal Law, Volume Three: Harm to Self* (New York: Oxford University Press, 1986); J. Feinberg, *The Moral Limits of the Criminal Law, Volume Four: Harmless Wrongdoing* (New York: Oxford University Press, 1988).

[40] Feinberg, *Harm to Others*, 11.

Put less concisely:

[I]t is legitimate for the state to prohibit conduct that causes serious private harm, or the unreasonable risk of such harm, or harm to important public institutions and practices... [S]tate interference with a citizen's behaviour tends to be morally justified when it is reasonably necessary... to prevent harm or the unreasonable risk of harm to parties other than the person interfered with.[41]

Note that, unlike Mill, Feinberg is deliberately tentative when it comes to the harm principle, initially saying only that it is '*a* valid legislative principle',[42] not necessarily the only legally valid liberty-limiting principle. I will return to this point in due course.

In view of the application to which I want to put Feinberg, it is important to be clear, and as specific as possible, as to what actually is the 'harm' identified by Feinberg's *harm principle*. For Feinberg, 'harm' here represents the overlap of two possible senses of the term. In the first sense, 'harm' is to be understood as 'the thwarting, setting back, or defeating of an interest'.[43] And Feinberg explains 'interest' in the relevant sense as follows:

One's interests... taken as a miscellaneous collection, consist of all those things in which one has a stake, whereas one's interest in the singular, one's personal interest or self-interest, consists in the harmonious advancement of all one's interests in the plural. These interests, or perhaps more accurately, the things these interests are *in*, are distinguishable components of a person's well-being: he flourishes or languishes as they flourish or languish. What promotes them is to his advantage or *in his interest*; what thwarts them is to his detriment or *against his interest*.[44]

The second sense of 'harm' is 'a kind of normative sense which the term must bear in any plausible formulation of the harm principle',[45] and this is the sense of harming *as wronging*:

To say that *A* has harmed *B* in this sense is to say much the same thing as that *A* has wronged *B*, or treated him unjustly. One person *wrongs* another when his indefensible (unjustifiable and inexcusable) conduct violates the other's right, and in all but certain very special cases such conduct will also invade the other's interest and thus be harmful in the sense already explained.[46]

Feinberg concludes that, in application of the harm principle, 'only setbacks of interests that are wrongs, and wrongs that are setbacks to interest, are to count as harms in the appropriate sense'.[47]

And this brings us to a key piece of wisdom in Feinberg. He writes:

One class of harms (in the sense of set-back interests) must certainly be excluded from those that are properly called wrongs, namely those to which the victim has consented.

---

[41] Ibid.  [42] Ibid, 12.  [43] Ibid, 33.
[44] Ibid, 34.  [45] Ibid.  [46] Ibid.
[47] Ibid, 36.

These include harms voluntarily inflicted by the actor upon himself, or the risk of which the actor freely assumed, and *harms inflicted upon him by the actions of others to which he has freely consented.*[48]

To return to the question of there existing other legally valid liberty-limiting principles, Feinberg identifies three candidates: the *'offense principle', 'legal paternalism'*, and *'legal moralism'*. I do not have the space to provide detailed analyses, but some general points can be made. It may already be clear that, like Feinberg, I reject both legal paternalism and legal moralism.[49]

## 4.3 Offence

I have always been inclined to something like what Feinberg describes as the 'extreme liberal position',[50] whereby, in line with Mill, only the harm principle can provide good reasons for criminal prohibitions. Feinberg devotes Volume Two[51] of *The Moral Limits to the Criminal Law* to the concept of offence, and I cannot hope to do justice to his treatment in one paragraph. In brief, he sees *offence*, however serious, as distinct to *harm* (as he has characterized 'harm' in his harm principle). The offence principle states: 'it is reasonably necessary to prevent hurt... or offense (as opposed to injury or harm) to others.'[52] And let us not be delayed by the notion of 'hurt'; sufficed to say, in adjectival terms, Feinberg's distinction is between, on the one hand, 'harmful,' and, on the other, 'disliked but not harmful,' and *hurts* and *offences* fall as sub-categories under the latter head.[53] What it is important to note is that, on Feinberg's analysis, '[i]f these unpleasant experiences are intense or prolonged enough... or if they recur continuously or occur at strategically untimely moments, they can get in the way of our interests'.[54] And, ultimately, he concludes that 'conduct that is *profoundly* offensive can legitimately be criminalized'.[55]

The question begged is: how is this exception to the harm principle, let us call it the *profound offence principle*, to be specified? Which is, in a way, to ask: what is it that marks out *profound* offences as justifying the limiting of liberty, and thus being a legitimate part of the domain of the criminal law, from other offences

---

[48] Ibid, 35 [my emphasis].

[49] Note, in this regard, Feinberg perceives legal moralism as providing 'grounding for statutes prohibiting deviant sexual activities—homosexual or extramarital sexual intercourse and *"perversions" especially shocking to the legislators*, even when performed in private by consenting adults...' (ibid, 13 [my emphasis]).

[50] Ibid, 26.

[51] Feinberg, *Offense to Others*.

[52] Feinberg, *Harm to Others*, 12.

[53] Ibid, Diagram 1, 47. For Feinberg's discussion of the distinction between 'hurt' and 'offense', see ibid, 46 ff.

[54] Ibid, 46.

[55] L. Alexander, Larry, 'The philosophy of criminal law' in J. Coleman and S. Shapiro (eds), *The Oxford Handbook of Jurisprudence and Philosophy of Law* (Oxford: Oxford University Press, 2002) 854 [my emphasis].

that do not? Feinberg's answer is that such conduct as causes offence must be conduct that occurs in public for it to be classified as causing profound offence. And note this well:

*Bare knowledge that such conduct is occurring in private, no matter how disturbing, cannot justify criminalizing its private occurrence.*[56]


## 5. Application to *Brown*

While Feinberg's restricted, (*profound*) *offence principle* is intellectually attractive,[57] I am happiest to stick to my guns, and to claim that it is the harm principle alone that is the appropriate philosophical underpinning of the criminal law, and that properly demarcates its rightful domain.

Applying this to *Brown*, it seems fairly straightforward to say that the conduct that led to these men's imprisonment did not fall foul of the harm principle. Straightforward? Yes. Recall that 'only setbacks of interests that are wrongs, and wrongs that are setbacks to interest, are to count as harms in the appropriate sense',[58] and that '[o]ne class of harms (in the sense of setback interests) must certainly be excluded from those that are properly called wrongs, namely those to which the victim has consented'.[59] Put more forcefully:

The harm principle will not justify the prohibition of consensual activities even where they are likely to harm the interests of the consenting parties; its aim is to prevent only those harms that are wrongs.[60]

I suspect that it may take more work to demonstrate that the conduct in *Brown* did not fall foul of the offence principle in its standard, broad form, but if Feinberg is correct about the *profound* offence principle, then it seems clear that this, at least, does not apply, as great care was taken by the parties involved to ensure that their activities were not conducted in public, and, indeed, no one other than those consenting adults involved would have known anything about it if the police had not kicked in their doors.

If I am right about all of this, then it seems to me that the various rulings in *Brown* clearly fall under the head of *legal moralism*.[61]

---

[56] Ibid, 854–5 [my emphasis]. On the 'bare knowledge problem', see Feinberg, *Offense to Others*, 61 ff.

[57] I am being deliberately cautious over the offence principle because I have yet to fully satisfy myself that, even in its restricted, Feinbergian form, it does not ultimately collapse into legal moralism (cf Alexander, 'The philosophy of criminal law', 859 ff.).

[58] Feinberg, *Harm to Others*, 36.

[59] Ibid, 35.

[60] Ibid, 35–6.

[61] Which is manifestly a bad thing!

My position on *Brown*, then, is something like this: Personally, I am not interested in 'BDSM';[62] indeed, I find the notion aesthetically unattractive;[63] but I will defend your liberty to pursue such conduct, just so long as it is (optimally) mutually consensual, and just so long as it is done in such a way that obviates the harming of others.

## 6. Implications for health care

### 6.1 Consistency in the law: 'proper medical treatment'. On what is the medical exemption based?

The real issue for me is the justification of limits to be placed on those acts to which one's consent may be legally valid, and the very notion that there may be acts to which a competent person's *consent* might not be valid strikes me, at an intuitive level, as philosophically unsound. At the risk of redundancy, let me emphasize again that, like Mill, and like Feinberg, I am not talking here of limits imposed on the consent of children, or others whose autonomy may be questioned. My focus here is on fully-fledged moral agents. If limits on consent are to be justified by anything other than the harm principle,[64] it seems to me that we thereby devalue personal autonomy. How much respect can one muster for a society that, on the one hand, embraces the doctrine of informed consent, and, by implication, espouses the significance of personal autonomy, and, on the other hand, seems to send the strong message that your autonomy is only to be viewed as significant if it grounds the choices that *you* make that are in line with *our* moral worldview?

### 6.2 Reasonable surgery

As a layperson, it seems to me that one thing I may reasonably expect of the law is consistency. There are many areas in health care where harm is done to a person.[65] Most often, the harm is judged to be necessary for the person's own good, his or her welfare; if the surgeon does not now cut open the patient and remove the

---

[62] From *Word IQ* at <http://www.wordiq.com/definition/BDSM>:

*BDSM* is a portmanteau acronym that stands for 'bondage & discipline' (B&D), 'domination & submission' (D&S) and 'sadism & masochism' (S&M), and describes an [sic] number of related patterns of human sexual behaviour involving amongst other things sexual sado-masochism in a context that is according to precepts of explicit informed consent by all parties involved. This is sometimes referred to as SSC (safe, sane and consensual) though others prefer RACK (Risk Aware Consensual Kink). Because of the explicit consent involved, parties involved in BDSM activities see BDSM as quite distinct from sexual abuse, which they regard as non-consensual by definition.

[63] On this, see Alexander, 'The philosophy of criminal law', n 122.

[64] And, perhaps, the profound offence principle.

[65] Of course, the competent person can refuse even life-saving treatment, and, if one believes acts and omissions to be morally equivalent, one might argue that in many situations in the medical setting we effectively have a trump card which allows us to 'consent' to harm.

offending cancerous tumour, for example, the patient will, in due course, suffer a worse harm. And consequentialists will likely have no problem with such cases of doing bad to do good.

In these kinds of circumstances, the patient's informed consent is taken as sufficient to morally and legally justify the act. Simplistically, the perceived necessity, benefit to the patient, and informed consent account for cases of, for example, 'reasonable surgery'.[66] I have it on good authority that there exists no statutory, or uniform definition of 'reasonable surgery'.[67] The Law Commission has, however, considered 'proper medical treatment or care'.[68] This is a term used by Lord Mustill in *Brown*:

Many of the acts done by surgeons would be very serious crimes if done by anyone else, and yet the surgeons incur no liability. Actual consent, or the substitute for consent deemed by the law to exist where an emergency creates a need for action, is an essential element in this immunity; but it cannot be a direct explanation for it, since much of the bodily invasion involved in surgery lies well above any point at which consent could even arguably be regarded as furnishing a defence. Why is this so? The answer must in my opinion be that proper medical treatment, for which actual or deemed consent is a prerequisite, is in a category of its own.[69]

As the Law Commission points out, this is in line with Lord Mustill's earlier judgment in *Bland*,[70] where, inter alia, Lord Mustill asserts that 'bodily invasions in the course of proper medical treatment stand completely outside the criminal law.'[71] He continues:

The reason why the consent of the patient is so important is not that it furnishes a defence in itself, but because it is usually essential to the propriety of medical treatment. Thus, if the consent is absent, and is not dispensed with in special circumstances by operation of the law, the acts of the doctor lose their immunity.[72]

Following the lead of the Criminal Codes of New Zealand and Canada,[73] the Law Commission provisionally recommends a 'medical exemption',[74] a 'Class I exception',[75] according to its scheme, 'in relation to proper medical treatment

---

[66] This is the term used by Lord Jauncey of Tullichettle in *Brown* (*R v Brown* [1993] 2 All ER 75, as quoted in *Laskey, Jaggard and Brown*, para 21).

[67] M. Brazier, (personal communication, 22 May 2005.)

[68] Law Commission, *Consent in the Criminal Law*, 117, para 8.50.

[69] *R v Brown* [1994] 1 AC 212, 226F–G, per Lord Mustill, as referred to in Law Commission, *Consent in the Criminal Law*, 102–3, para 8.3.

[70] *Airedale NHS Trust v Bland* [1993] AC 789.

[71] Ibid, 891.        [72] Ibid.

[73] See Law Commission, *Consent in the Criminal Law*, 104–5, paras 8.7–8.11. Note, however, that the Law Commission recognizes that s 61 of the Criminal Code in New Zealand, and s 45 and 216 of the Canadian Criminal Code are 'mainly concerned with legitimising surgical treatment carried out on a patient who lacks the capacity to consent, rather than with creating a general medical exemption from criminal liability for an offence against the person' (104, para 8.7).

[74] Ibid, para 8.50.

[75] That is, an exception which legalizes the causing of a 'higher level of non-fatal consensual injury' (ibid, 20, para 2.19). This is part of a three-tier classification of exceptions that 'derogate from a general principle that a person with capacity should be able to give a legally effective consent

etc'.[76] The recommendation is worded thus (and bear in mind that we are only considering non-fatal offences here):

8.50 We therefore provisionally propose that—

(1) a person should not be guilty of an offence, notwithstanding that he or she causes injury to another, of whatever degree of seriousness, if such injury is caused during the course of proper medical treatment or care administered with the consent of that other person;

(2) in this context 'medical treatment or care'—

    (a) should mean medical treatment or care administered by or under the direction of a duly qualified medical practitioner;

    (b) should include not only surgical and dental treatment or care, but also procedures taken for the purposes of diagnosis, the prevention of disease, the prevention of pregnancy or as ancillary to treatment; and

    (c) without limiting the meaning of the term, should also include the following:

        (i) surgical operations performed for the purposes of rendering a patient sterile;

        (ii) surgical operations performed for the purposes of enabling a person to change his or her sex;

        (iii) lawful abortions;

        (iv) surgical operations performed for cosmetic purposes;
        and

        (v) any treatment or procedure to facilitate the donation of regenerative tissue, or the donation of non-regenerative tissue not essential for life.[77]

What *actually* constitutes 'proper medical treatment'? It seems to me that we do not have to work too hard to shoehorn some procedures[78] into this category that may surprise many.

### 6.2.1 *Apotemnophilia and /or body integrity identity disorder*

Consider, for example, a treatment for apotemnophilia.[79] Apotemnophilia is a rare form of body dysmorphic disorder,[80] first described in

---

to any injury up to a level which [the Law Commission] will be describing as "seriously disabling injury." ' (ibid).

[76]  Ibid, 117, para 8.49.

[77]  Ibid, 117, para 8.50. For a discussion of the Law Commission's so-called 'quantitative approach', its characterization of 'serious disabling injury', which it sets as the limit on the defence of consent, and its qualification on who may perform such 'proper medical treatment', see P. Alldridge, 'Consent to medical and surgical treatment—the Law Commission's recommendations', *Medical Law Review* 4 (Summer, 1996) 129–3.

[78]  All performed 'by or under the direction of a registered medical practitioner' (ibid).

[79]  Also known as Body Integrity Identity Disorder (BIID), or Amputee Identity Disorder (see G. M. Furth and R. Smith, with an introduction by E. Kubler-Ross, *Amputee Identity Disorder: Questions, Answers and Recommendations About Self-Demand Amputation* (Bloomington, IN: 1stBooks Library, 2000).

[80]  According to Bensler and Paauw, writing in 2003, '[f]ewer than a dozen case reports of apotemnophilia currently exist in the literature' (J. M. Bensler and D. S. Paauw, 'Apotemnophilia

1977,[81] and has been defined as: 'self-desired amputation driven by the patient's erotic fantasy of possessing an amputated limb and overachieving despite being handicapped'.[82] There seems to be some confusion in the recent 'literature' over whether apotemnophilia ought to be distinguished from Body Integrity Identity Disorder (BIID). What seems to separate the two views is the erotic component. Thus, those who see no distinction between apotemnophilia and BIID would see it as similar to acrotomophilia, but differentiated by the fact that in apotemnophilia the desire is 'for *oneself* to be an amputee as opposed to *one's partner* having an amputation'.[83] I suppose I mention this simply on account of the nature of the offences in *Brown*, and I am actually quite happy to run with BIID. Those who see the distinction would say that in BIID 'an individual desires an amputation without an accompanying sexual component to this desire'.[84] According to the BME[85] Encyclopedia:

BIID has been most commonly compared to Gender Identity Disorder (GID) in that one common factor is that in both conditions, the individuals report that their feelings and urges have been present since their pre-adolescent years...Individuals with BIID who are unable to secure an amputation can become increasingly anxious and depressed, feeling that they can never become 'complete' which can lead to increasingly dangerous behaviors such as self injury to achieve amputation by using guns to injure a limb beyond the medical community's capacity to save the limb, burning or deliberately infecting wounds in the hopes of 'forcing' a doctor to perform the amputation...A small number of hospitals are beginning to recognize BIID as a legitimate disease that is 'curable'

masquerading as medical morbidity', *Southern Medical Journal*, 96/7 (2003), 676). From <http://www.biopsychiatry.com/bdd.html>:

Body dysmorphic disorder (BDD), a distressing and impairing preoccupation with an imagined or slight defect in appearance, is an 'OCD-spectrum disorder' [OCD = obsessive-compulsive disorder] that appears to be relatively common. BDD often goes unrecognized and undiagnosed, however, due to patients' reluctance to divulge their symptoms because of secrecy and shame. Any body part can be the focus of concern (most often, the skin, hair, and nose), and most patients engage in compulsive behaviors, such as mirror checking, camouflaging, excessive grooming, and skin picking. Approximately half are delusional, and a majority experience ideas or delusions of reference. Nearly all patients suffer some impairment in functioning as a result of their symptoms, some to a debilitating degree. Psychiatric hospitalization, suicidal ideation, and suicide attempts are relatively common. While treatment data are preliminary at this time, selective serotonin reuptake inhibitors (SSRIs) appear to often be effective for BDD, even if symptoms are delusional. Cognitive-behavioral therapy is another promising approach. While much remains to be learned about BDD, it is important that clinicians screen patients for this disorder and accurately diagnose it, as available treatments are very promising for those who suffer from this distressing and sometimes disabling disorder.

    [81] J. Money, R. Jobaris, and G. Furth, 'Apotemnophilia: Two cases of self-demand amputation as a paraphilia', *Journal of Sex Research*, 13 (1977), 115–5. Note that Money et al 'remarked that apotemnophilia was first brought to public attention in the September and October issues of *Penthouse* magazine in 1972' (Bensler and Paauw, 'Apotemnophilia masquerading as medical morbidity', 676).
    [82] Bensler and Paauw, 'Apotemnophilia masquerading as medical morbidity', 674.
    [83] S. Larratt and BMEZINE.COM, 'Apotemnophilia', *The BME Encyclopedia*, at <http://encyc.bmezine.com/?Apotemnophilia> [my emphasis].
    [84] Ibid.        [85] Body Modification Ezine (BME).

through amputation. However, the mainstream medical community tends to give these hospitals so much backlash after they perform such procedures that they are often forced to stop.[86]

This is pretty much what happened in the Falkirk and District Royal Infirmary cases, which caused a stir in the UK press in 2000. It came to light, in February of that year, that two men, one English, one German, had each had a leg amputated above the knee by consultant surgeon Robert Smith as treatment for BIID.[87] The operations had been performed in September 1997 and April 1999 respectively, but the Chairman and Board of the Forth Valley Acute Hospitals NHS Trust only became aware of them when, in Summer 1999, Mr Smith made it known that he was assessing a third patient, an American, for the same procedure.[88] In February 2000, the Trust ruled that no more such operations would be carried out on private patients at the hospital, although patients within the Forth Valley Acute Hospitals NHS Trust would be considered if the local health board gave its approval.[89]

The two successful amputees were private patients who had been refused treatment 'at hospitals across Europe',[90] and each paid the hospital (not Mr Smith) an estimated £3,000. Apparently, Mr Smith was moved by the fact that BIID sufferers 'often resorted to self harm—for example by shooting their leg off or lying on a railway track'.[91] He told the BBC: 'It gave me considerable pause for thought and it took me a year and a half of investigation before I agreed to do the first patient.'[92]

On reflection, it seems to me that these amputations *should* fall within the ambit of 'proper medical treatment', particularly where, as in these cases, other avenues of treatment have failed. According to Mr Smith, he had become 'increasingly convinced that the patients had had very little success from their treatments by psychiatrists and psychologists over the years'.[93] He also pointed out that '[t]hese two patients had been fully assessed by two psychiatrists, one of whom has an interest in gender reassignment disorders, and also by a psychologist'.[94] However, it would seem that Dennis Canavan, MP for Falkirk West, had more of a grasp of public opinion when he said that 'he found it "incredible" that a surgeon would

---

[86]  S.Larratt and BMEZINE.COM, 'Body Integrity Identity Disorder', *The BME Encyclopedia*, at <http://encyc.bmezine.com/?Body_Integrity_Identity_Disorder>.

[87]  C. Dyer 'Surgeon amputated healthy legs', *British Medical Journal*, 320 (5th February, 2000), 332. Note that, while Dyer refers to apotemnophilia, if the above distinction is valid, these were clearly BIID cases.

[88]  Ibid.

[89]  Anon, 'Trust bans "private" amputations', BBC News Online (1 February, 2000), at <http://news.bbc.co.uk/1/hi/scotland/627183.stm> (accessed 8 May 2007).

[90]  Ibid.

[91]  C. Dyer, 'Surgeon amputated healthy legs'.

[92]  Anon, 'Surgeon defends amputations', BBC News Online (31 January 2000), at <http://news.bbc.co.uk/1/hi/scotland/625680.stm> (accessed 8 May 2007).

[93]  Ibid.      [94]  Ibid.

amputate a healthy limb'.[95] He stated: 'I would have thought that the General Medical Council would have an ethical code forbidding such a practice.'[96] In this connection, it would be interesting to know what is Mr Canavan's view of the removal of a healthy kidney from a living donor for transplantation, and whether he believes the GMC should forbid this too.

What we have here is a procedure which may be deemed 'necessary' for the patient's (psychological) welfare. Indeed, it was reported that the English patient had been close to suicide prior to his amputation,[97] and so one might even argue that the procedure was life-saving.

## 6.3 Aesthetic surgery

What of procedures that are judged to be *not* 'necessary'? We tend to think here of elective 'cosmetic', or 'aesthetic' surgery. The range of such procedures available to us these days is daunting.[98] But let us begin with a procedure that has been available for some considerable time, rhinoplasty.

### 6.3.1 Rhinoplasty

As a reconstructive procedure, rhinoplasty dates back to the ancient Egyptians, but since the 1950s it has become one of the most commonly performed aesthetic surgical procedures. I am, by nature, squeamish, and when I watched the performance of a 'nose job' in a Discovery Channel documentary, I came very close to fainting—there is no doubt in my mind that this act constitutes a *harm*. However, let us assume, for the sake of the argument, that I am made of stronger stuff. I am a tad dissatisfied with my prodigious proboscis; you could not call it a deformity,[99] it is just not quite how I want it. And, let us assume, further, that I am not an university lecturer and can actually afford to go under the knife, the chisel (forgive me, 'osteotome'),[100] and the hammer. Why is it that the Offences Against the Person Act 1861 does not come into play *here*? Is not this level of injury rather greater than that which occurred in *Brown*?[101] Why is it that I can consent to an osteotomy[102] without fear of ending up in the dock next to my surgeon? As far as I know, no one will make anything of the fact that I and my surgeon do not consider the procedure 'therapeutic'—my previous nose functioned as well as the

[95] Ibid.       [96] Ibid.       [97] Ibid.

[98] See, for example, S. L. Gilman, *Making the Body Beautiful—A Cultural History of Aesthetic Surgery* (Princeton, NJ: Princeton University Press, 1999) 6–7.

[99] Please remember: this is a thought experiment.

[100] Osteotome—'any of various surgical instruments used to cut bone' (*Oxford English Dictionary* at <http://dictionary.oed.com/>).

[101] For those of great intestinal fortitude, step-by-step photographs of the procedure are available at <http://www.facialsurgery.com/INTRAOP1.HTM> (accessed 8 May 2007).

[102] Osteotomy—'surgical division, or partial resection, of a bone, esp. in order to correct a deformity; an instance of this' (*Oxford English Dictionary* at <http://dictionary.oed.com/>). In this case, the narrowing of the bridge of the nose.

next man's, and, whilst it is my preference to have a more streamlined nose, any psychological benefit will be, at most, minimal. I opted for the procedure simply for aesthetic gratification. Is this a superior ground, morally and legally, than that of sexual gratification found in *Brown*?

## 6.3.2 Phalloplasty

Let us consider another aesthetic surgical procedure, phalloplasty.[103] 'Phalloplasty surgery encompasses penis lengthening surgery, penis widening surgery in the flaccid and erect state and glanular enhancement.'[104] Suppose Mr Blue wishes to undergo one of these techniques. His motivation may well be aesthetic and/ or psychological in nature, resulting from, for example, so-called 'locker room envy', or 'locker room phobia'. However, it is also the case that his motivation may be, ultimately, sexual gratification.[105] And if it is this last, in what significant way does this act of consensual harming differ in substance from the acts in *Brown*? Why might this qualify as one of the well-known exceptions to the purview of the 1861 Act? Is it because Mr Blue's 'inflicter' is a qualified surgeon? According to Lord Jauncey of Tullichettle in *Brown*:

The line falls properly to be drawn between assault at common law and the offence of assault occasioning actual bodily harm created by section 47 of the 1861 Act, with the result that consent of the victim is no answer to anyone charged with the latter offence... unless the circumstances fall within one of the well known exceptions such as organised sporting contests or games, parental chastisement or reasonable surgery... the infliction of actual or more serious bodily harm is an unlawful activity to which consent is no answer.[106]

Is phalloplasty surgery to be construed as 'reasonable' surgery?

## 6.3.3 Labiaplasty

What of labiaplasty? If you go to The Reed Clinic in Miami[107] for your labia minora reduction, the surgery will set you back some $2,000. For this fee, '[o]verly pigmented and unattractive labia can be reduced with a V-plasty technique that converges freshened margins in a neat concealable line. Delicate, minimally reactive, self absorbing plastic surgery suture is employed... Surgery

---

[103] And I shall *not* be using *myself* as an example here, thought experiment or not.

[104] New York Phallo at <http://www.new-york-phalloplasty.com/main.html> (accessed 8 May 2007).

[105] It may be that we can usefully chop logic here. If it was Mr Brown, and not Mr Blue (who, it turns out, does not enjoy 'surgery' at any level) who was undergoing the phalloplasty, I suppose we could say that there is a significant difference, in that Mr Brown may be sexually gratified by the very act of surgery, whereas Mr Blue's prospective sexual gratification comes of the ultimate result of the act. It is not clear to me how this would make a significant difference in terms of the application of the 1861 Act. (And it is my guess that the convictions in *Brown* would have been handed down even if the relevant body areas had been anaesthetized prior to whipping with stingy nettles, etc.)

[106] *R v Brown* [1993] 2 All ER 75, as quoted in *Laskey, Jaggard and Brown*, para 21.

[107] <http://www.srsmiami.com/> (accessed 8 May 2007).

can be performed on an outpatient basis. Sexual activity may be resumed in 6 weeks. Excessive clitoral hood tissue may also be trimmed during this procedure as requested and is covered by our comprehensive fee.'[108] Apparently, the procedure is offered to women who 'suffer from *unsightly contour lines*',[109] as there may be some physical discomfort associated with this 'condition'.[110]

'Reasonable' surgery? Perhaps.

## 7. The normative domain of medicine

Is it reasonable that what separates such consensual harming in the aesthetic surgical sphere, for example, from the kind of consensual harming that occurred in *Brown* is the involvement of a health care professional? Miller, Brody, and Chung have suggested that 'cosmetic surgery is ethically questionable from the perspective of the internal morality of medicine, which makes it at best a peripheral medical practice'.[111] Some may wish to go further, and claim that cosmetic surgery falls outside the domain of medicine altogether.[112] I certainly would not wish to go this far.

Medicine is: 'the science and art dealing with the maintenance of health and the prevention, alleviation, or cure of disease.'[113] Miller, Brody, and Chung, however, seem to question the relevance of this definition to modern medical practice. For them, medicine 'is a professional practice governed by a moral framework consisting of goals proper to medicine, role-specific duties, and clinical virtues'.[114] And it is this framework that they refer to by the phrase 'the internal morality of medicine'.

From my current perspective, it is the notion of 'goals proper to medicine' that is of interest. And for a characterization of this notion, Miller, Brody, and Chung adopt 'a comprehensive list of four goals'[115] recommended by 'an international group of scholars, convened by The Hastings Center':[116]

[108] <http://www.srsmiami.com/labiaplasty-surgery.html> (accessed 8 May 2007). I think that the layperson may be forgiven for asking what, precisely, marks such procedures out as distinct from the kind of 'surgery' envisaged by our Female Genital Mutilation Act 2003, or the Federal Prohibition of Female Genital Mutilation Act of 1995 in the US jurisdiction.
[109] Ibid [my emphasis].
[110] 'Such women report pinching or chafing when sitting or walking, hindrance during intromission, and difficulty maintaining hygiene during menses or after defecation' (ibid).
[111] F. G. Miller, H. Brody, and K. C., 'Cosmetic surgery and the internal morality of medicine', *Cambridge Quarterly of Healthcare Ethics*, 9 (2000), 362.
[112] See, for example, D. A. Hyman, 'Aesthetics and ethics: the implications of cosmetic surgery', *Perspectives in Biology & Medicine*, 33 (1990), 190–202.
[113] MedLine Plus Medical Dictionary, at <http://www.nlm.nih.gov/medlineplus/mplusdictionary.html>.
[114] Miller, Brody, and Chung, 'Cosmetic surgery and the internal morality of medicine', 353–4.
[115] Ibid, 354.
[116] Ibid.

(i) 'the prevention of disease and injury and promotion and maintenance of health'; (ii) 'the relief of pain and suffering caused by maladies'; (iii) 'the care and cure of those with a malady, and the care of those who cannot be cured'; and (iv) 'the avoidance of premature death and the pursuit of a peaceful death.'[117]

How are we to fit aesthetic surgery into this classification? Does it really lie on the periphery of, or even outside medicine? My research in this area[118] leads me to fully accept that there is a real *need* for many cosmetic procedures in a great many cases, a need that is often to be understood in terms of identity and psychological burden, rather than anything physical, but as I have tried to indicate, in certain cases, the former may be just as life threatening.[119] There are, of course, questions to be asked about the impact of duress on patient autonomy, but one could ask such questions of many interventions that Miller, Brody, and Chung would readily accept as lying well within the internal morality of medicine.

What of cases of whimsy, such as my rhinoplasty example? Should I be denied my new nose simply because I don't *need* it enough? Surely, the real issue here is the question of whether public resources should be deployed in such a case. And I would argue that if I am prepared to pay the price, and I can find a surgeon who has no conscientious objection to performing the operation, and there are no other opportunity costs associated with it, and no third parties harmed by it, then my autonomous choice should not be frustrated. For sure, it may turn out to be a daft choice, one that I will come to regret, but I do not see how we might justify foiling daftness as a public policy, particularly in advance of knowing whether the choice was daft or not.

## 8. Conclusion

If, as my attempt at a lay perspective would seem to suggest, there is inconsistency in how various people are treated for similar actions under the law, the presumption in favour of autonomy and liberty should prevail, and should ground our default position as a society. Let me try to be clear about this. Under our current system, I am in favour of the 'medical exemption'. However, I would far prefer it if we could develop a more seemingly just notion of offences against the person that

[117] Ibid. Their reference is to D. Callahan, 'The goals of medicine: setting new priorities', *Hastings Center Report* [Special Supplement] 25/6 (1996), S1–S26.
[118] I spent three years, from 1998, working on a major international research project entitled 'Beauty and the Doctor: Moral Issues in Health Care with Regard to Appearance', funded by the European Commission, under its 4th Framework Programme, and coordinated by Inez de Beaufort of Erasmus Universiteit, Rotterdam. Whatever initial doubts I may have had about the 'medical necessity' of various cosmetic procedures were wiped away by this experience.
[119] I do not believe that there are many (competent) people who would consent to such treatments on the kind of *whim* that characterized my formulation of the example of rhinoplasty.

did not necessitate the inclusion of *any* kind of 'exemption'.[120] That is to say, as a citizen, I wish to see across-the-board consistency in the law. And if this implies that we are *not* to send people down for acts of BDSM conducted in private, and with optimal mutual consent, so be it. Go ahead, have your penis enlarged, or your labia trimmed, or your genitals whipped with stingy nettles. Just so long as this is an optimally autonomous, mutually consensual act, and just so long as it does not cause harm to non-consenting others, that is fine.

I am *not* saying that the way the law views certain medical procedures ought to be brought in line with how the law treats those who perform what seem, at an essential level, to be very similar acts in the non-medical setting; quite the reverse, I want to argue that the medical exemption ought to be expanded universally, that, just so long as we avoid non-consensual harming, consent as a defence in criminal law should not be limited.

It may sound as though I want to argue that any Tom, Dick, or Harry ought to be permitted to take an osteotome to someone's nose, just so long as he has the optimally informed consent of his competent victim, and it is not done in public. And perhaps that *is* a result of my argument. *So be it!* Autonomy, it seems to me, brings with it responsibility, including responsibility for the results of one's whimsical, and silly, and stupid choices. I do not believe that even a 'Nanny State' should extend its responsibility for protection of competent citizens this far, to protection from themselves; if we are to demand our autonomy, and the rights that come with that, then we must also face up to our responsibility for the results of bad choices, for ignoring the advice and remonstrations of our parents, our wiser friends, and even the good advice of the State (in its moments of lucidity). It is not as though, with the provisos inherent in the harm principle, that such a policy is likely to lead to anarchy and the fall of democracy. Despite the tyranny of the majority, surely democracy must, at a basic level, ensure protection of individual liberty in the way that is marked out by the harm principle.

---

[120] Medical, sporting, or, as my daughters would say in the face of potential parental chastisement, '*whatever*'.

# 15

# Medicalizing Crime—Criminalizing Health? The Role of Law

*Jonathan Montgomery*

## 1. Introduction

This chapter explores the question of when using the criminal law is desirable in the context of health and health care concerns. It looks at two case studies, aspects of both of which have been extensively discussed earlier in this collection of essays, in order to identify when criminal law seems an appropriate tool, and when it appears to bring unwelcome pressures and incentives into play.[1] In this way, the proper role of the law can be considered, and judgments made as to when, and how legal regulation can make a constructive contribution to general social goals.

John Harris has suggested that we should explore this question in relation to two themes.[2] The first is whether the use of the criminal law would promote a better health care system. Specifically included within this is the question of whether criminal liability would contribute to, or obstruct, the task of maximizing patient safety. The secondly is the desire to do justice, including the proper punishment of wrongdoing. These two concerns can be described as, first, the imperative to promote health and, second, the need to do so justly. These themes can provide a helpful framework for our case studies, which concern first the role of criminal law in the response to mistakes made by health professionals and secondly the impact of criminalizing disease transmission. In both areas, the question arises of whether the health context makes a difference to general expectations. Should we medicalize the criminal law by introducing exceptions and exemptions to the normal expectations of liability when wrongs happened to occur in the health care context? That might be right if criminalization would undermine our chances of improving our health care and reducing ill-health.

---

[1] My analysis will focus upon the criminalization of mistakes made by health professionals and of disease transmission.

[2] J. Harris, 'Introduction', *Criminalising Medicine—Doctors in the Dock*, International Conference, 26–27 May 2005, University of Manchester.

Or are we failing to do justice by seeing criminal sanctions as inappropriate when health concerns are raised? If so, should we be prepared to do more to criminalize unhealthy activities?

## 2. Is health law special?

A perennial question with which medical and health care lawyers grapple is whether their subject is distinct from other areas of law. What is it, if anything, which makes the health context different and justifies a particular sub-specialty of law? Is it merely a 'composite of principles derivative from other legal disciplines such as the standard principles of criminal law... and of civil law?'[3] It is reasonably easy to show that these principles have sometimes been applied differently in the health care context,[4] but it does not follow that they should be.

Three lines of argument might be used to suggest that it is acceptable to develop a distinctive approach to what justice requires in the health care context. The first is that the delivery of effective health care is a complex business that needs to be conceived as a corporate activity not an individual one and the usual individualized principles of justice need to be displaced by a more public law conception of maximizing the effectiveness of State services.[5] On this basis, the concern of the law should be with how to change the behaviour of organizations more than individuals and the value of bringing prosecutions should be judged with this in mind.

A second approach is to suggest that the purpose of health care law is not to resolve problems but to provide a framework within which resolution can be sought by those professionals and patients intimately involved.[6] On this view, the courts have adopted a position that assumes the integration of various institutions of society to ensure that difficult decisions about health care issues are handled as moral questions for which the actors must accept moral responsibility. The solutions cannot necessarily be formulated in terms of actions that will always be prohibited because the moral dilemmas do not lend themselves to that sort of uniform precision. Indeed, the law would dilute moral responsibility by taking it upon itself to prejudge the answers to the dilemmas. Further, from this perspective, the use of the criminal law may be problematic if it focuses on the responsibility of the perpetrator with little consideration of the responsibilities of others,

[3] Discussed by T. Hervey and J. McHale, *Health Law and the European Union* (Cambridge: Cambridge University Press, 2004) 17.
[4] J. Montgomery, 'Time for a paradigm shift? Medical law in transition', *Current Legal Problems* 53 (2000) 363–408, 365–7.
[5] See discussion in Montgomery, 'Time for a paradigm shift?', 371–99.
[6] This approach is explored in J. Montgomery, 'Law and the demoralisation of medicine', *Legal Studies*, 26 (2006), 185–210.

or on the competing obligations that people may face.[7] Both these concerns suggest that use of the criminal law will tend to undermine the moral legitimacy of there being a range of options. Faced by ethical uncertainty as to the appropriate way forward, judges have been reluctant to accept that the law should establish clear and precise conclusions on the issues with little scope for adaptability to the circumstances.[8] If such flexibility cannot be achieved when criminal sanctions are involved, then the use of the criminal law should be avoided.

A third approach considers that public health considerations—maximizing the health and well-being of society—may sometimes be more important than the normal expectations of justice. On this view, it would be acceptable for principles that would generally lead to civil or criminal liability to work differently in the health context if their impact would be to undermine public health. Assessing whether this is appropriate depends on balancing collective interests in public health with individual concerns. Arguably, the traditional deference to medical opinion in the interpretation of legal rules illustrates such an approach and reflects an implicit social contract under which health professionals are allowed special treatment in order to secure an effective health service.[9] That social contract is not fixed and must be reassessed to see whether it remains attractive.[10] Fundamental to this approach is the possibility that public health policy may sometimes constitute a more important public value than punishment of individual wrong-doing.

## 3. Social and personal wrongs

Another way of considering the demarcation between the provinces of the civil and criminal law is to consider the issue in terms of who is 'wronged' by an action. It can be suggested that in the case of *civil wrongs* it is the impact on the 'victim' that explains why the law is brought into play but that actions become classified as *crimes* because of the impact on society. The categories are not mutually exclusive. Many crimes are also civil wrongs because they constitute not only a breach of society's rules, which society is entitled to enforce, but also adversely impact

---

[7] In the civil law context, the risk of competing obligations has been used to justify judicial non-intervention in favour of reinforcing prevailing professional approaches. See, for example, *F v West Berkshire HA* [1989] 2 All ER 545 and *X v Bedfordshire CC; M v Newham LBC; E v Dorset CC* [1995] 3 All ER 353.

[8] See, for example, the reluctance of the House of Lords in *R (Pretty) v DPP* [2002] 1 All ER 1 to see euthanasia as an issue that should be settled by the European Convention on Human Rights rather than by national states (esp Lord Steyn, para 56). For consideration of the legitimacy of using medical law to adopt particular positions in cases or moral pluralism, see J. Montgomery, 'The Legitimacy of Medical Law' in S. McLean (ed.), *First Do No Harm: Law, Ethics & Healthcare* (Aldershot: Ashgate, 2006) 1–16.

[9] See J. Montgomery, 'Medicine, accountability and professionalism', *Journal of Law & Society*, 16/3 (1989), 319–39.

[10] See, for example, Lord Woolf, 'Are the courts excessively deferential to the medical profession?', *Medical Law Review*, 9 (2001), 1.

on the particular individuals who are victims. This can be seen by steps over the past few years to increase the involvement of victims in the criminal process, and the influence of 'restorative justice' as a role for the criminal justice system.[11] Nevertheless, the different characters of civil and criminal justice captured by this perspective are helpful in illuminating the question of the role of criminal law in relation to health care practice.

A number of consequences follow from this way of characterizing the distinction. The first concerns control over whether cases proceed. Where a civil wrong is concerned, then it will generally be up to the 'victim' to choose whether to bring a claim. The wrong is conceived as directed primarily at them and they are free to waive their right to sue. In relation to crimes, however, as the wrong is perceived to be against society, then it is the State (through its organs such as the Crown Prosecution Service) that decides whether or not to bring the case. Indeed, the State may choose to prosecute even where the 'victim' is not concerned about the actions—such as in the sado-masochism example discussed by Erin in this volume,[12] or in the case of consensual, but illegal procedures (for example, terminations of pregnancy outside the terms of the Abortion Act 1967, or euthanasia).

The distinction is not a neat one. Prosecutions will be harder to prove if the 'victim' does not cooperate, so the views of the victim can be more significant than the model implies. There are also circumstances when private prosecutions may be brought, so that State control is not comprehensive. However, thinking about questions of criminalizing medicine in terms of whether the wrongs in question are best considered as being against individuals (and therefore only actionable if that person is unhappy with what has happened) or as transgressing societal canons of behaviour (so that the State determines whether the law should be brought into play in any particular case) is a useful guide in deciding whether wrongs have been appropriately classified.

A second way of considering the different rationales of civil and criminal law can be found in the consequences of winning in the courts. Civil litigation is essentially concerned to protect the position of the individual. Occasionally, such

---

[11] See, for example, R. A. Duff, 'Restorative justice and punitive restoration' in L. Walgrave (ed.), *Restorative Justice and the Law* (Cullompton: Willan, 2002) 82–100; R. A. Duff, 'Restoration and Retribution' in A. von Hirsch, J. Roberts, A. E. Bottoms, K. Roach, and M. Schiff (eds.), *Restorative Justice and Criminal Justice: Competing or Reconcilable Paradigms?* (Oxford: Hart Publishing, 2003); R. A. Duff, 'Probation, punishment and restorative justice', *Howard Journal of Criminal Justice, 42 (2003)*, 180–96; E. Elliott and R.M. Gordon (eds.), *New Directions in Restorative Justice: Issues, Practice, Evaluation,* (Cullompton: Willan, 2005); I. Edwards, 'Restorative justice, sentencing and the Court of Appeal', *Criminal Law Review,* [2006], 110–23; A. Crawford and T. Burden, *Integrating Victims in Restorative Youth Justice,* (Bristol: The Policy Press, 2005); D. Cornwell, *Criminal Punishment and Restorative Justice: Past, Present and Future Perspectives* (Winchester: Waterside Press, 2006); J. Shapland, A. Atkinson, H. Atkinson, E. Colledge, J. Dignan, M. Howes, J. Johnstone, G. Robinson, and A. Sorsby, 'Situating restorative justice within criminal justice', *Theoretical Criminology,* 10/4 (2006), 505–32. I am grateful to Suzanne Ost for directing me to these sources.

[12] C. A. Erin, 'The rightful domain of the criminal law', in this volume.

as in the use of injunctions to restrain behaviour, this operates in advance to prevent wrongs occurring. More typically, however, the outcome of a civil case will be payment of money by the person who has done wrong to compensate the victim for what they have suffered. This seeks to restore the balance of justice between the people concerned.

In civil cases, the amount of money in question is determined by the scale of loss to the victim, not the degree of blame of the perpetrator. Thus, the same negligent mistake might lead to payment of substantial damages in one case and a nominal payment in another, depending on whether it did or did not cause major harm. This is perhaps most clearly seen in the context of maternity care, where a minor error can sometimes have a catastrophic impact leaving a severely disabled baby in need of constant nursing care for its whole life. This will lead to millions of pounds of damages. Yet an elementary and blatant error that would be seen as far more culpable may result in only minimal damages if, in fact, the harm suffered can be remedied cheaply or not at all (in the case of death). Thus, it can be crudely stated that it is 'cheaper' to kill patients than to maim them.

The rationale on which the damages are fixed is that we should separate two questions. First, *who* should bear the costs of a mishap? It is fairer that a person who has done some wrong should bear the costs of its consequences, rather than that the 'victim' of that wrong should be left to cope with them. This is more about the relative position of the two parties, rather than expected standards of conduct. Thus, the threshold for liability can be quite low because the victim is more innocent than the person who makes even a mildly careless mistake. Once it has been decided who should bear the costs of the damage suffered, then the second question of what that *damage* has actually been will be examined. On this model, we should not measure the degree of culpability by the financial value of the harm suffered. Rather, the question is who should bear the financial risk (and perhaps insure against it) of things going wrong.

Criminal sanctions have a different rationale. The wrong is against society, and the balance to be restored is not amongst individuals, but between the individual and the State. Thus, the consequence of a conviction will be punishment, rather than compensation. If money changes hands, it will generally be seen as a fine, and go to the Treasury, rather than compensation for the victim. The justification for sanctions will be found in concepts of deterrence, retribution, and the protection of society. The scale and form of penalties will therefore be determined according to whether they are severe enough to provide a sufficient disincentive (deterrence), adequately reflect the culpability of the perpetrator (retribution), or effectively protect society through imprisonment or other restrictions.

This last dimension of the comparison between social (criminal) and personal (civil) wrongs also challenges us to consider whether the binary distinction between criminal and civil justice gives us an adequate description of the legal armoury available to regulate health issues effectively. A third legal field of activity should also be considered that may provide more satisfactory solutions to the problems in question. This can be seen as an aspect of public law—the regulatory role of the State—broadly defined. Regulatory powers can be seen at work in both the case studies in question. In relation to the question of how errors should best be addressed, there are professional bodies with the power to remove or restrict people's licence to practise that may be more effective in protecting the public than criminal justice agencies. In relation to disease transmission, control powers may be available to enable intervention to restrict people's activities so as to reduce the risk of them infecting others. Deciding when to use the criminal law may depend on assessing whether these regulatory powers will be the most effective means of achieving the desired ends.

## 4. Should health care mistakes be criminal?

The characterization of the difference between criminal and civil wrongs as one that distinguishes wrongs against society from those that are merely against individuals can provide a tool for the consideration of the potential criminal liability of health professionals for manslaughter by gross negligence. Where professionals show a disregard for the common principles by which we live, such as the value of life, then they could be said to be violating their duties to society and properly subject to the sanctions of the criminal law. An inadvertent error that causes harm may well indicate that the professional was more to blame than the victim (and thus properly liable in civil law because it would be a greater affront to justice to force the victim to bear the full consequences of the mishap than to require the professional to provide compensation). However, it would not indicate that the professional had challenged the authority of society.

These considerations would suggest a rather different pattern for the use of criminal offences than seen in the gross negligence manslaughter cases. The essence of those cases is that there are some mistakes that merit something more than civil sanctions, but on the current formulation of the law, they remain cases of mistake rather than wicked intentions. They are very different from situations such as Harold Shipman—the mass medical murderer, who may have got away with murder more easily because he was a doctor, but was not claiming that murder was proper medical practice.[13] More marginal cases, such as those of Dr Bodkin Adams[14] and Dr Nigel Cox,[15] turn upon the decision of the jury as to whether the proper categorization of the doctors' actions is medical treatment or deliberate killing. There is an implicit assumption that they must be either one or the other, and cannot be both. Thus, the direction to the jury in *Adams*[16] indicates that a

---

[13]  See *The Shipman Inquiry*. Available online at <http://www.the-shipman-inquiry.org>.
[14]  *R v Adams* [1957] 1 Crim LR 365.
[15]  *R v Cox* (1992) 12 BMLR 38.
[16]  *R v Adams* [1957] 1 Crim LR 365.

defence to allegations of murder can be built out of 'right and proper treatment'. In Adams, the Judge directed that the jury should acquit Dr Adams if they were satisfied of three things, despite the fact that he had administered a drug that he knew would probably have shortened his patient's life: first, that the patient was already terminally ill; secondly, that using the drugs in question was 'the right and proper treatment'; thirdly, that the motivation for using the drugs was the relief of suffering. These seem to be a set of conditions aimed to determine whether the doctor was seeking to do the best for his patient and remaining within the enterprise of providing medical care rather than pursuing an evil purpose to which the medical context was merely the opportunity rather than the essence of the activity. Criminalization is not appropriate for those who try to do the right thing, but fail, only for those who set out to disregard the value of life that is protected by the criminal law.

Similarly, challenges to the substance of the rules themselves—such as that envisaged by Diane Pretty when asking for dispensation against the prohibition of euthanasia—are properly the province of the criminal law because they are in essence a challenge to societal values.[17] Thus, it is appropriate that they are understood as bringing individuals into conflict with the state rather than merely other individuals. That is why it is thought to be irrelevant that Diane and her husband believed they were doing the right thing and why the issue was regarded as more than merely a private matter between them.[18]

This suggests that justice does not require the use of the criminal law in the case of medical mistakes, but only where professionals set out to do wrong. Resistance to the use of gross negligence manslaughter can also be justified from the point of view of promoting good health. First, culpability is rarely solely on the individual, and patient safety requires corporate action to improve systems. Health and safety responsibilities on organizations seem a more appropriate response than prosecution of doctors.[19] Secondly, the focus needs to be on improving care rather than punishment. Single mistakes usually give little indication of a professional's current or future general competence. Regulating the right to practise through professional disciplinary procedures and ensuring the quality of care through clinical governance responsibilities seem to offer a more promising regulatory approach. Thus, criminalizing medical practice is not generally attractive and offences should be limited to cases of deliberate wickedness where the context might be clinical but the intention of the perpetrator is not therapeutic.

---

[17] *R (Pretty) v DPP* [2002] 1 All ER 1; *Pretty v UK* [2002] 2 FCR 97.

[18] For discussion of how far medical law deals with private or public issues, see Montgomery, 'The Legitimacy of Medical Law'.

[19] Following the case of *R v Misra and Srivastava* [2004] EWCA Crim 2375, the hospital Trust concerned was later convicted of offences under health and safety legislation for failing to provide appropriate supervision and fined £100,000—a step more likely to incentivize better protection for future patients than convicting the two doctors involved.

## 5.  Are health crimes different?

The previous two chapters have considered how the application of the criminal law to individual and intimate behaviour seems to have developed differently in the health context. Here, the questions concern whether conduct that would be regarded as criminal if the health issues were ignored should be treated differently because of that context. Which should take precedence—the criminal or medical paradigm?

Broadly, Erin suggests that the respect for privacy and autonomy over one's own body that has been displayed in the health care context is preferable to the moralistic paternalism that the criminal law has applied to sado-masochistic sexual practices.[20] Thus, the rules that have been developed for medicine to prevent surgery being regarded as criminal should be applied more generally. There is said to be sufficient commonality of the issues that we should not regard the health care context as intrinsically different. The 'progressive' principles that have been developed to deal with health care, so that it has not been held back by traditional taboos about the integrity of the body, should be matched by a similar liberal and enlightened regime to deal with sexuality. This suggests that we should not overplay the special circumstances of health care.

In contrast, Bennett argues that normal criminal sanctions should not be applied to disease transmission because the issues at stake are different from other circumstances in which harm is caused by one person to another.[21] Setting out to poison someone with a noxious substance is a classic criminal archetype. Yet in the context of sexually transmitted diseases, we are less clear that this is an appropriate way of analysing what is at stake. This suggests that we should pay particular attention to the special issues that the health context raises and consider whether they displace the traditional reasons for criminalizing the infliction of harm.

This section considers two arguments that might be raised to support the claim that the health context is sufficiently different from the general one, so that it is acceptable for principles of criminal liability to work differently there without contravening the requirements of justice that Harris reminded us would need to act as a constraint on well-meaning public health policy. The first can be described as the public health case that using the criminal law will lead to greater net harm than limiting legal intervention to the civil and public law. The second explores concerns that using the criminal law in the health context would hit people who were already 'victims' because of their health problems and this would be an unjust 'double whammy'. This raises the fear that there will be circumstances when the burdens placed on those with a particular disease status

---

[20]  Erin, 'The rightful domain of the criminal law'.
[21]  R. Bennett, 'Should we criminalize HIV transmission?', in this volume.

by the shadow of the criminal law over them would become so onerous as to be unjustly discriminatory against them.

## 5.1 The public health case

The essence of the public health case for not applying the criminal law is the claim that the net impact of criminalizing behaviour might be to increase the likelihood of disease transmission. If this were so, then society would need to determine the relative priority it gives to protecting future 'victims' and the punishment of perpetrators. Although this is an issue that would, in principle, be susceptible to empirical resolution, it will tend to be driven largely by political considerations, and often short-term pressures. Thus, the way in which the question about criminalizing behaviour is answered may depend in large part on the interplay between the use of the criminal law and prevailing public health strategies.

This can be illustrated by the contrast between Virginia Bottomley's brave resistance, when Secretary of State for Health, to media pressure to create an offence of transmitting HIV, based on the advice of public health professionals, and the fact that recent prosecutions for transmission seem to have been uncontroversial amongst the public health community. The key difference lies in the fact that in the 1990s, the principal public health strategy was to encourage people to take responsibility for their own health by taking steps to protect themselves, while now the focus is on ensuring that those who are HIV positive act responsibly in relation to the risk they might pose to others. Current self-protection messages are targeted at raising awareness of more common sexually transmitted diseases, such as chlamydia, rather than HIV.

The original strategy emphasized that the risk of exposure to AIDS is a matter of shared responsibility, that we all must actively manage this risk to protect ourselves, that it was a problem for people 'like us' ('Don't die of ignorance' was the slogan of the Government's campaign in 1987).[22] In that context, the suggestion that those who transmitted the disease were criminals would encourage people to think that they were a different type of person from those whom we know—encouraging a dangerously naive syllogism:

So long as I do not consort with criminals I will be safe.
I do not consort with criminals.
Therefore, I am safe.

This early public education campaign aimed to make everybody accept that they were at risk from AIDS and that they should therefore take precautions. It sought to minimize the feeling that people with HIV, or those at risk of infection, were in any way different from the general population. Now, HIV infection is

---

[22] Department of Health and Social Security, 'Don't Die of Ignorance' leaflet (London: Department of Health and Social Security, 1987).

not singled out for special consideration and the communication strategy is not aimed to maximize people's awareness of the specific risk of HIV so much as of sexual health more generally.

There are many reasons for this shift in public health policy. In the 1980s, there was considerable reluctance to force people to ascertain their HIV status because of the possibility that a positive result would lead to refusal of life assurance and therefore bar people from access to home ownership due to the resulting inability to raise a mortgage. Consequently, public health strategies were not based on the assumption that people should be aware of their own HIV status, but rather should proceed without knowing whether they (or others) were infected. With better understanding of the nature and incidence of AIDS, the insurance market has matured and this is less of an issue.

Increased understanding of the virus and the availability of medication to reduce the risk of AIDS developing have also superseded the view that there was limited value in knowing that you have contracted HIV. Thus, the earlier resistance to the possibility of testing for HIV without counselling has been replaced by active consideration of home HIV tests. HIV is now less a sinister, alien, and incomprehensible plague than an endemic disease that has become a public health 'fact of life'. Most HIV transmission is now through heterosexual activity. Protective measures against contracting HIV are not limited to specific risky practices and are no longer differentiated from other sexual health issues. The public health campaign against the virus has, in effect, been mainstreamed. In this context, the possibility of criminal liability for disease transmission has become less of a public health issue because its impact on public health policy has diminished.

The nature of this interaction between public health activity and the criminal justice policy can be captured by considering the contribution of the law to the shaping of the metaphors by which health issues are understood. Susan Sontag has shown how we make sense of illnesses through the development of a metaphorical language that brings nuances to our understanding of what is at stake and shapes our responses.[23] High profile criminal prosecutions for disease transmission nurture a metaphor of disease carriers as markedly different from 'normal' members of society who become stereotyped as external 'threats' to ordinary citizens.[24] The impact of this 'folk devil'[25] construction is to encourage people to think of the transmission of disease as the province of evil criminals, not people like them. The effect of this metaphor was amplified by the prevailing association by the media of HIV with 'deviant' groups—intravenous drug (ab) users and promiscuous homosexuals. Such a metaphorical conception of the

---

[23] S. Sontag, *Illness as Metaphor* and *AIDS and its Metaphors* (London: Penguin, 2002).
[24] J. Montgomery, 'Victims or Threats? The Framing of HIV/AIDS', *Liverpool Law Review*, XII/1 (1990), 25–53.
[25] S. Cohen, *Folk Devils and Moral Panics* (Oxford: Martin Robertson, 1980).

challenge of AIDS was antithetical to the public health strategy, which was to encourage every member of society to face up to the possibility that they might be at risk and to take responsibility for their own protection. Thus, in the context of this strategy, criminalization was resisted as undermining the important message of universal risk.

The metaphors that lie behind the current debate about criminalization are different, although there are still grounds for concern. Those being prosecuted are demonized less for their disease status than as sexual predators, and coverage shows a strong racial overtone. Searching the BBC website coverage of a recent case, it can be seen that all thirteen features covering the story mention Feston Konzani's African origins.[26] The coverage of 13 and 14 May 2004 is typical, where he is described as 'an African asylum seeker living in Middlesbrough'.[27] While living in Middlesbrough may not carry stigma, the African nationality, and asylum-seeker status are attributions that serve to stress the difference of Konzani from English citizens rather than his common humanity.

This has moved the debate away from public health into a more mainstream criminal justice context. AIDS is no longer presented as a gay plague but an African one. Even more clearly the protection of victims from aggressors has emerged as the rationale for criminalization, obscuring public health issues. The innocence of the victims and the evil of the aggressor are stressed:

A teenage girl was kept captive by a musician who infected her with the HIV virus when he had unprotected sex with her at the age of 15, a court heard... The girl told Teesside Crown Court Mr Konzani took her virginity and had sex with her on a daily basis during which he kept her locked inside their house.[28]

In this presentation of the case, the public health issues are subsumed into more general concerns about violence. Even if there was a case for treating the crime differently because of its health aspects, to argue it in the face of this account of the facts would seem to be supporting evil against innocence. There may be circumstances when the benefits to public health require such a bold stance, but it would take considerable moral courage. Whether this is called for will largely depend on what incentives are provided by criminal liability.

Perhaps, the criminalization of disease transmission could be harnessed to provide encouragement for protective behaviours, for example to encourage people to disclose their HIV status. Disclosure obligations could be seen as a step which will enhance people's ability to protect themselves and encourage those who

---

[26] The official legal account of these proceedings is found at *R v Konzani* [2005] EWCA Crim 706.

[27] Anon, 'HIV man no duty to reveal virus', BBC News Online (13 May 2005), at <http://news.bbc.co.uk/1/hi/england/tees/3712711.stm> (accessed 5 May 2007); Anon, 'HIV man is jailed for 10 years', BBC News Online (14 May 2005), at <http://news.bbc.co.uk/1/hi/england/tees/3714749.stm> (accessed 5 May 2007). The same description is used in both articles.

[28] Anon, 'HIV accused "kept girl captive"', BBC News Online (7 May 2004), at <http://news.bbc.co.uk/1/hi/england/tees/3695205.stm> (accessed 4 May 2007).

are infected to take precautions. The issue is now less whether there should be a criminal offence, so much as whether the terms in which the offence is couched can encourage the desired behaviour. Criminalization could have the potential to reinforce public health messages and therefore be appropriated into the public health strategy. From this perspective, offences which depend on causing harm, and thus the accident of actual transmission, are less helpful than offences committed by the running of inappropriate risks or those where the transgression consists in denying others the information that they need to decide how to protect themselves. Offences in the latter categories are more easily aligned with public health messages.

Risk based public health offences already exist in English law. Under section 17 of the Public Health (Control of Disease) Act 1984, it is an offence for anyone who knows that they are suffering from a 'notifiable' disease, to put others at risk of infection by their actions in a street, public place, place of entertainment, club, hotel, inn, or shop.[29] The mechanism by which such offences could contribute to public health policy would seem to lie in the theory of deterrence—that fear of approbation and punishment will deter people from behaving inappropriately. There are many difficulties with the smooth operation of deterrence in the context of sexual behaviour. It works best when people weigh up carefully the consequences of their actions; but this may be doubtful where intimate activities are involved and legal ramifications may be far from their minds, where they are not aware that the law regards their actions as criminal. How many people know the terms of the 1984 Act, or believe that they are unlikely to be caught or prosecuted (because their activities are private and consensual)?

These doubts about the deterrent possibilities of the law are exacerbated when the complexities of the case law on the offences currently being used to prosecute those who infect others with HIV are examined. Key ambiguities exist in relation to the extent to which the knowledge of the perpetrator that they are HIV positive has to be established. Is it sufficient that they were aware, or should have been aware that they might be infected? A second set of ambiguities concerns the relevance of consent of the 'victim'. Are they entitled to consent to the risk of infection at all? Is HIV infection in the same category as sado-masochism, where the risks cannot be consented to in law? If they can be accepted by sexual partners, is awareness that activities are risky sufficient to constitute consent? How much detail about the risk is required to raise such awareness? Does there need to be explicit disclosure or does awareness of the person's sexual history suffice? Should the law presume that everyone is aware of the risks presented so that they should be taken to have accepted a risk of transmission unless there has been a representation of past chastity?

---

[29] Notifiable diseases are those specified in regulations, and do not, for the purposes of s 17, include HIV at present. There are other risk-based offences in the Act.

The challenges of fitting real people's knowledge into such categories can be seen in *R v Konzani*.[30] The 15-year-old victim in that case gave evidence that she was aware of the risks of becoming pregnant and of catching a disease and was prepared to take those risks. Yet, she also said that she did not think at any time there was a risk of her contracting a serious sexually transmitted disease and would not have slept with Konzani if she had. In addition she gave evidence that she was not aware of the HIV problem in Africa and had not really got to grips with what AIDS was about from school lessons. A second victim, aged 27, was aware of the African AIDS problem. She was aware that unprotected sex carried a risk of infection, 'but...didn't think about it at the moment'.[31] The third victim gave evidence that Konzani had deflected questions about sexually transmitted disease by implying that there was no issue—indicating both awareness of the risk on the victim's part and deception on his.[32]

The point here is not the proper interpretation of the law on these difficult questions of consent and disclosure—that has been discussed elsewhere.[33] The point is that such ambiguities and complexities make the connection between the law and public health campaigns a fairly crude one. The subtleties of legal doctrine cannot be expected to impact on perceptions of risk of disease and the details of legal obligations cannot be expected to impact on individuals' behaviour. They are simply too obscure for citizens to be aware of them. The deterrent impact of criminalization needs to lie in the bald fact of whether or not prosecutions occur and, from a public health perspective, the attractiveness of criminalization lies in the extent to which this deterrent impact will align with wider health education strategies.

## 5.2 Victimizing victims?

A different form of public health argument about the proper role of criminal law concerns its impact on those who are ill. Here, the public health objective is to minimize the impact of ill-health on the 'victim' of disease. At its crudest, this is captured by the question of punishment. Is sending someone who is already dying to prison an appropriate step to take in a civilized society? Should we fine those whose illness is preventing them from working? There is, however, a broader perspective that needs to be considered about the criminalization strategy itself. The paradigm here is perhaps best seen as a discrimination issue. If long-term illness is seen as an 'onerous citizenship'[34] then society should be wary of increasing

---

[30] [2005] EWCA Crim 706, paras 12–14.
[31] Ibid, para 19.    [32] Ibid, para 25.
[33] See Bennett, 'Should we criminalize HIV transmission?'; R. Bennett, H. Draper, and L. Frith, 'Ignorance is bliss? HIV and moral and legal duties to forewarn', *Journal of Medical Ethics*, 26 (2000), 9–15; M Weait, 'Criminal law and the sexual transmission of HIV: *R v Dica*', *Modern Law Review*, 68/1 (2005), 121–34.
[34] L. Moran, 'Illness: A more onerous citizenship?', *Modern Law Review*, 51/3 (1988), 343–54.

the burdens by exposing those who are ill to additional constraints—increasing rather than relieving their burden. This issue manifests itself in the principle of social solidarity that lies behind the UK's nationalized health system which seeks to ensure that funding of services is according to means (taxation) and not determined by need (as would be the case in an insurance system with higher premiums for the ill or elderly). Distribution of services, in contrast, is based on clinical need without regard to the individual's ability to pay.

In the criminalization debate, the question is raised whether some forms of offence would impose an unacceptable and discriminatory burden on the victims of disease—further victimizing them in the same way that some say the criminal justice system further victimizes rape victims by exposing them to unnecessarily traumatic trial processes. The key to this issue is the terms in which criminal offences are cast. The law needs to maintain a degree of proportionality between the extent to which those infected with diseases are required to bear additional burdens and the public good achieved by such constraints.

The proportionality point can be best illustrated by the way in which public law control powers, such as quarantining, seek to maintain balance between the interests of individuals and wider society through a combination of due process, criteria for the restriction of liberty and careful limitation of the adverse impact on individuals. Thus, even under the somewhat dated provisions of the Public Health (Control of Disease) Act 1984, compulsory removal to hospital of those suffering from infectious diseases can only be permitted on a magistrate's warrant after it is shown that there is a serious risk of infection and adequate precautions are not being taken.[35] These are attempts to balance the public interest against the opportunity of individuals to take responsibility. The law has stopped short of permitting compulsory treatment—that being a step encroaching too far upon the autonomy of the individual. People can be kept apart from society to prevent infection, but must be left with the ability to choose what happens to their own bodies. Thus, any legal intervention needs to bear in mind the impact on the individuals concerned.

This has direct implications for the terms of possible offences. Some have argued that the concept of recklessness should be extending to ensure that those who know that they *might* have been infected should come within the scope of the offence, because that would maximize their incentive to take precautions. The difficulty with this line of reasoning is that it will necessarily impose the burden of criminal liability on specific groups—gay men, sex workers, people from Sub-Saharan Africa—who could be taken to know that they are always at significant risk even if they have taken precautions against being infected.[36] It therefore becomes discriminatory, in that this burden is imposed upon them because of categorization, not choice.

---

[35] See ss 35–38.
[36] This is well illustrated in M. Weait, 'Taking the blame: criminal law, social responsibility and the sexual transmission of HIV', *Journal of Social Welfare & Family Law*, 23/4 (2001), 441–57, 445–6.

Some formulations of criminal offences exacerbate this tendency. If it were argued that consent is not a defence to harm,[37] then the effect would be that no gay person could engage in sexual activity without being exposed to the risk of prosecution should it transpire that they have passed HIV on to their partner. This would be true even if they did not know that they were themselves infected, shared their uncertainty with their partner and their partner was prepared to take a fully informed decision to run the risk. It would seem a wholly disproportionate response to bar those already burdened with the HIV infection from normal sexual activity.

While this exploration has assumed a series of policy choices about the definition of criminal offences that run contrary to the expressed policy of the Government,[38] it does not go beyond the scope of commentary and judicial speculation.[39] The point is that such a development of the law would take us to a place in which those in high risk groups had hanging over them not merely the burdens of fear of HIV, but the additional threat of criminalization. Imagine that the arguments were extended to genetic 'flaws'. How different is the suggestion that adults who are aware of genetic abnormalities in their family should be prosecuted for 'harming' their children by inflicting upon them the burdens of an inherited disease such as muscular dystrophy? The illness is caused by an agent (the gene) that has been transmitted through sexual activity where there was at least a degree of knowledge of the risk. While public health policy might seek to enhance the information available to people making reproductive choices in such contexts, it would not seek to dictate the solutions by saying that the state is entitled to penalize people who choose to risk passing on their genes.

## 6. Conclusion

The cases that have driven interest in criminalization of disease transmission have drawn attention to vindictive infection where there has been little sympathy for the transgressor. Public health policy needs to take a broader view and lawmakers need to consider the importance of reinforcing good public health and health care practice. This chapter has argued that the key considerations lie in the extent to which those who may be rendered criminals should be seen as taking on the moral norms of the State. Those who set out to challenge such norms may legitimately expect to feel the strong arm of the criminal law. However, those who inadvertently cause harm even where their carelessness deserves approbation should better be seen as doing acceptable things badly. The development of gross negligence manslaughter has taken English law beyond the line suggested

---

[37] Following *R v Brown* [1994] 1 AC 212.

[38] *Violence: Reforming the Offences Against the Person Act 1861* (London: Home Office, 1998).

[39] See the critical discussion in Weait, 'Criminal law and the sexual transmission of HIV'.

as acceptable. Disease transmission can properly be seen as criminal where it is the deliberate infliction of harm, but beyond these stark and rare cases there are significant costs to society's health in the messages given by extending the scope of the criminal law. On balance, this chapter suggests that the medical paradigm offers more than the criminal one in the context of public health and patient safety. The circumstances in which justice requires the incursion of criminal law into health matters should be seen as strictly limited.

# *Index*

**health care** (*cont.*)
  harm principle  247, 248
  health and safety law  263
  health care management
    criminal liability  54
    financial resources  52
    staffing levels  52
  iatrogenic harm  67, 92, 94
  improvements  35
  informed consent  248
  interventionist approach  36
  justice, need for  257, 258, 263
  law
    civil litigation  260, 261
    civil wrongs  259, 260
    corporate responsibilities  258
    criminal sanctions  261
    distinctive nature  258
    framework for resolution  258, 259
    legal reasoning  5
    legal regulation  4, 36, 94–5, 257, 262
    measure of damages  261
    moral responsibilities  258
    personal wrongs  259, 260, 262
    restorative justice  260
    social wrongs  259, 261, 262
  medical practice
    avoidance of death  255
    care and cure  255
    definition  254
    internal morality  254
    moral framework  254
    normative domain  254, 255
    prevention of disease  255
    relief of pain  255
  need for  92–3
  open reporting  93–4, 96, 97
  palliative care  167, 170, 171
  patient safety  51, 52, 257, 263
  public health considerations  259
  public trust  36, 37
  punishment of wrongdoing  257
  quality  32, 35, 36
  reasonable surgery
    body integrity identity disorder (BIID)  249, 250, 251
    medical exemption  248, 249, 255
    proper medical treatment  249, 251
  safety  32, 35
  social attitudes  32, 35
**health care professionals**
  absence of blame  70
  civil proceedings  68–9
  corporate killing  6
  corporate liability  6, 14
  criminal liability  51

  criminal prosecutions  68–9
  disciplinary proceedings  68
  human error  7
  immunity from prosecution  69
  New Zealand *see* **New Zealand**
  professional reputation  68
  public trust  36, 37
**HIV transmission**
  consensual sexual contact  225, 226, 228
  consent
    bodily harm  229, 231, 235
    defence  229, 230
    informed consent  231–34
    risk of infection  231, 232, 268
    self-inflicted harm  231
    sexual contact  231, 232
  convictions  225
  counselling  228
  criminalization
    discrimination  227, 236
    generally  3, 12, 13
    moral harm  236
    public health considerations  227, 228
    punishment  229, 230–2
    stigmatization  227, 236
  defences
    consent  229–31
    informed consent  234–5
  disclosure
    HIV status  227, 229, 231–3
    legal duty  227, 230, 267, 268
  forewarning  226, 227, 229–3, 236
  harm
    bodily harm  229, 231, 235
    harm principle  13
    risk  230
    self-inflicted  231
    self-protection  265
  infection
    actual knowledge  228
    awareness  227, 228, 232, 268, 269
    exposure to infection  235, 236
    risk of infection  228, 230–2, 235, 265, 266, 268, 269
  moral obligations  232, 233, 235, 236
  moral wrong  232, 233, 235, 236
  mutual consent  12, 13
  offences
    offence of exposure  236
    offence of transmission  236
  prosecutions  225, 229
  public health measures  265–7
  reckless transmission
    assault  226
    awareness of infection  227, 228, 232
    criminalization  225, 227, 228

*Index*

Printed and bound by CPI Group (UK) Ltd, Croydon, CR0 4YY